Charles M. Russell

Charles M. Russell, *The Bronc's Lodged in the Top of An Old Cottonwood*.
Pen/ink on paper, illustration for "Bronc Twisters" in *Rawhide Rawlins Stories* and
Trails Plowed Under. Permanent Collection, C. M. Russell Museum, Great Falls, Montana.

Charles M. Russell
The Storyteller's Art

Raphael James Cristy

with a Foreword by B. Byron Price

UNIVERSITY OF NEW MEXICO PRESS ☾ ALBUQUERQUE

13 12 11 10 09 08 07   1 2 3 4 5 6 7

First paperbound printing, 2007
PAPERBOUND ISBN 978-0-8263-3285-1

LIBRARY OF CONGRESS CATALOGING-IN-PUBLICATION DATA

Cristy, Raphael.
Charles M. Russell : the storyteller's art / Raphael James Cristy ;
with a foreword by B. Byron Price.
p. cm.
Includes bibliographical references and index.
ISBN 0-8263-3284-6 (cloth : alk. paper)
1. Russell, Charles M. (Charles Marion), 1864–1926—Literary art.
2. Western stories—History and criticism. 3. Literature and history—
West (U.S.) 4. West (U.S.)—In literature. 5. Storytelling—West (U.S.)
6. Local color in literature. I. Title.

PS3535.U677Z63 2004
813'.4—dc22

2004010255

☾

Book and cover design and type composition:
Kathleen Sparkes
Body type in this book is Minion 10/14, 31P6
Display type is Mona Lisa Recut and Poetica

❦

For my father,

James C. Cristy, Jr.,

who shared my appreciation for

Charlie Russell's ironic humor

❦

Contents

~

List of Illustrations

FIGURES

FIGURES

(continued)

Plates

(following page 172)

Foreword

From James Fenimore Cooper to Mark Twain to Garrison Keillor, accomplished story-tellers have always held a special place in American life. They have shaped the way Americans think of themselves, poked fun at their mores, and helped define their heroes. No American tale teller was more celebrated in his own time than Charles M. Russell. The yarns he shared around a campfire, transferred to canvas with paint and brush, molded into clay and conveyed in the printed word, communicated the romance and adventure of the western frontier life he loved and kept it alive for subsequent generations.

Russell's stories drew their power from the close observation of both man and nature. Whether painted, written, or spoken, his narratives appealed to universal emotions and transcended social, cultural, and national boundaries. Russell's talents as a homespun raconteur, said to have rivaled those of his friend, renowned humorist Will Rogers, not only entertained listeners but also helped develop and nourish patrons for his art.

In the volume that follows, Raphael Cristy examines, from a literary and historical perspective, Charles M. Russell's published stories, many of which have been obscured by the passage of time and the spectacular success of his art. The author explores the origins of these tales, their relationship to Russell's art, their place within the context and tradition of American folk literature, and their value in interpreting the American West in the late nineteenth and early twentieth centuries. He argues persuasively for their narrative distinctiveness and confirms what the cowpunchers of the Judith Basin, Will Rogers, and the rest knew all along— Kid Russell could augur with the best.

B. Byron Price
Director, Charles M. Russell
Center for Art of the
American West
University of Oklahoma

Preface

FIG. 1. Charles M. Russell, *Horses Resting* (n.d.). Pen/ink, courtesy of the C. M. Russell Museum, Great Falls, Montana. Published in Bertha M. Bower, *The Lure of the Dim Trails* (New York: Grosset & Dunlap Publishers, 1907), 160. While the horses rest, the cowpunchers spin yarns.

This book discusses Charlie Russell's stories and essays without quoting most of them in full, allowing selected passages to provide highlights of his published writings. A basic purpose of this book is to encourage readers to look closely at *Trails Plowed Under* by Charles M. Russell. Copies can be found in many public libraries, better used bookstores, and many internet book dealers. Since 1996, a paperback version (minus color illustrations) has been available through retail bookstores from Bison Books—University of Nebraska Press.

In the 1970s I first encountered Charlie Russell's writings in *Trails Plowed Under* and *Rawhide Rawlins Stories,* as well as some of his illustrated letters in *Good Medicine,* while working as a partner in Chimaera Books, a used book and LP record store located in Palo Alto, California. In 1976 I drove to Montana to visit the C. M. Russell Museum in Great Falls and the Montana Historical Society in Helena, plus the Buffalo Bill Historical Center in Cody, Wyoming, gathering much information and inspiration about Charlie Russell's life and work. In 1985, I moved household and family from California to Montana to continue my research and to begin staging my one-man theater show, "Charlie Russell's Yarns" (a continuously evolving project). Subsequently, hundreds of performances have happened in theaters, museums, banquet halls, schools, colleges, festivals, and historic sites located in thirty states, three Canadian provinces, and two Australian cities. For seven years I lived in the Montana towns of Helena, Kalispell, and finally in Missoula, where I earned an M.A. degree in American History at the University of Montana. In 1992, I relocated to Albuquerque, New Mexico, finishing a Ph.D. in American History at the University of New Mexico in 1999. The performances plus the Master's thesis and doctoral dissertation all led directly to this book. Portions of the chapter "Stories of the Indians of the Northern Plains" were published in "Charlie's Hidden Agenda, Realism and Nostalgia in C. M. Russell's Stories about Indians," *Montana The Magazine of Western History* 43:3 (summer 1993): 2–15.

Acknowledgments

*A*cademic mentors who were crucial to the early formation of this work include University of New Mexico Professor of History Ferenc Morton Szasz and Professor H. Duane Hampton of the University of Montana's Department of History as well as UNM History professors Richard Etulain and Margaret Connell Szasz. UNM Professor of English Gary Scharnhorst; Dr. James Moore, Director of the Albuquerque Museum of Art and History; as well as Professor Brian Dippie of the Department of History at Canada's University of Victoria, B.C., and Russell author Ginger Renner have all been encouraging as readers of this work when it was cast in the form of an academic dissertation. History professors David Emmons at the University of Montana and Paul Hutton at UNM provided friendly wisdom and crucial employment assistance. Byron Price, Director of the Charles M. Russell Center at the University of Oklahoma, UNM English Professor David K. Dunaway, University of Montana English professor William W. Bevis, the New Mexico Endowment for the Humanities, and the Charlie Russell's Riders Foundation have been very helpful with crucial assistance.

Archivist Dr. Dave Walter and fellow staffers at the Montana Historical Society have supplied important research assistance, especially with the Montana Newspaper Association collection. Over several decades, the directors of the C. M. Russell Museum, including Ray Steele and Lorne Render, as well as curator Liz Dear and registrar Kim Smith, have been generous with time and access. The special help of Rick Stewart, Director of the Amon Carter Museum; Jan Brenneman, Director of the Sid Richardson Museum of Western Art; Dr. Van Kirke Nelson; and the late Fred Renner have all been crucial to this work. The especially helpful registrars and curators at the Gilcrease Museum in Tulsa, Oklahoma; the Buffalo Bill Museum in Cody, Wyoming; the Taylor Museum at the Colorado Springs Fine Arts Center; the Glenbow Museum in Calgary, Alberta; the National Cowboy Hall of Fame in Oklahoma City; Michigan's Kalamazoo Institute for the Arts; and the Rockwell Museum of Western Art in Corning, New York, have all been prompt and cordial in providing images and materials that are essential to this project.

Carol Christiansen at Bantam Doubleday Dell has been helpful in permitting the use of stories and illustrations appearing in *Trails Plowed Under* and especially the Harry Maule correspondence with Nancy Russell. Tara Wenger at the Harry Ransom Humanities Research Center, University of Texas—Austin, assisted me in locating the J. Frank Dobie papers on C. M. Russell and connecting me with the J. Frank Dobie Library Trust. Permissions to publish privately owned art works, archival materials, and photographs have been granted graciously by Sandra Curry, Wally McRae, Jim Combs, Sally Hatfield, Glenna Buck, Mr. and Mrs. W. D. Weiss, Martha Parfet, Woody Boudeman, Bill Skelton, Jack Hoover, Loren Smith, Rebecca Joe Wearin Pulk, and Mrs. Martha Wearin Rasmussen. Jack Lepley of the Fort Benton Museum and Mariellen Crosmer of the Judith Basin County Museum in Stanford, Montana; Joe Dekker of Glacier National Park, the Glacier Natural History Association; Beth Dunigan and Deirdra Shaw of Glacier National Park Library and Archives have been very helpful with historic photographs and other assistance.

Other individuals whose assistance and encouragement have kept me on course have included: Barbara S. Cristy, Jack Russell, Vivian Paladin, Dick Flood, Chuck Rankin, Steve Rose, Tom Rulon, Werner Quasebarth, Sarah and Rick Stevens, Kitty Wright and Peyton Huffman, Carol MacGregor, Bob Morgan, Buckeye Blake, Fr. John Russell, John O. Green, Sonny Trask, Floyd Forbes, Bruce Anfinson, Steve Fox, Peter Holter, Phil Tawney, Sam McCarthy, Monique Cristy, Paul Zarzyski, and especially Dr. Susan V. Richards.

Raphael Cristy

Introduction

FIG. 2. Charles M. Russell, *Chuck Wagon Meal.* Pen/ink, published in Owen Wister, *The Virginian* (New York: The Macmillan Company, 1916), 494.

*W*hen Charlie Russell was in the right mood and let his natural basso voice tell a story, other voices paused, other speakers listened. Accomplished raconteurs, ranging from fellow Montana cowboys to a national celebrity like Will Rogers, deferred to Russell's extraordinary, soft-spoken talent. At other times, when Charlie Russell transferred his narrative skills into painting on canvas or shaping clay into three-dimensional figures, his work attracted high praise and high prices from wealthy buyers. When he put his narrative impulses onto the printed page, however, he generated few dollars, but he captured local history and the cultural vitality of the American West like few other writers.

The published stories and anecdotes by western artist Charles M. Russell (1864–1926) form a local-color collection that serves as a vehicle for studying the cultural history of the American West. These brief writings by the popular "Cowboy Artist" focus on specific western people and events in the nineteenth and early twentieth century. Although Russell's published stories might not match the artistic accomplishments of his paintings and sculptures, the synthesis of many cultural elements in his writings can outweigh the frozen moment of information embedded in specific pieces of his fine art. Most of the stories offer distinctively vivid depictions of accelerating cultural changes in western America at the turn of the nineteenth century. Russell delivered most of his published tales in ironic rural voices, developing many of his stories as his own original narratives and reworking others that he had gathered from fellow storytellers, refining all of them into his own distinctive style. The author/artist employed half-a-dozen different fictional narrators, including the best-known, "Rawhide Rawlins," to deliver his tales in print. Most of these narrators reflect the author's personal values, although a few do not.

Russell's use of unlettered narrators and heroes continued earlier American humor traditions that began in the 1830s with "Jack Downing," continuing with Peter Finley Dunn's "Mr. Dooley" in 1899 and Ring Lardner's "Jack" in the 1920s.[1] Charlie Russell's published writings stand out from many other American local-color stories in their accurate portrayal of local people and culture. Especially important to the local-history content in these narratives was Russell's personal connection with a large number of typical rural westerners in Montana. His close links with the locals helped to make Russell's works distinctive from most other published narratives depicting the American West. The historical value of the specific local incidents and characters that fill Charlie Russell's sculptures, sketches, and published stories, as well as his popular paintings, fit closely the conclusions of Montana historian and author Dave Walter:

> The genuine vigor of Western history survives today in the arena of local history. Here stalwart, robust, truly exciting people lived, and fundamental, pivotal, amazing events occurred. Through local history, Montanans glimpse the real characters and incidents of the past—ones that lived and occurred on familiar ground. . . . In an era of dreadful Western stereotypes, local historical people and local historical events constitute Montanans' primary anchors to the truth. . . . This is not precise science; it is not chemistry, biology, or even geology. Local history is researched storytelling. It rests much closer to the oral tradition than many academic historians would like to admit.[2]

The stories that Charlie Russell told aloud and later published conform to larger traditions in American folk literature. Like many of the writers of local-color humor in the early nineteenth century, Russell first published his yarns in regional newspapers. In the early years of the United States, the published efforts to capture the magic of popular, face-to-face yarn spinning typically involved small-town newspapers where writers could mimic the storytelling process in print. Helpful for historians, the same rural Montana newspapers that first printed Russell's anecdotes also provide articles with corroboration of his basic themes, characters, and details.

Printed versions of tales and jokes from the Old Southwest frequently depicted local, rural dialects by means of phonetic spelling. Appearing in print in the decades before the Civil War, these rough yarns often included crude episodes of violence, coarse allusions to sexuality, petty crime, and racial stereotypes. These tales featured such fictional rascals as "Simon Suggs" and "Sut Lovingood." This was the rough humor of America's antebellum southern and western frontier districts. These tales included the kind of ribald material attributed to Abe Lincoln throughout his life, anecdotes that circuit-riding judges and attorneys shared with sales agents and other travelers at country inns, on riverboats, and in boardinghouses. Not to be categorized with oral-tradition fairy tales, or spiritual legends, these Old Southwest narratives became popular with English-speaking Americans as some of the country's earliest "local-color" anecdotes. It seems fitting that Charlie Russell's Missouri home overlapped with part of the "Old Southwest" region where this writing flourished.

Some novelists have employed elevated versions of local-color narratives in the nineteenth century, including Mark Twain in *The Adventures of Huckleberry Finn* and Harriet Beecher Stowe in *Uncle Tom's Cabin*. These novels represent a high point in local-color writing, although a few later-era critics reject Twain's and Stowe's depictions of simple people and their dialects as perpetuating negative racial stereotypes. The local-color genre has also been associated closely with the western writer Bret Harte. Like these fiction writers, academic folklore collectors have recorded oral-dialect storytelling on paper (as well as audio and video tape), but the local-color writers often expanded their works to portray the storytelling context and process along with the story itself. As they portray specific storytellers and their speech patterns, their local-color stories rise to fill the middle ground between fiction writing and the folklorists' unembellished recording of one person's voice. Charlie Russell helped to perpetuate local-color writing by transplanting Old Southwest humor techniques into the prairie and mountain western states. In his writings, Russell avoided the more crude themes and ideas from earlier frontier stories and the sentimental pathos of other local-color writers, as he sustained nineteenth-century American humor writing traditions in the early twentieth century.

Charles M. Russell's published tales offer a wide variety of themes and formats, but most fit into four general topic groups: (1) Indians, (2) humorous encounters between humans and wild animals, (3) vivid characters working on the unfenced western cattle ranges, and (4) nineteenth-century westerners adjusting to quickly evolving situations in the early twentieth century.[3] These four categories offer slight references to several important western topics, such as ethnic minorities (other than Indians), the mining industry, timber and railroad activities, farming, sheepherding, and the distinctive experiences of women. Especially intriguing are Russell's lighthearted tales that take place during the first three decades of the twentieth century. These narratives carry references to automobiles and World War I as well as the emergence of women and urbanization in the West—subjects that seldom appear in the thousands of Russell's narrative pictures and sculptures.

In the first topic category, Charlie Russell's Indian tales express his understanding of and appreciation for the persistence of Native American people and cultures in the face of extreme pressure to assimilate into Euro-American society. Russell's Indian stories raise such issues as the famine years following the demise of the wild buffalo as well as the genocidal killings of Indians by white settlers. He expresses friendship and appreciation for mixed-blood people as well as for the typically more traditional full-blood Indians. He also honors the frequently scorned Euro-American men who married Indian women and lived within tribal society. The blunt realism of these Indian stories contrasts with Russell's lighthearted ironic exaggeration in other writings.

The second group, Russell's nature and hunting stories, present both grim survival and humor in encounters between humans and wild animals. Human errors that generate confrontations with dangerous critters provide some of his best narrative humor among all his writings. In addition, Russell savors exaggerated descriptions of the animal-human encounters when his narrators retell their adventures by indulging in bragging and lying to outsiders.

Human destruction of dangerous bears, wolves, and buffalo concludes several wildlife stories, but, surprisingly, the author shows little of the disapproval or regret that he expressed privately about animal depletion. Bears, buffalo, elk, and wolves encounter humans with results varying from sudden death to complete escape, but Russell's narratives focus more on the comic human circumstances than on the deadly impact on wildlife. His narratives mix extreme danger with humor, portraying the killing of animals for food or self-defense as being natural and acceptable. On the other hand, the frivolous killing of wildlife proves to be perilous for any greedy hunter in these stories. Even in his most desperate survival tales, however, Russell found ways for the paradoxical opposites of comedy and death to coexist.

Charlie Russell spent eleven years working as a youthful cowpuncher on Montana's unfenced prairies, an experience that shaped most of his narrative artworks. His stories about the nineteenth-century western cattle ranges, our third topic category, emphasize humor over regretful nostalgia. Russell's open-range narratives focus more on the foibles of colorful individuals operating within the cattle culture and less on tales of minding herds and living the ranching life. Typically, Russell's cattle-range humor operates at the expense of individual cowpuncher friends who became the butt of his humorous narrative "roasts." The author employs outrageous exaggerations to tell about their predicaments—a form of rustic American humor that honored close friendships with good-natured insults. Only one of Russell's cattle stories, "Longrope's Last Guard," expresses nostalgic sentimentality for the cattle-range life, while telling about a tragic sacrifice during a long cattle drive from Texas to Montana. In general, Russell's cattle-era writings, both stories and essays, reflect the swift transition from open-range to fenced-pasture ranching to express more wry humor than a bitter sense of loss.

In his stories about the twentieth-century West, the fourth topic category, Charlie Russell contradicts many latter-day critical assumptions that he was unable to focus his artistic attention outside a nostalgic preoccupation for the nineteenth-century West. These tales demonstrate Russell's knack for satirizing "modern" twentieth-century topics including automobiles, tourism, World War I, and the common inability among many western men to adjust to women's changing roles. Progressive social reforms of the century's first decades, such as prohibition and mechanization, also appear as targets for Russell's satirical narratives. The people in his yarns, especially his heroes, are challenged to wake up and adjust to the accelerating changes in western life during bewildering new social circumstances requiring more adaptation than resistance. Russell enjoyed crafting narratives about his companions' dilemmas and discomforts with "modern times" in the early twentieth century because he shared their inability to adapt gracefully to the new situations. These stories reflect as much about Russell's own maladjustment to modernity as the plights of his hapless story characters.

Beyond Russell's published writings, any direct evidence of his legendary, numerous *orally* transmitted tales has survived in few documents. Even when preserved in print, few versions of Russell's oral tales, as his contemporaries recalled them for publication, seem reliable or amusing. Only the convincing recollections of his friend Frank B. Linderman appear to be plausible and reliable. Several of Russell's friends, including Will Rogers, have suggested that the artist's own published versions of his stories may be good reading, but his direct telling of tales was more impressive. Russell's own printed stories might have seemed less effective for those few lucky readers who had witnessed his narrative delivery in person, but these published yarns are, nevertheless, the ones that he decided to preserve in print. And in the years since the deaths of all firsthand witnesses, Russell's printed tales remain amusing as they supply useful understanding of the nineteenth- and early twentieth-century West.

In contrast with his published stories, Charlie Russell's illustrated personal letters have become widely known in the decades since his death through the successful publication of several volumes. Although his letters are especially revealing of his private thoughts, Russell's correspondence served a function different from his published tales. He sent these letters to individual friends and occasionally to small groups, such as the patrons of a particular saloon. In contrast, he published his stories to address a much wider public audience. Shortly after Russell's death, his widow Nancy published a valuable collection of his illustrated correspondence, titled *Good Medicine.* Then in the late twentieth century, scholar/writers Fred Renner and Brian Dippie separately published worthwhile collections of the letters with their own detailed, well-informed explanations. For evaluating Russell's published stories, his letters are useful as they reveal his opinions and a few alternative versions of incidents mentioned in the printed tales. Ultimately, it is Russell's published stories and essays that form his definitive literary statements.

The vivid moments in the lives of local people in Russell's stories remind viewers familiar with his paintings and sculptures that the expression of *local history* was more important to the writer/artist than creating fine aesthetic statements in color and form. Overall, Charlie Russell's pictures and sculptures make more sense as story-based illustrations of local and regional topics than as refined objects destined for intellectual art criticism. When regarded in the context of art history in late twentieth-century viewpoints, Russell's pictures have become entangled in critical arguments over the relative influence of other artists on his painting and sketching, as well as the possible impact of the commercial marketplace's demand for "Wild West" exaggerations in his straightforward works. With art-history critiques by intellectual observers in the final decades of the twentieth century tending to dominate formal discussions of Russell's significance, general appreciation for his narrative priorities and the local/regional significance of his work seemed to recede. If considered through the lens of his published stories, however, Russell's accomplishments as a cultural historian find a clearer focus that also seems closer to the artist's expressed intent for his fine art works. In other words, if art viewers seek to understand more about the content and significance of Russell's paintings and sculptures, they must consider his published stories.

CHAPTER ONE

Telling Stories

"...a compelling urge to talk in an entertaining manner."
—Joe DeYong

*A*t the root of Charles M. Russell's artworks lived his stories. His delivery of yarns to a receptive audience of one person or more gave him special pleasure. He told stories many ways—through spoken words, prose, poetry, pencil sketches, paintings, and sculptures. In his days on the cattle range, storytelling with a fellow cowboy might begin as they sat in the shade of their horses. Decades later in his log-cabin studio, he might overlap his methods when he talked and sculpted at the same time, or, on rare occasions, when he sketched or painted as he spoke. Frequently he sculpted the air as he told stories heard from Indians, using the northern plains native sign language to add visual counterpoint to his spoken words. When Russell's voice was silent, his pencil, paintbrush, sculpting tools, or graceful hands still told stories. Inevitably, narrative ideas coalesced into works of art.

From the beginning of his eleven-year career as an open-range cowboy in nineteenth-century Montana, Charlie Russell combined storytelling and the making of artworks. The eighteen-year-old raconteur from St. Louis may have been crude in both practices, but his companions remembered that he was nearly always effective. Russell's first range boss, Horace Brewster, remembered the teenage kid he had hired as a night herder for the Judith Basin Pool Roundup.

> [Brewster] recalls, as though it was yesterday, the time he employed Russell as a horse wrangler.... "He could tell stories even then; drew pictures that looked like some of the boys, and was always wantin' to know things."[1]

In later years young Charlie Russell's questions proved to be part of his firsthand research for the stories he told throughout his life about the people and history of the American West. Aside

FIG. 3.   Charles M. Russell, "The Mountains and Plains Seem to Stimulate A Man's
Imagination." Pen/ink, courtesy of the Montana Historical Society, Helena.
Published in *Trails Plowed Under* (New York: Doubleday, 1927). Storytelling
could begin in the shade of their horses.

from serious inquiries, however, many of his range sketches had a humorous purpose. Brewster
recalled his own difficulties after spending several hours wearing down an especially wild horse.
The next day, Brewster had trouble walking upright and was unable to saddle his regular mount.
Charlie saw him go behind the wagon to apply liniment, "treating some sore places. Unbeknown
to me, the kid penciled me in the act. They all said it looked like me. . . . It caused much laughter
about the camp. It was hung up in a conspicuous place where all could see it."[2] At that moment,
as the foreman of the outfit, Horace Brewster was in a position to end "Kid" Russell's first job as a
cowboy. Instead, he joined in the laughter and they became lifelong friends. Some forty-four
years later, in October 1926, Horace Brewster was honored, among thousands of Russell's cowboy
friends, to be selected as the lone horseman riding in Charlie's funeral cortege.

Late in Charlie's life, it was a rare occasion that he found receptive and congenial friends
for his stories as he spent his final winters, mingling with southern California art patrons.
Once, a Santa Barbara newspaper reporter noticed the relationship between Russell's paintings
and his speaking voice when "he showed me his paintings—wonderful, virile, throbbing pictures of a by-gone day. . . ." Some forty years after experiencing a campfire on the open range,
Russell painted himself standing off to the right on a coffee break from his job of solitary night-
herding, as he listened to a humorous storytelling session over a campfire (**see plate 2**).

Hearing and seeing the artist present such vivid pictures, the same newspaper writer and
former cowpuncher Frederick Richardson paid closer attention:

> Powerful, colorful tales, those paintings tell, and one marvels that their creator
> should show them with a half-apologetic air of nonchalance—he really doesn't
> sense their fineness because to him the canvas, the brushes and the pigments are
> just a way to express feelings he cannot put into words.[3]

Russell was unenthusiastic about his paintings because rendering stories through paint daubed on canvas was hard work, and the results seldom satisfied him as the complete story or as acceptable art. Yet the results of his stories in paint and canvas, ink and paper, or clay and bronze have more than satisfied and entertained generations of viewers.

Bringing Russell back into the realm of spoken words in such an alien California setting could be a challenge for his companions. An important story-instigator in Santa Barbara was Russell's longtime Montana friend and occasional collaborator, writer Frank Bird Linderman, who spent one lucky winter in Santa Barbara living along the beach near Charlie Russell. "At dinners and other social occasions," Linderman recalled, "I had told Western stories until I was beginning to repeat some of them." As Linderman put it,

> Charley's coming promised relief for both our Santa Barbara friends and myself. "Invite the Russells," I urged a lady with whom we were sufficiently acquainted to allow of such a request, "Charley is the best of storytellers. . . . I'll try to get him started at storytelling, but please don't let anyone ask him for a story outright. Stories have to be suggested by incidents." I knew from experience that nothing is more difficult than to begin storytelling from a standing start and nothing easier, for a good storyteller, than following up a suggestion. I knew that Charley would balk if asked outright; particularly as he was among strangers.[4]

Santa Barbara reporter Fred Richardson wrote about a gathering where both Russell and Linderman had been storytelling. He happened to observe an occasion when Linderman was not the one who sparked Russell's yarn spinning. In fact, it was the reporter himself who knew enough of the old cowpuncher's friends and habits to move the artist into a talkative mood. When Russell crossed the room to show one of his paintings, Richardson recognized the occupational source for the artist's distinctive walk and subdued speaking mannerisms:

> I saw before me the typical cowman—the most typical I have seen in years—and in the early eighties I knew cowmen of the plains—well. It was not until I mentioned some of the old names, and the old places that the transformation of the features came. . . . Those grey eyes lit up, they shone, and more than once came that silent inward chuckle that shook the frame—while never a sound escaped his lips. And how the eyes would laugh at some memory of men and incidents agone [*sic*].
>
> Then Frank Linderman—another cowman, now a literary genius, joined the circle, and he, too, knew the old fellows and the old days. But those features had relaxed. The "squint" lines deepened as the grey eyes smiled over some memory . . . [such as] the chap who couldn't be sympathized with when he was sick because it made him sicker—so when the boys began to divide up his belongings and talk about how long he could last, he recovered after he had warned them, cursing that "damn you coyotes, I aint dead yit." And the chest trembled under suppressed amusement at the memory—but never the sound of a laugh.
>
> But [Russell] realized he was talking over old times with old timers—and he

limbered up—recalled the old days—the old scenes. The real man—with his wist-
fulness for the plains and the buttes, the horses of the range, the coyotes and the
wolves, the winds, the stars of the clear nights and the rocking of the saddle under
him, shone out, transforming him. . . . It was a rare afternoon, to watch him as he
talked of the old days and the old friends, then to see them on the canvases.[5]

The reporter observed how Russell's personality and experiences gave colorful depth to his
tales as well as the artworks that the stories had inspired. And he verified that the figures in
most Russell paintings depicted specific people and events.

Without reflecting typical storyteller's envy, Frank Linderman recalled the impact of
Russell's low-key domination of the yarn-spinning session in that Santa Barbara setting: "On
and on went Charley's stories of Montana, different from any the guests had ever heard. He
kept them merry for hours. No other man could have told the stories as he did, and even if he
learned them word for word, he could never have said or written them. He was a master teller."
Linderman had learned from firsthand experience that when another person repeated a Russell
story, the impact was never as good as the original. For approximately fifteen years, he gave
occasional public readings of Russell narratives, generating positive responses, and even published his versions among his own original writings. Apparently, these secondary versions,
written or spoken, always provided full attribution to Russell.[6]

The storytelling aspect of Charlie Russell's personality was especially popular with his
contemporaries in Montana. Although not everyone who knew him was able to activate
Russell's congenial tale-telling, those who did frequently remembered the moments.
"[Charlie] was a man of whom you didn't ask questions," L. E. Falk told a would-be Russell
biographer in 1937, "although he was kindly and a most pleasant companion for a stroll along
the street." Falk added:

I resided for a time in the same block where his residence stood. . . . If one entered
[his studio] and he did not look up from his work, it was sign he was busy and all
who knew him would make their exit as graciously as possible. If he laid down his
brushes and palette and reach [sic] for his tobacco and made ready to roll a cigarette, the gods smiled on the visitor, for that meant a most delightful half-hour of
talk about everything that might be on his mind and incidentally a story. For I pre-
sume you have learned by now he was a capital story teller and even so famous a
story teller as the late Will Rogers wrote of him, "there was no one ready to try, if
Charlie was in a mood to tell another." Most of his stories, at least the best of them,
you will find in his book "Trails Plowed Under."[7]

Published by Doubleday in 1927, *Trails Plowed Under* formed the ultimate printed format for
Russell's storytelling.[8]

Charlie Russell's storytelling began almost a decade before his 1880 arrival in Montana at
the age of sixteen. As a bright lad growing up in St. Louis, Russell frequently entertained his
siblings, parents, and family friends. His sister once recalled:

By the time he was eight or ten [Chas] afforded much amusement to the family, as he always saw things in a funny light & would call forth many a laugh when he told us about anything he had seen, or described any "show" to which he had been taken. He was always a great mimic.[9]

Russell also enjoyed visiting the family's coalmine and brick factory in the St. Louis suburbs. Here he would banter with his father's employees who spoke English through the filter of their Scottish, Irish, Cornish, or Welsh accents. Sister Sue recalled that Charlie could "reproduce their oddities of pronunciation in a very amusing way."[10]

Russell's family might have been amused by little Charlie's version of an Irish brogue or a Cornish turn of speech. They were less amused when Charlie later revisited St. Louis fresh from the Montana cattle ranges, addressing family and friends in the rural vernacular of uneducated cowpunchers. "The family were surprised," wrote Russell's literary-minded nephew, Austin,

to see how he had changed and grown up, and what a good story teller he had become, but were shocked at the way his English had deteriorated—full not merely of westernisms but plain bad grammar. His spelling, always a minus quantity was now minus minimus.[11]

The wealthy Russell family had struggled for years to persuade Charlie to remain in school through his sixteenth birthday, efforts that included corporal punishment as well as a brief stint at the Burlington military academy in New Jersey. They also employed special tutors. And one family tradition in which every child, including little Charlie, read aloud from Shakespeare and the King James Bible, had a subtle impact years later on Charlie's adult speech and writing patterns.[12] In special gifts to friends Charlie created bits of remarkable poetry that showed he not only retained a fond memory of Elizabethan-era words and speech patterns, he could also manipulate them into humorous rhymes. Nevertheless, despite his education and his upper-class family's dismay, after 1880 Charlie Russell immersed himself in the cultural life of Montana's mountains and cattle ranges, totally absorbing the speech patterns of that region. In addition, from his earliest days as a teenager in Montana, Charlie Russell wore a (French/Indian) Métis sash, identifying himself with the often-scorned mixed-blood Indians.

Russell's popularity as an entertaining figure in the Judith Basin district of central Montana did not develop immediately. While still a teenager, he initially earned the title "that ornery Kid Russell" by being uncooperative and stubborn, especially in the face of authority figures. A fellow Judith Basin cowpuncher, Silas Gray, wrote an unsympathetic account of this side of Charlie Russell's personality. He recalled the time in the Missouri River village of Fort Benton during the early 1880s when Russell had asked to ride with "Old Man" True's cattle outfit, joining the cowboys and their boss to borrow one of their horses for the fifty-mile trek back to the Judith Basin. Along the trail, "True and uncle Billy were preparing supper," recalled Gray, "Russell sat smoking a cigarette." Then

True asked the Kid to get a bucket of water for supper, but the Kid kept on with his

FIG. 4. Charles M. "Kid" Russell, ca. 1881, age sixteen or seventeen. Photograph courtesy of Montana Historical Society, Helena. From his earliest days as a teenager in Montana, Charlie wore a French/Indian Métis sash, typically worn by mixed-blood Indians.

smoke regardless, a few minutes passed, when True asked him again, still the kid did not move, then True got hot, walked over to the Kid, an[d] said by God you get that water or you don't get any supper. I knew that settled the water question as far as the Kid was concerned. for he was just as stubborn as True, we had supper, but not the Kid, no coments [*sic*] were made we had Breakfast but the Kid did not partake, we had dinner, but the kid smoked instead, supper time we were home. The

Kid ate somewhere else, and perhaps he learned a good lesson, for it is sure bad taste, to be a drone about camp. If each one does a little it tends to make things more pleasant for all.[13]

Although local legends persist around the Judith Basin about young Russell's "ornery" personality, few specific accounts remain. Russell's nephew wrote that by the time Charlie was thirty, most people in the north-central district of Montana "had entirely forgotten 'that ornery Buckskin kid' stuff and thought of him as not only a good mixer but a wonderful storyteller—he could keep the whole house laughing all evening."[14]

For most of his first two years in Montana, Russell camped and hunted in the Belt Mountains with trapper/hunter Jake Hoover. The young man had a chance to mature through some of his "ornery" phase while learning the behavior and anatomy of wilderness animals. Russell also got a dose of yarn-spinning from Hoover, the cantankerous mountain man who also "was a great storyteller," according to one local observer, "and liked to tell the tender feet about how he kiled [sic] lions, bear, etc. bare-handed."[15] In addition, Russell made occasional and sometimes prolonged visits to L. B. Diver's place, "Lying" Babcock's cabin, and other homesteads around the Judith Basin.[16] These visits may have challenged him to soften his stubborn streak and sharpen some of his social skills, as well as his ability with a musical instrument. Charlie "always carried his banjo with him," recalled Miss Lolly Edgar, whose father's homestead-ranch frequently welcomed the footloose and romantic young Russell.

> He knew all the popular songs. His fund of good stories and his keen sense of humor made him a popular guest at any of the cattle ranches through the long winters. I think they used to vie for his company & offer bribes to get him at many of the ranches.[17]

After unsuccessfully courting Lolly, Russell gave up the banjo. Most accounts indicate that his singing voice was fit only for longhorn cattle. His unusual skills as a comedian and storyteller, however, soon became the talents preferred by local Montana folks. He developed a sense of humor that set him apart from most people. "He was one of those rare persons who could make a story funny," wrote Montana Supreme Court Justice Lew Callaway, who socialized with Russell in Great Falls salons and saloons. "The same story told by another would be mediocre; told by Charlie it would be a side-splitter."[18]

By the time Russell had landed his first job with Horace Brewster's cattle outfit, in 1882, he was well on his way to becoming the entertaining companion who was dubbed the court jester of the Judith Basin by fellow range rider John Barrows. "At camp and elsewhere," recalled another former cowboy, "Charlie Russell was always the center of attraction.... always had a meal time story and the boys circled around him as close as possible, eating with legs crossed, plates on knees."[19]

Russell was not alone in giving priority to yarn spinning. Whether in the bunkhouse or beside the open campfire, western range men took turns in storytelling, always a favorite pastime. Nearly every cowpuncher had at least one sure-fire, amusing yarn ready for the assembled bunch.[20] Russell enjoyed participating in what could be a competitive storytelling arena. "He often stopped of a night by the I. J. Ranch on the head of MacDonald Creek," remembered I. D. O'Donnell:

> In the evenings in the bunk house the crowd usually got to spinning yarns and telling stories or singing songs. Charlie would be mum until everyone else had finished and then he would tell his story that out classed them all, and then he was mum.[21]

The lives of nineteenth-century Montana range hands were filled with verbal amusements, and Charlie Russell absorbed this narrative material as he steadily perfected his story timing and delivery. The apprentice cowboy from wealthy St. Louis earned his assimilation into the ranks of the working-class Montana range riders by amusing the others with his yarn-spinning skill.[22]

Russell's careful verbal style often set him apart from his contemporaries. A Great Falls neighbor noticed that Russell "was quiet, meditative, and, when he spoke, his voice was low and his words few. When Charlie spoke, he rarely opened his mouth, but spoke from out of the corner."[23] Russell's apprentice Joe DeYong recalled that his mentor "habitually spoke deep in his chest and with little lip movement"[24] to shape his gentle, Missouri drawl.[25] Western artist Maynard Dixon once observed that Russell "was a noted storyteller; but told his yarns so casually that you'd almost believe he was thinking of something else meanwhile, and would slip over the point so quietly that hearers who had not lived in the West would be apt to miss it."[26] In his understated delivery, Russell had subtle ways to hold the attention of a listener. One of Russell's victims recalled several of the artist's low-key mannerisms. "He seemed able to look clear through another man with his calm eyes," he said.

> [S]ometimes I felt like turning my own eyes away from him. He held me plainly speechless by his stories. At times he would string stories out like letting a big pen full of steers out through a gate to the open range. His supply of stories seemed to have no limits. . . .
>
> He was a constant roller and smoker of cigarettes. When a cigarette was smoked out, he invariably stopped talking while he deliberately rolled another. During the process he would not speak a word, even if he was in the middle of the climax of a story. He knew how to "make 'em wait." Most of his stories were humorous, made so by Charlie's vivid language and characterizations. He never smiled even while provoking rolls of laughter in others.[27]

Russell's slow, drawling delivery became part of a powerful means of narrative control that galvanized his listeners. The deadpan delivery that Russell maintained during his humorous stories was typical for nineteenth-century professional humorists, such as Artemus Ward and Josh Billings, as well as the most famous of them all, Mark Twain, who once referred to the straight-faced style as "a 'dead' earnestness that was funny enough to suffocate a body."[28] Of the few descriptions of Russell laughing, Joe Thoroughman recollected that Russell "never laughed.

FIG. 5. Henry Keeton and Charlie Russell. Detail of photograph courtesy of Montana Historical Society, Helena. Taken outside his log cabin studio, this is a rare image of Charlie Russell laughing.

He'd go kinda, 'Huh, huh, huh,' but he never laughed like other people."[29] A writer/editor and friend similarly recalled that Russell

> seldom indulged in a real laugh. In the company of friends with half-closed eyes and an out-thrust chin, he merely talked and smiled and chuckled while his audience laughed and laughed over his outrageous stories until their tears ran furrows down their cheeks. And he hugely enjoyed all of it.[30]

Contributing to Russell's reluctance to laugh out loud in his later years were his dentures. If moved to laughter, Russell usually covered his mouth with his hand.[31]

While storytelling, Russell sometimes acted out the tale, "and that," said Thoroughman, "was what made it so good."[32] Fellow professional artist/illustrator Philip Goodwin appreciated Russell's precise release of narrative information within his entertaining, storytelling manner:

> He has the true old-time plainsman's and trapper's gift at spinning yarns, and his equal as an original campfire raconteur will rarely be heard. He is decidedly

human, with a very keen sense of humor and daring imagination, is naturally droll, has perfect control of his remarkably striking features, has a pleasingly mellow bass voice, excellent powers of description and tells a story as a gambler plays poker.[33]

Russell's careful narrative control presented each story element with the purposeful revelation of a turned-over card. As DeYong observed, "people hung on his every word like so many kids. When his deadpan, delayed-action manner of delivery finally put across a slow-fused 'sneaker,' their delight was unmistakable—often whole-heartedly explosive!"[34]

In the open forums of western saloon and campfire storytelling, a subdued delivery, a straight face, and subtle timing in delivery were storytelling assets. They were not absolute requirements for success, however. One western author knew a cowboy storyteller named Brice who regularly employed this blustery introduction for his tales: "'I was drunk, ragged an' lousy! Broke flatter'n eggs on a plate, damn ol' Missus Mitchell.' Then Brice would go from there."[35] Nevertheless, there was one inflexible storytelling rule in Russell's Montana. "The narrator might tell about his own misadventures but, unless he was willing to be nicknamed 'Windy,' he avoided bragging about his exploits."[36] Russell's storytelling style stayed within this limit, according to observers such as one Butte newspaper writer:

> Low in voice and modest in demeanor, he attracts but never repels; charms but is never the least aggressive, and when drawn out reveals the most delightful and refreshing style of repartee. As a storyteller he stands without a peer, weaving through his accounts, which are always brimful with vim and sparkle the color of originality, with never a suggestion of "shop," but on the whole so entertaining and fascinating that the artist is lost in the genial man and companion.[37]

Additional storytelling sites emerged for Russell when the cattle range overlapped with mining districts in the mountain clusters that bordered the Judith Basin. In the Judith Mountains north of the eventual site of Lewistown, the mining camp called Maiden included "a saloon operated by a humorous old Scotchman, Buck Buchanan, and his brother Bill." According to one Russell biographer:

> The place was frequented by cowboys, ranchers, miners and the usual drifters. . . . When Charlie met [freighter] Johnnie [Mathewson] in Buck's saloon the three would attempt to out-tell each other with ridiculous stories. The sociable clientele, eager for entertainment of any kind, crowded around these fabulists.[38]

When storytelling, friendship, and a competitive atmosphere coincided in a place like Buck Buchanan's log shack, the yarn spinning could take on a different shape. The boys often expressed their friendship in elaborate insults that were spiced with ridiculous exaggerations. As Walter Lehman, a Judith Basin shopkeeper, described the scene, "They made up the worst stories on each other, and told them with a straight face in front of the whole crowd in some saloon."[39] Lehman also recalled that such yarn-spinning men "told a lot of things they knew

FIG. 6. Charles M. Russell with (left to right) Buck Buchanan, John Mathewson, and Bill
Deaton at Chico Hot Springs. Photography courtesy of the Montana Historical Society,
Helena. Charlie often spoke quietly from the side of his mouth, in this case, probably
commenting about the photographer, his friend Con Price.

were not so in order to get a 'raise' out of their victim in front of a saloon crowd and so make
him buy the drinks for all hands."[40]

Russell could embarrass a friend with exaggerated yarns but he also enjoyed "roasting"
himself. As one journalist observed, "If the joke happens to be on him—and many of those he
tells are—he takes an added relish in the telling."[41] The congenial roasting of friends in face-to-
face storytelling was a process Russell continued to enjoy in his later years while wintering in
southern California. A Los Angeles newspaper recorded Russell's continuation of this technique in the 1920s.

> One of [Russell's] boon companions when in Los Angeles is William Chambers
> Tyler of 1323 Third Avenue, who many years ago lived for a time in Montana. Tyler
> too rode the range, but he also cooked.
>
> In a round of calls on friends the Russell and Tyler stories differ strikingly as
> to how the latter escaped from the occupation of cooking. According to the artist,
> there was a unanimous desire in camp to hold funeral services for the cook, but the
> Los Angeles man solemnly swears that the fame of his appetizing grub is still the
> subject of song and story in Montana.[42]

Russell published several stories that continued this basic "roasting" routine.

Although he was adept at the storytelling roast and other popular western yarn-spinning forms, such as lie-telling, Charlie Russell was unique when he included art-making during the narrative give-and-take. One fellow cowpuncher recalled that the situation might involve several different art techniques and the entire situation could become a performance.

> [Charlie] was not known much at that time as an artist. But just the same all us cow punchers loved him. As an entertainer he could not be beat. Sitting at a card table at Jack Graham's saloon CM would take a stack of poker chips. Talking all the while, he would draw your picture, a Horse or coyote. Take a piece of moulding wax from his Pocket and make a perfect cast of a buffalo or horse. And put on a real good show.[43]

Sometimes Russell's barroom sculpting included holding his hands under the table or behind his back while his cronies tried to guess the figure in the narrative that would soon emerge. The loser had to buy the next round of drinks for the assembled crowd. Meanwhile, the finished figure would abruptly disappear into the blackened wax lump in Russell's hands.[44]

The sculpting process, however, was not always linked exclusively to joking and story-telling. One observer noted that, during a conversation, Russell "would have his hands working with a piece of wax,

> moulding figures in a few minutes he would have a bear, start over and a buffalo would materialize with never a glance at his hands; his eyes would be on the person he was talking to. Unless you watched close the figure would be destroyed and he would be starting on another. If you were quick enough and inquired, "What have you there, Charlie?" he would show you, and immediately resume his conversation and moulding.[45]

The purpose of this nimble exercise was not to produce a finished, three-dimensional work of fine art. Rather, the figure served as an accompaniment, or counterpoint, to the narrative. The sculpted figure often reflected as much of Russell's sense of his listener as the subject of the conversation or story. The artwork was secondary to the narrative idea.

The variety of Russell's storytelling settings increased dramatically when he left the cattle range in 1894, and especially when he married Nancy Cooper two years later. Even before marriage, the footloose artist had shifted his base of operations from Fort Benton and Helena to Great Falls, a raw settlement of shacks and larger buildings on the upper Missouri River. Years later, a Great Falls bank president recalled that wherever Russell appeared, "a crowd gathered to hear and enjoy the humor of his stories and his friends in all walks of life were legion."[46] One of Russell's friends, fellow Montana cowpuncher Jim Thornhill, also recalled that when Charlie would appear on the street men gravitated around him to hear him tell stories and jokes.[47] A newspaper reporter who happened to be present on the streets of Great Falls when Russell returned in 1904 from his first trip to New York City recorded one of these public narrative moments:

FIG. 7. Charles M. Russell. Photograph courtesy of the C. M. Russell Museum, Great Falls, Montana. Russell (center) is sculpting and talking to staff and guests on Howard Eaton's expedition into the Grand Canyon.

> Russell's reappearance on the streets yesterday was a glad sight to his scores of friends and he was kept busy shaking hands and saying "Howdy," to the many who pressed around him to welcome him back . . . he is the same old "Charley" and his comments and stories on the east kept his auditors in a roar of merriment.[48]

Russell adapted easily to life around Great Falls. As long as he had a close rapport with the local people, as expressed in his bantering and storytelling, he remained comfortable in the small-town West.

In a spontaneous moment during the year (1895) before his marriage to Nancy Cooper in Cascade, Charlie Russell took the opportunity to swap yarns on the town's railroad platform during an encounter with a national political celebrity. Traveling as a Democratic presidential candidate, William Jennings Bryan stepped onto the rear platform of his two-coach special train when it paused at the little village on the way north to Great Falls. Instead of a crowd, Bryan faced only Charlie and the livery-stable employee. According to one version based on the liveryman's memory, the candidate said, "Not many people in your town, is there." To which Russell replied, "They've all gone down to the Falls to hear that windjammer." Probably disarmed by Russell's lighthearted candor, Bryan stepped off the train and walked to the depot building as Charlie began telling amusing stories. Soon, the two men had progressed from leaning against the wall to sitting on the platform, all the while trading tales back and forth. Two or three times, the conductor came along and shouted "All aboard!" but the older man did not stir. Russell warned his fellow yarn-spinner to get on the train or be left behind, but the great orator (who would deliver the famous "Cross of Gold" speech a year later to win the Democratic Party's nomination for president) stayed to tell and hear more. After another "All Aboard!" and a warning from Charlie, Bryant said "Oh no. I don't think they'll leave without me." Finally he arose and shook hands with the entire Cascade contingent, saying, "Boys, this is the most enjoyable half-hour of my life." Stepping onto the rear coach's platform, he turned and said, "My name's Bryan," as the train pulled out. According to the local legend, that was precisely the moment when Charlie Russell realized who had been sharing stories with him.[49] As the nineteenth century was nearing an end, a lively storytelling session could distract a distinguished politician from his campaign routine as easily as pulling an upstart painter from his easel.

Charlie Russell's 1896 marriage in Cascade changed his life even more than his leaving the cattle range. Nancy Russell made a great influence on her husband's artistic career, including an impact on his storytelling. "When there were guests in Chaz's home after he married," a St. Louis observer of Russell family history observed,

> his wife used to start him to telling stories until everyone laughed throughout the meal. And in his home, when Chaz became quiet and picked up his brushes, guests never knew quite how it happened, but they would find themselves in another room and Chaz's wife would be doing the entertaining.[50]

Nancy assumed the role of "regulating" Russell's social storytelling so as to maximize his output of paintings—for the paintings proved the most saleable form of his narrative artworks.

Charlie Russell seemed especially willing to let storytelling distract him from his artistic work when his audience was children. The youthful company, especially in later years with his adopted son Jack, brought great enjoyment to the artist. In a rare written statement, Jack Russell commented on his few personal memories of his father, who had died when Jack was only ten years old.

> My recollections of my father are dim in details. . . . The many hours he spent with me—telling me stories of the animals and of the people he knew and loved—the details of the stories are long gone but I well remember that they were always told from the viewpoint of the animals or people he was telling about. Gentleness and tolerance came through clearly.[51]

Jack Russell's perspective is consistent with the artist's interactions with other children on several occasions when he shared Indian stories and sign language.[52] "You know he was a great lover of children," one friend recalled,

FIG. 8. Charles M. Russell on the lawn of Lake McDonald Lodge, Glacier National Park, Montana. Photography by Ed Neitzling, photograph courtesy of the Amon Carter Museum, Fort Worth, Texas. Drawing and speaking simultaneously, Charlie held a magnetic rapport with children of all ages.

and one night when Charlie and Mrs. Russell came over I found him with his back to the kitchen sink, sitting on the floor, telling my small child the story of "the three bears," as he modeled the bears from a bar of laundry soap, and I am sure I don't know which one was having the better time.[53]

A younger woman recalled the time when Russell entertained herself and his son Jack with "shadow pictures—charging buffaloes, birds and all kinds of wonderful images made with just those wonderful hands of his."[54] One of Frank Linderman's daughters recalled how Russell made small sculptures, with one hand in his pocket, just to amuse himself and the little people nearby.

Evenings as we sat visiting in our living room I would see Mr. Russell pull one of his wee wax figures from his pocket. He would set a tiny pig with curly tail on the arm of his chair, giving it a punch here and there, and just as I was about to say "May I have it?" his deft fingers would flatten it out and drop it back into his pocket, to come out next as a cocky rooster, feathers and all. I never heard of anyone else who could do this.[55]

Russell's rapport with children involved many different forms of narrative delivery. Talking and sketching (or talking and sculpting) simultaneously, Charlie could charm children of any age. Among Russell's many storyteller paintings and sketches, however, only one or two depict the speaker with a graphic representation of his words (**see plate 3**).

Aside from his compulsive sculpting, Charlie Russell's frequent storytelling activity seems typical of many nineteenth-century western characters. The same Montana Newspaper Association that first printed many of Russell's stories in small-town newspapers throughout the state also carried articles about other colorful individuals from earlier days. One of these pieces involved this 1926 profile of John F. Yancy,

> who was usually called "Uncle John" by the sons and daughters of the old timers . . . Like many other old timers he did not often say much about his past life, but when the spirit moved him in this direction, the conversation was enjoyed by all who were fortunate enough to be present.[56]

In many cases, these old-timers stimulated their storytelling impulses with whiskey or other alcoholic drinks.

Russell's married-life transformation included a voluntary abstinence from alcohol during his final eighteen years. Although he still visited certain Great Falls saloons almost every afternoon to sip mineral water and share stories, Russell's life no longer included the boisterous evenings spent drinking and carousing with other men. Joe DeYong lived with the Russell family for some of these years and observed moments when Nancy might be absent on art business and Russell's need to deliver a few stories suddenly surfaced in his feelings. "In the evenings," recalled DeYong, "his loneliness sometimes found expression in a compelling urge to talk in an entertaining manner. Stories which were in all-modesty wasted since they were worthy of a larger and more important audience. And yet, he at such times 'gave of himself' as freely as is possible to imagine."[57]

For many years after his mentor's death, DeYong attempted to write about Russell's shifting moods, which varied from remotely introverted to brilliantly extroverted, but the apprentice never published most of his writings. Nevertheless, his first-draft attempts provide an inarticulate but intimate view of Russell's behavior when the impulses to tell stories surfaced abruptly. "There were certain times—moods rather," DeYong noted in one rough draft,

> Sort of an almost drowsy absentmindedness—a state of mind—of his entire being, rather—when to "come back to the surface" even for the answering of some simple, necessary question appeared to be a definite struggle; on the other hand there were also unpredictable occasions when the urge to "talk" came to the surface amount[ing] almost to a hunger!
>
> The first, being well-known to his family and small circle of intimates, was accepted without any seeming need for discussion—surely never resentment; while the other extreme was much less apt to arouse any reaction other than spontaneous

delight . . . since his was at such times the genial, magnetic quality—expansive personality on which his friendships—far more often with men than with women—were based.[58]

Apparently, the dynamic, crowd-pleasing, public-entertainer quality of Charlie Russell that so many Montana people recalled in the man they typically considered to be their personal friend was only one aspect of the complex narrative artist.

As part of managing the business affairs of her impractical, storytelling husband, Nancy Russell arranged for the construction of a log cabin to serve as an art studio located beside their Great Falls house. Occasionally the cabin also served as a social-gathering spot and story-telling site. One of the men who helped to build the structure out of decommissioned telephone poles recalled the congenial setting in the rustic building:

> Many a good time I had in that old log cabin studio. Charlie'd ask a bunch of us up there. He'd bake a batch of biscuits in a Dutch oven, and when we'd brag about them, he'd come mighty near dancin' a jig. He was a fine camp cook. We'd eat and then sit around the fireplace smoking and listening to him tell stories. He was the best story teller I ever heard.[59]

Another friend recalled that a certain "bunch" would spontaneously "know" to gather at his cabin on Sunday mornings and enjoy his humorous stories.[60] Judge Callaway was one of the favored few who arrived on the Sabbath after Nancy had gone to church. While crouching over his heels in the manner of furniture-free Indians and cowpunchers, Charlie would varnish his latest picture and entertain his friends with his yarns.[61] Nancy Russell understood that this cabin studio functioned as an inspiring place for Charlie to tell stories. "Charlie was saying," she wrote about his (delayed) enthusiasm for the place,

> "that's going to be a good shack for me. The bunch can come visit, talk and smoke, while I paint." From that day to the end of his life he loved that telephone pole building more than any other place on earth and never finished a painting any-where. . . . Sitting on his heels he would roll a cigarette with those long, slender fingers, light it, and in the smoke drift back in his talk to times when there were very few, if any, white women in Montana. It was Nature's country. If that cabin could only tell what those logs have heard![62]

For more than twenty years, the log-cabin studio served as the primary physical site that unit-ed Russell's narrative activities of storytelling, sketching, painting, and sculpting.

Beyond the magical Great Falls cabin, Russell could still hold the attention of listeners, sometimes to the point of inconveniencing others. Lila Mackenzie recalled how she had waited with her mother in the family's horse-drawn "democrat" wagon while her father conversed with men in a hotel in the southern Alberta town of Lethbridge. "Finally they came out onto the sidewalk," she recalled, "and still stood talking away, laughing and having quite a good time.

Finally my dad came over to the democrat and said, 'Well, by gosh, when Charlie Russell gets telling stories its pretty hard to walk away and leave him.'"[63] Russell visited southern Alberta throughout his life and felt comfortable sharing conversations with local Canadians in Medicine Hat, Lethbridge, Standoff, and other rural towns.

Charlie Russell traveled more than most Montana people, especially when Nancy Russell wanted to sell his art in distant urban markets. Several incidents of Russell's storytelling while traveling by rail proved especially memorable. Montana resident Wilford Johnson was a boy in 1919 when by chance he joined Charlie Russell and the artist's longtime friend E. C. "Teddy Blue" Abbott on a train to Miles City. "Russell told stories, most of them containing raw meat," recalled Johnson,

> but every one of them as clever and brilliant as stories could be made—for five or six hours, without a break. Abbott would occasionally find a place to cut in with one of his stories, always about some funny happening in a roundup or saloon, but Russell carried the ball most of the time, and provided me with one of the most interesting episodes of my life.[64]

When the Russells first went to New York in 1904, Charlie's fellow artist and urban guide, John Marchand, sparked the soft-spoken cowboy artist into telling stories on the train, entertaining the men who gathered around while passing the long ride in the smoking car.[65] Russell's return trip apparently was less enjoyable. Without his friend Marchand to get him started, the artist was on his own to generate a conversation with other passengers. Charlie blamed his lack of success on regional behavior styles. "If you go into a smoking car east of Chicago," Russell told a spontaneous welcome-home party,

> sit down beside a man and start talking to him by saying, "This is a fine country through here," he'll mumble "yes" and look the other way. You can't get anything out of 'em. I guess they're afraid you'll spring a shell game on 'em or try to sell 'em a gold brick."[66]

Russell often faced eastern indifference to his narrative western artworks.

On his first trip to New York in the winter of 1903–1904, however, Russell found a brief moment when his storytelling held the attention in literary and artistic circles at the Players' Club. This elite Manhattan location provided a gathering place for influential men typically dressed in tuxedos to enjoy fine food and drink, cigars, stories, and social one-upmanship. Author Hamlin Garland noted that "the noisy crowd" who frequented the Players' Club usually included such celebrities as "Twachtman, Simmons, Reid Metcalf and [Frederic] Remington and (quietly) Augustus St. Gaudens," in addition to less-frequent appearances by such notables as Mark Twain, Andrew Carnegie, and Theodore Roosevelt.[67]

Three professional New York illustrators, John Marchand, Albert Levering, and Will Crawford, honored their friend Charlie with a dinner at the club in 1904. Russell attracted curious stares with his everyday attire, which included a red sash, high-heeled riding boots, and western hat to complement his dark suit and tie. "He made no effort to be anyone but himself," explained John Marchand's sister, Lila Marchand Houston.

> Then my brother and [Crawford and Levring] began to draw him out and gradually he lost his shyness and story followed story as he forgot his surroundings and lived again in the wild west he had always known. The men who at first regarded him as a western curiosity were soon hanging on his every word. Here was something new and fresh. He imitated the sounds made by animals, he silently told stories in the Indian Sign Language and other conversation became dull and commonplace. Soon it was Russell who was doing the entertaining and others watched and listened. "Charlie" Russell was a success in New York.[68]

A large, illustrated article in the *New York Press* immortalized that night when Charlie Russell told stories at the Players' Club. Under the headline "Smart Set Lionizing Cowboy Artist," the *Press* described Russell's life in Montana and included photos of the artist riding a horse, as well as several of his paintings and one sculpture. After the event Nancy must have supplied the photos to the newspaper because, by that New York trip, she had made herself into a thoroughly professional press agent.[69] No record suggests that Russell met fellow western artist Frederic Remington or any other celebrity at the Players' Club on this occasion. And, despite his clear triumph in this critical arena, there is no indication that Russell ever returned to that setting to tell another story.

The momentary success of Russell's storytelling at the Players' Club contrasted with the typical New York society indifference to his verbal talents. The incident that best reflected this disinterest in Russell's storytelling took place during a *New York Times* interview in 1911, on the occasion of his first one-man gallery show in Manhattan. The full-page story in the *Times* looked grand, with large photographs of the artist and several of his paintings. But in the accompanying article, the unnamed interviewer seemed skeptical, referring sarcastically to Russell's state of mind and artworks depicting the nineteenth-century West as "Dreamland Montana, the mysterious mountain-land that has melted away never to return . . . dotted with the bones of murdered and scalped palefaces."[70] In the conversation that led to this article, Russell's typical shyness with interviewers stifled any long responses to the questions. The impatient writer observed, "That's how Russell talks when he is interviewed. He is hopeless."[71] The interview had nearly ended when Russell started to tell a story. Westerners like Great Falls resident L. E. Falk would see this as a moment when "the gods smiled" on the listener,[72] but the *Times* interviewer had heard enough when this uncooperative, bumpkin painter

> plunged, with huge relief, into anecdotes utterly irrelevant to the interview, and the interviewer pocketed his pencil in despair, and a pair of Russell's friends, realizing the situation, gently but firmly eliminated the big Westerner entirely from the interview, and started in themselves to tell about the picturesque career which the artist himself seemed entirely incapable of divulging.[73]

The *Times* writer accepted, without question, Russell's New York friends' inaccurate versions of

the artist's life story, even though the subject sat silently before him. Readers might have concluded that Russell had walked out of the meeting room ten minutes before the conversation ended.
Yet, despite an unsympathetic interview in an influential newspaper, Russell's gallery show proved
a success. Because of the interviewer's resistance to western storytelling, however, *The New York
Times* lost an opportunity to sample Charlie Russell's conversational narrative magic.

Stressful newspaper interviews notwithstanding, Russell could perform well in the limelight of popular attention, but he could just as easily sit through a cordial social gathering
silently engulfed in personal thoughts. Among strangers, he usually required gentle coercion by
knowledgeable friends to begin his storytelling. On the other hand, adulation and lavish praise
made him especially uncomfortable. As a St. Louis newspaper phrased it, "With the true artist's
dread of being lionized, Russell is at his best when, among a few friends, he recounts his adventures in the cow camps, holding his auditors spellbound by his soft vibrant voice and his compelling, magnetic personality."[74]

After 1904, the Russells returned to New York almost annually for the next fifteen years.
There are few accounts of Russell performing stories on these trips like he did at the Players
Club, however. Nevertheless, on one rare occasion in New York, Russell sparked himself out of
a somber mood and into his most lively storytelling self. A Great Falls neighbor and family
friend recalled that a high official of Montana's Anaconda Corporation had decided to offer his
friends the opportunity to meet Charles M. Russell and hear his stories over a fancy dinner.

> He prepared his friends by telling them that they were to hear one of the greatest
> story tellers and one of the wittiest men he ever knew. Charlie went to the dinner—
> perhaps Nancy made him—but he was in no frame of mind to enjoy himself. He
> didn't like New York. He didn't like the polished and sophisticated New Yorkers.
>
> The dinner began, the dinner progressed. Charlie sat there unimpressed and
> silent. With each passing moment his host became more and more frustrated. He
> struggled in every way to bring Charlie out. Finally, as he was too distraught to do
> anything but bring the dinner to a close, the many kinds of wine hit Charlie and he
> turned to his host and drawled, "You know our cows in Montana in the hot August
> sun is nearer dead than that beef served tonight." From then until dawn, Charlie
> told story after story, and the guests went home reeling with laughter, and perhaps
> with wine.[75]

This scene probably took place between 1904 and 1908 because Russell stopped drinking alcohol
altogether during the latter year. Maynard Dixon reported meeting Russell in New York in 1908,
aware of his reputation as a heavy drinker. At a restaurant gathering, Dixon observed: "At table he
refused a cocktail, but took one glass of wine with dinner and let it go at that. For this he had my
immediate respect.—and kept it."[76] After 1908, only Russell's unpredictable spontaneity, rather
than excess wine, would have moved him to break into comment on the especially rare beef.

The most comfortable urban setting for Russell was Great Falls. And for many years,
most of the people in this town reacted to him with appreciation and affection. Russell's
Montana contemporary Earl Talbot told researcher James Rankin about the banquet honoring

Russell on his 1911 return from his first solo exhibition in a major New York art gallery. Talbot recalled that Russell responded to the party crowd in Great Falls's familiar Rainbow Hotel by sharing versions of yarns that eventually were published in books of his stories. This was a rare moment when Russell performed such material aloud in front of a large audience. For groups larger than about thirty people, Russell most often spoke in silent sign language through an interpreter or not at all.

Charlie Russell's primary scene for storytelling included certain locations along Great Falls's busy Central Avenue. In early years, before 1900, a favorite site was the old Park Hotel. In subsequent years, according to Joe DeYong, Russell typically ended his afternoon visits to the main-street saloons at Goodman's Cigar Store next to The Mint saloon, and at Hillgard's Post Office newsstand. Sid Willis's Mint has been the bar most often associated in Montana legends with Charlie Russell because the artist frequented the place almost daily. During his out-of-town travels, he sent his friend Sid many amusing illustrated letters. Also, he supplied Willis with the grandest collection of his artworks to be found anywhere in public until the second half of the twentieth century. But The Mint was not Russell's favorite saloon. DeYong noted that Russell preferred Bill Rance's smaller Silver Dollar saloon, across the street from The Mint. He visited it regularly until the Prohibition laws in 1919 forced the Silver Dollar's closure. At that time, Rance sold most of his Russell artworks to The Mint, which survived Prohibition as a restaurant and ice-cream parlor. Russell responded sharply to DeYong's observation that The Mint was the more popular bar along Central Avenue.

> [Bill] Rance's place was small, darkly pannelled [sic], and the gathering place for the "elite"—the "quality-drinkers" of the town.... The Mint—large, usually crowded—catered to the Smelter Workers, and much often—noisly [sic] expansive types. And when I happened to remark "It looks like the Mint gets the trade!" Charlie explosively and with—for him—an extremely rare expression of scorn in his eyes, blurted: "Its all five-cent stuff!"[77]

In the early twentieth century, Great Falls was changing, and the industrial workers who relaxed over a nickel glass of beer probably ignored the Russell art covering The Mint's walls. They were less likely to pay close attention to older men quietly sharing droll stories about trappers, Indians, cowpunchers, or other Old West characters. Nevertheless, DeYong recalled one of the urban-industrial workers who appreciated Russell's old-fashioned stories:

> In one instance a certain workman of the Lunch-Bucket type who worked at a refinery across the River remarked after Russell's death, "I used to try to get off early and hurry up to the cigar store to hear Charlie tell stories; but now I go straight home."[78]

This working man was an exception among the changing population that became less likely to gather around Charlie Russell in the street to hear the artist's spontaneous humor.

Russell regretted his growing sense of alienation from Montana people. He commented once to his range pal Tommy Tucker that "we usto know every body but time has made us strangers but we got no licence to kick we got the cream let these comletlys have the skim milk[.]"[79] His old cattle-range friends were dying off or had moved away. The cattle ranges had been transformed into wheat farms and smaller, fenced ranches. His friends among the Indian tribes struggled to survive on impoverished reservations. The mechanized twentieth century was replacing companionable horses with noisy automobiles, trucks, and tractors. Large industrial smelters and refineries fouled the Great Falls air. And perhaps most important, fewer people cared to remember characters and adventures of the earlier days in stories about the "Old West." In addition to these disappointments, Russell contributed to his detachment from local people with his long absences from Great Falls to sell artworks in major cities, to spend winters in California, and to spend summers at his cabin in Glacier Park.

Even though there were fewer opportunities for spontaneous storytelling with Great Falls locals, Russell still found congenial circumstances where he could keep his narrative flow active. There were many stories told at the Russell's private cabin, "Bull Head Lodge," located inside the eventual boundaries of Glacier National Park. One Kalispell-area friend recalled that Russell "would sit on the porch of the Lewis Hotel [by Glacier's Lake McDonald], and start telling stories to maybe only John Lewis or some other friend. Before long somebody else would approach to listen, then others, until everybody at the hotel would be around listening to Charlie tell stories."[80] Russell occasionally rode on the pack trips through Glacier that dude-ranch innovator Howard Eaton organized. On one Eaton trip, the novelist Mary Roberts Rinehart was impressed by Russell's storytelling. "And there was supper and the camp-fire," Rinehart recalled:

> Charley Russell, the cowboy artist, was the campfire star. To repeat one of his stories would be desecration. No one but Charley himself, speaking though his nose, with his magnificent head outlined against the firelight, will ever be able to tell one of his stories.[81]

Glacier's astonishing mountains and lakes must have invigorated Russell's energy and imagination. One relative who visited the Russell cabin on Lake McDonald observed that almost nothing could stop Charlie's continuous flow of stories.

> Most of our ablutions were performed on this pier with the clear cold lake as a wash basin. I'll always remember Charley starting a story and keeping going strong all the time he was dousing his face in the lake, taking out his store teeth for cleaning. There wasn't much of anything that could stop that bird from talking.[82]

The icy waters in Lake McDonald, recently melted from mountain snows and glaciers, took the breath away and made most swimmers' teeth chatter, no doubt contributing to Russell's nonstop yarn-spinning during personal scrubbing and washing.

Charlie Russell shared a seemingly bottomless well of tales when he attended the Pablo/Allard buffalo roundups on Montana's Flathead Indian Reservation in 1908 and 1909.[83] "We sat around the large campfire all evening telling stories and talking," noted a *Toronto Globe*

FIG. 9. Charles M. Russell, Howard Eaton (left), and two guest riders, 1915. Almeron J. Baker, Portland, Oregon, photographer; photography courtesy of the C. M. Russell Museum, Great Falls, Montana. Charlie is sculpting and talking to dude-ranch innovator Eaton and two guests on a horse-riding trip into Glacier National Park.

reporter who attended and wrote about the roundup and sale of Indian-owned buffalo for shipment to Canada.

> Here the personalities of the different members of the party came out. The star per-former was Charlie Russell, the ex-cowboy and present artist of western life. He is fine and voluable, constantly talking and full of stories. These are the greatest collec-tion of wit combined with vulgarity I ever heard. He is also a star as a swearer, for in men's company his language is a succession of oaths and petty exclamations.[84]

The prim Canadian reporter may have been encountering his first dose of the everyday profanity typically shared among American men talking around a campfire. Apparently, cow-boys of the American West displayed a special talent for a sudden blast of profane words and phrases. Western writer Stewart Edward White once attempted to describe this phenomenon, but he admitted "to observe the riot of imagination turned loose with the bridle off, you must assist at a burst of anger on the part of one of these men." White declared:

It is most unprintable, but you will get an entirely new idea of what profanity means. Also you will come to the conclusion that you, with your trifling damns, and the like, have been a very good boy indeed. The remotest, most obscure and unheard-of conceptions are dragged forth from earth, heaven, and hell, and linked together in a sequence so original, so gaudy and so utterly blasphemous that you gasp and are stricken with the most devoted admiration. It is Genius.

Of course I can give you no idea here of what these truly magnificent oaths are like. It is a pity, for it could liberalize your education.[85]

Mark Twain did not limit the mastery of profane diatribes to western range-riders, stating, "when it comes to pure ornamental cursing, the native American is gifted above the sons of men."[86] Twain's examples for this tribute were, nevertheless, western miners.

Beyond the Toronto reporter's astonishment, one of the few published observations of Russell's profane capabilities was a reference to a relatively innocent outburst, recorded by a friendly townswoman. "I think he enjoyed his neighbors, especially our small fry of a son," wrote Jesse Lincoln Mitchell.

These two soon sealed their friendship over a dead mother robin. Russell was a great lover of all wildlife and he had helped his mother robin with her nest in the back-yard. He and Son were together when they heard the wild cries of the mother bird, and rushing too late to her aid, they found an old alley cat had killed her. Son stood in awed fascination at the words that rolled from the corner of Russell's mouth. Then they sat down on the lower step and were quiet. Finally, Son turned to the man next to him and said, "Do you like cats?" This was where I left the scene.[87]

Mitchell had observed Russell overstepping a basic rule of profanity among nineteenth-century westerners, limiting the use of such language to the company of men.

Russell was generally sensitive to normal propriety and confined his use of narrative profanity to oral stories shared with men and kept it out of his published works. Even his private letters were free of any words rougher than "damn" or "hell." Of course, Russell was immune to guilt pangs over routine profanity used among his pals. He joked to a friend, "if cusing is wrong we'l stay in Hell not till the cows come home but till the buffalo come back. but I cant think of a bunch I'd rather be in Hell with[.]"[88] Among his many friends the opinions seemed split between those who claimed he never used rough language and those who best remembered all the roughest stories. Witnesses to Russell's banter-filled visits to Senator Paris Gibson's office in Great Falls asserted that all his language was clean.

CMR frequently visited Paris Gibson's offices in the afternoons. "That reminds me—" and is off on a story—never repeated, never off-color, . . . told incidents, character sketches, to illustrate a point in conversation not to mold people . . . didn't laugh at his own stories much—smiled, twinkle in his eye. Never used profane language beyond a damn.[89]

New York artist John Marchand once told his sister that he never heard Russell "use a word or tell a story which could not be repeated to a company of ladies. . . . Russell had an innate refinement. He was a cowboy, but a gentleman."[90]

In contrast with this well-meaning sentiment, Great Falls Bank President Lee Ford knew that Russell was quite capable of adapting stories and language to the inclinations of his audiences. "Charlie had stories for any and all occasions," Ford wrote, "and if called he could appear before the meeting of a ministerial association, a convention of school teachers, W.C.T.U.'s, bar tenders, or Civil War veterans and convulse the several audiences with most appropriate stories."[91] In truth, Russell was never called for such duties and avoided speaking before most groups. But Ford's evaluation holds true for the spontaneous storytelling that Russell shared with informal clusters of friendly people.

One of Russell's few formal talks occurred before the assembled students at Great Falls High School just a year before his death. Students present at this occasion recalled later that while he spoke quietly from a front corner of the stage, Russell continuously rolled cigarettes that were soon discarded unlit because they had each lost all their tobacco fragments in his nervous hands.[92] Nancy Russell stood nearby to reassure him and to interpret her husband's sign-language story. The student newspaper reported the event with a front-page article and photo of Charlie in his studio.

> Mr. Russell told in his talk that the school systems of the olden days differed with the system practiced today, as a man had to have much muscle in order to hold his position then. The artist stated that he held no love for schools and the work attached to them when he was a boy, but was forever devising ways of getting out of doing the work. The story in the sign language ended his speech.[93]

Looking back in the 1930s, many of the artist's cronies verified the artist's skill with off-color language and narratives, but none dared to provide written examples that they still remembered. One Great Falls friend told researcher James Rankin that he worried about violating federal anti-obscenity laws if he were to send a version of an off-color Russell story through the mails. He explained that Charlie had lived during a rougher era and never pretended to be "a parlor story teller."[94] Similarly, Aldee Bessette explained that many Russell stories that he remembered "couldn't be published, he was a man's man and told stories mostly for men's ears. I know a lot but can't quite publish them if I ever see you I'll tell them."[95] Julius Hillgard described the story swapping that happened at his mother's Great Falls Post Office newsstand, near The Mint. "Everyday Charlie Russell used to come down there and meet with five or six old-time cowhands and swap stories," Hillgard told researcher Forest Crossen.

> I could have probably become very wealthy publishing those stories. But some of them were off-color. Some of the finest privy stories I have heard in my life were told by Charlie and Jimmy Denean and Jimmy Casey and the other old cowhands. They were wonderful stories; they depicted the spirit of the old west and what the boys used to do on the range and otherwise."[96]

In telling his stories, Russell frequently created works in other art forms that corresponded to the topics he told aloud. It is not surprising, then, to find that Russell's narrative range extended beyond propriety in the other techniques as well. A few Russell paintings depict sexual situations between men and women. These pictures were probably related to the Russell stories that his friends remembered vividly but refused to write down. Bessette referred to one of Charlie Russell's more infamous examples of barroom pornography: "You should see [t]his cowboy and squaw picture Sid has [:] it's a 'mens only' one [.]"[97] The Mint's art collection included the picture *Joy of Life* that Sid Willis had secured from the Silver Dollar. It depicts a cowboy and an Indian woman copulating inside a tepee. An attached leather flap representing the outer part of the tepee wall covers the figures, but viewers wishing to see a graphic depiction may swing it up from the surface. A less-explicit Russell watercolor, the third in a four-picture set, titled *Just a Little Pleasure,* depicts a bedroom scene where a prostitute helps a drunken cowboy remove his boots.[98] Russell's portrayal of sexual themes in works of art appears to have ceased with his marriage in 1896. In an effort to raise Russell's artistic and social stature, Nancy Russell attempted to destroy all examples of her husband's sexually oriented art and she nearly succeeded.[99] Nevertheless, sexuality and other unseemly topics most likely continued as story themes that were shared discretely with select cronies. Repetitions and rumors of these unseemly stories added to Charlie Russell's negative reputation with wives of his cronies as well as the "moralists" and more dignified residents of urbanizing Montana.

In refined company, Russell could be reluctant but capable in conversation. Jessie Lincoln Mitchell recalled the night that Russell spontaneously assumed the limelight of an intellectual discussion group. When invited to join the Roundtable Club, "Russell declined," wrote Mitchell, "by saying they were too high brow for him. His field was painting, not writing." She continued:

> But they would not take no for an answer. . . . The first night he was present, one of the most brilliant minds of the club had a paper on the German philosopher, Nietzsche. When the masterpiece was finished, Charlie was the first to comment, and my husband said no one that evening opened his mouth except to scream with laughter, for Charlie was at his best. He was among men he liked and there was Nietzsche whom he didn't like. Dignified ministers and sober doctors threw back their heads and laughed till their faces were crimson. As they left the meeting, the writer of the paper said, "And to think I spent a year writing that paper, and instead of a Nietzsche night, it was a spontaneous Charlie Russell night!"[100]

Despite his success in making somber men laugh about issues raised by Nietzsche, Russell was disinclined to speak as a literary critic. He avoided participating in most intellectual discussions. Austin Russell recalled a pretentious conversation in the Russell home when Nancy was encouraging a visiting author to express his opinions about "Modern Art," a topic that her husband distained. Charlie interrupted the discussion, pushing away from the dinner table, stating, "Well, you people can sit up as late as you like but this is Saturday night and I'm going to take a bath if it chokes the sewer."[101] He genuinely preferred vivid anecdotes about unsophisticated western characters over intellectual issues examined in lofty discourse.

FIG. 10. Will Rogers and Charles M. Russell, 1921. Photography by Sinclair Bull. Photograph
courtesy of the Homer and Helen Britzman Collection, Taylor Museum, Colorado
Springs Fine Arts Center. Russell was visiting Rogers on the set of the silent film
A Poor Relation, at the Goldwyn Studios in Los Angeles.

Russell's narrative abilities occasionally met their match among men of parallel interests.
For more than twenty years humorist Will Rogers and Charlie Russell both enjoyed the
moments when their professional careers enabled them to spend time together. One mutual
friend of those years was Ed Borein, a successful western artist who had cattle-range experience
in Mexico and California similar to Russell's in Montana. Mrs. Borein recalled when Rogers
and Russell visited the Borein hacienda in Santa Barbara. "They told stories before dinner, during dinner and after dinner . . . far into the wee hours of the morning," she reported to her husband's biographer:

> There was no drinking and no off-color stories. They were just like little boys. I
> went up to bed, and at 3:00 a.m. came down to find out if Ed intended to sleep at
> all. The three were amazed to learn what time it was—they had lost themselves
> completely in their story telling. They smoked Bull Durham, rolling their
> own . . . and next morning the tobacco was inches thick on the rugs.[102]

Will Rogers, Jr., told Davidson that when literary humorist Irvin S. Cobb socialized with his father, Will Rogers, Sr., the two "would have a shouting match, because Dad was used to the center of the stage, and Cobb wasn't going to yield it very easily." He added:

> My memory is that Ed [Borein] wasn't as sparkling as the rest of them, and he wasn't as talkative, but of course, he was in pretty high-class company. Russell was a great storyteller; in fact, the dope I get is when he started to talk, everybody else stopped talking. He must have had quite a dominating personality.[103]

Cobb told his own daughter that his idea of heaven would be "a campfire in the woods . . . listening to Charley Russell tell stories."[104]

Will Rogers wrote the "Introduction" to Charlie Russell's posthumous collection of stories, *Trails Plowed Under,* and included his own idea of heaven. In this imagined afterlife, Charlie Russell would be exchanging good yarns with the likes of famous nineteenth-century American humorists Abe Lincoln, Mark Twain, Bill Nye, and James Whitcomb Riley. Although Russell had been more inclined to share stories with everyday ranch hands and townspeople than with celebrities, Rogers was right to imagine that storytelling would be the activity of choice for the angelic Charlie Russell, rather than sketching, painting, or sculpting. Storytelling was his favorite pastime activity among all others. "But with old Charlie, if he had quit talking to you and started painting, you would-a got sore," wrote Rogers:

> It wasn't what you wanted. What you wanted was to hear him talk, or read what he said. . . . If he had devoted the same time to writing that he had to his brush, he would have left a tremendous impression in that line. It's cropping out in every letter, in every line, his original observations, original ways of expressing them. He was a great storyteller. Bret Hart[e], Mark Twain or any of our old traditions couldn't paint a word picture with the originality that Charlie could. He could take a short little yarn and make a production out of it. What a public entertainer he would have made. So few writers can tell their stuff.[105]

Story and narrative were Charlie Russell's primary preoccupations and telling tales aloud to receptive people provided the easiest means of delivering good stories, followed by sketching, sculpting, painting, and, dead last, writing them down on paper. Only with the greatest effort did Russell overcome his resistance to saving narratives in writing. The few Russell stories that have survived in print are the result of his sluggish initiative, his wife's persistence, the determination of his friends, and sheer luck. Nevertheless, long after the paint dried on thousands of his pictures and the dozens of bronzes had acquired a rich patina, a handful of Russell tales still come to life on paper, confirming the descriptions of family and friends of the absolute primacy of storytelling in this artist's life.

CHAPTER TWO

Stories into Print

The west is dead my friend
But writers hold the seed
And what they sow
Will live and grow
Again to those that read[1]

Charlie Russell relished telling stories among supportive and knowledgeable friends, but he was far less enthusiastic about publishing them. For Russell, writing was the most difficult form of narrative expression. As he once remarked, "as a talker I am better than a green hand but with the pen I am Dam nere deaf and dumb[.]"[2] Russell told fellow storyteller and author Frank Linderman, "the pen to me is the same as the pick. Its work and Im one of the men that sweats when I write."[3] Joe DeYong provides the most vivid account of Russell's all-out struggle to write even a casual letter to an old friend:

> Usually he would grasp the pen in one hand and the ink bottle in the other and while staring blankly straight ahead—exactly like the steersman holding onto the spokes of the wheel of a ship in rough weather, with the sweat streaming down his forehead, he appeared to actually struggle over every word—it being extremely rare for him to write a complete sentence with out having to stop and think before going further. One, two, three words at a time and always slow. . . . he had little idea of spelling and none whatever of punctuation other than the period, sometimes a question-mark and—though rarely—a few chance commas squeaked in like so much pepper and salt.[4]

Indeed, Russell's first publishing venture lacked words altogether. In 1889, at the urging of his friend Ben Roberts, Charlie Russell painted a dozen black-and-white pictures to be published in 1890 as a portfolio-styled book under the title, *Studies of Western Life.*[5] Within the same year, Roberts published a second edition of the book, including comments about each picture as written by pioneer Montana cattleman Granville Stuart. Roberts reported later that Russell had initially resisted the idea of depicting aspects of life in the West in a series of pictures, but he finally agreed and painted the twelve in just eight days.[6] Whatever ideas Russell had in mind for each image, the task fell to Stuart, the owner/operator of the DHS cattle outfit, to put appropriate words with the black-and-white paintings.

EARLY DAYS ON THE BUFFALO RANGE AND MEDICINE ARROW

Seven years passed following the publication of *Studies of Western Life* before Russell published a story of his own in a national publication. The April 1897 issue of *Recreation* carried "Early Days on the Buffalo Range," plus three illustrations, all by "C. M. Russell."[7] Although the events of the story took place in 1857, seven years before the author was born, Russell used a first-person narrator. In this fictional autobiography, the twenty-year-old "narrator" has camped among the Blackfeet Indians as member of a traders' group. Most of the tale focuses on the narrator's participation in a buffalo hunt, as part of a band chasing and shooting the stampeding animals from the backs of hard-running horses. Many elements of the story bear direct similarities to one Russell revised and published twice more during the next forty years, entitled "How Lindsay Turned Indian." The narrator's language here is more grammatically correct and less idiomatic than the slang that Russell's narrators used in most of the stories published later. Russell seems to have struggled in writing the text, achieving only a stiff formal style. Nevertheless, a comparison between the final magazine version and the author's handwritten draft shows that the magazine editors made surprisingly few changes beyond correcting Russell's characteristic spelling and punctuation errors.[8]

In 1897, Russell had overcome his chronic reluctance to write when he produced his sixteen-page draft of "Early Days on the Buffalo Range." Although there is no evidence about Russell's motive, several scholars have concluded that newlywed, uneducated, eighteen-year-old Nancy Russell had maneuvered her thirty-one-year-old cowboy husband into creating this work.[9] In contrast, one friend recalled that Russell had turned to writing "after years of suggestion on the part of his friends [when] he put into type yarns of experience and romance in the days when men and things were rough and red, wild and wooly in the cow country of Montana."[10] It also seems plausible that Russell's literate friends and mentors ranging from Granville Stuart to such local writers as James Willard Schultz[11] and Robert Vaughn also may have convinced the stubborn young painter that the difficult story-writing and publishing process might help secure illustration contracts and sell more artworks.

Writing the magazine story must have been unsatisfactory for Russell. Apparently, he had so little interest in the process that just one year after the appearance of "Early Days on the Buffalo Range," the author gave away a story for publication rather than write it himself. Instead, the January 1898 issue of *Sports Afield* carried a fable by Anna P. Nelson titled "The

Medicine Arrow."[12] The magazine also published three illustrations for the story by Charles M. Russell, including the picture used on the issue's cover page. According to the author's daughter, Elizabeth Nelson Greenfield, Russell often told her stories, including "The Medicine Arrow," when he visited the Nelson ranch, which was located between Cascade and Great Falls. "One reason my mother wrote the story was because I was so full of it," wrote Greenfield sixty-six years after Russell had first shared the story with her.

> I had told and re-told it as Charlie had told it to me. It was a legend, so Charlie said, about a sad young Indian whose arrows never found their mark. Charlie told it while we were sitting on the sandbar between our ranch home and the Missouri River. . . .
>
> After the visit when Charlie told me the Medicine Arrow story, my mother got an idea. Why not write it up and get Charlie to illustrate it, then send it to some magazine and perhaps a sale would develop that would help Charlie win the recognition he so badly needed. For in those early years Charlie and Nancy were very hard up. . . . So She wrote up the legend in elegant language that was not like Charlie's at all.[13]

The Medicine Arrow fable echoed Russell's own situation of inadequate art sales. Even if this legend was not autobiographical, it provided a remarkable match between an Indian legend of a warrior who couldn't bring home food and Russell's own lack of art sales. Greenfield's mother apparently believed that Russell was oblivious to the benefits of publishing a story. And the daughter's explanation is consistent with other descriptions of Russell's spontaneous rapport with children. As Greenfield remembered it, Russell was preoccupied with storytelling.

> Charlie could never sit long without telling a tale. Indeed, I would not have let him. Usually he modeled a bit of wax as he talked so that at tale's end there was his leading character sitting on the palm of his hand. No wonder children adored him![14]

Russell enjoyed the company of children and may have anticipated having some of his own, since he had been married to Nancy for two years. His gift of "The Medicine Arrow" to this little girl, and his consent to have her mother rewrite it for publication, shows that story *telling* was clearly more important to him than story *publishing*.

A Savage Santa Claus

Nine years after his first printed story, Russell published another. On December 16, 1906, the *Great Falls Daily Tribune* featured a special section in its Sunday edition, offering a sampling of Christmas stories by local writers. Positioned at the top of the section's front page was Russell's story "A Savage Santa Claus," accompanied by a sketch of two men firing rifles at an attacking bear.[15] This tale, with its vivid illustration and headline title, overpowered the other pieces on the page.

FIG. 11. *"It's Like Hell on a Holiday."* Pen/ink illustration for the story "A Savage Santa Claus,"
Great Falls Daily Tribune, December 6, 1906; reprinted in *More Rawhides* (Great Falls:
Montana Newspaper Association, 1925), with the title *"The Bark of Beaver's Henry
Brings Me Out of the Scare."* Charlie redrew the sketch for *Trails Plowed Under.*

"A Savage Santa Claus" broke new ground for the writer Charlie Russell. It was his first
published story that featured a narrator speaking in rural Montana slang. This format would
characterize most of Russell's subsequent tales. The narrator, however, was not the "Rawhide
Rawlins" figure who would later become the fictional storyteller for half of Russell's subsequent
yarns. The voice telling "A Savage Santa Claus" belongs to the story's lead character, whom
Russell named "Bedrock." Coincidentally, a man identified as "Bedrock" Jim Bercham lived in
the Little Belt Mountains along the west side of the Judith Basin near Utica.[16] The nickname
would certainly have been humorous to Russell and anyone else familiar with local characters
of that area. In contrast with the reliable solidity of the mining term, the man called "Bedrock"
was an eccentric, unpredictable miner. This Bedrock stayed around the gold-mining camp,
known as "Yogo," long after the gold ore had "played out" to reduce the mountain boomtown
of the late 1870s to an abandoned ghost town. In the years that followed, Bedrock appeared
occasionally in the nearby stagecoach-stop village named Utica to trade bits of gold dust for
supplies before retreating back into the hills, where he gradually became a recluse, living in a

cave and shunning human contact.[17] By giving his narrator and main character the name "Bedrock," Russell established a humorous mood for his audience, who may already have heard rumors or stories about the Montana miner by that name. Independent gold panners inspired the artist to create many prospector images, including a watercolor foreshadowing the arrival of mining industry buildings (**see plate 4**).

Beyond the subtle joke of his narrator's name, Russell's brief Christmas tale gives Bedrock the extra irony of sympathetic intellectual and emotional depth. The narrator shifts from spinning jokes about cold weather, and a horse who seems to tell the miners when to dismount for shelter, to telling a ghost story about a life-or-death struggle with a monstrous grizzly bear and the startling discovery of the bones of the cabin's original owner. In contrast with the story's second character, "Beaver," who cares only about the dead man's gold stash, Bedrock understands the tragic side to the cabin owner's death. He gives the dead man's remains a decent burial before the two visitors solemnly depart. By the time this tale ends, Bedrock has experienced a sobering brush with death in the jaws of the great bear that the men had nervously called "Old Santy Claus." In addition, Bedrock has gained an appreciation for another man's lonesome demise that deserves respectful closure. At the conclusion of this violent Christmas ghost story, Bedrock Jim, the joking narrator, has become a serious person worthy of respect. And the author, Charlie Russell, has proven that he could preserve his storyteller's subtle craft on paper.

This tale reappeared in the Montana Newspaper Association (MNA) weekly newspaper inserts in 1922, in Russell's second book of stories, *More Rawhides*,[18] and, ultimately, in 1927 in *Trails Plowed Under*. From the first typed manuscript[19] through three subsequent printings, the story remained intact with only a few words altered for the 1927 version. By using a fictional character/narrator speaking in rural slang Russell had found an effective style for transferring his spoken yarns onto paper. Whether the narrator would be "Rawhide Rawlins," "Dad Lane," "Bedrock Jim," or an unnamed rural voice who seems to be Russell himself, the narrative format that mimicked the speech of an unlettered, but perceptive, rural storyteller became Russell's primary story-writing style. "A Savage Santa Claus" proved to be a milestone, for it marked the practical beginning of Charlie Russell's professional writing career.

The appearance of Charlie Russell's Christmas story also signaled another milestone—the involvement of his wife, Nancy. As revealed in a newspaper interview four years later, Nancy had quietly begun to participate in Russell's storytelling to ensure that the tales appeared successfully on the printed page. "The artist's wife acts as his manager and markets his work," explained a St. Louis newspaper, "and recently launched him as a writer." The piece continued:

> It was necessary for Mrs. Russell to learn shorthand to do this. The artist has profound confidence in her judgment, but she couldn't persuade him that he could write. Caspar Whitney, editor of Outing, who visited the Russells in the West, thought he could. Whitney said that if Russell would write the story of some of his experiences just as he told them, and illustrate it, the product eagerly would be sought by magazines. But Russell was obdurate. He was not sure whether he could paint, but he knew he could not write.

So Mrs. Russell learned shorthand and surreptitiously took down his stories as he told them to friends. Together they edited them, and he illustrated them. Several have appeared in recent magazine issues.[20]

By having Nancy transcribe his stories as he told them aloud, Charlie bypassed the self-conscious formality that weighed down his 1897 story-writing experiment, "Early Days on the Buffalo Range." The reporter may have overstated the situation in saying that Nancy "surreptitiously" transcribed Charlie's spontaneous narratives.[21] Although Nancy may have been discreet when taking notes while Charlie spoke, he would have been fully aware of her presence and purpose. Russell told quite different stories when only men were present, and it would have been unlikely for Nancy to transcribe one of Charlie's "men only" stories. Nevertheless, the newspaper account of Nancy's transcriptions confirms her involvement in this stage of her husband's story writing and raises the question whether she also directed his first story-writing effort. Nancy's shorthand transcriptions were important because they assured that Russell's tales maintained the immediate sense of his spoken words. As a young sculptor and friend of Charlie's once observed, "To write a story told by Russell, so it would go over [it] would have to be told exactly the way he told them [for] if that was not done the story looses its 'kick.'"[22] If Nancy transcribed "A Savage Santa Claus" the way it appears in both typed manuscript and final printed form, then Russell's use of "Bedrock" as a fictional narrator would have been an oral-transmission technique—written down by Nancy as he told a story out loud. It is also possible that the fictional narrator could have appeared at some later time when Charlie and Nancy edited the piece for the first typed manuscript.

The newspaper readers around Great Falls could see that Charlie Russell wrote a good story. They also learned in the same edition that the "Cowboy Artist" would soon publish more stories in a national magazine. The same Sunday paper announced, "So far, Russell has written a series of short stories, to be called 'Line Camp Yarns,' which are advertised as a feature in the attractions listed for the coming year by the *Outing* magazine."[23] A year later, the *Tribune* proudly predicted that his writings would be as successful as his paintings and spoken stories.

> Charles M. Russell, Great Falls' famous cowboy artist, is in the spotlight in the February number of Outing, . . . Russell, among his acquaintances, is as well-known for his ability as a story teller as he is famous throughout the country as a painter of western life, and it is very probable that his literary efforts will make him even better known than he is now.[24]

The local reporters assumed that publishing success would come easily to the hometown artist with a growing national profile. The process, however, proved to be much more difficult.

The *St. Louis Post Dispatch* referred to the Russells' interactions with Caspar Whitney and *Outing* magazine. Nancy's persistent efforts to find illustration work for Charlie when they visited New York in 1904, 1905, and 1906 succeeded when she secured contracts from several national magazines, including Whitney's *Outing*. As one of the higher-quality publications in the twentieth century's first decade, *Outing* was among the few national publications still interested in pieces about the West. Although five Russell stories received national distribution in *Outing,* the communication with Whitney proved frustrating for Nancy Russell.[25] Whitney had enthusiastically accepted the tales and even commissioned Charlie Russell to create artworks in Old Mexico for another writer's stories, but Nancy anticipated a larger project. On their return from Mexico, the Russells spent several days in Los Angeles. There, a newspaper reporter told of Nancy's wish that Caspar Whitney publish a book of Charlie's stories and illustrations. Nancy Russell also stated that Whitney had also "informed Mr. Russell that these stories are to be made into book form after they have run in the magazine."[26] Whitney may have hinted, or even agreed, with Nancy's typically blunt questions about such a project. But he never moved beyond the magazine publication of the Russell stories that he printed in 1907 and 1908.

While *Outing* was printing Charlie's tales, Nancy pressed harder for more illustration assignments, story placements, and a book project. Whitney responded directly to the artist himself with manipulative flattery that veiled his negative message.

> Dear Charlie Russell:—
> . . . Don't you get impatient Charlie Russell,—you are doing all right. You are putting on canvas a phase of life that is fast passing, and you are making a name for yourself as an illustrator and really a historian. Good luck to you!
> I wish this magazine was my very own and I could combine the business as well as the editorial management in one. If I could, I would have you in the magazine every month; and that's no mere boquet that I am throwing at you. . . . [27]

Whitney was not rejecting the Russells completely, but he was "stringing them along."

The early years of the twentieth century brought a diminished market for western magazine subjects, other than pulp-format, romantic western fiction.[28] From 1888 through 1905, dominant publications such as *Harper's* had published western stories and/or pictures by Frederic Remington in almost every issue.[29] By 1907, however, this had come to a complete halt. In the declining marketplace for Charlie Russell's tales, Caspar Whitney and Nancy Russell exchanged letters frequently for about two years. The artist's wife regularly offered more stories for *Outing,* and Whitney regularly declined. Then, just as Whitney began to hint about perhaps printing a few more stories, the editor abruptly changed jobs. With the new year, he greeted the Russells as editor of the "Outdoor America" department of *Collier's Weekly.* It proved to be bad news for Charlie and Nancy Russell. Whitney's 1908 letter said that he was forbidden to compete with *Collier's* by publishing any fiction in "Outdoor America." As he told the Russells, "I can use the romance of travel and adventure, if it's a true story; or I can use anything in fact that isn't fiction."[30]

After congratulating Whitney on his new position, Nancy's response revealed her confusion over the role that fiction and fact played in her husband's writings: "Chas. says he does not know whether his stories would be called fiction or not. They are taken from stories fellows have told and a good many of them are from happenings of friends of his. This article, 'The Cowboy as he Was' is absolutely true as near as Chas. could get it. It is really a bit of history."[31] The same confusion between history as documented events and history as secondhand "word-of-mouth" yarns also could apply to most of Russell's paintings. Russell's artworks typically depict a moment in some incident that involves specific people in a specific location, but they never attempt to be an "exact" photographic rendition of a certain moment. The artworks are generally accurate but not precise representations in the manner of photographs. In her appeal to Whitney, Nancy did not claim that Charlie had created the stories himself, but only that he was relaying narratives from reliable sources. For Nancy, this process made the stories "true," not at all fictional. To add to the confusion, Russell's historical essays or extended editorial comments, such as "The Cowboy as he Was," seemed like nonfiction to Nancy and Charlie, even though they often contained semifictional digressions. "The Cowboy as he Was," which later also appeared under the titles "The Story of the Cowboy" and "The Story of the Cowpuncher," opens with a joke about cowboys being half-human. It later describes a narcissistic cowpuncher nicknamed "Pretty Shadow" and closes with the narrator's supposedly autobiographical tale about his nearly disastrous trip to Chicago. As Charlie told Joe DeYong, "part of most of those stories really happened."[32]

For her part, Nancy Russell was willing to claim that *all* of her husband's stories were nonfiction if that would get them published. She concluded with a plaintive question that appeared in several letters to Whitney, "Will it be possible for Chas to get all these little yarns together in a book someday?"[33] Because Whitney was unable to continue accepting stories, Nancy never received a direct answer to her book question. In 1909 Whitney wrote about transferring several of Charlie's story manuscripts to the weekly *Collier's* fiction department, while declining any further pieces for his own publication.[34] Evidently Caspar Whitney admired Russell's verbal and graphic art works, but he never published other individual essays or the hoped-for book of stories.

In 1916, seven years after Caspar Whitney's apparent farewell letter, Charlie Russell's stories began to appear in small-town weekly newspapers throughout Montana. A partnership that a former Butte newspaperman, W. W. "Bill" Cheely, formed as the Montana Newspaper Association (MNA) in Great Falls served the 140 weekly newspapers throughout the state.[35] The MNA provided a "ready-print" service of four blank pages onto which each paper printed its own local news and advertisements, in addition to four more pages pre-printed with national ads, regional feature stories, and historical articles. As noted in a history of Montana newspapers,

> Bill employed at least one competent writer who filled one page with a Montana historical feature. Most of these were researched at the Montana Historical Society library in Helena. . . . Bill also reproduced some of Charles M. Russell's art, and he was the first to put into print some of the CMR stories.[36]

A Miles City journalist saluted Cheely's MNA "as a medium for the preservation of anecdotes and history of the state of Montana."[37] The MNA's obituary for Cheely described him as having trained "a staff of writers and editors in the field which held for him the greatest interest, the history of the old west . . . a staff which could supply an almost endless amount of the feature material."[38] Another writer characterized Cheely as a man who loved a good story, stating, "Whenever he picked up a good one, he was prone to write about it in his own style in one or more of his publications."[39] Russell's humorously exaggerated tales and illustrations harmo-

FIG. 12. Charlie Russell and Percy
Raban. Detail of full photograph with E. C. "Teddy Blue"
Abbott and George Calvert
in Miles City, 1919. Courtesy
of John Riggs, Miles City,
Montana.

nized with the other MNA pieces that ranged from well-researched essays to anecdotal reminiscences by elderly western characters, all accompanied by fine photography and line illustrations. From 1916 through 1921, twenty-two Russell stories appeared in the weekly inserts. The
MNA reprinted most of them several times until the insert service closed in 1942.

Although the MNA editors would have welcomed more Russell tales during their first five
years of operation, Russell's writing production was erratic. He produced only six short pieces in
1916, nine in 1917, three in 1918, two in 1919, one in 1920, and two in 1921. His editors, Bill Cheely
and Percy Raban, found that motivating the artist to write was "like pulling teeth."[40] Russell spent
most of his time producing larger oil paintings, smaller oils and watercolors, sculptures for
bronze castings, and a considerable number of detailed pen/ink sketches. The MNA used these
sketches frequently to illustrate articles and stories by other writers in their insert sections. In
addition to his distaste for the writing process, Charlie Russell's considerable production of art
prevented him from supplying more stories for the MNA weekly inserts. Nancy Russell was
always monitoring her husband's artistic output, making sure that she had a steady supply of
paintings for the couple's periodic journeys to gallery exhibitions in larger cities.

THAT WAS SOME HORSE TRADE
WHEN DeHART WAS A COWMAN

Charles M. Russell, the cowboy artist, a few years ago had a half interest in a cattle ranch in Teton county with Con Price, a noted old-time cowpuncher and cattle man, who now resides on the Flathead reservation.

Jake De Hart, Montana's game warden, for years a cowman, was then manager of the famous Flying U ranch near Choteau.

Price, who was managing the Price-Russell ranch, met De Hart in Choteau one day told him he was looking for a heavy saddle horse that he could make into a good roping horse for corral work.

"I've got just what you want," said De Hart. "Big bay that could hold a mountain on a rope. What

brand a bunch of calves. Toward noon, De Hart arrived with his part of the bargain and took the roans over to the Flying U.

A day or two later Price returned and found Charlie Russell at the ranch, having come up from Great Falls.

"What's that thing in the corral, Con?" Russell inquired.

"Must be the horse Jake De Hart traded me," replied Con, who hadn't seen the animal yet.

"Horse, nothing," replied Russell. "I thought it was a buffalo first, but it ain't the right shape. You could make good money with it in the side show business, but I don't see just what good it would be around a ranch.

This Is Horse Jake Traded Off.

have you got that you'll swap for him?"

"What will he weigh?" inquired Price.

"Better than 1,010 pounds," De Hart replied.

"Well," said Price, after a minute's deliberation, "I've got three small roan three-year-olds. I'll give you the three for the big fellow."

"I'll bring the big horse over to your ranch tomorrow," De Hart agreed.

"I may not be in, but leave him in the corral," said Price. "I'll run in the roans and leave them in the corral."

The next morning Price left the ranch for the Sweet Grass Hills to

"I hope you didin't buy it by the pound," Russell continued, "because it weighs over a ton. It looks like a good sleeper. I haven't caught it with its eyes open yet."

The cowboy artist continued to make remarks about his partner's trade while Con walked over to the corral and took a look at it.

In silence Price surveyed the 1,900 pound relic of a workhorse that stood in troubled reposed on its battered legs and sore hoofs.

"Well," he finally observed, "I don't know that we're much better off with this monument of decrepitude than Jake De Hart is with the three roan runts I traded him. Every one of 'em's locoed."

FIG. 13. "That Was Some Horse Trade When DeHart Was a Cowman," as printed in the *Jordan Gazette* (MNA), October 1916. This piece may be the first collaboration in print between Charlie Russell's oral narration and Percy Raban's transcription and editing.

That Was Some Horse Trade When DeHart Was a Cowman

Russell's friendship with fellow Elks Lodge brother Percy Raban was especially significant for transcribing stories onto paper. Raban was part owner, writer, and editor for the Montana Newspaper Association. The MNA's weekly deadlines sometimes compelled Raban to transcribe Russell's unfinished story from the artist's dictation.[41] Apparently, a few story manuscripts carry the handwriting of both men. "I was very close to Russell from 1898 until his death in 1926," Rabin told researcher James Rankin,

> and transcribed most of the stories which appeared in his book—Trails Plowed Under—published after his death. Most of these were included in the two booklets—Rawhide Rawlins and More Rawhides published by my publishing company [Montana Newspaper Association].[42]

Raban may have overstated his claim that he transcribed most of *Trails Plowed Under*. Original manuscripts are not available for the majority of the MNA-published stories, but Rabin probably had a hand in less than half of the forty-seven published pieces.[43] Joe DeYong also claimed to have helped in editing Russell's tales, stating, "I also was present when he wrote his stories that made up his book 'Trails Plowed Under.' In fact and in all modesty—edited some following his death."[44] Nevertheless, Russell's early manuscripts and final published versions show little evidence of DeYong's influence. Certainly, Nancy Russell did not transcribe the MNA stories. She appears to have been relatively uninvolved in this stage of Charlie's publishing career.[45] In the years from 1916 to 1921, Nancy was parenting their adopted son Jack and managing the Russell household while also arranging Charlie's gallery exhibitions in major cities in the United States and Canada. She proved a superb manager, securing prices for single paintings that rose 100 percent—moving up from five thousand dollars[46] in 1915 to ten thousand dollars[47] in 1921. Selling stories for a few dollars to small-town Montana readers must have been a low priority for this ambitious and successful businesswoman.

Three Stories in *the Great Falls High School Roundup*

In contrast to his wife's hard-driving business momentum, Charlie Russell gave away three stories to the local high school yearbook during this same period. Russell's anecdotal essay, "The Story of the Cowboy As It Was Told To Me By An Old-time Rider Of The Range" appeared in the MNA inserts in the fall 1916. In June 1917, it reappeared in the *Tenth Annual Great Falls High School Roundup*.[48] This was the same piece, then titled "The Cowboy As He Was," that Nancy Russell had been trying to sell nine years earlier to Caspar Whitney for his nonfiction magazine. Also in June 1917, Russell published a description of his life as a teenager with hunter/prospector Jake Hoover in the MNA supplements, titled "Hunting And Trapping On The Judith With Jake Hoover."[49] One year later, in 1918, Russell gave this piece, retitled "A Slice of Charlie's Early Life," to the same student yearbook.[50] The third story that Russell provided for the *Roundup* appeared in the yearbook on June 20, 1919, under the title "The Olden Days."[51]

Just ten days later, the MNA published the same story statewide under the title "The Pinto."[52] Although it seems likely, in the absence of any business records, that the MNA was paying Russell a meager amount for his stories, it seems equally certain that the school printed the artist's stories and illustrations for no fee. There is at least one indication that Nancy kept her eye on these gifts, however. Eight years later, while negotiating with Doubleday to publish Charlie's stories, Nancy could still recall that the Great Falls High School had not copyrighted the story when it printed "The Olden Days" in the yearbook.[53]

The Story of the Cowboy

Charlie Russell's generosity with these written works could have grown out of his ambivalence toward some unsatisfactory narrative experiments. In his twenty-two pieces that appeared from 1916 until 1921, the year when the MNA republished seventeen of them in *Rawhide Rawlins Stories,* Russell tried writing in different styles with various recurring elements. He used several different narrators, including himself (unnamed), naming others "Bedrock," "Bill Weaver," "Dum Dum Bill," "Hank Winters," "Dad Lane," and, most frequently, "Rawhide Rawlins," all of whom used similar rural slang to tell a story. When the stories reappeared in subsequent books, the "Rawhide Rawlins" narrator had supplanted most of the others, and, except for a few title changes, the stories survived essentially as first written. The three pieces that Russell gave to the high school students were not humor writing like the others, although the "Story of the Cowboy" tells a joke at the beginning and offers a lighthearted anecdote at the end. Each of the three employs different means to depict the writer's own experiences, in contrast with his other published works that focus exclusively on people other than the author. Most distinctively, two of the three gift-story narrators use grammatical English, not Russell's characteristic rural slang.

Hunting And Trapping On The Judith With Jake Hoover

In contrast with the rural voice of "The Story of the Cowboy," Russell employed an unnamed narrator in "Hunting And Trapping On The Judith With Jake Hoover." The narrator speaks as if under the influence of a high school English teacher who has translated his typical slang, phrase by phrase, into acceptable prose. A likely rewriter for Charlie's autobiographical piece would be the faculty member who was editing the *Tenth Annual Roundup* for Great Falls High School. Charlie's rural slang would have seemed especially inappropriate in a book for and about students who were, no doubt, being challenged to write grammatically proper sentences for their classes. This piece provides details about Hoover's and Russell's outdoor life hunting and camping in the Central Montana mountains during the early 1880s—colorful information not available from any other direct source. The narrator always uses language correctly, but it seems awkward and unnatural when compared to Russell's everyday speech and storytelling banter. Whether it was the result of Russell's writing experiment or of someone else's editing, this very informative but artificial article never reappeared in print, either in the MNA pages or in any subsequent book.

The Pinto

Like the earlier Jake Hoover piece, "The Pinto" presents Russell during his late teenage years, a period of likely interest for the high school yearbook readers. The narrator for "The Pinto"—

an omniscient third-person voice—delivers information directly in a spare, low-key style that seems written especially for twentieth-century urban high school readers, who could have been less amused with rural slang than the author's older audiences. At the end, the narrator reveals that he is one-and-the-same with the young owner of the story's main character—the pinto horse. As with the Jake Hoover piece, no earlier drafts have surfaced, either handwritten or typewritten, leaving researchers to guess whether or not someone other than Russell altered his typical storytelling style. In subsequent years, a sales sheet describing the original manuscript suggests that Russell wrote this story almost exactly as published, with Percy Raban's handwriting showing that he transcribed certain segments from Russell's narration.[54] "The Pinto" is, overall, distinctive writing, superior to most other Russell stories. Although it did not appear in either of the two *Rawhide Rawlins* books, the Doubleday editors wisely included it in *Trails Plowed Under,* titled "The Ghost Horse."[55]

For unknown reasons, Russell chose not to demand the continued publication of the Jake Hoover piece. Whether the readers disliked or enjoyed the essay's sanitized narrative style, the author apparently saw it as appropriate to share only with the Great Falls students. The popularity for "The Pinto" is apparent with the MNA reprinting in 1922.[56] "The Story of the Cowboy" also received several reprintings. Russell presented these three different narratives to the next generation of Montana residents, partly to amuse and partly to inform. "The Pinto" ends with the arrival of horse and teenage rider in the newly established town of Great Falls— another aspect of the story that could appeal to the local students. Russell experienced Montana's transition from the 1880s to the twentieth-century urban West as unpleasantly abrupt. He evidently wanted the students to know how different life had been only a few years earlier. By the end of his life, this wish became strong enough for him to overcome a lifelong aversion to public speaking and moved him to address the assembled high school students in October 1925. His three yearbook stories were gifts that successfully passed on to the next generation of Montana residents a sense of life on the cattle range, in the mountains, and among the Indians—a personal view of moments in western history.[57]

In October 1921, the MNA published the first book of Charlie Russell's stories, illustrated with his pen/ink sketches. *Rawhide Rawlins Stories* presented seventeen yarns and a brief introduction. It omitted six pieces that had appeared previously in the weekly insert sections and included three new ones that Russell had never published before. The editors did not choose any of Russell's more serious stories, such as those that had appeared in *Outing* or the three that he gave to the *Roundup.* The slim volume's seventeen selections were all brief, humorous yarns, except for the lighthearted essay "The Story of the Cowpuncher."

At the time *Rawhide Rawlins Stories* appeared, Montana was caught in a drought and postwar economic depression that did not begin to lift until 1922.[58] Russell knew that the rural and small-town audience for this book could spare little money for nonessential purchases and he encouraged the publishers to keep the price of the book affordable. "These are hard times with a lot of folks," the author observed in a newspaper interview. "If this book is going to give anyone a laugh, I want the price low enough so that people to whom a dollar means a dollar will feel they're getting their money's worth."[59] Accordingly, the MNA priced the volume at one dollar and the book's sales volume required four printings in its first year, with final sales of

Irvin S. Cobb

America's Greatest Living Humorous Writer,

CALLS

Rawhide Rawlins Stories

BY

Charles M. Russell

A worth-while contribution to the literature of the real west."

IRVIN S. COBB

IRVIN S. COBB
REBEL RIDGE
OSSINING
· N. Y

Mr. Charles Russell,
Great Falls, Mont.

My dear Charlie Russell:
Thank you
for your book.   have read it and reread
it with pleasure. It is full of good local
color, good character-drawing, and good lines
Personally, I regard 't as a worth-while
contribution to the historic literature of
the real West.

With sincere regards,

Yours cordially,

Dec. 23, 1921.

FIG. 14. This advertisement for *Rawhide Rawlins Stories* appeared occasionally in Montana Newspaper Association insert sections. The nationally popular humor writer Irvin S. Cobb wrote this endorsement letter four years before meeting Russell in person.

approximately fifteen thousand copies.[60] The MNA inserts carried some advertising for the book, including a generous endorsement from humorist Irvin S. Cobb. The book sold primarily inside Montana but attracted some long-distance praise from friendly journalists.[61] Nancy Russell apparently was not closely monitoring the business of publishing Charlie's stories in the MNA's inserts and the *Rawhide Rawlins* book. She was surprised to discover in 1926 that Charlie had agreed to anthologize two of his *Rawhide Rawlins* pieces in different 1922 editions of *Short Stories Magazine,* all for the grand sum of fifteen dollars.[62]

In addition to the insert service for Montana weekly papers and the successful publication of *Rawhide Rawlins Stories,* two MNA partners Bill Cheely and Percy Raban sold a series of fifty-two historical articles to newspapers around the United States in 1922 and 1923. As the Cheely-Raban Syndicate, they used large, detailed pen/ink sketches by Charlie Russell to illustrate their well-researched articles on famous historical characters, military forts, Indian battles, and other selected highlights of history in the American West. Subscribing newspapers received a story and illustration each week for a year under the general title *Back-Trailing on the Old Frontiers.*[63] In 1922, encouraged by the success of *Rawhide Rawlins Stories,* Cheely and Raban also published fourteen of the fifty-two syndicated articles in another slim book that was intended to be the first of three volumes. Although the syndication of articles from March 1922 until February 1923 was initially successful, the book, also titled *Back-Trailing on the Old Frontiers,* was not. By October 1923, Percy Raban had left Montana and the publishing business to sell real estate in California. In a personal letter he simultaneously apologized to Nancy Russell for being late in his payments on her personal loan to him, while also handing over to her the Cheely-Raban share of the copyrights for both *Rawhide Rawlins* and *Back-Trailing* for a dollar "and other valuable considerations."[64] Cheely and Raban had high hopes that a book of brief history essays illustrated by C. M. Russell would sell to schools, libraries, and the newspaper readers who had enjoyed the history articles. But the volume failed to match the successful sales of Russell's humor book.

Nancy Russell had provoked Raban's return of the copyrights by writing to him about her visit to the MNA offices in Great Falls and her inspection of the company's financial records. She was suspicious about the lack of regular checks from Cheely-Raban during the past year. At that time, Charlie was ill, confined to bed with a painful back condition for at least six months, and unable to paint or write.[65] Despite her successes in selling single paintings in 1921 and 1923 for ten thousand dollars,[66] plus other art sales and the launch of *Rawhide Rawlins Stories,* Nancy was worried about income and determined to secure any outstanding funds. She pressed Rabin bluntly for the balance of the MNA's *Back-Trailing* bank account. "[T]here are no outstanding accounts against the books," Nancy observed at the finish of her letter. "The cash now on hand amounts to $282.08 or there abouts. Will you please authorize Mr. Cheely to make Chas. a check for that amount. It will help us a little. It sure don't pay to be sick."[67]

Only a month later, with control of the *Back-Trailing* inventory and copyrights, Nancy became a bit more optimistic. She seemed determined to make the best of selling books at a dollar apiece. "We may not get anything out of this stuff," Nancy wrote,

> but I do believe some day it may add to Charlie and you as historians of the
> Old West so that is why I think it should be kept together in ship shape so it can be

gotten at some time. We sold about fifty books this summer at the lake. Of course they were at Lewis's but I was glad to see half of them were "Back Trailing." From the way Mr. Cheely talked and from your letter this has been a very unfortunate venture all the way round. I surely am sorry you lost so much of your money and time. You will remember Charlie could not do anything else while he was working on Back Trailing stuff.[68]

The prestige associated with being "a historian" clearly motivated Nancy to try to market these books and to publish more of Charlie's own stories, despite the meager financial gain. After being somewhat aloof from the publishing business for nearly fourteen years, by the end of 1923 Nancy Russell was back in full control.

Charlie Russell's spouse must have been strongly in favor of Cheely publishing a second book of the artist's stories. When the MNA brought out *More Rawhides* in December 1925, just in time for Christmas sales, the contents included three of the five *Outing* stories that Nancy had prepared for publication two decades earlier.[69] Charlie Russell told Joe DeYong that the MNA had planned to publish these longer, more serious tales in the newspaper inserts. "Rabon was going to use them in his paper,"[70] he scribbled on a note to his understudy. In contrast with the pieces in *Rawhide Rawlins Stories,* none of the *More Rawhides* tales, besides "A Savage Santa Claus," had appeared in MNA newsprint prior to the book's appearance. The other thirteen stories were similarly new to the eyes of the Montana readers. In a shift from the all-humorous first book, *More Rawhides* included five serious-minded pieces, including the murderously violent "Mormon Murphy's Misplaced Confidence" as well as the somber "Longrope's Last Guard."

A Few Words about Myself

The most striking piece in the book was not one of the stories, however, but a brief autobiographical preface titled "A Few Words About Myself." In just 344 words, the humorist/cowpuncher/artist/author sums up his life. Russell's health had continued to decline and he seemed to sense that his time might be up. Indeed, this section was written approximately twelve months before his death in October of 1926.

A Few Words About Myself

The papers have been kind to me—many times more kind than true. Although I worked for many years on the range, I am not what people think a cowboy should be. I was neither a good roper nor rider. I was a night wrangler. How good I was, I'll leave it for people I worked for to say—there are still a few of them living. In the spring I wrangled horses, in the fall I herded beef. I worked for the big outfits and I always held my job.

I have many friends among cowmen and cowpunchers. I have always been what is called a good mixer—I had friends when I had nothing else. My friends were not always within the law, but I haven't said how law-abiding I was myself. I haven't been too bad nor too good to get along with.

FIG. 15. One of many advertisements for *More Rawhides* appearing statewide in 120 MNA subscribing weekly newspapers, including the *Judith Basin Press* of November 23, 1925.

Life has never been too serious with me—I lived to play and I'm playing yet. Laughs and good judgment have saved me many a black eye, but I don't laugh at other's tears. I was a wild young man, but age has made me gentle. I drank, but never alone, and when I drank it was no secret. I am still friendly with drinking men.

My friends are mixed—preachers, priests, and sinners. I belong to no church, but am friendly toward and respect all of them. I have always liked horses and since I was eight years old have always owned a few.

I am old-fashioned and peculiar in my dress. I am eccentric (that is a polite way of saying you're crazy). I believe in luck and have had lots of it.

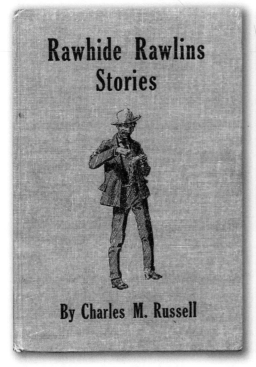
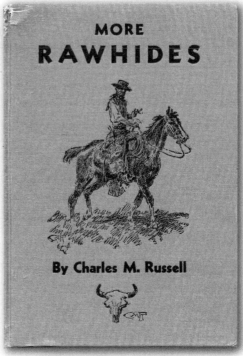

FIG. 16. Cover designs of the two "Rawhide Rawlins" books produced by W. W. Cheeley's Montana Newspaper Association in 1921 and 1925. The books were reprinted in 1946 by Homer Britzman's Trail's End Publishing of Pasadena, California.

> To have talent is no credit to its owner; what a man can't help he should get neither credit nor blame for—it's not his fault. I am an illustrator. There are lots better ones, but some worse. Any man that can make a living doing what he likes is lucky, and I'm that. Any time I cash in now, I win.[71]

Russell clarifies his modest cowboy skills as a cowboy, neutralizing erroneous publicity and gossip. He remembers that when friends were his only wealth, his sense of humor saved him from harm. He acknowledged his past as a public drinker and his eccentricity. The artist says he is merely "an illustrator"—neither the best nor the worst; just lucky enough to make a living doing what he likes. Then he finishes his self-examination—a satisfied man—stating that anytime the game of his life stops, he feels like a winner. The words may be few, but they seem complete enough.

Despite the calm in Russell's self-description, the business side of *More Rawhides* seemed slightly frantic. Cheely was shameless in using the MNA newspaper inserts to promote all the books he published, including *More Rawhides*. Numerous large advertisements and several promotional pieces masquerading as news articles appeared throughout the inserts, urging his readers to get the latest Russell book of stories. Despite the self-serving purpose, however, one public-relations article provided a valuable observation that the origins of these tales began with actual Montana people. The piece states that the humor of these yarns and the pictures illustrating them will be the delight of thousands of Montanans, many of whom, as was the case in the first book, will recognize various characters who are woven into the narratives. Some of these are called by name while others are so portrayed that their friends will rapidly recognize them.[72] Although Russell's stories were largely humorous exaggerations, the promotional piece points out that these stories were based enough on actual people and events to be considered "realistic." Additionally, the writer of another MNA public-relations piece makes a plausible case for knowing the author's intent.

> It may be said that these yarns of Mr. Russell's are not a serious effort at literature on his part. If the truth were known, he wrote them more to amuse himself and the old-timers of the state whom he has known for more than 40 years, than for the public at large, but that very fact and the manner in which they are written makes them of greatest interest to anyone—old-timer or newcomer, for they reflect western wit and western fun that were characteristic of Montana men at the times they portray.[73]

These stories have unusual value, the writer suggests, because they were intended to amuse the surviving old-timers of a previous era. Thus, the reading public could be better informed about that era by seeing what amused the former participants.

More Rawhides received only one printing (of unknown quantity). The MNA maintained plenty of inventory, continuing to advertise the book until the insert service shut down in 1942. The marketing process had begun at the moment the book appeared in print. Cheely sent a letter to inform the Russells, who were conducting a gallery exhibition in New York, about his sales efforts. The details in this letter suggest that the Russells were substantial business investors in this third publishing adventure. "Our book went on the market yesterday," Cheely announced,

> and we are starting out with fair sales. The manuscript was just a little short, two or three pages of type and we had to use 20 cuts [illustrations] for fillers. However, they are all appropriate and fit into the scheme of the book all right. Of course I would have liked to have had your approval, but it was an emergency and we had to get to press as soon as possible.
>
> We dug up all our coupons through which our mail customers ordered "Rawhide Rawlins" five years ago, and sent every one a post card, copy of which I enclose.
>
> I sent out a story to the daily newspapers with a couple of cuts and last Sunday practically every daily newspaper in the state ran this story, giving us a circulation of about 100,000, so the book is well exploited. Then I dug up through Dunn's Mercantile agency the name of every possible dealer in the state—probably twice as many as we had before—and circularized them with a coupon hooked into their circular, and this is getting fair results.[74]

Cheely's letterhead proclaims a readership of four hundred thousand people, and his efforts to reach those readers and other potential book buyers seem thorough and professional. Yet sales of this second book of Russell stories undoubtedly suffered from Doubleday's national distribution of the 1927 book that incorporated the yarns in both *Rawhide* volumes, plus several more pieces, in the volume that would be titled *Trails Plowed Under*.

CHAPTER THREE

Stories about Northern Plains Indians

The Red man was the true American
They have almost gon, but will never be forgotten
The history of how they fought for their country is written in blood
a stain that time cannot grinde out
their God was the sun their Church all out doors
their only book was nature and they knew all its pages[1]

*T*aking a closer look at the groups of Charlie Russell's stories, those about Indians fit chronologically and socially for first consideration. Since Russell held Indian cultures in highest esteem and since their stories predate the arrival of Euro-Americans in the West, these narratives naturally stand first for closer reading. Russell's Indian stories also provide a model for his other narratives in expressing his social awareness. Among the other three categories, only his twentieth-century stories reflect the author's social sensibilities as much as the Indian tales. The wildlife and cattle-range story groups, preoccupied with individual adventures and foibles, seldom reflect a wider view of the social forces of their times.

In words, pictures, and sculptures Charlie Russell expressed a strong wish to share his appreciation of Indian people and their cultures with his fellow non-Indians. Most viewers of Charlie Russell's Indian pictures or sculptures have perceived his positive feelings and ideas while few writers have expressed doubt or uncertainty about his affinity for Native Americans. Some art critics and biographers in the late twentieth century too quickly categorize Charlie

FIG. 17. Charles M. Russell and mounted Blackfeet Indians. Photograph courtesy of
    C. M. Russell Museum, Great Falls, Montana.

Russell with other western artists' patronizing or unsympathetic views of Indians in the American West. Writing about the Taos artists, Julie Schimmel made this mistaken conclusion:

> By 1900, the West of Frederic Remington, Charles M. Russell, and Charles Schreyvogel dominated popular images of the fine and popular arts—the West of violent confrontation in which white men were good guys and red men were the bad guys.[2]

In his written works, Russell's true affinity for Indians stands out clearly. Schimmel's oversimplified *good guys–bad guys* equation is swept aside in the subtle force of Russell's humorous suggestions that the Indians' lives may have been superior in many ways to anything experienced by the most "advanced" Euro-Americans.

Throughout his life, Charlie Russell was fascinated with the plains Indian cultures and their collisions with American and European settlers. His own family history contributed to his preoccupation with Native Americans. Charlie Russell's great-uncles—the brothers to his grandmother, Lucy Bent Russell—founded Bent's Fort in 1834 in what is now southern Colorado.[3] William Bent married first one and, when she died, then another daughter of a key Cheyenne tribal leader. Ultimately he became the primary advocate to the federal government for all the plains Indians. The artist's nephew, Austin Russell, confirmed that the Bents' experiences

> had such an effect on their St. Louis [grand-] nephew, Charlie Russell, that to tell his story it is necessary to tell theirs. Because what the Bents did—and what was done to them—explains how Charlie felt about the whites and the Indians. And

THE SIDNEY HERALD

BACK-TRAILING ON THE OLD FRONTIERS
Drawing by CHARLES M. RUSSELL

When a comprehensive history of the southwestern United States is written, its beginnings will cover many an interesting chapter on the Santa Fe trail, great highway from the Missouri river to New Mexico along which the commerce of the prairies was carried from 1820 to the coming of the railroads. Its northern extremity was Independence, Missouri, and it extended to the ancient town of Santa Fe, which still disputes with St. Augustine, Florida, the honor of being the oldest town in America. In the early days the Santa Fe trail lay half in American and half in Spanish territory, for the ford of the Arkansas river in Colorado, where the boundary was crossed, was almost exactly midway, between its extreme ends.

When expeditions first began to be made from Missouri to Santa Fe they followed up the Arkansas river to the vicinity of where La Junta, Colorado, now stands, and then turning south, went first to Taos and then to Santa Fe. Even after the shorter trail was established across the desert, the route by the Upper Arkansas continued to be used. On this branch of the trail Bent's Fort on the Arkansas was the great stopping place, and it was in every respect the most important outpost of the southwest, ranking with Forts Union, Pierre and Laramie. It was the great crossroads station of the southwestern country and the trading point of an enormous area.

Bent's Fort was built by the trading firm of Bent & St. Vrain, which ranked next to the American Fur Company in the amount of business it transacted in the period about 1840. It was situated 530 miles from Independence, Mo., and stood on the left bank of the river, half way between the present towns of La Junta and Los Animas, in Colorado. The date of its beginning was 1828, but it took until 1832 to complete.

Bent. George Bent was on the Upper Missouri rier, in what is Montana today, as early as 1816 in the employ of the American Fur Company. William Bent's first adventure into the western wilderness was also in the employ of the American Fur Company among the Sioux Indians.

In 1824 William Bent built a trading post on the Arkansas river

ism characteristic of the race of strong men from which he came. In 1828 William Bent, with St. Vrain, another noted Indian trader, began the construction of the celebrated Bent's Fort on the Arkansas river, about 15 miles from where Pueblo stands today. It took four years to complete it, and it was of adobe brick construction. It was destined to become one of the most famous of all the western trading

mounting which a flagstaff rose. This watch tower consisted of a single room, with windows on all sides and a spy-glass mounted on a pivot. Here was stationed continuously a sentry, with a chair and a bed for his convenience, and if anything unusual were noticed through the telescope he gave notice and proper precautions were immediately taken. A huge bell in the watch tower sounded the hours,

en, walking swiftly about the courtyard and on the roofs of the houses, clad in long buckskin dresses and bright moccasins, were full of interest; while the naked children, with perfect forms and the white of the Saxon race showing through the darker line of the mother blood, excited his enthusiasm. He wondered at the novel manners and customs that he saw;

it greatly impressed the Indians, who until now had not realized that there were half as many men in the whole "white tribe." Swinging to the left as it neared the fort, the column marched up the valley, forded the river to the Mexican bank and went on its way. Part reached Santa Fe, part marched through to California and part went to meet the troops marched by. Charles Bent entertained in his quarters in the fort a group of officers, serving mint-juleps. A few months later some of these men marched from Santa Fe to Taos to avenge the murder of Charles Bent.

By 1850 the fur trade had begun to decline, the beaver having been pretty thoroughly trapped out of many of the mountain streams. Besides that the silk hat had been invented and was rapidly taking the place of the old beaver hat. The mountains were full of idle trappers, and a colony of these settled on the present site of the city of Pueblo, where they farmed in a limited way and smuggled much whisky from Mexico to the plains country.

The stagnation of the beaver trade, of course, affected the trade of William Bent, whose chief business was now in buffalo robes and horses. The establishment at the fort was much reduced, and in the early 50's Bent tried to sell it to the government for a military post. As too small an amount was offered, in 1852 he laid charges of gunpowder in the buildings and blew the old fort into the air.

Bent thereafter built a new fort below Fort William and leased it to the war department. In the late 60's he built still another post, where he died in May, 1869. His friend, Kit Carson, died at Fort Lyons, Colorado, just a year before.

George Bird Grinnell, in his interesting narrative, Beyond the Old Frontier, tells of visiting the site of Bent's Fort 10 years ago and

Bent's Fort, Oldest and Largest of Fur Trading Posts of the Great Plains, Stood for Years as an Impregnable Outpost to Hostile Reds of Southwest

FIG. 18. "Bent's Fort on Arkansas River." Pen/ink, illustration for the essay series *"Back Trailing on the Old Frontiers,"* *The Sidney Herald* (MNA), November 12, 1922. Russell did not write this or any of the essays in the series.

that affected his art: he never, except on order, painted American soldiers killing American Indians.[4]

For Charlie Russell, the racial and cultural relationship between Indians and Euro-Americans defined an essential part of life in the American West. The artist contributed to historical definitions of the western racial equation through his stories as well as his paintings and sculptures by interpreting and explaining Indians as well as the Indian/white relationships to his peers and customers.

Russell's associations with Indians began early in his life in the West. During his first years in Montana, he made numerous personal contacts with the Indians in his region. The new Judith Basin town of Utica and the nearby Little Belt Mountains, where Charlie Russell lived off and on with Jake Hoover, occupied part of the traditional route connecting the Blackfeet at Browning and the Crow reservation at Hardin. When the Indians camped near Utica, they often came into the small town to sell their beaded crafts, buy tobacco, or trade horses.[5] In his first years in Montana, Russell made Utica his base of operations.

Russell frequented Utica in 1880 and 1881, while out in the adjacent Judith Basin, bands of starving and desperate Indians, including Bloods, Blackfoot, Sarcees, and Crees from north of the United States/Canada border, combined forces with Blackfeet (Southern Piegan) and Crows from south of the border to hunt the final remnants of wild North American buffalo.[6] Charlie Russell had plenty of opportunities to observe or contact the Indian buffalo hunters with little difficulty. Also, during this general period, he briefly joined a small band of Crow Indians. As one early-day friend recalled:

> I think it was the spring of '82 that he took pot luck with a band of Indians that were passing through, in order to get a close-up study of their characteristics. He stayed with them until they camped at what was then known as Haymaker Coulee near Martinsdale. He said he got by pretty well for a while, but the outstanding item on the menu card being Dog Stew, a-la-mode, it began to get monotonous.[7]

The young artist interacted with numerous Indians, accidentally and by design, without having to leave his immediate surroundings in the Judith Basin district.

Although Russell showed no signs of wishing to live permanently among Indians, later in his life he continued to seek out native contacts, typically with the serious intent of clarifying details in his depictions of Indian life. At that time, one of his many intermediaries was fellow artist Lone Wolf, or Hart Merriam Schultz (1882–1970)—the son of popular author James Willard Schultz (1859–1947)[8] and his Piegan-Blackfeet wife, Fine Shield Woman. Russell had caroused with the elder Schultz during his range-riding days and in later life he occasionally spent time with the younger Lone Wolf and his friends among tribal elders,[9] hearing stories full of details about Indian life that could be reworked in paintings, sculptures, and oral tales.

In his later years, even though he lived the settled urban life of a successful artist in Great Falls, Russell still counted many Indian people among his everyday friends and acquaintances. His contacts included the Cree leader Young Boy, who was a helpful collaborator on cultural details. Like fellow cowboy Con Price, or fellow artist Phillip Goodwin, Young Boy occasionally stood or sat as a painter's model on the rare occasions when a project of Russell's required a live human figure. The artist paid Young Boy for these and other chores, thereby helping the impoverished Indian in much the same way Russell paid occasional non-Indians who also needed money, including the young Wallace Stegner, who subsequently grew up to become a nationally prominent author.[10] Russell also spontaneously gave art works to Young Boy and other Indian friends such as Angus Monroe.[11] Josephine Wright, the Blackfeet woman who was a lifetime friend of Nancy's and Charlie's, also became an occasional model. These individual Indians and many others were welcome visitors in Charlie Russell's art studio and home.

Charlie Russell's stories and artworks depicting Indians frequently focused on the period of the horse and buffalo economy of the northern plains—the initial two-thirds of the nineteenth century—when horses were plentiful, guns were becoming more available, and Euro-Americans were not yet numerous. Some of Russell's stories, such as "The War Scars of Medicine Whip," reflect the early reservation period, whereas others provide information about interactions of settlers and natives in the later periods. Russell's stories and many of his paintings frequently portray the *interactions* of Indians with explorers, prospectors, cattlemen, and early settlers as much as showing these groups by themselves. Some of the artist's comments show that he found the earlier periods to be more picturesque and thereby more enjoyable for making narrative art works. His attraction to the nineteenth-century West seems to have been stimulated by a heightened sense of adventure associated with experiences in those less civilized times.

Russell perceived the nineteenth century on the northern plains, the West's greatest buffalo-hunting years, as a period worth commemorating and celebrating in his vivid stories and numerous pictures and sculptures. One historian of western environments has noticed that the best times for abundant wildlife seemed to have reached their peak early in the nineteenth century, calling it "a meteoric time indeed."[12] According to Dan Flores, the best times for wild buffalo herds were declining by 1850, well before 1864, the year of Russell's birth. The terminal buffalo decline appeared somewhat later for the northern plains, but the buffalo culture for Indians was essentially finished by the time the teenaged Charlie Russell arrived in the Judith Basin in 1880.

Because of the lack of easily accessible written records, Russell's representations of Indian tribal history necessarily have relied on oral accounts by reliable participants and observers. This process carried the risk that his human sources might not survive long enough to tell him their stories or be able to recall accurately. And the risk also included the possibility that Russell's own limitations and preconceptions would distort even the best source material. Historian Robert Berkhofer, Jr. concludes that the overall history of "white" images of Indians reflects the inability "of one people to understand another in mutually acceptable terms."[13] Some Native American responses to Russell's art suggest that he made works that fairly represented Indian life. Moreover, many well-qualified academic critics, such as John Ewers, have found Russell's work to be especially reliable as cultural history.

Several critics in the late twentieth century have pointed out that Russell's nostalgic longing for the nineteenth century overwhelmed his objectivity during his final years in the early 1920s. The historian and expert Russell author Brian Dippie argues that Russell's later paintings shifted "from documentary realism to what might be more accurately called romantic realism grounded in nostalgia. His portrayal of the Indian is a case in point." Dippie maintains that "Nostalgia shaped his artistic vision,"[14] and many subsequent critics have agreed. Certainly nostalgia figures strongly in Russell's works, yet a less personal emotion, more of a historian's compulsion to record moments of nineteenth-century culture of Montana and the West, seems to provoke his urge to create objective narrative writing, painting, and sculpting.

The War Scars of Medicine Whip

Although Russell's preference of artistic focus certainly reflected some nostalgia for earlier days, he also displayed a tougher, less sentimental preoccupation with the past in his published writings about Indians. Among these local-color narratives, his story "The War Scars of Medicine Whip" conveys that dry-eyed, realistic consideration of earlier times in specific detail. Russell accepted twentieth-century Indians the same way he accepted twentieth-century cowpunchers—as friends. He simply preferred to focus his talents on the more picturesque people and events of the nineteenth century.

FIG. 19. Charles M. Russell, *Counting Coup* (or *Medicine Whip*), 1902. Oil on canvas, courtesy of the Sid Richardson Collection of Western Art, Fort Worth, Texas.

Without hesitation, Russell took up the challenge of depicting some of the least popular aspects of Indian life in the eyes of the Euro-American settlers, such as the brutal violence of intertribal warfare. In "The War Scars of Medicine Whip"[15] Russell respectfully focused on an unassimilated old Indian warrior. This hero had earned his story-title name years earlier as a young man when, in a fierce battle with Sioux warriors, he sustained a near-fatal tomahawk blow to his face while striking his enemy with a short hand whip. With his survival following the battle, he had gained his new name, "Medicine Whip."

The old Indian's account of this intertribal incident inspired Russell to depict the battle's climax in three disciplines: painting, sculpting, and writing. While in Canada during the summer of 1888, Russell apparently heard the account from an aging Blood Indian. Twelve years later Charlie Russell painted a picture based on the battle story, which he titled *Counting Coup*. He also provided the picture's first buyer with a brief chronicle of the incident that he had painted.[16] Three years later, Russell produced a bronze sculpture depicting a three-dimensional version of the same battle's climactic moment, as shown in *Counting Coup*.[17] Then, in 1908, Russell completed an especially vivid oil painting, *When Blackfeet and Sioux Meet*, depicting the climax of that same story from an especially dramatic viewpoint (**see plate 5**). Also in 1908, Russell finished writing an expanded version of the tale that he had begun with his explanation of his 1902 picture. He titled this story "The War Scars of Medicine Whip."[18] Some observers have noted that Russell occasionally sketched or painted from a clay model, working out his subject in three dimensions before committing it to paper and canvas. In fact, the narrative idea, as in the case of the Medicine Whip story, preceded his efforts in clay, paper, or canvas.[19]

FIG. 20. Charles M. Russell, *Counting Coup*, 1905. Bronze, cast in 1905, no. 1961.116, Amon Carter Museum, Fort Worth, Texas. Medicine Whip is the figure (center) reaching down to the crouching figure.

In 1902 Charlie Russell wrote an informal summary of the deadly Blackfeet—Sioux skirmish, with himself as the story narrator, retelling a tale that apparently he had heard from the battle's victor. He illustrated his explanation with a sketch depicting himself inside a tipi listening to the old warrior/storyteller as he relates the battle. Six years later, however, when Russell wrote "The War Scars of Medicine Whip," he made his first narrator, seemingly his own personal voice, invite a character named "Squaw Owens" to tell about the old, scar-faced survivor living on the Blood Indian Reserve in Alberta.

By having once been married to an Indian woman, the fictional Owens had become a "squaw-man" in the eyes of his non-Indian peers; thus his special name. In Russell's lifetime, this was a term of derision, but in his writings he often referred to "squaw-men" with an ironic respect. The term *squaw* has been in use since European settlers first arrived to colonize Massachusetts,[20] and Russell used it freely to refer to Indian women, as well as the term *buck* to refer to Indian men. Russell used these terms in his writings without apparent derisive intent. In the late twentieth and early twenty-first century, these racial/gender terms are widely considered to be unacceptably offensive to Indians and women for written or oral-story delivery.

As a squaw-man, "Owens" speaks as a knowledgeable insider on Indian matters, enabling the author to inform his readers about Indian cultural values and to deliver social commentary about nineteenth-century race relations in Montana and the West. Russell's urge to inform his peers and readers in subsequent generations lifts his Indian narratives such as "The War Scars

FIG. 21.　Charles M. Russell, *Russell in the Lodge of Medicine Whip,* 1902. Pen/ink on paper, published in Harold McCracken, *The Charles M. Russell Book* (Garden City: Doubleday and Co., 1957). The picture illustrated Charlie's letter to the buyer of the painting *Counting Coup.* The old warrior seems to be making the sign for the word *dog.*

of Medicine Whip" beyond the level of mere adventure storytelling. Russell disguised his narratives as local-color elaborations of oral folk tales to deliver plains Indian cultural information ranging from warfare to interracial marriage.

As literary realism about intertribal warfare, "The War Scars of Medicine Whip" is especially violent. For late twentieth-century Americans of urban sensibilities, face-to-face oral storytelling typically suggests an innocent pastime appropriate for children. But Russell's storytelling environment included the roughest men of his frontier days. Accordingly, his story about Medicine Whip contains enough bloody violence to merit exclusion from most younger audiences.

Russell's narrator "Squaw Owens" reminds the reader that the old warrior was capable of hair-raising tales. "That old savage is the real article," warns Owens, "an' can spin yarns of killin's and scalpin's that would make your hair set up like the roach on a buck antelope." Near the story's end, Medicine Whip recovers just enough from his own severe battle wounds to inflict ritual mutilation on the dead bodies of his defeated enemies. As "Squaw Owens" describes the situation:

Plumb locoed with the pain of his wound, he starts butcherin. . . . [T]he way he trims that Sioux that called him names is sure scandalous. Every cut he makes means somethin' to an Injun, an' as these people believe a man lands in the next world in the shape he leaves this one, it won't be hard, he thinks, to identify this Sioux as a liar an' thief in the happy huntin' ground.[21]

Through Owens's rural voice, Russell was presenting this description as a blunt statement of alternative cultural and religious values. In publishing such material, the writer accepted the risk that he would offend many readers and listeners of the early twentieth century. This passage effectively contradicts the misperceptions of Russell as being basically sentimental and nostalgic about Indians. Despite the risk of alienating romantic enthusiasts for Indians in his audience, he addressed this disturbing aspect of tribal warfare as being a valid part of the historical and cultural values of pre-reservation plains Indians.

In another realistic touch, Charlie Russell voiced the common racist language typical of nineteenth-century Montana and the West in the narration of his Indian stories. As these local-color stories demonstrate, Russell was a master of ironic statement. In several stories the author loaded a negative term like *savage* with a sense of admiration suggesting an inverse meaning, in the same way he used *gentlemen* when referring to the hunters he despised for annihilating the wild buffalo.[22] Charlie Russell seemed to appreciate the unassimilated independence of Medicine Whip as much as narrator "Owens," who says:

> I admire this red-handed killer. The Whites have killed his meat and taken his country, but they've made no change in him. He's as much Injun as his ancestors that packed their quivers loaded with flint-pointed arrows, an' built fires by rubbin' sticks together. He laughs at priests an' preachers. . . . He's got a religion of his own an' it tells him that the buffalo are comin' back. . . . When he cashes in, his shadow goes prancin' off on a shadow pony, joinin' those that have gone before, to run shadow buffalo. He's seen enough of white men, an don't want to throw in with them in no other world.[23]

In many stories, Russell's narrators comment on the ironic parallels of Indian culture to that of the supposedly more advanced white settlers. For Russell, the comparative merits of civilized society in the West to Indian life often favored the so-called savages.

Only a few of Charlie Russell's fellow Montana citizens shared his curiosity and admiration for Indian life. Russell admired but also differed with the prominent Judith Basin cattleman Granville Stuart. Married to a full-blooded Shoshoni woman, Awbonnie Tokanka,[24] Stuart nevertheless limited his sympathy for her people, demanding compulsory assimilation for all Indians[25] and the suppression of Indian activities off the official reservations.[26] Russell likewise ignored the opinions of local farming advocate Robert Sutherland, whose popular weekly newspaper, *The Rocky Mountain Husbandman,* proclaimed that the Indians would have to stay on the reservations or face extermination. Another Judith region newspaper was especially blunt about advocating harsh suppression of Indians in the region where Russell worked as a cowboy. Under the title "The Red Devils," it stated:

> During the past summer small lodges of Bloods, Piegans and Crows have been prowling around the Musselshell Judith and Missouri valleys, killing stock and stealing horses . . . the property and belongings of white settlers. . . . There should be no further favoritism shown the thieving red devils by the military authorities. . . . The Noble (?) Red Man will speedily realize that if he desires to exist on this sphere he must remain on the grounds set aside for his exclusive occupation. This is as it should be, yet the big-hearted, philanthropical, goggle-eyed, heathen-converters and Indian civilizers of Yankeedom cannot understand it and will probably resist.[27]

In contrast with these 1880s sentiments, Russell's 1907 narrator, Owens, expressed understanding for Medicine Whip's perspective, stating: "The Whites killed his cattle [the wild buffalo], an' he can't see where it ain't right to knock over a spotted buffalo [the Texas Longhorn] now and then."[28]

As a boisterous cowboy with a notorious social life, Russell probably paid little attention to local newspaper editorials. It is even less likely that he took time to read nationally prominent writers. In Mark Twain's 1870 essay entitled "The Noble Red Man," Russell would have encountered absolute contempt for all Indians. On the other hand, if Twain ever read Russell's story "The War Scars of Medicine Whip" he would have been quite unamused by Russell's appreciation for Blackfeet spiritual belief in an afterlife and especially by Medicine Whip's post-battle mutilation of his dead enemies.[29] In his essay, Twain calls every Indian

> ignoble—base and treacherous, and hateful in every way. . . . His heart is a cesspool of falsehood, of treachery, and of low and devilish instincts . . . the scum of the earth. . . . All history and honest observation will show that the Red Man is a skulking coward and a windy braggart, who strikes without warning—usually from an ambush or under cover of night.[30]

Whether author Samuel Clemens agreed with his narrator, "Mark Twain," or simply vented extreme hatred as an exercise in ironic prose construction, his essay "The Noble Red Man" stands out as an exaggerated condemnation of all Native Americans. Among prominent nineteenth-century writers, Twain was not alone in his negative opinion of Indians. Theodore Roosevelt's western writings from the 1890s refer to "sly, lurking, bloodthirsty savages," and expresses more sympathy for the soldiers attempting to protect the endangered settlers than for any displaced, starving Indians.

In contrast with either the advocates of eliminating Indians or the well-meaning supporters of assimilation, Charlie Russell seemed to be more of a sympathetic preservationist. Without wanting to be an Indian himself or to live among them full time, he still valued their culture and history. He sought historical realism in his works, especially in his story narratives and in his explanations of Indian culture in his private letters to friends. Russell provided blunt and sometimes violent accounts that his peers accepted as historical. In the late 1980s, the respected Canadian historian Hugh Dempsey supported the plausibility of Russell's Medicine Whip story as oral history, stating, "the adventure that Russell recounted could easily have been told to him, as he said, while he was in camp along the Bow River."[31] Russell sought to preserve narrative accounts of events like the fight that he transformed into pictures, a sculpture, and a story about Medicine Whip.

Finger-That-Kills Wins His Squaw

Like Mark Twain, Charlie Russell used humor to present his message, but instead of encouraging his audience to distrust and dislike Indians, Russell's ironic style encouraged contemporaries to be more attentive to information about Indian courage in the harsh conditions of their everyday lives. By creating entertaining local-color narratives, Russell informed his listeners and readers about the Indians' extreme hardships. Most of his peers ignored information about how the demise of the buffalo in the early 1880s had brought famine to the natives of the northern plains.[32] At the beginning of his story "Finger-That-Kills Wins His Squaw," Russell introduces the issue of the Indians' famine conditions with his first references to the main character. At the same time he shades words with irony while shifting his tone from lighthearted to serious. Once again, Russell's narrator is "Squaw Owens," who recalls:

> There's an old Injun comes visitin' our camp, an' after he feeds once you can bet on him showin' up 'bout noon every day. If there's a place where an Injun makes a hand, it's helpin' a neighbor hide grub, an' they ain't particular about quality—it's quantity they want. Uncle Sam's Injuns average about one good meal a week; nobody's got to graze this way long till a tin plate loaded with beans looks like a Christmas dinner.[33]

Here, Russell accommodates a typical Euro-American assumption that Indians would be helpful or willing to work only when the time comes to "put away" food. As a masterful, straight-faced storyteller, Russell would have noticed anyone who laughed inappropriately at his references to people being forced to "graze" on beans for a fancy meal. Russell meant to touch both the sympathies and the outrage of listeners and readers with his blunt image of people starving at the whim of the government.

After beginning with references to Indian sufferings, the story of "Finger-That-Kills" develops into an adventure about violent conflict between northern plains tribes—in this case the Blackfeet and the Gros Ventre (Atsina).[34] Building his story line, Russell's narrator, "Owens," precedes the warfare with contrasting examples of Blackfeet courtship and marriage, comparing his own failure as a squaw-man with Finger-That-Kills's success as a young warrior/bridegroom. Apparently, Owens's only "success" with his Indian wife proved to be in the art of quarreling, at which they were the equal of "civilized folks in harness."[35] Once again, Russell offers an idea that many in his audience might think absurd or ludicrous to the point of being humorous, that Euro-American society was actually no better (and possibly worse) than Indian life regarding such basic human matters as marriage compatibility.

In general, Owens tells the story of how "Finger-That-Kills" lost several fingers during his quest to capture horses from a rival tribe, thereby earning the right to marry his tribal leader's daughter.[36] The story's crisis arrives when an enemy, a Gros Ventre warrior, stuns the hero with

FIG. 22. Charles M. Russell, *"The Gros Ventre Begins Hackin' the Fingers Off"* (or *Reaching for the Jeweled Hand*). Pen/ink, illustration for the story "Finger-That-Kills Wins His Squaw," *Outing Magazine,* April 1908, and *Trails Plowed Under.* This may be the only Russell depiction of post-battle mutilation.

a nearly fatal bullet. While the hero pretends to be unconscious, the Gros Ventre becomes distracted momentarily from killing and scalping by noticing the victim's trading-post jewelry. He delays the kill long enough to harvest three of his victim's right-hand fingers and collect their attractive brass rings. In this violent story, Russell shows his audiences how the capacity to withstand severe pain, a highly prized trait among many Indian cultures, enables the hero to feign death long enough for his comrades to catch up and rescue him.

In depicting the stoic response to pain, Russell provides another cultural contrast. The Indian warrior faces torture and "takes his medicine without whinin'. If he makes any talk its to tell ye you're a green hand at the business; of course he don't cuss none, he don't know how. That art belongs to civilized folks. . . ."[37] Among fellow western men, Russell could be impressive with profanity, so he knew he was comparing himself with the Indians and coming up short regarding this Indian's self-control. The author's friends would have appreciated Russell's joke on himself. "Civilized" people also suffer ironically in comparison with an injured warrior.

Russell delivers another joke with Owens's clarification of the hero's priorities: "Finger-That-Kills is glad he's livin' an's got his hair, but he's sure sore 'bout losin' those rings."[38] The author portrays a nineteenth-century plains Indian's regret for lost jewelry as being greater than his sense of loss for three irreplaceable fingers from his hand. This joke accelerates an audience's awareness of conflicting cultural values. In many cases the response to this moment is the laughter of recognition by people who, especially in Russell's time, would have been unsympathetic to Indian cultural motives. Some of the audience laughter would be a response to nervous recognition of the so-called "logic" of mutilating a defeated enemy. And any unsympathetic listeners might simply have laughed at the absurdity that Russell paid any attention to such Indian matters whatsoever.

At his story's opening, before he could simply introduce the one-fingered hero, Russell addresses his audience's typical distaste for Indians. He cannot automatically expect his turn-of-the-century listeners and readers to appreciate the Indian cultural values at the heart of this yarn unless he has softened some of their racial assumptions. Twain expressed a typical bias about Indians, stating: "the Red Man is a skulking coward and a windy braggart, who strikes without warning—usually from an ambush or under cover of night."[39] Russell's first words through the voice of his narrator "Squaw Owens" acknowledge the "ambushing-coward" stereotype, but then he immediately inverts it:

> Injuns is born bushwackers; they believe in killin' off their enemy an' ain't particular how its done, but prefer gettin' him from cover, an' I notice some of their white brothers play the same way. You watch these old gun-fighters an' you'll see most of 'em likes a shade the start in a draw; there's many a man that's fell under the smoke of a forty-five—drawn from a sneak—that ain't lookin' when he got it.[40]

Having established the relative equality of murderers for both racial groups in his first paragraph, Russell's narrator reveals himself as a skeptical expert on Indians with a grudging respect for their self-control when under excruciating pain:

> I've had plenty experience amongst Injuns, an' all the affection I got for' 'em wouldn't make no love story, but with all their tricks an' treachery I call them a game people. It's their religion to die without a whimper; in olden times when a prisoner's took, there's no favors asked or given. He's up agin it. It's a sure case of cash in—skinned alive, cooked over a slow fire, or some such trail to the huntin'-ground—an' all Mister Prisoner does is to take his medicine without whinin'.[41]

Despite the risk of alienating his audience by tampering with widely held racial assumptions, Russell has his narrator, Owens, finish his opening remarks with wry humor that deflates presumed white cultural superiority. The storyteller is cultivating a neutral, if not altogether sympathetic, audience for a tale about Indians. Now Russell may begin his tale with a typical local-color ploy: the continuation of a topic: "Talkin' about an Injun's nerve reminds me of an old buck I run onto on the Blackfoot Reserve a few years ago."[42]

Russell's preface to delivering a realistic story about Indians addressed widespread white indifference to Indians in turn-of-the-century America. Indian characters were often not utilized in the plots of western stories destined for major publications. According to one observer of popular western publishing, by 1922 Curtis Publishing (*Saturday Evening Post* and *Ladies Home Journal,* among others) no longer bought western stories in which Indians were characterized.

"Indian characters might be present," states Jon Tuska, "but if they were, they must be portrayed as renegades or fill only minor roles." In popular stories and films, this was a time for Indians to vanish, not intermarry.[43] Russell's local history–based stories about Indians ran counter to American mass-consumption trends of early twentieth-century publishing and after 1910 he stopped trying to publish them in national mass-circulation magazines.

How Lindsay Turned Indian

Challenging Euro-American sensitivities about interracial marriage in the early twentieth century, Charlie Russell brought the sensitive topic of Indian/white marriage into open discussion in his story "How Lindsay Turned Indian."[44] Interracial marriage between Indian women and white men happened with some frequency and typically generated controversy in polite Euro-American society of the nineteenth and twentieth centuries. (Apparently, marriages between white women and Indian men were so extremely rare as to be unthinkable.) Russell seldom painted or sketched this topic, with the exception of the oil painting titled *When White Men Turn Red*, depicting a white man with his two Indian wives, but he did explore Indian/white marriage in several stories as a way to discuss cultural differences. In the painting *When White Men Turn Red*, Russell shows the three mounted figures approaching what appears to be the future site of Fort Benton, Montana. Regarding the lodges down along the river, the younger wife signs to her husband, "What follows?" as the white horse calls ahead to fellow horses in the encampment (**see plate 6**).

White men participating in interracial marriages typically experienced lower stature in Euro-American culture in the West and often preferred to live within the Indian community or tribe of their wife's people. Early fur trappers who took Indian wives, according to one historian, were the ones "the settlers hated the most, alleging against them every villainy that should be alleged against Indians."[45] These sentiments faded slowly, if at all. In 1937, eleven years after Russell's death, a Montana woman gossiped in a letter to a Russell researcher, "I think I told you I saw James Willard Schultz in Great Falls at the Rainbow [Hotel]. . . . He impressed me as the sort of man who would love his Indian wife the best because he would like the servility."[46] Even though such disapproval expressed the bias of a judgmental school-marm, her assessment of white, male motivation proved fairly accurate. Russell's lifelong friend from their early days as cowpunchers, Teddy Blue Abbott, wrote:

> I wasn't the only one [attracted to Indian women] by a long way, because there was plenty of cowpunchers in that early day who were not ashamed to marry an Indian girl. You couldn't blame us. We were starving for the sight of a woman, and some of these young squaws were awful good-looking. . . . Those Indian women made wonderful wives. The greatest attraction in a woman, to an Indian, was obedience. They were taught that and they inherited it. Their husband's will was their law. Every white man I ever knew that was married to an Indian—like Granville Stuart—thought the world of them.[47]

Both Stuart and Abbott, who had married one of Stuart's mixed-blood daughters, lived on cattle ranches near Lewistown, Montana, and enjoyed relatively high stature in the community. If an interracial couple resided on tribal lands, however, western white society typically dismissed the husband as a "squaw-man." According to Texas literary historian J. Frank Dobie, "Any English-speaking frontiersman who took up with the Indians was dubbed 'squaw-man'—a term of sinister connotations."[48]

Within these prevailing sentiments, Russell began his intermarriage story with a revealing dialogue between his two primary Indian story narrators, "Dad Lane" and "Squaw Owens." These two voices quickly show their personal views on the matter:

> "Most folks don't bank much on squaw-men, but I've seen some mighty good ones doubled up with she-Injuns," says Dad Lane. "Ain't you, Owens?"
>
> "I told you my short experience with that Blood woman; I wasn't a successful Injun, but the comin' of white women to the country's made big changes; men's got finicky about matin'. I guess if I'd come to the country earlier, squaws would a-looked good enough, an' if there wasn't nothin' but Injun women, it's a cinch that all married men would be wearin' moccasins."[49]

This relatively open-minded and tolerant conversation then leads directly into the story concerning the ultimate squaw-man, known simply as "Lindsay."

Many observers have speculated incorrectly that Russell's sympathetic approach to intermarriage was based on his own personal experience. A Russell biographer has guessed that Lindsay simply served as a fantasy wish-fulfillment for the author.[50] In fact, several moments in this story of Lindsay's life contain episodes that are similar to the life of legendary Montana squaw-man Hugh Monroe. More than parallel to Lindsay, Russell's experiences with Indian women probably resembled the failed interracial romance of narrator "Squaw Owens."

Charlie Russell's friends and associates have expressed conflicting opinions about the young artist's romantic involvement with Indian women. The author James Willard Schultz, who knew Russell before the artist's marriage to Nancy Cooper, stated simply that Charlie "never had an Indian girl."[51] Another friend stated, "Now you asked about his girl friends. The only friends I knew him to have were the red-light girls, squaws or Indian girls. He played them some. Nearly every cowpuncher played the same as he did."[52] Fellow cowpuncher Con Price thought Russell had opportunities for sexual encounters with Indians while in Canada in 1888, but Phil Weinard, who had brought Russell north of the border that summer and lived near where Russell stayed, disputed Price's opinion.[53] Russell may have fed his friends' confusion. He tended to make jokes about his possible involvement with Indians, such as his letter to a fellow cowpuncher in which the twenty-eight-year-old night herder states:

> I was surprised to here thet you were married. . . . and hope that you will settel down and live like a whit man I never expect to be that lucky. I expect if I ever get married it will be to [t]his kind [sketch of small hand pointing to drawing of Indian woman wrapped in a blanket] as there is a great many [of] them here and I seem to take well among them.

> I had a chance to marry young louses daughter he is black foot chief It was
> the only chance I ever had to marry into good famley but I did not like the way my
> intended cooked dog and we broke of[f] our engagment[.][54]

Many observers, including Phil Weinard, Fred Renner, and Brian Dippie, have noted that the Blackfeet firmly abstained from eating dog meat. Russell obviously was joking in this letter as much about marrying an Indian as about eating dog. Other accounts of Russell's encounters with Indians suggest that he shared the Blackfeet's revulsion over eating canine companions.[55] Charlie Russell's jokes about dog meat and his references to marrying an Indian woman demonstrate that he was not above lighthearted ridicule of a few aspects of Indian cultures. Nevertheless, his sensitivity and appreciation for their circumstances at the end of the nineteenth century stand out clearly in his stories, in contrast with most of his peers and contemporaries.

A 1998 biography challenges the sense of Russell as having been compassionate toward Indians. Author John Taliaferro argues that Russell's depiction of Indian women in several sexually oriented paintings negates his stature as a sincere Indian sympathizer. Although Russell painted as many as a dozen sexually suggestive paintings (some of which Nancy may have destroyed) among his estimated forty-five hundred artworks, he painted just as many involving Euro-American women as Indian women. More significantly, the vast majority of Indian women portrayed in his art demonstrate lives of independence, beauty, and courage, as in *Beauty Parlor* (**see plate 8**). In *Returning to Camp*, Russell depicts several generations of women transporting and protecting meat for their families while nurturing the next generation of hunters (**see plate 7**). Rarely did Russell show them as victims of oppression. Russell's depiction of drunken seduction between a cowboy and a white prostitute, titled *Just a Little Pleasure*, demonstrates that, in his few sexually oriented paintings, Russell's gender insensitivity extended to all women, not simply to Indian women.[56]

Russell's tale about intermarriage is also his best story about white encounters with Indian life. "How Lindsay Turned Indian" adapts a pivotal moment in the legendary life of Hugh Monroe (1799–1896), who is widely considered to be the first white man accepted into Blackfeet tribal life.[57] Russell put several of Monroe's experiences into the "Lindsay" character.

In Lindsay's autobiographical yarn, the crucial moment of his acceptance by the Piegan Blackfeet took place when he lit a chief's ceremonial pipe using sunlight focused through a magnifying glass. This narrative moment mirrored the historical event that had enabled young Monroe to live and travel with the tribe. In Russell's version, the white man's technology saves young Lindsay's life, but the stoic Indians mask their initial reactions.[58] "Squaw Owens" tells Russell's audience about the astonishing powers of self-control that Indians could exercise in the presence of such an unnerving magical device as a piece of glass that can burn tobacco with the sun's light. This looking-glass episode displaced a moment in his 1908 published version of the story involving Lindsay shooting a mounted rider who was galloping over to force the boy to return to the fort and white civilization.[59] Russell revised his fictional device of supernatural sunlight that suddenly breaks through clouds following the dramatic gunshot. Instead, the artist/writer opted for a historical model for his narrative. Essentially, Russell chose realism over fantasy as he portrayed the intrusion of optical technology into the lives of nomadic natives in the West.

FIG. 23. Charles M. Russell, *Just a Little Pleasure*, ca. 1898. Transparent and opaque watercolor and graphite on paper, no. 1961.285, Amon Carter Museum, Fort Worth, Texas. From a quartet of rough watercolors—*Just a Little Sunshine, Just a Little Rain, Just a Little Pleasure, Just a Little Pain*—that hung for years in the Silver Dollar Saloon, Great Falls, Montana.

The realism of Lindsay's story demonstrates Russell's ability to gather information about events that predated his own arrival in the West. Russell had met Hugh Monroe at least once as the elderly man lived out his final years on the Blackfeet Reservation near Browning, Montana.[60] Russell also had ample opportunity to read the accounts published in the same MNA inserts to which he was supplying his own stories. In later years, Russell also had many

FIG. 24.

Charles M. Russell, *Just At the Crack of The Gun The Sun Breaks Out Through a Cloud Hittin' The Kid.* Illustration for the story "How Lindsay Turned Indian," in *Outing Magazine,* December 1907. After this magazine appearance, this fanciful episode and illustration disappeared from all subsequent printings of the story.

friendly contacts with Monroe's grandson, Angus.[61] Nancy Russell referred to these interactions when she spoke to a local women's club:

> Mr. Russell could paint a picture of life a hundred years before his time, because when he first came west he met old men who had used the flint-lock rifle and they told him stories of their lives and tales that their grandfathers told them. These campfire stories that were told this impressionable boy of fifteen [actually sixteen], when his mind was like wax, have held until there is an unlimited store of subjects to choose from.[62]

Russell knew numerous squaw-men, both his own age, like Jack Griffin,[63] and some almost as old as Hugh Monroe. Russell's fictional, elderly squaw-man, "Lindsay," most likely represents a composite of several individuals.

Russell focused his interest on the lifelong squaw-men, the ones who lived most of their lives among Indians and whose experiences overlapped with the Euro-American settlement of the West. The author clearly wanted his audience to appreciate the presence of this aging

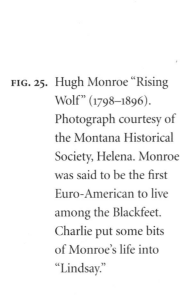

FIG. 25. Hugh Monroe "Rising Wolf" (1798–1896). Photograph courtesy of the Montana Historical Society, Helena. Monroe was said to be the first Euro-American to live among the Blackfeet. Charlie put some bits of Monroe's life into "Lindsay."

human history book, who would typically be dismissed as a lowdown "squaw-man" by many Montana whites. Narrator Owens observes: "This old boy could string the best war and buffalo yarns I ever heard. It's like readin' a romance; any time he calls I'm sure of a good yarn."[64] The storytelling process is crucial for enjoying Lindsay's presence, beyond simply learning facts about a strange old man's remarkable life. To Russell, the old man's yarns are a rich reward unto themselves.

Like many Montana readers of the MNA inserts, Russell was intrigued by the idea of a white man immersing himself in an Indian culture for most of his life. As a young man, Charlie Russell shared the wish of his range buddy Teddy Blue Abbott, to have lived among an earlier generation of Indians. Abbott described the day he first realized that Russell shared this wish:

Coming back up Dog Creek, I met Russell. I said: "God, I wish I'd been a Sioux Indian a hundred years ago," and I told him the story [just heard from an Indian about their lives in earlier years]. He said: "Ted, there's a pair of us. They've been living in heaven for a thousand years, and we took it away from 'em for forty dollars a month."[65]

In his more mature years, Russell seemed less inclined to wish that he had been an Indian and more motivated to help other non-Indians appreciate Native American people and their cultures. He told fellow western artist Maynard Dixon about how difficult it would be to fully understand even one tribe, expressing what Dixon called "the impossible mental-spiritual-psychological abyss that exists between us and the old time Indian."[66] Charlie Russell was a realist about his limitations for fully grasping Indian culture, but the stories he published showed that he considered the effort worth trying.

Much of Lindsay's story involves a buffalo hunt. This high-adrenalin adventure of surprising a buffalo herd, then racing horses bareback among the thundering animals and killing as many as possible with arrows or primitive guns provides the story's climax. On that day, the fourteen-year-old Lindsay rides in his first buffalo stampede, kills at least one animal, and "lunches on raw liver, like any other Injun," concludes narrator Owens, who then adds with dry irony: "Looks like this short run has turned him savage." At the end, there can be little doubt that Lindsay is happy that he lived out his life among Blackfeet Indians. Russell's narrator leaves the final words to his subject:

> "My boy," says Lindsay, finishin' up his yarn, openin' an' shuttin' his hands like an Injun—I savvy he's countin' winters—"that's been sixty-five years ago as near as I can figure. I run buffalo till the whites cleaned 'em out, but that's the day I turned Injun, an' I ain't cut my hair since."[67]

With this ending, Lindsay's tone seems composed and defiant, giving Russell's listeners and readers a better understanding of both buffalo-era plains Indians and dedicated squaw-men.

DAD LANE'S BUFFALO YARN

The crucial role of wild buffalo in the story of Lindsay also dominates the two sections of "Dad Lane's Buffalo Yarn." As with many of Russell's serious stories, this tale opens with an explanation about Indian cultural practices and conditions in the nineteenth-century West. An editorial statement about the bloody demise of the wild buffalo herds takes up the first quarter of the story. The initial narrator, "Long Wilson," exposes the very unromantic side of buffalo slaughter with long-range rifles, telling how the professional hunters did their bloody work, killing dozens of animals at a time from a hidden vantage point:

> Whenever one tries to break out of the mill, there's a ball goes bustin' through its lungs, causin' it to belch blood an' strangle, an' it ain't long till they quit tryin' to get away an' stand an' take their medicine. Then this cold-blooded proposition in the waller settles down to business, droppin' one at a time an' easin' up now an agin to cool his gun. . . . These hide hunters [are] the gentlemen that cleaned up the buffalo . . . [68]

Russell shared the widespread belief that the shooting of buffalo herds by white hunters for their hides or for mere sport accounted for the nearly complete extinction of the North

American bison.[69] Russell's narrator "Long Wilson" expressed the author's bitter sarcasm about the process, identifying with obvious contempt the hunters as "gentlemen."

Long Wilson's description of buffalo destruction provides only a preliminary statement to Russell's main story, opening the way for narrator "old Dad Lane" to tell about his survival in the midst of intertribal warfare with an Indian partner who has a dual identity. Although he is a full-blood Piegan Blackfeet, this Indian has been raised by whites and has adopted some of their ways, including an anglicized name, "Joe Burke." Just beneath the exterior of his white man's clothes, name, and language, however, resides his Indian identity and name, "Bad Meat." Although this translated name seems negative in English,[70] Bad Meat proves himself a good partner. As the two men face a life-or-death attack from another tribe, Dad Lane's partner sheds his Anglo clothing:

> When it's light I'm surprised at Bad Meat's appearance. Up till now he's wearin' white man's clothes, but this mornin' he's back to the clout, skin leggin's an' shirt. His fore-top's wrapped in otterskin an' from his hair to just below his eyes he's smeared with ochre. The rest of his face is black, with green stripes. He notices my surprise an' tells me it ain't good medicine for an Indian to die with whitemen's clothes.[71]

Bad Meat reveals his own submerged identity because, just under the surface, he is still a full-blood Indian with religious and cultural beliefs that resurface in response to extreme stress. Russell demonstrates how the reemergence of Bad Meat's essential culture and personality ultimately holds a positive benefit for his white companion by saving his life.

In the same moment of crisis, Russell's narrator Dad Lane also reveals his own hidden identity—a racially minded bigot. The old narrator admits that the nighttime attack and theft of their horses put him in a profane state of mind. And then Bad Meat mentions that he had anticipated the Indian attack on their camp.:

> I'm cussin' an' goin' on when I hear Bad Meat kind o' chucklin'. He calls me from his blankets. "I knowed it," say he.
>   "If you knowed," says I, "you're a little late breakin' the news. What's the use of you holdin' out all this knowledge?" An' I cussed him up a batch. I'm in the wrong all right, but ain't in no humor to own up to it—specially to an Injun."[72]

In his own description, Dad Lane reflects an awareness of his misplaced racial pride but carries on, nevertheless, because he isn't in a mood to humble himself, "specially to an Injun." The narrator's contrary self-revelation must have been a source of humor for Russell's white audience but, conversely, for an Indian audience, a less humorous confirmation of this narrator's insensitivity. In a similar fictional situation, Mark Twain's character Huckleberry Finn could put aside his sense of racial superiority to apologize to his close companion and presumed inferior, the runaway African American slave Jim: "It was fifteen minutes before I could work myself up to go and humble myself to a nigger—but I done it, and I warn't ever sorry for it afterwards, neither."[73] In both cases, the authors (Twain and Russell) allow their rustic narrators to reveal their internal struggles with racial bias toward their presumed racially inferior companions who have actually just proven their superior intelligence. The narrators' struggles with self-awareness appear as potentially humorous, moral lessons for their readers.

The works of both Russell and Clemens share a vulnerability to criticism in the later generations for racial language that may have seemed vulgar in contemporary nineteenth-century usage, but was not considered derogatory to their immediate readers. As Samuel Clemens/ Mark Twain biographer Justin Kaplan has observed:

> "Huckleberry Finn" is in constant trouble with teachers, librarians and parents because of its iterations of "nigger," a word that has pre-emptive force today that it did not have in Huck Finn's Mississippi Valley of the 1840s. As far as I can tell, there have been no comparable objections to the frequent use, again by black characters as well as whites, of the word in Uncle Tom's Cabin.[74]

Russell uses "nigger" only once in his books of published stories—as a description of extreme darkness brought on by a nighttime storm. In the words of "Rawhide Rawlins," "Finally it darkens up so I can't see him at all. It's black as a nigger's pocket; you couldn't find your nose with both hands."[75]

Russell's four dozen brief stories do not attract the widespread acclaim awarded Mark Twain's prolific writings (except, perhaps in Montana, where the artist remains a folk hero). But even in the Treasure State, Russell's stories seldom appear as curriculum reading in secondary schools, especially in the state's seven Indian reservations. Russell's frequent use of terms such as *buck, squaw, Injun, savage, half-breed, breed, red,* and *redskin* make his writings authentic and colorful, but they are also just as unwelcome with Native Americans as the frequent appearance of *nigger* makes *The Adventures of Huckleberry Finn* unpalatable to most twenty-first-century African Americans.[76] Twain's use of *nigger* notwithstanding, his staunch support for nineteenth-century African American rights effectively contradicts charges of racial hatred. Ironically, the same cannot be said for Mark Twain's attitude toward Indians. Conversely, Charlie Russell defended Indian people and cultures, contrary to the scornful indifference of mainstream American society. Except for the slave York, however, whom he depicted in several paintings of the Lewis and Clark expedition (**see plate 9**), Russell expressed no comparable interest in African Americans. Charlie told his apprentice Joe DeYong, "That is Clark's slave. The Indians did not believe he was black. They thought it was paint."[77]

One of the few indications of Russell's attitude toward African Americans can be found in a brief conversation note to his teenage understudy, Joe DeYong. Russell comments candidly, "I don't think any man is better than another till he proves it I wouldn't want to mix with niggers but theres some good ones an some that can ride Some of the old niggers were mighty good to there masters after the war[.]"[78] Although he rose above typical western attitudes about Indians, Russell's disdain for the social company of Blacks and focus on the loyalty of former slaves all seem typical for wealthy southerners of the post–Civil War era. Nevertheless, Charlie Russell made friendly contacts with some Montana African Americans, including the young Judith Basin ranch hand Walter Jackson[79] and Molly Reingold, the older Negro woman

FIG. 26. Charles M. Russell, *The Next Thing I Know I'm Amongst His Horns,* 1908. Watercolor, illustration for the story "Dad Lane's Buffalo Yarn," *Outing Magazine,* February 1908. Subsequent publications of the story omitted this illustration showing "Bad Meat" shooting the buffalo while Dad Lane clutches its head for his life.

who lived near Utica.[80] Jackson recalled that his occasional encounters with Russell were cordial.[81] The artist's live-and-let-live attitude extended tolerance to many racial groups.[82] But with his ethnic interests primarily focused on Indians, he missed opportunities for more inclusive narrative works about other ethnic groups living in the nineteenth-century West.

The dual character Bad Meat/Joe Burke apparently held little appeal for Charlie Russell as a subject for paintings or sculptures, but for the storyteller/author, the dual character stimulated his story-writing impulse. His only illustration for the story shows Bad Meat/Joe Burke in his Indian attire shooting to kill the buffalo while "Dad Lane" clutches the galloping animal's horns and head for sheer survival. Russell shows that Indian companionship and practical know-how have the highest value in life-or-death situations. Tales like "Dad Lane's Buffalo Yarn" reflect an urge to communicate his ideas and values. Russell clearly wanted his white Montana contemporaries to understand the value of the persistence of Indian cultures and personalities despite assimilation policies being enforced on western Indian reservations.

In Charlie Russell's lifetime, more than mere cultural trappings, such as clothing styles and long hair, were disappearing from the American West. Russell noted that Indians as well as other vivid characters from frontier days seemed to be melting away as more settlers arrived in the early twentieth-century West. When a professional card-player told Russell that

> an Injun had no more right in this country than a Coyote. I told him what he said might be right, but there were folks coming to the country on the new rail road that thought the same way about gamblers and he wouldn't winter many times till he'd find the wild Indian would go but would only break trail for the gambler.[83]

The gradual disappearance of Indian people corresponded with a measurable decline in Indian population, a decrease that spawned a turn-of-the-century perception of Indians as the "vanishing Americans."[84] Like most Americans of his time, Charlie Russell believed that this downward spiral of Indian populations would probably eliminate Indian tribal and racial identities, either by military force and starvation or by federally mandated assimilation under the Dawes Act. Russell, however, believed that such a fate was unjust, and he expressed compassion for those who resisted or fell victim to the accelerating changes in the West.

Charlie Russell translated his pro-Indian sensibilities into public action by supporting the plight of the wandering bands of Cree and Chippewa Indians who were collecting in squalid camps outside Helena, Great Falls, and a few other Montana towns in the early twentieth century.[85] During an especially severe period of winter weather in 1909, Russell joined former Senator Paris Gibson, writer Frank B. Linderman, and several other prominent men to set up a relief fund. In a discussion with a *Great Falls Tribune* reporter, Russell made these candid observations:

> It doesn't look very good for the people of Montana if they will sit and see a lot of women and children starve to death in this kind of weather. . . . Lots of people seem to think that Indians are not human beings at all and have no feelings. These kind of people would be the first to yell for help if their grub pile was running short and they didn't have enough clothes to keep out the cold, and yet because Rocky Boy and his bunch are Indians, they are perfectly willing to let them die of hunger and cold without lifting a hand. I know that the majority of people in the state are not that way, however, and if they are called upon they will be glad to help the Indians out.[86]

Russell's participation in the relief effort reflected his sense of personal connection with the migrant Indian bands that he visited occasionally on the outskirts of Great Falls. There he developed friendships with tribal leaders like Young Boy (Chippewa) and Little Bear (Cree), among others. Despite consistent personal connections, however, Russell's public leadership in the drive to provide aid in 1909 stood out as uncharacteristic for the artist. Although Russell entertained many people with the extroverted, comic storytelling side of his personality, he remained a relatively private person. When he spoke publicly to the *Tribune* about the freezing and starving landless Indians and dropped the first cash into the collection hat, he was expressing an

Miss Montana, "Father I have thrown my lands open to the world There are Americans, have I nothing for them?"
Uncle Sam, "No My child not as long as the land hog has control He is the only animal known that lives with out a heart."

FIG. 27. Charles M. Russell, *Uncle Sam and the Land Hog* (also called *Russell Was the Indian's Friend*). Watercolor on paper, courtesy of private collection. Russell offered this cartoon to help Frank Linderman secure land for Montana's so-called landless Indians, on what ultimately became the Rocky Boy's Reservation.

especially intense concern. Ordinarily, his expression of political, religious, and family attitudes remained restricted within his private household.

Charlie Russell joined one other political effort on behalf of Indians, helping Frank Linderman in the effort to gain a reservation for the Cree and Chippewa on the site of a decommissioned army fort located between Great Falls and Havre, Montana. Linderman led this unpopular struggle from 1908 until final success in 1916,[87] and Russell provided ideas and encouragement, a political cartoon, and a blunt letter to U.S. Senator Henry L. Myers.[88] Ewers has confirmed that this effort to secure a reservation for the homeless Indians lacked popular support, "for neither whites nor Indians living on reservations expressed much desire to have these so-called renegades settle on lands near them."[89] Russell's political sketch may never have reached publication, but the reservation effort succeeded nevertheless.

Although the attitudes of many fellow Montana citizens about the appropriate treatment of Indians differed with Charlie Russell's opinions and activities, he had little to fear from public disapproval. His wide popularity, based on his personality, artworks, and ever-increasing professional success, tended to minimize local, negative responses to his Indian advocacy. Both Great Falls newspapers enjoyed his companionship, printed favorable profiles, applauded his successes, and generally agreed with his Indian ideas including the push for a Cree/Chippewa reservation.[90] In addition, Russell's art sales seemed to be buffered from adverse local opinions in Montana. Nancy Russell raised her prices on his works with each passing year, thereby leaving fewer Montana people able to afford them. Most transactions involved wealthy collectors in distant urban markets leaving no risk from loss of local sales. Russell's preoccupation with art production and long-distance sales trips probably contributed to his social "tunnel vision," which, in turn, limited his political activism. "Dad Lane's Buffalo Yarn" dramatized a cautious friendship between two men of opposing cultures who were thrown together by survival necessity. Russell's few instances of political advocacy originated in his friendships with specific Indians and his appreciation for those he knew at a distance.[91]

Mormon Murphy's (Misplaced) Confidence

Despite his support for Indian cultural survival and socioeconomic well-being, however, Charlie Russell did not ignore the history of warfare and violent conflict among natives and white settlers in the West. Indeed, not every Russell story portrayed Indians as exemplary heroes or victims. In particular, his story "Mormon Murphy's (Misplaced) Confidence"[92] provides an example of ambiguous values about Indian/white violence. In this tale, an Indian murders a good-natured white man and then, in turn, falls under the gun of the story's narrator, a participant in several Russell tales named "old Dad Lane." The deadly violence happens suddenly, without apparent provocation, and Dad Lane avoids his own death only through a combination of seasoned intuition and quickly aggressive self-defense. In this tale, Dad Lane is both the narrator and the leading participant in the story. This narrative is less about the title character, Mormon Murphy, who is "good-hearted till he's foolish, an' so honest he thinks everybody else is on the square,"[93] and more about the narrator. This story of the swift murder of a good person also shows the hardening of Dad Lane's negative attitude about Indians.

After describing the quick exchange of deadly gunshots, Dad Lane spends a quarter of this narrative reflecting on the results. As a typical nineteenth-century western man, he struggles to express his emotional feelings about burying his partner Murphy, saying "I tell ye, fellers, I don't know when I cried, it's been a long time ago, an' I didn't shed no tears then, but I damn nigh choked to death at that funeral." Conversely, his extreme anger at the dead Indian must be suppressed:

> I don't scalp the Injun—not that I wouldn't like to, but I ain't got time to gather no souvenirs an' I'm afeared to hang around, cause Injuns ain't lonesome animals; they band up, an' it's safe bettin' when we see one there's more near by.[94]

"Dad Lane" then admits that if he had started to scalp the dead murderer, his fury would have driven him to skin the body entirely. "I'd a-peeled him to his dew-claws," he states.[95] Only Dad Lane's all-powerful sense of threatened survival prevents him from acting like Medicine Whip and mutilating his dead enemy. Here Russell shows his audience how the compulsion to mutilate a vanquished opponent dwells within Euro-Americans as well as Indians. Russell missed his chance, however, to note that, in this case, the non-Indian has controlled his feelings in contrast with Medicine Whip's venting of his fury on a dead enemy.

FIG. 28. Charles M. Russell, *The Injun Pulls Murphy Toward Him, And At The Same Time His Left Hand Pulls The Trigger,* 1907. Watercolor on paper, illustration for the story "Mormon Murphy's Confidence" in *Outing Magazine,* August 1907, and in *Trails Plowed Under.*

Of all the fictional narrators in his stories, Russell's character "Dad Lane" seems the most remote from the author's experience or viewpoint. In "Mormon Murphy's Confidence," more than any of the other three stories to which he contributes, "Dad Lane's" manner of expression makes him distinctive. He opens the story with expert testimony about the antiquated use of a sling or loop to carry a rifle on a saddle and refers to himself as "an old coyote like me." Most important, many of his phrases, "used ter," "got ter," "acrost in front of ye," "ye can tap yerself, he ain't lyin'," "a skift of snow," "that-a-way," "I got him on a limb," and "I damn nigh choked," are distinctive to this character. Those phrases and such words as "arger" for argue, "ye" for you, "clost" for close, "fust" for first, and "a-feared" for afraid appear neither in other stories by Russell nor in his personal letters.[96] No other Russell character or narrator speaks this way. Russell not only names him "old Dad Lane," he proves his seniority with antiquated figures of speech and an older man's hardened attitude about Indians. Although some of Russell's narrators may be thinly disguised alter egos of the author, "Dad Lane" seems to be the most distinctive personality, the narrator least likely to represent Russell's personal values. Instead, "Dad Lane" speaks the views of an earlier generation of white settlers, such as friends of Russell's like Bob Thoroughman and Robert Vaughn, who harbored deep mistrust and hatred for Indians that contrasted with their younger friend, C. M. Russell.[97]

In "Mormon Murphy's Confidence," Russell establishes a historical context to create more than a mere anti-Indian parable about a random act of murderous violence. Early on, Dad Lane explains that the events took place "back in '78, the same year that Joseph's at war agin the whites." Later his suspicions rise when an Indian approaches riding an Appaloosa horse, a breed closely associated with the Nez Perce tribe of eastern Oregon and northern Idaho. At the story's end, the narrator concludes that the Indian must be part of the runaway Nez Perce band under Chief Joseph, who were hurrying across Montana's northern prairies in a vain attempt to escape into Canada from the U.S. Army. His references to the Indian's origins are perfunctory:

> "Guess this Injun's a Nez Perce, all right, because a short time after the killin' of Murphy there's a bull-train jumped an' burned on Cow Creek, an' it ain't long till Joseph surrenders to Miles over on the Snake."[98]

For an old-time skeptic like Dad Lane, no more need be said. The dead Indian was Nez Perce, passing through with Chief Joseph. For most of Russell's Montana audience, however, that connection would be enough for recognition of the Indian's origin in Dad Lane's narrative.

By the turn of the century, westerners knew some details of the Nez Perce Indians' ordeals. After conflicts with white settlers and illegal seizures of their tribal lands, they made their desperate flight through Montana in 1877 to a potential refuge in Canada. In the process, the Nez Perce threatened many Montana townspeople and ranchers living in their path. The Indians' desperation increased following brutal battles with army and militia forces along the way. A few whites, like Russell's fictional characters Dad Lane and Mormon Murphy, experienced harm or death when they unwittingly encountered violently desperate members of the Nez Perce band. But in subsequent years, a growing number of non-Indians in Montana and elsewhere saw the Nez Perce as tragic victims rather than marauding renegades. From 1916 to 1940, the sympathetic pages of the Montana Newspaper Association's weekly inserts often carried articles about the doomed Nez Perce and their leader, Chief Joseph. Russell's friend, State Supreme Court Chief Justice Lew Callaway, contributed one piece that called the conflict "unjust" for the Nez Perce.[99] Americans in other regions who saw "Mormon Murphy's Misplaced Confidence" in *Outing Magazine* in 1907 may not have noticed Dad Lane's brief reference to the Nez Perce, but western readers, especially those familiar with the Nez Perce in Montana, Idaho, and eastern Oregon, would have experienced some recognition and probably the discomfort of conflicting feelings.

Russell's brief story carries a dual sense of values. From Dad Lane's perspective, the attacking Indian whom he called "that damn snake"[100] deserved death and mutilation for killing Murphy and thereby confirming the old man's worst thoughts about Indians. For Nez Perce sympathizers, however, the story's Indian raises questions. Was this Nez Perce Indian a cold murderer or simply riding in advance of the fleeing tribe as a guard to protect his people's chance for survival? Russell's careful hints in this narrative show that he knew more about the Nez Perce than his narrator.

Ironically, the author told his story through the perceptions and words of "Dad Lane," a

FIG. 29.
Charles M. Russell, *Chief Joseph,*
1900. Oil on board, gift of the
Federation of Great Falls
Women's Clubs, courtesy of the
C. M. Russell Museum, Great
Falls, Montana.

wary old-timer with no sympathy for the Nez Perce's extenuating circumstances. Dad Lane kills the Indian as a matter of self-defense and tells his story from that perspective. Nevertheless, Russell guides his narrator to include enough information to suggest a Nez Perce perspective in this incident. The old narrator never mentions this alternative viewpoint, but the more alert members of Russell's audience could appreciate that the Nez Perce antagonist also acts from self-defense. Dad Lane's speech patterns demonstrate that he does not speak for Russell. Nevertheless, by shaping Dad Lane's presentation of this story, Russell shows that he understood the Indians' and settlers' opposing sides on matters of violent conflict. In "Mormon Murphy's Confidence," the author's personal conflict over his sympathies for Indians gleams through the cracks of Dad Lane's fury at "that damn snake." This duality makes "Mormon Murphy's Confidence" one of Russell's most intriguing tales.

Curley's Friend

In contrast with the uncertainty of "Mormon Murphy," Russell's complex story "Curley's Friend"[101] tells of an attempted massacre with a clearer pro-Indian point of view. Russell's nar-

rator, "Curley," tells how he came to forcibly interrupt a fellow cowboy in the act of systematically shooting an unsuspecting group of Bannock men and women. The narrator relates his
good deed, not to boast but to explain why his life was spared by a Bannock war party on a
later occasion. To gain the attention of Montana listeners and readers who might sympathize
with the murdering cowboy more than with the narrator, Curley must earn their trust. He
could not show too much compassion for the Indian victims or risk being rejected as a "big-
hearted, philanthropical, goggle-eyed, heathen converter,"[102] as a Judith Basin newspaper dismissed Indian sympathizers with characteristic verbal overkill. Consequently, Russell has
Curley begin with a disclaimer, "I ain't no Injun lover, . . . but I'm willin' to give any man a fair
shake." Among less-sympathetic nineteenth-century westerners, such a preamble would have
seemed generously liberal and open-minded toward the native inhabitants.

In 1924, three years before "Curley's Friend" appeared for the first time as a new story in
Trails Plowed Under, a remarkably similar and equally grim narrative appeared in the Montana
Newspaper Association inserts. This unsigned MNA piece told about cowboys working near
the Montana/Idaho border in 1878 who participated in reprisal raids against Bannock Indians
over the apparent theft of horses and cattle. Occasionally, the cowboys would locate and kill
small bands of Indians—men, women, and children—and cleverly deposit the dead bodies in
abandoned mine shafts. Hiding the human remains helped to avoid an all-out war with the
Bannocks, as well as to escape a reprimand by white law officers. The MNA writer made light
of how the cowboys hid the grisly evidence after the shooting stopped, stating that "all of the
Indians including the squaws, were soon in shape to be 'snaked' [roped and dragged feet-first
behind a horse] to the graveyard." And since that day, "The old shaft is the sepulcher of a dozen
or so braves, as well as a few squaws and papooses."[103]

Russell's handwritten draft of his similar story, "Curley's Friend," appears to have predated the 1924 newspaper accounts of the 1878 incidents involving the killing of Bannock
Indians.[104] None of the newspaper accounts includes evidence of a person who interrupts the
violence as narrator Curley mentions in Russell's story. Conversely, Russell's tale lacks any reference to bodies of Indians hidden in a mineshaft or deep well. Russell's inspiration or information source, therefore, appears to have been independent of the newspaper versions.

Yet, even if the character Curley were merely a figment of Russell's imagination, the
author created a plausible role model of an ordinary cowpuncher without idealistic motives,
who instinctively took appropriate action and forced a murderous comrade to interrupt a
small-scale massacre. Curley's moral act spared two Bannock women following the ambush-
killing of two men and the cold-blooded shooting of another woman who was begging for
mercy. Russell apparently adapted at least one oral account about atrocities against the
Bannocks to form his own tale, complete with the high-risk action that halts a genocidal incident. Whether this story was fact or fiction or a mixture of both is unimportant. Russell's story
purposely brought his skeptical or indifferent audiences face to face with the unpleasant dark
side of supposedly heroic transformation of the frontier West into civilization.

Curley's only reward for his good deed proves to be the gratitude of a warrior who later
spares him in the midst of a murderous Bannock raid that subsequently killed four white
settlers. In Russell's narrative, Curley's relief over being spared by the warpath Indians inspires

FIG. 30. Charles M. Russell, *He Shook Hands and Told Me To Go.* Pen/ink, published as an illustration for the story "Curley's Friend," in *Trails Plowed Under.*

him to negate a basic slogan of American frontier bigotry, stating, "I heard that all good Injuns were dead ones. If that's true, I'm damn glad the one I met that day was still a bad one."[105] Through personal storytelling and publishing his transcribed narratives as local-color stories, Charlie Russell challenged common western assumptions about Indians to present his divergent ideas to listeners and readers in a style that they could appreciate. Despite a confusing plot sequence, Russell's story "Curley's Friend" effectively raises the unpleasant but historic reality of genocide in the American West.

THE TRAIL OF THE REEL FOOT

In contrast with Curley's grim lesson about mass murder, Charlie Russell's "The Trail of the Reel Foot"[106] successfully mixes serious issues with humor. Russell selected "Dad Lane" to narrate this story about a partially disabled white trapper whose odd footprints in the snow confuse some Indian warriors. Russell assembled this story using local accounts of a specific mixed-blood Indian, "Clubfoot George Boyd," whose frostbite-amputated feet made tracks in snow that worried a band of Gros Ventre warriors during the winter of 1864–1865.[107] Russell adapted the legendary story about "Clubfoot George," whose feet consisted of stumps following the frost-bite amputation of his toes and forward half of each foot. In Russell's version, the story's main character, a white man whom the narrator calls "Reel Foot," has a fully reversed "club foot" condition or, as described by the unsympathetic narrator, Dad Lane, "His right foot's straight ahead, natural; the left, p'intin' back in his trail."[108]

FIG. 31. Charles M. Russell, ca. 1915. Photograph courtesy of the C. M. Russell Museum, Great
Falls, Montana. Charlie is smiling as he forms the sign for "over," "crossing," or "the
other side" while he is seated on the porch of his summer cabin, Bull Head Lodge,
on Lake McDonald in Glacier National Park.

"The Trail of the Reel Foot," like the stories about Finger-That-Kills and Lindsay, contains descriptive references to Indian sign language. Russell was able to speak only rudimenta-
ry bits of the Blackfeet language, but throughout his life he became more adept with the
universal plains Indian sign language.[109] Charlie's nephew, Austin Russell, recalled that his
uncle was quite effective when talking with his hands:

> Charlie could tell a story, make jokes and describe the country he had just traversed
> and the animals and people he saw, all in sign language. Being an artist and using
> his hands so well, he was as graceful about it as an Indian—it's fascinating stuff
> to watch.[110]

Russell's sign-language vocabulary was large and grew even greater after the young deaf-mute
Joe DeYong became a regular member of the Russell studio and household.[111] The artist's ability with Indian sign language was impressive to many people and enabled him to spend time
with Indians in ways that enhanced his narrative art and stories about Native Americans,
including the ironic humor in "Reel Foot."[112] In his painting *The Fireboat* (**see plate 10**), Russell

FIG. 32. Charles M. Russell, *Lost in a Snow Storm—We Are Friends,* 1888. Watercolor, no. 1961.144, Amon Carter Museum, Fort Worth, Texas. The Indian leader speaks with his hands: "other side," "over" or "cross over"—probably offering survival instructions.

shows the medicine man raising his hand with fingers fluttering to make the sign for fire. Another warrior covers his mouth in an expression of astonishment, suggesting a depiction of the first encounter for these Indians with Euro-American steamboat technology.

Humor can cut to the feelings in unexpected directions, however. From one angle, Russell's jokes in "Reel Foot" might seem to be patronizing supposedly simple-minded Indian superstition, as when the warriors decide that Reel Foot's opposite-direction footprints signify "two one-legged men travelin' in opposite directions."[113] Later, when the warriors examine Reel Foot's irregular feet at close range, they spontaneously respect his condition as being an honorable wound, presumably suffered in battle or under torture. They can imagine honorable warfare circumstances for the backward foot so they decide not to kill him when they have the chance. In Russell's portrayal, the Indian mind has a positive side worthy of respect and appreciation as well as ironic humor.

In "The Trail of the Reel Foot," Charlie Russell shows how Indian cultural values respect human disfigurement and thereby differ from the ridicule and disgust typically found in the author's white audiences. Narrator Dad Lane articulates that unsympathetic attitude in a joke, telling Russell's audience, "I never do look at him without wonderin' which way he's goin' to start off."[114] In contrast with Euro-American revulsion and sarcasm, the Sioux values about disfigurement effectively save Reel Foot's life. Russell's presentation of the humanistic nature of dangerous Indian warriors in a humorous context actively contradicts the common stereotype of bloodthirsty Indian "braves" and exposes significant differences between human values in the Indian and Euro-American cultures. On this occasion, Russell does not directly insinuate that Indian values might be superior to Euro-American society, but the outcome of this story leads to that conclusion.

Russell's crusty old narrator "Dad Lane" once again uses harsh racial terms such as *buck,* *squaw,* and *savage* as valid human categories and, in this story, refers to the disfigured hero as a *cripple.* This term may have seemed inoffensive in the late nineteenth and early twentieth centuries of Russell's lifetime, but it registers as rude disrespect to readers nine or ten decades later. Russell's historically accurate use of these terms disturbs many readers in later generations. In one of the more distracting passages, Russell's "Dad Lane" explains why there are so few "cripples" among the "Injuns":

> [T]he old men of the party say it is not good to kill a man whose tracks have fooled the hawk-eyed Ogalalys [Ogallala Sioux Indians]. Deformities amongst these people are few an' far between. In buildin' all wild animals Nature makes few mistakes, Injuns 're only part human, an' when you see a cripple among 'em, it's safe bettin' that somebody's worked him over.[115]

This abrupt generalization by Dad Lane echoes Russell's humorous narrator "Rawhide Rawlins," who observed in a different story that many whites also were only part human:

> It put me in mind of the eastern girl that asks her mother: "Ma," says she, "do cowboys eat grass?" "No, dear," says the old lady, "they're part human," an' I don't know but the old gal had 'em sized up right. If they are human, they're a separate species.[116]

Charlie Russell may have been joking about "part human" Indians, just as he was about "part-human" cowpunchers, but in the generations after Russell's lifetime many readers find Dad Lane's Indian references to be humorless reinforcement of unpleasant racist stereotyping. Even though the embittered fictional narrator ultimately expresses respect for both "cripples" and "Injuns," his harsh language prevents many latter-day readers from enjoying this otherwise humorous story.

Of various race categories in Russell's time, a "half-breed" or "breed" (mixed-blood Indian) typically attracted special scorn from non-Indians. In a favorite book of Russell's, *The Oregon Trail,* Francis Parkman's description of mixed-blood trappers articulates this negative point of view:

> the half-savage men . . . their hard weather-beaten faces and bushy mustaches looked out from underneath the hoods of their white capotes with a bad and brutish expression, as if the owners might be the willing agents of any villainy. And such in fact is the character of many of these.[117]

Despite his use of racially abrasive language, Charlie Russell enjoyed the company of many mixed-blood Indians, including such friends as Belknap "Bally" Buck, Pete Van, and Duncan

FIG. 33.

Charles M. Russell, *He's Wearin' The Garments of a Breed.* Pen/ink, illustration for the story "Mormon Zack Larson," in *Trails Plowed Under.*

McDonald, and published favorable stories about each man. Charlie Russell's friendships included other mixed-blood Indians, such as Lone Wolf (Hart Merriam Schultz), wood sculptor John Clark, and Hugh Monroe's grandson, Angus Monroe. At a time when white Montana society stigmatized mixed-blood people as untrustworthy "half-breeds" and scorned Indians in general, resenting their presence on impoverished reservations and ignoring their starvation in shanty-camps just outside town,[118] Russell's friendships and public advocacy for Indians were much more than an intellectual pose. These personal associations formed an everyday part of his life that he carried on despite overt social disapproval.[119] As for the racist language, Russell applied the common term for mixed-race people to himself when he joked about his affinity for another scorned racial minority, "Maybe I'm not Irish but my fondness for that race makes me believe I'm a breed."[120] In Russell's use, the term *breed* for mixed heritage seemingly held neither positive nor negative weight. He opens another story with the words "Dunc McDonald, the breed," where the use of Rawhide Rawlins as narrator, rather than Squaw Owens or Dad Lane, signifies a lighthearted tale, rather than a serious one about racial issues.

Dunc McDonald

Charlie Russell met Duncan McDonald (1849–1934) at the Ronan buffalo roundups held in 1907, 1908, and 1909. At this unique series of events, several dozen riders, including Russell and McDonald, struggled to gather and hold hundreds of Indian-owned wild buffalo destined for sale and shipment to Canadian buyers, thereby making room for government-sponsored white homesteaders on the Flathead Indian Reservation. McDonald's Scottish father, Angus, and his Nez Perce mother, Katherine, operated the last Hudson's Bay Company trading post in the United States at Fort Connoh in the Flathead Valley until 1871,[121] a line of work that their son Duncan continued for many years.[122] In addition, McDonald took upon himself to interview the tiny remnant band of Nez Perce Indians who had barely escaped to Canada following Joseph's flight from Idaho and surrender in northern Montana. With this insider's information he wrote historically useful accounts of the Nez Perce "break-out" for a newspaper in Deer Lodge, Montana.[123] McDonald also rediscovered the lake that now bears his name in what became Glacier National Park, coincidentally the same lake where Charlie and Nancy Russell located their summer cabin. As a willing conversationalist and storyteller, Duncan McDonald became popular in the 1920s and 1930s with faculty members at the University of Montana and with newspaper writers, especially the MNA reporters, who sometimes referred to him as "the Sage of the Flathead."[124] Dunc McDonald proved to be a knowledgeable insider/expert on Indian culture and history in northwestern Montana. In the twenty-first century, the McDonalds continue to grow as a leading Indian family on Montana's Flathead Reservation.

Duncan McDonald frequently told listeners a story about his close scrape and escape from a wounded buffalo. Long after Charlie Russell had heard McDonald relate his buffalo story in 1908, and years after Russell had published the story in *More Rawhides* and then in *Trails Plowed Under*, Dunc McDonald was still telling his own version. Russell had a clear memory for speech patterns and could have quoted McDonald himself. Instead, the artist/writer put the story into the ironic, rural speech of his fictitious narrator, "Rawhide Rawlins." McDonald spoke in a slightly stilted and formal style. He was well-read, self-educated, and spoke neither the French-English patois typical of mixed-blood people in the Northwest nor the pidgin English typical of tribal people struggling with a foreign language. At the story's climax, Russell has Rawhide Rawlins describe McDonald's decision to relinquish his grip on a buffalo's tail, stating, "Dunc ain't slow slippin' his hold."[125] By comparison, McDonald told one reporter about the same moment in his own careful diction, stating, "A fellow thinks fast in that kind of predicament."[126] In having Rawhide Rawlins tell the yarn, Russell maintains the narrative continuity with his other stories by relating Dunc McDonald's story in his Montana listeners' familiar speech patterns. On the other hand, Russell's readers missed a chance to witness the eloquence of a self-educated Indian.

FIG. 34.
Duncan McDonald. Photograph by George Grant, courtesy of Glacier National Park Headquarters Library and Archive, West Glacier, Montana. "Dunc" was the self-educated son of a Scottish fur trader and a Nez Perce woman. Lake McDonald in Glacier National Park bears his name.

Russell's story "Dunc McDonald" stands apart from his other tales due to the availability of a complete, alternative version told by the story's main character that was available in McDonald's own words in several newspaper editions. A record also exists of the circumstances when Russell heard the tale for the first time. The Toronto *Globe* reporter attending the 1908 Ronan buffalo roundup recorded several observations of both Russell and McDonald in his field diary:

Friday, May 20. . . . We sit around a large campfire all evening, telling stories and talking. . . . The star performer was Charlie Russell, the ex-cowboy and present artist of western life. He is fine and voluble, constantly talking and full of stories. May 22. . . . Duncan McDonald came along and regaled us with Indian stories & reminiscences of his own for upward of two hours. It was most interesting and we had quite a discussion over the relative standards of morality of the white and red men. He is well read and bright, though somewhat stolid, as befits men with red man's blood.[127]

FIG. 35. Charles M. Russell, *"There's Only One Hold," Says Dunc, "Shorter Than A Tail Hold On a Buffalo—That Of A Bear."* Pen/ink, for the story "Dunc McDonald," in *More Rawhides* and *Trails Plowed Under.*

One incident not mentioned in McDonald's 1934 account, which appeared in Russell's earlier published version as a poetic moment of Indian sign language, was translated by Russell into printed English. "The old man signs that the gun is loaded, and one ball is enough for any good hunter. The wolf hunts with what teeth he's got."[128] This last sentence translates easily into the figurative symbols and ideas of Indian sign language. McDonald appreciated Russell's knowledge and skills with signing. "Charlie was a great student of the sign language," the eighty-two-year-old man told one reporter, "and with his death passed the greatest white expert on the subject."[129]

Like many aspects of the transitional western frontier that Russell enjoyed, Indian sign language was disappearing from everyday use by the 1920s. Russell's basic attitude about most of the changes in the West became obvious when he made this statement near the beginning of "Dunc McDonald": "Like all things that happen that's worth while, it's a long time ago."[130] The acceleration of changes in the West, especially those affecting Native Americans, discouraged Russell and his like-minded friends, as indicated by his occasional nostalgic expressions.

Injuns

Charlie Russell presented his only narrative essay, "Injuns," through the voice of a fictitious character, "Murphy." Without a specific story to tell, Russell still had several Indian issues to discuss in writing for his turn-of-the-century audience. In "Injuns," Murphy presents a campfire editorial voiced in the conversational slang typical of most of Russell's other narrators. He offers no background credentials for his Indian knowledge, but expresses humility

FIG. 36. Charles M. Russell, *The Big Change Came When Old Cortez Brought Hosses Over.* Pen/ink, illustration for the essay "Injuns," in *Trails Plowed Under.* Russell apparently produced only this pen/ink depiction of the pivotal arrival of Spanish horses in the Western Hemisphere.

about knowing little Indian lore firsthand. "If I told only what I know about Injuns," admits Murphy, "I'd be through right now."[131] He challenges academic experts, "these wise book-learned men" (presumably meaning anthropologists) who deduce an Asian origin for Indians, "but they can't prove it." The only historical record for Indians that Murphy respects consists of "a few paintin's and carvin's on rocks." Nevertheless, the narrator agrees with turn-of-the-century anthropological thinking about the permanence of pre-contact Indian culture, stating, "What changes the red man has made, he took from his white brothers."[132]

Mostly, Murphy comments on the changes that Euro-Americans caused with their intrusions into North America. "The big change," explains Murphy, "came when old Cortez brought that three-cross brand of hosses over. Mr. Injun wasn't long afoot." The intrusions continue into Russell's twentieth-century West, with his descriptions of modern tourists' assumptions of open access to Indian dwellings. A passage about curious white intruders barging into Indian homes explains why the natives seemed humorless to outsiders. Russell's terse conclusions, "An Injun [being uncivilized] laughs only when it's on the square,"[133] echoes the ironic sense permeating his writings that Indians may have the superior society and culture.

Russell's narrator mentions the Indians' reputation among whites for theft, observing, "Whites will do the same, I notice, in war times. We stole every inch of land we got from the Injun but we didn't get it without a fight, and Uncle Sam will remember him a long time."[134] The tone of Murphy's indictment seems serious, but Russell often touched on the same issue of land seizures by the government in a relatively lighthearted fashion. Regarding a trip through the Arizona desert heat, he wrote to a friend:

The country we traveled belongs to Injuns an nobody is going to take it away from
them for a while. Uncle Sams might[y] good that way aneything he can't use he lets
the Injun keep Hell will be no surprise to those who live in Arizona[.][135]

In a similar vein, Russell observed in Florida that the whites allow the Seminoles "to have all the
lande thats under water."[136] Wetlands or dry, Russell told his listeners and readers, the Indians
received neither justice nor generosity from the Euro-American intruders.

At the end of Murphy's comments, he concludes that technology, especially firearms,
made the difference for white conquest and domination. "I believe if the white man had the
same weapons as his red brothers, Uncle Sam wouldn't own only part of this country yet
and we wouldn't need any game law." As for superior intelligence, narrator Murphy sarcastically concludes that whites have demonstrated their superiority primarily by playing golf
as a means to pretend to stay in shape. His final sentence suggests that intermarriage (a topic
as yet unmentioned in Murphy's remarks) will cause the final white assault on Indian cultural and racial continuity. "A few more generations an' there won't be a full-blood
American left."[137]

Not only were Indians deserving, in Russell's eyes, to be considered above the category of
scorned "heathen," the artist/author saw them as spiritually superior to their white critics, with
cultures worth preserving. In describing his painting *Sun Worshipers,* Russell told an art
patron, "all planes Indians I think prayed to the sun and were much more devout than their
Christian white brothers."[138] It did not bother Russell that the Indians were not all Christians,
but he did share the prevailing nineteenth-century romantic sense of Indians as being "Mother
Nature's children." His variation on that patronizing concept also happened to include the
open-range cowboy and, by extension, himself. As he told one friend, "Old Ma Nature was kind
to her red children and the old time cow puncher was her adopted son[.]"[139] As participants in
Russell's sense of nature, Indians and cowpunchers were on equal footing.

In his paintings, Charlie Russell depicted the Indians as colorful and picturesque but
always enacting some realistic narrative purpose. When describing himself to one friend,
Russell's modesty downplayed his own understanding of Indians, as he stated, "I have always
studied the wild man from his picture side."[140] Yet Russell also knew Indians from a storyteller's verbal perspective that did not always translate directly into paintings or sculptures.
Some ideas and events in his published narratives remained exclusively in the realm of words.
Appreciating Charlie Russell's view of Indians requires the consideration of these nine written
works. A sense of Russell through his pictures and sculptures alone seems incomplete and
sometimes vulnerable to misunderstanding. In the local-color mode of his published stories,
Russell's nostalgia about Indians of former times matures into a more concrete realism. The
storytelling side of Charlie Russell reflects his appreciation for the depth and nuances of Indian
cultures as well as their beneficial interaction with Euro-Americans.

Few indications remain of contemporary Indian responses to Charlie Russell and his
works. One revealing incident was noted by a newspaper report. Following the artist's death,
supporters began a fundraising effort to preserve Russell's log-cabin art studio as a public
memorial. During the process, one Montana reporter noticed:

Some of the Indians on the [Blackfeet] reservation took it upon themselves to circulate a petition among their members in order to raise a small sum to contribute to the memorial. The result was the receipt, Monday by Dan Conway, Secretary of the Chamber of Commerce Russell Memorial committee, of $6.60....

Contributions made by the Indians to the memorial fund follow: Joseph Iron Pipe, 25 cents; Paul Iron Pipe, 25 cents; Samuel Van Choate, $1; Frank Vielle, 10 cents; James Evans, 10 cents; William Rose, 25 cents; White Quiver, 25 cents; Peter Flint, $1; Joe Bullshae, 50 cents; Sure Chief, 10 cents; Nick Green, 5 cents; Emil Bellou, 25 cents, Homer R. Wolf, 25 cents...

Phillip G. Cole of New York, collector of Russell paintings, wired Mr. Conway his contribution of $500 for the fund.[141]

As a percentage of available funds, the donations by these Blackfeet probably exceeded the wealthy New York art collector. Generally, American Indians have not published many opinions about Charlie Russell's artistic effectiveness or his value as a cultural broker. Nevertheless, those Native Americans who knew him during his lifetime seemed to appreciate his works that depicted Indian life.

CHAPTER FOUR

Survival and Humor in Wildlife Stories

"It was nature's enemy the white man"[1]

*W*hen he encountered nature in Montana's wild animals and uncivilized forests, mountains, and prairies, Charlie Russell also gained humorous inspiration from Indian myths of the region. In certain artworks and personal letters, he depicted the mythic Indian character Napi, a northern mountain variation of Coyote or the "trickster" who is found in Indian mythic lore of some other regions. An illustrated Russell letter to Frank Linderman isolated the problem of environmental destruction as belonging to the insatiable "white man." Both Russell and Linderman appreciated the mythic traditions of the Indians who live in or near the northern Rocky Mountains. Frequently, they spoke about this Indian view that a semidivine agent called "Napa," "Napi," or "Old Man" had created the creatures and people of the Indian world.

In Russell's interpretation, Napi's powers had proved ineffective against the presence and actions of the European-Americans, as when Russell told Linderman:

> you spoke the truth when you said the old man had hidden many beautiful things. . . . The men he made were satisfied with what lay on the surface . . . but his caches would have lane till the end of time Had not another man come, one he did not make—a greater thief than all of his It was nature's enemy the white man This man took from under and more he stole from the water and the sky. he was never

FIG. 37. Charles M. Russell, *Napi Talks with Beaver and Wolf.* Pen/ink in first editions only,
How the Buffalo Lost His Crown, by John Beacom (Forest and Stream Publishing, 1894);
reprinted in *A Bibliography of Published Works of Charles M. Russell,* by Karl Yost and
Frederic Renner (Lincoln: University of Nebraska Press, 1971), 4.

satisfide It was he who raised the Old man's caches an still hunts the fiew that are
left When Napi saw the new thief he hid his face in his robe and left this world and
I don't blame him.[2]

Russell heard many Napi stories, mostly lighthearted ones but a few that include humor about
violence or sexuality that some Indians consider unsuitable for children, stories that he heard
when he was among the company of Indian men. Merely the mention of old Napi often brings a
smile to the faces of older Blackfeet like those men whose company Russell enjoyed. In this letter
to Linderman, Russell included a burst of anger against "nature's enemy the white man"—a condemnation of Euro-American arrivals into the wilderness seeking Old Man's "caches" of natural-
resource treasures. Rather than face such a greedy presence, Russell told Linderman, the magical
presence of Napi went into hiding, leaving nature unprotected. Such sentiments can resemble
environmentalist values of the late twentieth and early twenty-first centuries.

In addition to Napi, Russell also enjoyed referring to nature as a female deity as in variations
of Mother Nature in "Ma Nature" and "the old lady." He wrote Linderman to say that the Flathead
Lake district west of Montana's Rocky Mountain continental divide seemed especially inspiring.
"That country of yours is shure the place to bring storeys to a man. Everywhere you look is another page in old lady nature's book."[3] As cited in the previous chapter, Russell wrote that the Indians'
"only book was nature and they knew all its pages." Whether the work of old Napi or Ma Nature,
however, wilderness helped Charlie Russell recharge his psychic and artistic energies.

FIG. 38. Charles M. Russell, *White Buffalo Napi.* Pen/ink, Permanent Collection, C. M. Russell
Museum, Great Falls, Montana. For Indians of the northern plains and Rockies, Napi
is a semidivine trickster—the subject of many droll tales.

FIG. 39. Charles M. Russell, *How the Ducks got their Fine Feathers.* Pen/ink, courtesy of Dr. Van
Kirke Nelson, illustration for Frank Bird Linderman, *Indian Why Stories; Sparks From
War-Eagle's Lodge Fire* (New York: Scribner's Sons, 1915). Charlie may have sensed
aspects of Napi's playful personality in himself.

FIG. 40. Charlie and Nancy Russell at Bull Head Lodge, 1908. Photograph courtesy of the C. M. Russell Museum, Great Falls, Montana.

Through most of his life as a professional artist, 1898–1926, Charlie Russell lived in the burgeoning town of Great Falls (then competing with Butte to be the largest city in Montana) boasting a huge smelter north of town with a gigantic smoke stack, hundreds of feet high, that spewed raw toxic fumes over the windblown prairies and occasionally over the town. Sometimes Russell left his urban home and studio, riding a horse across rolling land where he had herded cattle decades earlier, for artistic inspiration and to revive his enthusiasm for painting and sculpting. In the summer months after 1906, the Russells relocated to their own rustic cabin on the west side of the Rocky Mountains in what soon became Glacier National Park. As Russell explained to one friend, "I spend my summers at Lake McDonald on the west side of the mane range where I have a cabon. its about as wild a place as you can find these day[s] an that is what I like[.]"[4] From a single-room cabin, Charlie and Nancy expanded Bull Head Lodge to several log structures that are now privately owned and hidden from public view (**see plate 11**).

Getting into the woods or onto the prairie proved to be a necessity for Russell. No amount of urban culture could satisfy his need for a regular dose of Mother Nature, in as free and unspoiled a circumstance as possible. He celebrated this same therapy in his message to a horse wrangler who worked for the "dude" pack trains that operated in Glacier:

> In spite of gasoline the bigest part of the Rocky Mountains belongs to God and as long as it dose thairl be a home for you and your kind to me the roar of a mountin stream mingled with the bells of a pack trane is grander musick than all the string or brass bands in the world.[5]

Charlie Russell responded to the nature he encountered in his Montana surroundings by trying to capture it in paintings, sculptures, and stories. Nevertheless, he told one range crony that his own creations seemed "like a poor imitation of the real thing when he looked at what Ma Nature had turned out."[6] His special knack for portraying animals appears most clearly with his simple sculptures of such animals as bears, deer, antelope, buffalo, elk, horses, and cattle. Russell's wildlife depictions benefited from his time spent with Jake Hoover, especially when his share of the chores included removing the hide from a dead animal and observing the muscles and bones that lay beneath the skin. As two western art historians have noted, "Charlie Russell skinned dozens of different wild animal species. His intimate familiarity with animal anatomy gave his art a vitality which few other wildlife artists ever matched."[7] The nineteenth-century author and illustrator Dan Beard noted his firsthand observation of Russell's three-dimensional depiction of animals:

> The thing that interested me most intensely was his intimate knowledge, not only of the Western people, Indians, cowboys, but of the animal life. While he talked to me he modeled with his fingers a wax antelope about four inches high. It was dainty as the animal itself, full of action, and correct anatomically. . . . His ability to model an animal like this from memory means more than skill; it means genius of high order.[8]

Charlie Russell published most of his stories about western wildlife between 1906 and 1925, when the wild animals of the trans-Mississippi West no longer thrived in the abundant numbers that he had witnessed on his 1880 arrival in Montana Territory. Russell's wildlife and hunting stories reflect his awareness of issues such as killing wildlife for human survival, the annihilation or recovery of certain species, the possibilities for humor related to human survival in the wilderness, and the responsibility of humans in environmental and animal destruction.

One of the most striking transformations in the shift from unregulated wilderness to settled Montana communities involved the dramatic depletions of wildlife species. Granville Stuart, the managing partner of the DHS cattle ranch in the Judith Basin, recalled the swift disappearance of the abundant wild animals:

> It would be impossible to make persons not present on the Montana cattle ranges

FIG. 41. Charles M. Russell, *Dancing Animals.* Pen/ink, courtesy of Dr. Van Kirke Nelson, illustration for Linderman, *Indian Why Stories.*

realize the rapid change that took place on those ranges in two years. In 1880, . . . thousands of buffalo darkened the rolling plains. There were deer antelope elk wolves and coyotes on every hill and in every ravine and thicket. . . . In the fall of 1883, there was not one buffalo remaining on the range and the antelope, elk, and deer were indeed scarce.[9]

The species depletion that Stuart noted took somewhat longer in Montana's mountains, enabling Russell to witness firsthand some of the soon-to-disappear animal abundance. In one of his first published pieces written for Montana newspaper readers, Russell described his earliest experiences as a St. Louis teenager living with the Montana prospector/hunter Jake Hoover. Russell recalled a pristine mountain oasis, teeming with wildlife, guided by a female goddess called "Nature":

Shut off from the outside world it was a hunter's paradise bounded by walls of mountains and containing miles of grassy open spaces more green and beautiful than any man-made parks. These parks and the mountains behind them swarmed with deer, elk, mountain sheep and bear, besides beaver and other small fur-bearing animals. The creeks were alive with trout. Nature had surely done her best, and no king of the old times could have claimed a more beautiful or bountiful domain.[10]

Russell's magnificently oversized painting *The Exalted Ruler* (**see plate 12**) reflects the pinnacle of his reverence for the Rocky Mountain elk and their dramatic habitat along the eastern slopes of the continental divide. In such a grand work of oil paint and canvas, Russell's graphic art talents overwhelmed his lighthearted verbal references to "Ma Nature" or "the old lady"[11] to communicate effectively his sense of awe for undisturbed wilderness in the American West.

In contrast with his personal letters, Charlie Russell's published stories seldom mention Napi directly. More frequently, Russell's stories deal with dramatic interactions between humans and wild animals. The author/artist witnessed the reduction of many wildlife species, although he seems to have had minimal involvement in taking the life of anything. Despite his apprenticeship with a professional game hunter, Russell chose not to participate directly in killing animals. Some personal friends like Frank Linderman and longtime Utica resident Finch David have described how Russell would join willingly in the work of skinning and butchering game that others killed, taking time to observe and sketch the muscle and bone structure for later artistic compositions. Con Price recalled that even though Charlie Russell enjoyed eating meat as much as anyone, he had once said, "when it comes to the killing I don't want to be there."[12] Even though most of Russell's wildlife stories involve hunting and the death of wild animals, he supported legal limits on the sport killing of wild game. Apparently, late in their lives Russell and Linderman disavowed hunting for sport even though Linderman occasionally hunted meat to feed his family.[13] More than any other subject for stories about nature, it was the dangerous and often deadly encounters between humans and buffalo, wolves, and bears that provided material for high adventure in Russell stories. Permeating every story, however, is the spirit of Napi's droll humor as expressed in Russell's subtle ironic view that colors even the most violent encounters.

A SAVAGE SANTA CLAUS

Like most of his paintings and sculptures, Charlie Russell's stories express his understanding that Mother Nature is not always gentle to humans. His stories about bears reflect the explosive reality of wilderness animals and the need for humans to kill for survival. His best bear story, "A Savage Santa Claus,"[14] tells of a close-quarters encounter between a grizzly bear and two gold-panning prospectors during a Christmas-Eve blizzard. "A Savage Santa Claus" also marked the first appearance of Russell's western-dialect writing style and launched his writing career.

In a national context, Russell's story appeared during the climax of the "nature faker" controversy, a quarrel that filled major newspapers and magazines with criticism and counter-criticism among animal-story writers, scientific naturalists, and even the president of the United States, Theodore Roosevelt. The public debate that lasted from 1903 to 1907 grew from turn-of-the-century American popularity for nature study, camping, bird-watching, butterfly collecting, and especially for the new story format known as the so-called realistic wild-animal story in which animals exhibited human feelings and motives. The anthropomorphism that authors such as Ernest Thompson Seton and the Reverend William J. Long portrayed in the sentimental narratives about animal adventures offended the more outspoken and scientifically minded writers, such as John Burroughs and Theodore Roosevelt.[15] Russell exhibited an awareness of Roosevelt's values, naming one cowboy painting *The Strenuous Life,* quoting an anecdote to his nephew from Roosevelt's book *The Wilderness Hunter,* and by painting a watercolor picture depicting President Roosevelt shooting a grizzly bear.[16]

There is no evidence, however, that Russell paid much attention to the "nature faker" controversy. Nevertheless, the primary episode in "The Savage Santa Claus" appears to support Burroughs's and Roosevelt's views that some animals are simply dangerous beasts and may be destroyed for human survival. In this story, the bear manifests no human thoughts, sentiments, or behavior (aside from making its den in an abandoned cabin), and the attachment of a

FIG. 42. Charles M. Russell, *In the Mountains*, 1905, gouache, courtesy of the Montana Historical Society. A noted Montana rancher, Colonel Wallace Huidekoper, donated this hunting portrait of Teddy Roosevelt to the Historical Society. Huidekoper was a veteran of the Spanish-American War and admired TR's legendary adventures in North Dakota, Wyoming, and Montana.

human name, "Santa Claus," could be merely a grim joke that the author has perpetrated through the story's narrator and main character, "Bedrock Jim."

Early in the story, however, the two prospectors hesitate to dismount and enter the abandoned cabin until one of their horses intuitively signals them to take advantage of the shelter from the blizzard. According to Bedrock:

> "'I guess we'd better take that cayuse's advice,' says Beaver pintin' to [the horse named] Baldy, who's got his ears straightened, lookin' at us as much as to say: 'What am I packin' fer Pilgrims; or don't you know enough to get in out of the weather? It looks like you'd loosen these packs.' So takin' Baldy's hunch, we unsaddle."[17]

FIG. 43. Frank Linderman, Chippewa medicine man Big Rock, and Charlie Russell, 1916. Photograph courtesy of a private collection. Big Rock shared stories that Linderman respectfully translated into the book *Indian Old Man Stories; More Sparks from War-Eagle's Lodge Fire* (New York: Scribner's Sons, 1920), illustrated by Russell.

In Russell's experience, a few horses may have intelligence equal to or higher than humans. Domesticated horses, however, were not in the same category and were likely to be less gifted mentally than wild animals. For this tale, Russell seems to agree with the Roosevelt/Burroughs naturalist faction regarding grizzly bears while, at the same time, humanizing a horse with human intelligence worthy of the "nature fakers." In this frontier Christmas story for Great Falls newspaper readers in 1906, Russell embraces the perspectives of both the scientific realists and the sentimental animal writers. Other Russell tales, to be discussed in later sections, demonstrate the heightened awareness and intelligence in some horses and lethal cunning in others.

Also in Russell's Christmas bear story, survivors of the unsettled American West had to take advantage of marginal opportunities, especially when hunger overruled food selectivity. "Savage Santa" shows how killing an animal to gain a food supply could happen by accident. The morning after their battle with the bear, Bedrock Jim and his partner "Beaver" (also referred to as "Jake Mason") ate part of the dead bear to augment their limited diet of dried beans and wheat flour, despite the meat's unappetizing flavor. As Russell has Bedrock describe the meal:

> He's an old boar, an' it's pretty stout, but a feller livin' on beans and bannocks [frying pan bread] straight for a couple of weeks don't kick much on flavor, an' we're at a stage where meat's meat.[18]

FIG. 44. Charles M. Russell, *Bear with Pipe and Indian.* Pen/ink, illustration for Linderman, *Indian Why Stories.*

Even though Bedrock and Beaver kill the bear in self-defense inside the cabin, they consume the unpleasant meat as if they had hunted it for days through the snowy woods. The meat is a gift.

In addition to telling an entertaining holiday story for Montana newspaper readers, Russell also expressed wildlife values that seem remarkably close to those in many Native American cultures. His narrator portrayed the bear as humanlike in its choice to spend the winter in a human dwelling, a dead prospector's log cabin. And despite the bear's lethal violence, Russell's characters accord him a human name, nervously referring to him as "Santa Claus." Ethnohistorian Calvin Martin has noted that North American Indian folktales frequently describe animals in human terms, including such anthropomorphic qualities as living in humanlike dwellings.[19] By calling this cabin-dwelling grizzly bear "Santa Claus," Russell provided a humorous European folklore name for an American Indian–style human/animal relationship, inserting joking merriment into an otherwise grim and violent story. Such naming is consistent with stories from the Old Southwest traditions that frequently called a dreaded bear "Old Ephram."

Charlie Russell enjoyed the nonsentimental humanizing that many Indians included in their mythic storytelling. His illustrations for Frank Linderman's translations of some Indian legends capture a whimsical sensitivity in his humanized animal portrayals that few people would mistake as scientifically accurate, but which gain greater impact by their realism. The second element of Indian values in "A Savage Santa Claus" involves the bear's gift of himself to the gold panners. Despite the violent battle, Beaver's statement made it clear that the bear's death provided two gifts: "he brought plenty of meat an' showed us the cache for we'd never a-found it if he hadn't raised the lid."[20] Martin has noted that, according to many native traditions, "animals in the Indian cosmology consciously surrendered themselves to the needy hunter."[21] Russell was communicating to his western audiences the role of game animals and their consenting involvement in a legitimate process of dying to supply food for human survival.

LEPLEY'S BEAR AND HANK WINTER'S BEAR FIGHT

As with "Savage Santa," Charlie Russell's other bear stories consistently show that, without the advantage of guns, individual men are no match for nature's powerful creatures. In another story of unpredictable forces, "Lepley's Bear,"[22] Russell describes an embarrassment for "Old Man Lepley,"[23] who survives without his gun in an encounter with a grizzly only because the bear's mood and direction changed abruptly. The scrambling, fleeing horse kicks up a branch that strikes the bear, causing it to reverse its direction and flee. At that same moment, Lepley's horse reaches the end of the tie-down rope, sending his rider, Lepley, to land on his face in his most vulnerable moment. Without the bear's sudden change in direction, he would have been on top of Lepley in an instant.

In "Hank Winter's Bear Fight,"[24] a grizzly mauls Hank, the hunter pursuing the bear into deep brush. Without warning, the prey counterattacks, inflicting deep cuts in Hank's arm and leg and forcing him to drop his rifle. Only the last-second appearance and fast shooting by his partner, "Bedrock Jim," saves Hank's life. Russell's narrator and main character, Hank Winters, lives to understand the vulnerability of a man facing an attacking bear without a firearm, explaining with wry humor: "I've heard about men fightin' bears with nothin' but a knife an' winnin', but if I ever get a chance to bet on that kind of fight I'll play the human with a copper."[25] Nevertheless, simply having a gun proves insufficient for Hank Winters. In this story, two men with guns equal just one of nature's more powerful creatures. The story of a life-saving intervention for a hunter caught by a grizzly bear must have intrigued Russell. He created at least four pictures of the same general subject.[26] One of these paintings, *The Price of his Hide,* is, according to Rick Stewart, "an

FIG. 45. Charles M. Russell, *His Hoss Stops at The End Of The Rope.* Pen/ink, illustration for the story "Lepley's Bear," in *More Rawhides* and in *Trails Plowed Under.* Too hurried by the onrushing bear, Lepley rode away without untying his horse and soon faced the consequences.

FIG. 46.
John Lepley, n.d. Photograph courtesy of the Montana Historical Society, Helena. Russell called this dignified Fort Benton cattleman "Old Man Lepley." Unlike "Lepley's Bear," most Russell tales focus on working-class people.

example of Russell's storytelling at its best. . . . [A]s always, the artist has chosen the perfect moment to stop the action of the story and present it to the viewer."[27]

In most of Charlie Russell's hunting stories, the hunters seek meat for survival. The "Hank Winters" story, on the other hand, demonstrates how ego satisfaction, a relatively frivolous pursuit of one of nature's most violent creatures, could provoke a deadly counterattack. Narrator Winters admits that Bedrock Jim had warned him twice against pursuing that bear. Russell's narrative about Hank Winters seems sympathetic to Native American values that Martin uncovered among eastern Algonquian Indians living prior to contact with Europeans. "The single most important deterrent to excessive hunting," observes Martin, "was the fear of spiritual reprisal for indiscreet slaughter."[28] Without that basic deterrent of cautionary fear, as shown by the Hank Winters tale, the hunter could bring about his own demise by unwittingly becoming the bear's prey. In contrast with sentimental writers like Seton and Long, Russell made no attempt to depict the bear's mind or strategy. On a practical level, an experienced hunter like Roosevelt knew that pursuing a "grisly" bear would always be especially dangerous, given the bear's notoriety for abruptly reversing the role of the hunter and the prey. Roosevelt observed:

The instances in which hunters who have rashly followed grisleys [*sic*] into thick cover have been killed or severely mauled might be multiplied indefinitely. I have myself known of eight cases in which men have met their deaths in this manner.[29]

Russell never published the Hank Winters story beyond the Montana Newspaper Association inserts. It did not appear in the Rawhide books or in *Trails Plowed Under*. The story served as a cautionary tale about greedy human folly, the same characteristic that Native American spiritual values disdained, as well as the practical danger understood by hunters like Roosevelt. Similar local stories about specific people making similar hunting errors may have made this narrative too commonplace for Russell to republish as either humor or surprising adventure.

BAB'S SKEES

Even though Russell's bear stories demonstrate sensitivity to right and wrong reasons for killing animals, he also showed his capacity to find humor in narratives of human survival in the wilderness. Russell frequently adapted formats of the exaggerated "lie" story or "tall tale" for excursions into humor writing that generated wide popularity among the storytellers of his lifetime. In one blatant lie called "Bab's Skees,"[30] Russell's mountain neighbor, "old Babcock," tells how he supposedly plummeted out of control on skis down central Montana's Snowy

FIG. 47. Charles M. Russell, *They're Leavin Their Beds When I Come Hurlin' Off The End of a Lodge Pole*. Pen/ink, illustration for the story "Bab's Skees" in *More Rawhides* only.

Mountains until he landed on the back of a bull elk. Falling off the bull, Bab continues on his downhill streak, gaining enough speed on his homemade skis that another animal collision kills an elk cow. At the end of his wild ski ride, Bab returns to the dead animal to salvage some meat and to acknowledge his lesson—to use snowshoes instead of skis, "if you aint in a hurry."[31] The consequences of misjudging a steep descent on untested skis, as well as collisions with Montana's abundant wildlife, added up as rough comedy in Russell's narrative treatment.

Some Liars of the Old West

In Charlie Russell's world of old-fashioned storytellers, "old Babcock"—David Babcock, who resided in the mountains near Utica, Montana, in "Pig-Eye Basin"—was a grand-master liar who could even joke about death. Bab had steadily cultivated his reputation as a notoriously entertaining prevaricator. While a young man, Russell visited Babcock's cabin in Pig-Eye Basin frequently, both because of its proximity with Jake Hoover's log shack and also for the entertaining storytelling sessions. According to the Reverend George Edwards, "Pioneer Presbyterian Minister," Old Bab enjoyed some wide popularity.

> There was an old-timer, affectionately called "Lying Babcock," because he could tell tall tales and stretch the truth a little further than any other old-timer in the Basin. That was his specialty. . . . Lying was simply an amusing game the old-timers played like joshing and Babcock generally came out ahead at the game.[32]

A historical thread lay deep within one of Bab's most popular lies—his tale about the time the Indians chased him into a dead-end canyon. When describing this adventure, Bab would pause in his delivery until an uninitiated listener would ask what happened next. Then he would whisper the punch line. "They killed me b'God."[33] In Russell's retelling of his friend's lie stories, the ultimate humorous absurdity contradicted nature so completely that a human who experienced death might live to tell the story.

In the folk traditions of American frontier life, the lie story grew directly from accounts of the natural wilderness, especially nature's eccentricities. Russell's collection of brief tall tales, titled "Some Liars of the Old West," explains the presence of so many skilled exaggerators in the region by pointing to environmental influences. Writing without resorting to a fictitious narrator's voice, Russell states directly:

> Speakin' of liars, the Old west could put in its claim for more of 'em than any other land under the sun. The mountains and plains seem to stimulate man's imagination. A man in the States [back east] might have been a liar in a small way, but when he comes west he soon takes lessons from the prairies, where ranges a hundred miles away seem within touchin' distance, streams run uphill and Nature appears to lie some herself. These men weren't vicious liars. It was love of romance, lack of readin' matter, and the wish to be entertainin' that makes 'em stretch facts and invent yarns.[34]

The author/narrator seems to be speaking tongue-in-cheek on the matter of lying. For Russell, the semblance of "Mother Nature" manifesting anything but the truth merely signaled that the observer had failed to perceive her correctly.

Rather than deceptive panoramas, however, the greatest source for western lying traditions grew from the disbelief and resistance that westerners typically encountered when trying to tell about awesome wilderness landscapes, animal abundance, and encounters with Indians in the West.[35] Many of Jim Bridger's immigrant clients showed the temerity to challenge the seasoned mountain man when his suggestions for grassy campgrounds near good water differed from their ten-cent guidebooks' advice. According to one account, "Sometimes he would sit for hours and act as if deaf and dumb, in order to put a stop to the silly questions of travelers."[36] One unnamed writer for the Montana Newspaper Association distilled Jim Bridger's dilemma in trying to tell the truth about Yellowstone's thermal wonders:

> Bridger had seen many wonderful things in the west, of which he told his friends, but the public was inclined to doubt his veracity. So when he tried to inform his acquaintances . . . of the marvels of the Yellowstone park, he was laughed out of countenance. That he was inclined to draw a long bow was well known, and the incredible stories he put in circulation discounted his truths. [37]

More simply, as Teddy Blue Abbott put it, "old timers have been laughed at so often for telling the truth that they retaliate by telling unheard of yarns."[38]

In the years following the immigrant surges, former fur trappers who had become guides often hired out to hunters and tourists. One such guide told MNA writer Mrs. M. E. Plassmann that the early tourists were so gullible that they became victims of many practical jokes. Apparently the early stage drivers found "pleasure in their credulity."[39] As a sixteen-year-old newcomer from the East, Russell found himself the victim of a joking stage driver on the occasion of his first stagecoach ride. Some years later, Russell retold the incident:

> "The driver of that stage," he said; "was a typical stage hand, an' he was just as entertainin' company as was most of his kind, for he talked a stream. I guess he had a lotta fun with me."
>
> "'Where yu from, Bud,' he asked me."
>
> "'I'm from Missoury!' I replied, straightenin' up with a whole lot of pride.
>
> "'My Gawd, boy, not so loud!' he whispered. 'Don't fer the life of yu tell ennybody in Helena yu be from Missoury. Why they got a tree there in the gulch what they're hangin' peeple from Missoury on right along jest as fast as they find 'em. Tell 'em you're from Indiany, Ioway, er enny other state; but fer Gowd sake, don't mention Missoory to these folks up here. I'm from Missouri, too, but I don't dare tell nobody 'bout it.'
>
> "An' I sure took 'im at his word, fer I didn't [t]ell nobody where I come from till I hit Billy Korrel's place over on the Judith."[40]

Lying and lie stories could deliver truth, nevertheless. The stage driver scared young Russell while also delivering useful information about social customs in Montana and the West.[41] Spontaneous lynchings still formed a part of Montana society in 1880, and Missourians consistently ranked high on lists of suspects for any crime. Also, a man's previous residence was his private information, especially for a man with a criminal past. Asking someone in the West about his original home could provoke a violent response or at least ominous silence.

Later in his life, Charlie Russell might show his own impatience with an outsider's foolish questions. Will Rogers noted in his syndicated newspaper column, "Charlie is the greatest storyteller I ever heard, and most of them are on himself." But apparently not every Russell story teased the teller. Rogers continued,

> "An eastern tourist was looking at a picture of an Indian who had just killed a buffalo. The tourist says 'But why did he kill the buffalo?' Charlie told him, 'Well they had a grudge against each other and they finally shot it out and the Indian killed him to get even.' Tourist says 'How extraordinary!'"[42]

Russell's intellectual nephew, Austin, noticed that his own arrival in urban, twentieth-century Great Falls awakened many old-timers' assumptions that their dated, lying jokes could provide a fair initiation for Charlie's greenhorn relative, fresh off the train from the East. Austin soon noticed that he was being treated as a foil for their jokes, a process he did not enjoy.

> But what impressed me about Great Falls [in 1908] was the people, especially the old-timers, Charlie's friends, they were so different from the people at home [St. Louis], and—as it seemed to my young ignorance—so crude. Spotting me as a pop-eyed tenderfoot, they discoursed to such effect that I concluded all Westerners were liars—silly liars.[43]

Austin Russell's reaction shows that his uncle's lie stories were out of style with literary-types by at least a decade before his Uncle Charlie first published them in the MNA newspaper inserts throughout Montana. By the time this droll humor appeared across the country in 1927, in *Trails Plowed Under,* the stories must have resembled quaint artifacts to anyone but rural sympathizers of William Jennings Bryan, die-hard westerners, and fans of Will Rogers who were surviving in America's urbanizing "Roaring Twenties." They were a far cry from the literary sophistication of such writers as F. Scott Fitzgerald, Ernest Hemingway, and the harsh, anti-rural cynicism of journalists like H. L. Mencken.

Safety First—But Where Is It?

Contrary to the national trend of increasing urban sophistication, however, the numerous versions of one of Russell's hunting and wilderness stories demonstrated the continuing interest in humorous narratives about human-animal conflict. Russell's story titled "Safety First—But Where Is It?"[44] begins with "Rawhide Rawlins" providing western examples of the shortcomings

FIG. 48. Charles M. Russell, *Jack Goes Back But He Don't Stay Long.* Pen/ink, illustration for the story "Safety First! But Where Is It?" in *More Rawhides* and *Trails Plowed Under,* titled *"Stay in that hole, you damn Fool!"*

of a typical Progressive Era reform—"Safety First." No safety can be found in a rocking chair during an earthquake, concludes Rawlins, nor in poorly canned food, nor by leaping to solid ground from a runaway stagecoach. These observations of the futility of seeking safety in Russell's West then leads into a brief tale about two hunters who carelessly allow themselves to be cornered without their guns by an injured bull elk. One hunter climbs a small tree for safety, and the other dives into a shallow cave only to emerge seconds later as the elk backs away from crashing his antlers on the sheltering rocks. The tree dweller shouts instructions to the caveman to remain in the safe shelter, finally bellowing, "'If you'd stay in that hole, you damn fool, that bull would leave and give us a chance to get away!'" On his third or fourth exit from the hole, however, the nervous cave dweller has heard enough. "This time when Jack shows, he yells up to Bedrock, 'Stay in the hole, hell! There's a bear in the hole!'"[45]

This tale provides the clearest example of Charlie Russell's adaptation of western folklore for one of his stories. Evidently, Russell added the safety theme and title to a widely shared hunting story about two men threatened by one dangerous animal, forcing one to seek shelter in a cave, only to be confronted by another equally dangerous beast. J. Frank Dobie recognized the basic plot. "This is a true modern *folk* story," he noted in the margin of his copy of *Trails Plowed Under.* "One version of it, not so good as Russell's, is in *Clay Allison of the Washita,* by O. S. Clark. . . ."[46] Western novelist Eugene Manlove Rhodes noticed another version in the November 21, 1931, edition of *Collier's* and angrily tried to make a *Collier's* editor admit that the author Channing Pollock's "Short Short Story" should be attributed to Russell, who had published his version in 1927; "I had heard him tell it, long before." Rhodes continued, "I think it most unlikely that Channing Pollard actually stole this story. He heard somebody tell it, probably. . . . Mr. Pollard's story is not identical with Charley's as to the actual words. But all essentials are exactly the same."[47] Frank Linderman recalled a slightly different version that he attributed to his artist/author friend.[48]

Russell may have seen another published version of the story because his New York friend and fellow artist John Marchand provided the illustrations. In this version, western author Alfred Henry Lewis had also embedded the same basic tale into a story, titled "Red Mike," that appeared in his 1913 book of tales, *Faro Nell and Her Friends; Wolfville Stories,* illustrated by Marchand.[49] Russell owned several other A. H. Lewis books and mentioned meeting the author briefly on his first visit to New York City in 1904. Some critics, including Rick Stewart, cite Lewis's use of a fictitious narrator, "the old cattleman," and his volumes of *Wolfville* tales in western dialect as the likely model for Russell's *Rawhide Rawlins Stories.*[50] In contrast with Lewis, however, Russell used more than one narrator for his stories and presented a much wider variety of story formats than the Wolfville books. Nevertheless, the cowboy artist seemed to enjoy the Wolfville books, some illustrated by Frederick Remington, and tolerated Lewis's blunt racism and his exaggerated phonetic dialect much more than readers in later generations.

Differing with Russell's version of this hunting adventure, in Lewis's story "the old cattleman" is both the narrator and the treed hunter, "Steve Stevenson" is at the cave, and the threatening animal is a wounded buffalo rather than an elk. In Lewis's version of western vernacular, "the old cattleman" relates the yarn's big moment:

> "'You dad-binged Siwash,' I yells down at Steve, 'whyever don't you-all stay in that hole, ontil the bull forgets whar you're at?'
>
> "'Go on!' Steve shouts back, as in he dives, head-first, for mebby it's the twentieth time; 'it's as simple as suckin' aiggs, ain't it, for you up in your tree? You-all don't know nothin' about this hole; thar's a b'ar in this hole!'"[51]

A critic might argue that Russell adapted his story in 1925 directly from Lewis's 1913 version, but the artist's numerous connections for oral sources of such widely known western folk tales as this one suggest that, more likely, Russell's version of this widely shared tale was a response to those that he had heard rather than one that he read in a published format.

The story of the bear in the hole has continued to evolve into the twentieth century. The list of folk-story motifs that Antti Aarne collected and that Stith Thompson translated refers to *Ozarks* by Randolph Strangers, dated 1951 and summarized as "Man crawls into hole to escape from a bull; there is a bear in the hole."[52] For another variation attributed to Russell in recent decades, Eddie's Cafe, located inside Glacier National Park at Apgar Village, just five hundred yards from Russell's summer cabin on Lake McDonald, published a shortened version of the tale on the back of the restaurant's chatty menu. In this rendering, attributed casually to Russell, the attacking animal is a moose.[53]

Folklorists like Richard Dorson express more certainty that a story is genuine folklore if a large number of versions survive through oral transfers, just as this story seems to have spread. Few of Russell's other stories follow standard folklore rules of multiple oral transfers, suggesting that he either originated most of them or discovered them close to their sources. For the serious folklorist, however, the creation of a new folk tale seems less significant than participating in a long sequence of repetition and relay by delivering a well-expressed version of an archetypal form. "The talent lies not in imaginative presentation of a new story," writes Dorson, "but in the imaginative presentation of an old one."[54] Nevertheless, Russell knew his sources, whether they were his own imagination, printed material, or another person. Supreme Court Chief Justice Lew Callaway, a companion of Russell's in many Great Falls barrooms, recalled:

> After Charlie's first book came out—I think it was Rawhide Rawlins—I met Charlie on Central Avenue in Great Falls, and said to him jovially, "I see you swiped one of my pet stories." "Which one?" "The one about the fellow the Indians chased up the box canyon." "Huh," Charlie said, "I heard that long before I heard you tell it."[55]

If Russell's source for the box-canyon tale was not Lying Babcock, as stated in "Some Liars of the Old West," he did not mention an alternative to Calloway. But the judge's claim shows that many versions circulated in the region at that time, attributed neither to Russell nor to Old Bab nor to the likely source—Jim Bridger.

Serious students of American folklore in the twentieth century have analyzed and celebrated the same rural vitality expressed in oral-tradition stories and humor that Russell enjoyed. In many ways, Charlie Russell was a folklorist, collecting and relaying stories from other people as much as creating new narratives. Few academic folklorists have paid much attention to Charlie Russell's stories, however, possibly because of his preeminence as a fine artist. But their motif categories and systematic numerical codes have included a few traditional themes and formats that Russell used frequently, including the lie stories. Stith Thompson, one of America's most influential scholars of folklore, observed that stories of lying and "foolery" were widespread and experienced popularity during the "opening up of the American continent, with its incredible events of everyday life." Thompson mentions the lie-telling format that Russell and other westerners enjoyed, even though admitting that his analysis of this popular phenomenon remains incomplete.

> Sometimes a storyteller teases his audience by stopping just as the interest has been aroused. . . . Or the tale may be essentially a game: the teller frames the story so that

the hearer is almost compelled to ask a certain question to which the story-teller returns a ridiculous answer (Z13, Type 2200). Folktale collectors have not always interested themselves in these unfinished tales and catch tales, and we cannot be sure that our knowledge of them is accurate.[56]

Thompson's apparent disinterest in these lie-telling formats suggests a lack of sympathy and a clear sense that such "catch tales" seem unworthy of detailed, academic analysis.

One prominent folklorist of the American West, Mody Boatwright, offers a useful discussion of "the catch tale," the lie story with the surprise ending:

> For the tallest of tall tales, as distinguished from mere tall talk, had logic and structure. The tall tale is logical in all points but one.... At the point of highest suspense there is a pause. Here the listener is sometimes induced to ask a question.... [H]e has not yet discovered the catch. [57]

Boatwright perceived an American literary tradition within the westerner's lying impulses. He saw that the settlers moving into the West carried little sense of "highfalutin theories of art." Although the settlers preferred realism, their heroic legends typically leaned toward comic exaggeration. "In the tall tale," Boatwright concludes, "they developed one of America's few indigenous art forms."

Lest Boatwright's readers assume, however, that the great nineteenth-century folklore exaggerators, like the semifictional figures Davy Crockett and Mike Fink, provided the only examples of this basic American literary tradition, Boatwright widened the scope of definition for western humor:

> Contrary to the conventional analysis of American humor, the folk liar does not depend upon mere exaggeration.... He knew that he must provide ludicrous imagery, an ingenious piling-up of epithets, a sudden transition, a non sequitur— something besides mere exaggeration if his audience was to respond to his tales.... [T]he folk artist knew the value of understatement and used it skillfully in his narratives of fact and fiction.[58]

The better storytellers, including Charlie Russell, employed many subtle "tricks of the trade" beyond mere exaggeration. Boatwright's collaborator, Southwest author J. Frank Dobie, identifies factual content as the key ingredient of successful lie stories. "The authentic liar," Dobie explains, "knows what he is lying about ... for his art is essentially realistic. His burlesque, like all good burlesque, rests on a solid foundation of truth." Dobie refers to Russell's "Some Liars of the Old West" as "a delicious chapter."[59]

Dog Eater

In one notable catch tale, Russell told a humorous death-yarn that used a longer format than Babcock's tall-tale structure about being cornered by Indians. In Russell's "Dog Eater," one

FIG. 49. Charles M. Russell, *Friendship Goes Yelping Into The Woods.* Pen/ink, illustration for the story "Dog Eater" in *More Rawhides* and *Trails Plowed Under.*

man's survival struggle in the wilderness becomes simply a struggle to find something to eat. Russell's narrator, "Rawhide Rawlins," begins by telling about a friend who unintentionally ate dog meat when camping with some Indians. Despite the shock of realizing what he has ingested, as Russell reassures his readers, "It was good and Bill held it."[60]

Charlie Russell enjoyed telling this story to tease sentimental dog lovers[61] and to demonstrate that this part of many Indians' diet might become acceptable to squeamish non-Indians if they were truly desperate for food.[62] Apparently, Russell did not create "Dog Eater" to make fun of Indian dietary customs. The artist could be respectful for those Indians whose traditions included eating dog meat,[63] although he favored the company of Blackfeet Indians who avoided using dogs for human food. "Rawhide Rawlins" narrates most of the story by repeating the words of an old prospector known as "Dog-Eating Jack."

This recollected narrative tells how Jack earned his special name through choosing between terminal starvation in Montana's mountain forests or eating his beloved companion, a dog he had named "Friendship." The prospector and the dog survive the ordeal through a non-negotiated compromise—the sudden amputation and cooking of Friendship's tail. Russell creates subtle humor in the self-contradictions and rationalizations that Jack considers before taking the tail:

After about four days of living on thoughts, Friendship starts watchin' like he's afraid. He thinks maybe I'll put him in the pot, but he sizes me up wrong. If I'd do that, I hope I choke to death. The sixth day [of nothing to eat] I'm sizin' him up.... He's a hound with a long meaty tail. Says I to myself, "Oxtail soup! What's the matter with dog tail?" He don't use it for nothing but sign talk, but it's like cutting the hands off a dummy. By the eighth day, with hunger and pain in my ankle, I['m] plumb locoed and I can't get that dog's tail out of my mind. So a little before noon I slip up on him, while he's sleeping, with the ax. In a second it's all over, Friendship goes yelpin' into the woods and I'm sobbin' like a kid, with his tail in my hands.[64]

The watery dog-tail soup sustains Friendship and master Jack just long enough for the weakening prospector to make a lucky shot, killing a large elk with a single bullet. In Russell's deft treatment, the agony of slow starvation, when combined with guilty discomfort over eating part of a cherished pet, reveal a darkly comic side of Charlie Russell's perspective on death in the wilderness versus pet sentimentality.

"Dog Eater" has earned critical praise as "the funniest of [Russell's] humorous anecdotes."[65] Another critic has determined that "the plot as well as the style of 'Dog Eater' is also probably taken from oral tradition" since many variations exist.[66] Actually, the story is Russell's blend of a widespread folk story and local anecdotal history. Someone known as "Dog Eating Jack" lived in Choteau County, in the vicinity of Fort Benton, Montana, in 1885—the same period that Russell worked as a cowboy in that area. The name "Dog-Eating Jack" appeared on a list, compiled in the 1940s, of a few of the approximately seventy locally notorious characters in nineteenth-century northern Montana who had taken or attracted especially colorful names. The others included "Gamblers Ghost," "Liver Eating Johnson," "Sweet-Oil Bob," "Seven-Up Pete," "Stink-Foot Bill," "Fred The Rattler," "Antelope Charlie," "Old Horse Eye," and "Old Tomato Nose." Most of these names included no explanation about their origin. For "Dog-Eating Jack," however, the writer stated simply that the old-timer "became lost and lived on his dog."[67] Obviously, Russell had plenty of story material explaining the origins of other colorful names in his area, but only a few like "Dog Eater" survive in print.

Charlie Russell seems to have based some grotesque story details, such as eating a pet for survival or the appearance of deformed footprints in the snow that disturb the Indians ("The Trail of the Reel Foot"), basically on local history and folklore. On the other hand, his story structures, characterizations, and narrative style seem to have been his own invention. Russell shaped this story's ending like a catch tale, having narrator "Rawhide Rawlins" ask the foolish question, "'What became of Friendship?' says I. 'He died two years ago,' says Jack. 'But he died fat.'"[68] To create a believable lie story, Russell filled his narrative with enough plausible data that it maintains historical accuracy. Like his paintings and other artworks, Russell anchored most of his narratives, however exaggerated they might seem for comic effect, in local legends concerning actual people and events. As a connoisseur of local history and folklore, Charlie Russell appreciated old-timers like Dog-Eating Jack and his quandary of having to choose between his own survival and his deeply ingrained, sentimental loyalty to a domesticated animal.

BROKE BUFFALO

Charlie Russell never objected to people keeping dogs and cats, but, other than a few horses that he kept nearby, he owned no household pets. One of his stories ridiculed an attempt to domesticate nature's wilder creatures. In "Broke Buffalo,"[69] Russell employed a narrative format reminiscent of the turn-of-the-century Indiana humorist George Ade,[70] presenting a light-hearted fable about an unnamed main character, in this case demonstrating the consequences of harnessing a wild buffalo to a buggy or a plow. In the narrative style of a parable, the story tells how a pair of yoked-up buffalo prove too strong for an ambitious farmer to control. They stubbornly hold their plowing direction and change course only when seasonal weather affects their migration instincts. Without adding a brief closing moral statement that George Ade typically put at the end of his fables, Russell simply mentions that the buffalo continue to plow on and on, northward or southward, depending on the season, with rumored sightings echoing back to the farmer. Russell wrote with more subtlety and understatement than George Ade and may have assumed that his western audience of cattlemen and their sympathizers would gather enough of a moral conclusion through their amusement with a greedy farmer, who is cast as the butt of a joke about the unnatural use of wild animals in the frontier West.

"Broke Buffalo" served as comic relief just as the North American bison was rebounding from the near annihilation of the species. Russell found humor in the juxtaposition of wild, powerful buffalo and farming, a practice despised by most cattlemen. In 1925, as this story first appeared in print, the U.S. government's new herd on the (recently designated) national Bison Range in Montana's Mission Valley steadily expanded. At the same time, Yellowstone National Park had already begun to sell surplus buffalo in an effort to limit the size of the park herd.[71] A

FIG. 50. Charles M. Russell, *Maybe These Hump-Backs Knows Where They's Goin' But The Driver Ain't Got No Idea.* Pen/ink, illustration for the story "Broke Buffalo" in *More Rawhides* and *Trails Plowed Under.*

Great Falls newspaper headline in 1921 proclaimed "Herds of Buffalo Increasing in West, American Buffalo is Far From Extinction Latest Census Shows. Are now over 3,000 in U.S."[72] With buffalo recovering from near extinction and achieving limited commercial availability, westerners among Russell's audience could enjoy a joke about the narrow-minded stamina of the formerly endangered animal.

When Pete Sets a Speed Mark

Another joking treatment of buffalo formed the context for Russell's roast of his friend Pete Van in the brief yarn "When Pete Sets a Speed Mark."[73] In this story, the slowest human in Montana suddenly discovers how to run very fast indeed when bucked off his horse in front of a stampeding buffalo. Unlike the more serious stories that ended with a human and a buffalo in mortal confrontation, such as "Dad Lane's Buffalo Yarn" and "Dunc McDonald," this buffalo survives the story's end as Pete and the bison seem to run on and on forever across the rolling prairie.[74]

Some Liars of the Old West

Charlie Russell also found humor in the legendary, gigantic herds of bison and other animals of the trans-Mississippi West. He used some of that humor in the closing segment of his mini-anthology of lie stories, "Some Liars of the Old West."[75] In this yarn, "Milt Crowthers" steps forward to provide proof in a wager negotiated between a traveling salesman and a local bartender named Coates.[76] The men make a bet whether anyone in town will take a solemn oath that they had ever seen as many as one hundred thousand buffalo at one time. Known to the smiling bartender but not to the outsider-salesman, the local trickster, Crowthers, who volunteers to take the oath, is a notorious liar in that district. Without being instructed, Crowthers senses his role and spontaneously responds to questions from the skeptical salesman by claiming to have seen, on certain occasions, two hundred thousand prairie antelope, "somethin' over a million" mountain elk, and "about three million billion" wild buffalo. In the cross-examination by the outsider, who has become the sucker/victim for this elaborate lying joke, Crowthers explains that all the three million billion bison were just the preliminary bunch and, "Lookin' back, here comes the main herd."[77]

The historically accurate but somewhat smaller herd numbers must have been as incomprehensible to a non-western newcomer as the inflated herd sizes that Crowthers cites to win the bet for the bartender and to embarrass the outsider. Granville Stuart's 1880 diary noted in the Rosebud Valley of south-central Montana, "The whole country is black with buffalo." A few days later, sixty miles east of the Snowy Mountains near the Judith Basin, he found "Buffalo by the thousands in every direction."[78] By the time Charlie Russell's lie story appeared in print, however, most signs of the buffalo, including remnants of bones and skulls, had disappeared from the landscape. All forms of wildlife had become so depleted that Russell commented in a personal letter to Stuart, "where once great bands of antelope fed theres not even a curlew now."[79] Crowthers's lie story ironically reflected the truth that buffalo herd numbers exceeded

You sleeping relick of the past
if I but had my way
Id cloth your frame
with meat an hide
an wake you up to day
C M Russell
1908

FIG. 51.
Charles M. Russell, *"You Sleeping Relic,"* poem and sketch, 1908. Pen/ink, published in Ramon Adams and Homer Britzman, *Charles M. Russell* (Pasadena: Trail's End Publishing, 1948).

normal credibility or everyday comprehension so much that humorous exaggeration left the "truth" unharmed. Both the pranks and the stories that fueled them seem to have been widespread among local folk customs. As Boatwright observed:

> hoaxing was one of the chief forms of frontier folk humor. The temptation to use superior knowledge to deceive the uninitiated is well-nigh universal except among the most sophisticated; and travelers in strange lands have always found it a hard temptation to resist.[80]

In this episode, it is the locals who succumb to the temptation to "deceive the uninitiated." Russell presents not only an amusing lie story, but his narrative dramatizes the social context for perpetrating the hoax. The reader can see what westerners might lie about and understand *how* they might trick an unsuspecting outsider whenever possible. Russell's story about Milt Crowthers's barroom lie exhibits the form that literary critic Henry Wonham identifies as the typical American literary tall tale. Wonham observes that Mark Twain "had learned from 'The

Jumping Frog' and other early pieces that the narrative interest in tall humor stems primarily from the interpretive drama that surrounds the performance of a tale." To capture the attraction of the tall tale on paper, "a writer must depict the relationship of the teller to his audience."[81] Russell portrayed this relationship in several of his "catch tale" formats, especially when the outsider/listener asks the narrator the fatal question at the end of "Dog Eater." Russell's presentation of Milt Crowthers's exchanges with the traveling salesman in the White Sulphur Springs saloon, more than any other stories in *Trails Plowed Under,* resembles the literary tall tales that Twain wove throughout many of his best works. In these tales, Wonham notes that "the narrative form works to bring characters with different styles and assumptions *into* rhetorical conflict."[82]

Despite the flippant humor of "Broke Buffalo" and Crowthers's buffalo-herd exaggeration, Charlie Russell genuinely cared about the fate of these animals. In 1925, Russell wrote to his friend Ralph Budd, then president of the Great Northern Railroad, to advocate a national day of remembrance for the buffalo comparable to honoring the turkey on Thanksgiving Day:

> the Rocky mountains would have been hard to reach with out him he fed the explorer the great fur trade wagon tranes felt safe when they reached his range he fed the men that layed the first ties across this great west Thair is no day set aside where he is an emblem. The nickle weares his picture dam small money for so much meat he was one of natures bigest gift and this country owes him thanks [83]

As indicated by numerous paintings, sculptures, and bits of poetry, Charlie Russell maintained considerable respect for the buffalo and deep regret for its near extinction.[84] He sketched the buffalo skull as his professional logo next to his signature on every finished work of art. Referring to the buffalo minted on the five-cent nickel coin, Russell's phrase "dam small money for so much meat" distills his sentiments perfectly.

BULLARD'S WOLVES

In the Russell wildlife stories, one animal seems destined for extermination. Charlie Russell's sympathy for endangered wildlife, such as the buffalo and the antelope herds, did not extend to the burgeoning packs of prairie wolves. In his story "Bullard's Wolves,"[85] an unidentified narrator's voice tells how Bill Bullard happened to rope two wolves that were sick from eating poisoned meat. Bullard's own greed for securing two wolf bounties motivates him to rope the second wolf by using the free end of the same lariat that holds the first. After tying the middle of the rope to his saddle horn, he drags the nearly dead animals behind his horse most of the way back to the cowboy's range camp. But the wolves, with their sickened eyes glazed and jaws snapping in a frothy frenzy of strychnine convulsions, happen to bounce too near Bullard's horse, which immediately bolts out of control. "He goes hog-wild," observes the wry narrator, "and wherever he's goin' Bill don't know, but the gait he takes it's a cinch they won't be late." After taking a few days to cool his temper, Bullard delivers the moral of this violent tale:

FIG. 52.

Bill Bullard. Photograph courtesy of the Montana Historical Society, Helena; L. A. Huffman, photographer, Miles City, Montana. This elegant gentleman was one of the roughest, most short-tempered cowpunchers that Russell encountered among Montana cattle outfits.

"maybe you'll kill two birds with one stone but don't ever bet you can get two anythings with one rope."[86] The message discourages greed, like a George Ade morality tale, but it also ignores any concerns about a wolf's perspective.

During Russell's eleven years as an open-range cowboy, stockmen systematically exterminated wolves from Montana and other western cattle-grazing areas.[87] One of Russell's earliest range companions recalled the harsh treatment that the cowboys gave to any wolves found out on their range:

> One of the major sports and unofficial assignments was roping wolves.... Kid Amby said, "We did a lot of it." Since the buffalo and other game animals were almost all gone, the wolves were forced to prey on domestic livestock for their food....
>
> According to Amby, full-grown wolves could only be roped when they were full of meat from a kill, so the cowboys watched for wolves at a carcass and for young wolves who were clumsy and just learning to run fast. A cowboy had to have a fast rope horse and one that would not spook when his rider hooked onto a wolf. The men found that some horses were so frightened by a wolf on the rope that they would buck and throw the rider or get the rope tangled up in the bush. If that happened the cowboy would have to cut the rope and let the wolf go.

FIG. 53. Charles M. Russell, *Right Then's When the Ball Opens.* Pen/ink, illustration for the story
"Bullard's Wolves," in *More Rawhides* and in *Trails Plowed Under.*

Roped wolves were killed with a "45" revolver or dragged to death. Roundup
bosses didn't get after their cowboys for roping wolves because they recognized
wolves as more devastating to their cattle herds than the Indians who often
demanded "toll" for cattle crossing their land.[88]

Even as the final surviving wolves in the northwestern Rocky Mountains died at the hands of
persistent hunters in the 1920s and 1930s, local newspapers characterized them as "The Most
Despicable of Animals."[89] Few, if any, of Russell's contemporary audiences harbored much
sympathy for the poisoned, strangled, and dragged victims in the Bullard story. Granville
Stuart summed up the typical perception of wolves and the cattlemen's callous, nineteenth-
century responses to them when he wrote:

> The winter of 1881–82 . . . predatory animals were quite troublesome especially the
> large grey timber wolf that surpasses any other animal in sagacity, fleetness of foot
> and powers of endurance. . . . In the summer the cowboys frequently found a den
> and then there would be great sport roping them and shooting the awkward
> sprawling whelps with their six shooters. Charlie Russell has immortalized this
> sport in one of his paintings.[90]

According to Nancy Russell's photo files, as preserved by Fred and Ginger Renner, Charlie Russell painted at least fifteen pictures of cowboys throwing ropes over the heads of running wolves from the backs of galloping horses, but none show the shooting of pups. Russell manifested no particular affection for the victims in "Bullard's Wolves," but he did reflect appreciation for their roles as hard-to-kill agents of natural wildlife, big varmints that could cause big problems for careless humans, even while the animals were half-dead. Nevertheless, in a private letter, Russell expressed appreciation for the wolf's smaller cousin, the coyote, writing:

> the Scientific man ain't slow in proving that that beast or bird should be wiped out. . . . Man can't win much fighting nature when the coyote was plenty thair was few gophers or rabbits now the hole west swarms with them[.][91]

Russell perceived the practical need for predator coyotes, even though they also preyed on sheep and calves, but expressed no specific regrets about civilization's demand for the extermination of the wolves that threatened the beef herds. Nevertheless, although the Bullard story shows no mercy for wolves, Russell did demonstrate how the tenacious underdogs of the West, although poisoned and roped, still gave a tormentor like Bill Bullard one very bad ride in exchange for his greed. Russell could sympathize with the wolf to illustrate folk stories and myths recorded by Frank Linderman and others, painting images that depict wolves speaking politely to humans (**see plate 13**). In his own published stories and serious artworks, however, Russell showed the wolf as far more dangerous—smart perhaps but also desperate and ominous.

In addition to his dozens of paintings depicting wolf ropings, at full gallop by horse-riding cowboys, Russell produced a dramatic oil painting, *The Lone Wolf* (**see plate 14**), showing a snarling, gray wolf loping across the open prairie. It provides a realistic depiction that could be interpreted as either impressive or despicable, depending on the viewer's attitude toward this predator. Alberta cattleman George Lane once told Russell about a surprise encounter with a wolf pack that had killed and eaten one of his beef cows. While Lane shot at and scattered four of the offending wolves, the largest male counterattacked him, biting off the toe-cover on Lane's stirrup before the cowman could shoot it dead. In response to his friend's vivid story, Russell eventually presented Lane with a picture of the rare event when a wolf fought back against a human on horseback (**see plate 15**). Several accounts of this incident state that when Lane examined the dead wolf he found a piece of the thick leather "tapadero" (stirrup covering) was still in the wolf's mouth, testifying to the animal's sharp teeth and powerful jaws.[92] The incident had become a popular local legend in southern Alberta years before Russell heard the story from its source, visited the site, examined the damaged saddle, and made this picture especially for Lane, a friend from earlier days in Montana.

This picture of an attacking wolf notwithstanding, Charlie Russell knew that wolves generally would retreat when confronted by a human, even if it meant taking second place for fresh meat. In writing "Finger-That-Kills," Russell describes the moment when the walking Indian warrior interrupts a wolf pack about to kill an injured buffalo. Narrator "Squaw Owens" states that as the Indian walks toward the hungry wolves just before they attack their injured target, the predators "go slinkin' off makin' faces at him; they don't like bein' busted in on at meal times."[93] In his essay, "Range Horses," Russell speculates about the human-wolf relationship of prehistoric times, in a period often referred to as "dog days." In the words of "Rawhide Rawlins":

> "The Injuns used to tame wolves to move their camps till the Spaniard came. . . . I'm guessin' that in those days that nobody knows about, the red men followed the wolf and when able, drove him from his kill, and the wolf had the best end of it. But with a hoss under him it was different. The wolf followed the red man and got part of his kill."[94]

He might portray the rare wolf who attacked a horseback-riding human, as inspired by his friend's story, but Russell's writings showed that he knew that such behavior is the exception for these predators.

The George Lane/Wolf picture can tell only part of one extraordinary incident. A written account by Russell would be more informative, providing other facets of the story before and after the attack. Even though a written account is lacking, and despite the violence of this wolf-attack image, Russell's appreciation for this demonized animal is apparent in his words and most of his artworks. He told Joe DeYong, "If a Blackfoot said a man was a wolf it was no insult it meant the man was very smart. In the sign language wolf and smart are the same."[95] Charlie Russell demonstrated his genuine respect for wolves in several especially sympathetic depictions of the animals in paintings and sculptures. As author Ginger Renner has observed:

> The grey wolf may have been a skulking, snarling scavenger of the plains, but in Charlie's eyes, the animal's keen senses set him apart. Time and again, Russell painted or modeled the wolf in a wary, alert, or forceful manner.[96]

Even when he was a full-time cowpuncher, Russell's depiction of nature themes attracted critical praise. "One of the best animal painters in the world is Charles M. Russell, of Cascade, Montana, who is popularly known as the 'cowboy Artist,'" wrote Charles Hallock for *Nature's Realm* in 1891.[97] Russell "told" his most subtle stories involving wolves and wolf behavior in his bronze sculptures. *The Last Laugh* portrays a wolf snarling at a human skull. *The Enemy That Warns* shows a wolf reacting to a rattlesnake coiled next to a buffalo skull. *To Noses That Read, A Smell That Spells Man* depicts a wolf reacting cautiously to an empty whiskey bottle. *Lone Wolf* or *Wolf With Bone* has a wolf seated on its hindquarters holding down a large bone with a front paw. *Range Father* represents a stallion chasing away a wolf with both animals running at full speed. This sculpture reflects a second reason for Russell to dislike wolves, in addition to sharing the cattleman's bias. Russell sympathized emotionally with horses, which instinctively react against the sight or smell of these predators. And so, if horses hate wolves, so would Charlie.

Charlie Russell's subtle and realistic depiction of a wolf's natural behavior placed him close to the values of the controversial author/illustrator Ernest Thompson Seton and other so-called nature-faker writers,[98] who were among the few people portraying wolves as anything but vicious demons. In the early twentieth century, an artist making favorable depictions of wolves and other meat-eating predators risked offending many people, especially westerners involved with live-

FIG. 54. Charles M. Russell, *Range Father,* 1926. Bronze, cast ca. 1929–1934, no. 1961.95, Amon Carter Museum, Fort Worth, Texas.

stock management, but Russell chose realism over popularity for his paintings and sculptures. As an illustrator for Frank Linderman's Indian-myth stories, however, Russell provided sketches of wolves with no obvious human characteristics, but that have much more engaging humanlike personality and subtle humor than other wolf depictions of his era.

An important asset in Charlie Russell's various narrative skills proved to be his powers of observation. He noticed and remembered the movements and behaviors of humans and animals in ways that served his representations in story, paint, and bronze. As one friend recalled years later:

> He was a matchless storyteller, with an almost supernatural ability to impersonate the character he was describing, whether human or animal. He told me a grizzly bear story once. As he described the charging bear, his teeth became fangs, his fingers became claws, and his snarl sent shivers up and down my spine. Anyone who ever heard him tell a story knows this is no exaggeration. It was uncanny.[99]

As suggested by such an account, Russell probably enacted the animal behaviors as he narrated this passage quoted as Squaw Owens's version of Finger-That-Kills driving some wolves away from a wounded buffalo:

> "This old buffalo's got three wolves around him; he's hamstrung an' down behind, but whirlin' 'round an' makin' a good standoff with his horns. When Mr. Injun walks up, these wolves go slinkin' off makin' faces at him."[100]

The artist's sculptures of wolves reflect a special sensitivity to their behavior that goes beyond his paintings and sketches. He successfully transferred his ability to mimic animal behavior into making static three-dimensional representations that prove to be equally "uncanny" as his personal storytelling.

In Russell's wildlife narratives, the animals typically resist human domination and a few can escape death, as in *Lepley's Bear* and *Broke Buffalo*. Others win outright over humans as the skunks do in *Man's Weapons Are Useless* (**see plate 16**), while others get the last laugh even though they die, as in *Meat's Not Meat 'Til It's In the Pan* (**see plate 17**). In these narrative paintings, the animals get the best of the humans.

Russell celebrated animal survival while living through an era of near extinction of the buffalo and the common white-tailed deer. Russell observed, in published stories and private letters, that humans gained the winning edge mostly with the help of firearms. In addition, he understood that technological advantage could have a double impact, affecting both native wildlife and Native Americans. Wildlife depletion, in Russell's view, was a direct result of European-American firearms superiority, not necessarily superior cultural values and wisdom.[101] Calvin Martin's analysis offers an elaboration of Russell's basic conclusion concerning the white man's destructiveness, stating, "European contact should thus be viewed as a 'trigger factor' . . . [that was] responsible for the corruption of the Indian-land relationship in which the native had merged himself sympathetically with his environment."[102] Broadening his own view, Charlie Russell assigned responsibility for ecological destruction in a eulogy for fellow Montana painter Edgar Paxson, writing a statement that the MNA published in newspapers across Montana. In this indictment, Russell saw the problem as not merely that of "the white man":

> Civilization is Nature's worst enemy. All wild things vanish when she comes. Where great forests once lived nothing stands but burned stumps—a black shroud of death. The iron heel of civilization has stamped out nations of men, but it has never been able to wipe out pictures, and Paxson was one of the men gifted to make them.[103]

In this slightly more mature view, Russell saw the enemies of nature as not merely white Euro-Americans, but any representatives of the industrial world, including himself.

Charles M. Russell clearly believed that artworks could preserve a memory of things destroyed or altered by civilization. He selected his art subjects carefully and chose not to depict many that were contemporary with his lifetime, including mining and smelting (two industries that were thriving in the Montana centers of Butte, Great Falls, and Anaconda), sheep ranching, wheat farming, logging, and the impoverished twentieth-century life on Indian reservations. And when he wrote to a Montana friend from his vacation in sunny California, he announced that he chose not to paint "fruit, flowers, automobiles or flying machines" (even though he sometimes included them in his personal letter illustrations), adding "but nature ain't lived here for a long time and that's the old lady Im looking for[.]"[104] Russell observed that southern Californians' artificial plantings of roses, orange groves, and palm trees, combined with suburban expansion and automobile congestion, precluded a natural environment. His environmental insight seems prophetic to subsequent generations. In the face of such accelerated change, he preferred subjects in the trans-Mississippi West that were disappearing or had already gone under "the iron heel of civilization." He used narrative ideas in paintings, sketches, sculptures, and writings to preserve aspects of life in the West that were disappearing with the increasing population and the use of technology. Russell's choice of stories about human encounters with wild animals portrayed human domination of wildlife and the natural environment. Nevertheless, he especially enjoyed relating tales through stories, pictures, and sculptures that gave a fighting chance to the disappearing wildlife.

Charlie Russell accepted the necessity of humans killing wild animals for safety and for food, while he avoided direct participation in these tasks. He regretted the near extinction of the buffalo and other species from the West, but less so the annihilation of the gray wolf. He caught a glimpse of the vast animal abundance in the American West just before it disappeared under the heel of human expansion into wilderness areas. And the historic memory of nature's wealth merged in his imagination with a degree of romantic nostalgia for earlier times.

Russell's motives for preserving parts of western life in narrative artworks involved an impulse to record past incidents like historic specimens, a feeling that included a degree of nostalgic longing. In his attempts to make sense of the human role in the destructive transformation of western wilderness, Russell mixed racial guilt with sarcastic denunciations of unstoppable urbanization and other human folly. Nevertheless, he transcended his own disappointment and feeling of loss with a wry sense of humor that could even make fun of death. A few weeks before his own death, Russell's final illustrated letter reflected his continuing reverence for nature as a female deity who lives in the present as well as the past:

> the camp you live in now can bost many man made things but your old hom is
> still the real out doors and when it coms to making the beautiful Ma natures got
> man beat all ways from the ace and Im glad to see that old gal still owns a lot
> of Montana[105]

Charlie Russell could craft a humorous story of Bill Bullard attempting to improve the former buffalo range for use by beef-cattle herds through the violent torture of dying wolves. Out of such a low point in the history of western wilderness transformation, Russell at least found humor in the embarrassing discomfort of his old friend Bullard—the initial "roasting" purpose for that story. By publishing animal and wilderness yarns, Russell provided entertaining information for his fellow humans in the rapidly civilizing and urbanizing American West.

Russell enjoyed trading bits of Indian myths and narrative lore through illustrations involving Napi, talking wolves, pipe-smoking bears, and dancing critters, but his stronger storytelling efforts in published yarns and in larger oil-on-canvas images, such as *The West*, expressed a vivid realism in portraits of living animals. *The West* also depicts a specific Montana location along U.S. Highway 87 connecting Great Falls and Lewistown where travelers in the twenty-first century can see the same view for themselves. Heading west along the well-graded two-lane stretch between Stanford and Geyser, the viewer sees the same perspective of the Highwood Mountain to the West, plus Round Butte to the right (called "Hay Stack" by earlier white inhabitants, as Russell remembered "when this was a game country").[106] Russell painted this work in 1913, when buffalo and harassing wolf packs were no longer present in the open, rolling prairie of the Judith Basin. Russell's painting title refers to both the direction of the view and the wildlife that once made this open valley their home before they

FIG. 55. Charles M. Russell, *The West.* Oil on canvas, 1915. Courtesy of the Rockwell Museum of Western Art, Corning, New York. Russell painted a view of specific landmarks on the western skyline of Montana's Judith Basin before roads, fences, houses, and towns filled the view—when wildlife was abundant and a confrontation between a wolf and a buffalo bull was high drama.

were killed off to make way for the "iron heel" of ranches, farms, gravel roads, railroad lines, and little towns. With Russell placing animals in his work that embody the greater West, this painting proves to be consistent with the majority of his nature stories about animals of the wilderness. Rather than publishing the sort of folkloric Indian fantasies of friendly animals that amused him and a few of his knowledgeable friends, Russell preferred to fill his published yarns and stronger artworks with the most realistically dramatic wild animals and natural settings of the West.

CHAPTER FIVE

Cattle Range Transitions

Here's to days of the open range
When the grass that God planted was free
An' there wasent a fence from the Mexican Gulf
North to the Arctic Sea
But they aint no use kickin, Wallace
Th' cowmans had his day
The nesters here with his fence and plow
An it looks like hes here to stay[1]

*F*or eleven years (1882–1893), Charlie Russell participated directly in Montana's open-range cattle business as a horse wrangler and night herder. In contrast with his Indian tales, Russell's stories of the cattle-range era reflect only a few glimmers of social commentary. Despite debates by generations of western settlers and cattlemen, Russell's cattle stories seldom mention such controversial issues as water rights, irrigation priorities, railroad policies, and the rivalry between cattle, sheep, and farm interests. Although range-stock management and urbanization shaped several story themes, it was individual people who provided the primary focus for these stories about the transitional changes for the western cattle ranges in the nineteenth-century, trans-Mississippi West.

The experiences and relationships of the individuals involved in the open-range cattle business provided Russell with the focus for his published narratives. As his cattle stories emphasize remarkable moments in the lives of individuals, however, these tales also exemplify the storytelling process in the West of the nineteenth century. Shared experiences of dangerous work and long hours in the saddle strengthened lifelong friendships and bonds of personal loyalty among cattle-range participants. The process of storytelling tended to reinforce this interpersonal linkage that was typical of the cattlemen's dominant era. The pattern of sharing stories among cattlemen also provided Charlie Russell with an opportunity to collect exceptional bits of narrative history and folklore from the relatively brief frontier phase of the unfenced ranges. In the "Foreword" to his first book of these tales, Russell wrote:

> When I came to Montana, which was then a territory with no railroads, reading matter of any kind was scarce. Where there's nothing to read men must talk, so when they were gathered at ranches or stage stations, they amused themselves with tales of their own or others' adventures. Many became good storytellers. I have tried to write some of these yarns as nearly as possible as they were told to me.[2]

The common, preindustrial pastime of oral storytelling flourished with the open-range cattle business. Small groups of men found themselves isolated out on the prairie grasslands for weeks or months, living far away from other people and stimulating entertainment. Whatever cattle outfit he was working for, Russell provided some of the solution to their boredom and isolation. As one of his range companions recalled, Charlie

> could tell all kinds of yarns and that was something valued in a cow country. I can remember when the wagon was 265 miles from a post office so you can readily see we needed someone to entertain us. We have went for six months without seeing a decent woman and damn few of the others.[3]

Charlie Russell enjoyed sharing anecdotal history through the perspectives and experiences of individual people. He savored the spicy fragments and lively moments of personal histories. Russell's cattle-range yarns offer especially revealing portrayals of his quirky contemporaries. As Phil Weinard recalled, "His greatest interest was in telling amusing stories about old timers."[4] Russell's preoccupation with his cattle-range days focused on the amusing people and personalities he encountered. For humorous and colorful material useful in stories, pictures, and sculptures, he merely recalled well-known local characters like "Slick, Slim, Shorty, Bowlegs, Brocky, Pike, Bed-Rock, Panhandle, Four-Jack Bob, Jim-the-Bird, P. P. Johnson, Old Bench Legs and Fighting Fin." Writing to a friend who also remembered these figures, Russell observed:

> This bunch John are all most extinct. most of them have crossed the range, maney of them wore crime stanes, but among them were good men not made good by law but because there guts lay above there short ribs. . . . [T]he memory of one of these dead friends good ore bad meanes more to you and me than the boughten friendship of a million of these come latelys.[5]

Russell held western men in highest esteem, even if they participated in crimes, especially those men who spontaneously would be unhesitatingly honest. He valued the friendship of such men above subsequent settlers in the West, who might have purchased his artworks but

FIG. 56. The Judith Basin Roundup, 1883 or 1884. Photograph courtesy of the Montana
    Historical Society, Helena. At breakfast with the village of Utica in the background,
    Russell is seated second from left, with his hand on his knee. Such settings
    encouraged storytelling among hands assembled from several cattle outfits.

had not gained his full admiration. It was the colorful people of the range-cattle years (and
before) that Russell preferred for his narrative-art focus, along with their struggles with the
subsequent transitions from untamed frontier life into more civilized society in the West.
Russell's narratives celebrate those individuals who faced the need, figuratively, to wake up and
adapt to the accelerating evolution of the open cattle range in the trans-Mississippi West.

THE GHOST HORSE

Among Charlie Russell's published stories and essays, one odd piece, different from all the
rest, links the world of the Indians with the cattle culture of the Euro-Americans. The story of
Russell's favorite mount, titled "The Ghost Horse,"[6] connected the artist/author personally
with the buffalo hunts that his pinto pony had been bred to join. In turn, Russell introduced
this horse to herding open-range cattle. When Russell painted his self-portrait, *When I Was a
Kid,* Monte, the "Ghost Horse," had just died after twenty-four years with the storyteller/artist.
Nancy Russell kept this picture in her home and printed it on the cover of *Good Medicine,* her
1929 book of her husband's illustrated letters. The site depicted is a steep trail, still in use, providing access to the South Fork Valley of the Judith River in Montana's Little Belt Mountains
(**see plate 18**).

Written for the high school students in Great Falls in 1919, "Ghost Horse" uses uncharac-
teristically "correct" grammar to tell the story of a horse that the Crow Indians raised to be a
buffalo runner, which the Piegan Blackfeet stole in a bloody raid, and which a would-be cowboy

FIG. 57. Charlie Russell on Monte, near Utica, ca. 1883. Photograph courtesy of the Montana Historical Society, Helena. Monte was bred by the Crow Indians to be a buffalo runner, stolen by the Blackfeet, shot (unsuccessfully) in the neck to accompany a dead warrior, and survived to be traded to teenager Charlie Russell, his ultimate companion.

bought from the Indians for a low price. Much of Russell's narrative attention in this story describes the horse's experience with Indians, including the horse-stealing raid that nearly caused the young horse's death and earned it the negative name of "Ghost Horse" (a negative term to the Blackfeet who had once tried to kill it). When the small pinto finally becomes the cowboy's property, and is renamed "Monte," the animal encounters the white man's cattle grazing the prairies that wild buffalo had occupied for centuries.[7]

Near the story's end, Russell's narrative focus shifts slightly, enabling the reader to see events through the horse's eyes. When the author makes this narrative adjustment, his point of view approaches that of the idealistic writers such as Ernest Thompson Seton and others who were ridiculed as the "nature fakers."[8] Tied outside a saloon full of cowboys, the horse witnesses a fatal gunfight. The reader learns that the horse comprehends an important human value that few of Russell's contemporaries appreciated. Rather than depicting the horse's mental process, however, the narrator simply explains, "Paint knew then that the white man was no different from the red. They both kill their own kind." Russell's viewpoint, expressed through the horse, leaves no room for a sense of racial or species superiority. Russell's horse seems to understand basic cultural relativity and racial equality. Charlie Russell granted no other horse such powers of perception. He saw Monte as unique—a sentient being.

FIG. 58. Charles M. Russell, *Packing Monte,* Russell leading Monte, illustration for "The Pinto," *The Moore Independent* (MNA), June 30, 1919, and in *More Rawhides* for the story "Mormon Murphy's Confidence." Russell may have extended Monte's life by packing more than riding him.

In the final paragraphs of the story, Russell highlights a frontier urban transformation when the horse and his cowboy master, accompanied by another horse and rider, enter the cow town Great Falls:

> and their ponies, which knew no lights but Nature's, jumped the great shadows made by the arc lights at the street crossings. They passed rows of saloons, dance halls and gambling houses.... Both men were dressed as cow hands, and the only difference in their clothes was a bright colored, French half-breed sash, worn by the light-haired man.[9]

In this passage, Charlie Russell brings the buffalo horse into the garish cow town on the western urban frontier. Charlie's red Métis sash, out of sync with the rest of cattle-range culture, appears for its only mention in all of his stories. This fragment of mixed-blood Indian life linked Russell with the outcast, non-reservation French/Indians and set him apart from most non-Indians. And as the cowboy and his buffalo-culture horse arrive in Great Falls, Russell's writings also arrive at a new phase—the period of open-range cattle ranching.

In contrast with "The Ghost Horse" that was written for adolescent readers, most of Charlie Russell's cattle-era narrative stories drew their form and inspiration from the peculiar ways that Russell and his range contemporaries expressed their friendships within the male saloon culture. Instead of receiving a story as a direct compliment, the favored friend often felt the impact of an insult, delivered in person, at close range, and spiced with ridiculous exaggerations. As Walter Lehman recalled, "They made up the worst stories on each other, and told them with a straight face in front of the whole crowd in some saloon." Lehman's advice for James Rankin, a would-be Russell biographer, clarified the personal element of Russell's story-telling in Montana's saloon culture:

> if you catch his underlying humor and not seem too coarse in the telling it will be fine. After all, men did a lot of things in those days which they knew were not so in order to get a "raise" out of their victim in front of a saloon crowd and so make him buy the drinks for all hands.[10]

If the teller could provoke the target of his roasting story to denounce the tale as a lie, the victim might be obliged to buy the teller a drink. And if the victim exploded in vehemence, denouncing the tale as a "damn lie!" the cost of renewed harmony might require him to supply a round for everyone present.

In this cultural tradition, Charlie Russell created spontaneous entertainment and honored his closer friends through the telling of personal "roast" stories. If the focus of the roast could "take it"—even enjoy the insult as Horace Brewster accepted the sketch Russell made of him doctoring his hindquarters back on Charlie's first range job—the resulting friendship could last a lifetime. Some of those insulting roasts appeared in Russell's favorite humorous print formats: the Montana Newspaper Association's weekly inserts, the Rawhide Rawlins books, and, finally, *Trails Plowed Under*.

How Louse Creek Was Named

In the case of especially strong friendships, Charlie Russell satirized some men more than once. He made Pete Van's lack of swift personal mobility the focus of "When Pete Sets a Speed Mark."[11] Then, in "How Louse Creek Was Named,"[12] Russell maligned Pete Van in several altogether different ways, suggesting that Pete had started his own cattle herd by stealing unbranded "maverick" calves from other ranchers.[13] Russell's very brief story announces that Pete helped to name a Judith Basin stream as "Louse Creek" when he was found smashing his lice-infested shirt between two boulders beside the stream. The writer was celebrating his longtime friendship with Pete Van by granting him the dubious honor of giving an embarrassing name to a special site and then accusing Pete of being ungrateful for the privilege. Russell made humor out of the shameful but common frontier inconvenience of body-lice infestation.[14] The author subtly avoids making a direct reference to the unsavory little creatures beyond the story's title. When Rawhide Rawlins discovers Van slamming the seams of his shirt between the rocks, all we hear him say is "'I'm damned if this don't get some of the big ones!' Well, from this day on, this stream is known as Louse Creek."[15] Such a backhanded tribute to an old friend demonstrates the irony of a vulgar cowboy joke about body lice that could create a lasting name for a geographical site on the prairie.

Charlie Russell made no claim to have invented the roast-story format (nor any of his other story structures). Typical of his other yarns, Russell's roasts of close friends followed an existing folk tradition. Samuel Clemens noticed the art form of the roasting yarn (as well as the composed,

FIG. 59. Pete Van, detail of photograph, "Cowboys at Umbrella Spring near Denton, Montana, 1883." Photograph courtesy of the Montana Historical Society, Helena.

even-tempered response of the victim) while residing with his favorite California storyteller in the gold-mining camps of the Sierra foothills near Yreka. According to his narrator:

> I spent three months in the log-cabin home of Jim Gillis and his "pard," Dick Stoker, in Jackass Gulch. . . . Every now and then Jim would deliver himself of an impromptu lie—a fairy tale, an extravagant romance. . . . Jim always soberly pretended that what he was relating was strictly history, veracious history, not romance. Dick Stoker (the hero of these stories), grey-headed and good-natured, would sit smoking his pipe and listen with a gentle serenity to the monstrous fabrications and never utter a protest.[16]

Twain supposedly visited Gillis and Stoker in Jackass Gulch in 1865, at the time when Charlie Russell was a mere infant, only a year old.[17] Russell's subsequent continuation of the roasting format brought the humorous style into the twentieth century, extending the life of an American folklore and literary tradition.

In his spoken and written roasts, Charlie Russell honored friends with his assumption that they could control their tempers, like Dick Stoker, in response to his outrageous jokes. The irreverent roast actually reflected deep respect for a friend's "grit" and emotional strength,

FIG. 60. Charles M. Russell, "___*! I'll Get The Big Ones Anyway.*" Pen/ink, illustration for the story "How Louse Creek Was Named," in *Rawhide Rawlins Stories* but omitted from *Trails Plowed Under*. Russell depicts Pete Van delousing his infested shirt by cursing and smashing it between two rocks, but shows his horse employing the hoof-in-ear method, minus the profanity.

despite the public discomfort, or in other words, assumed that he could "take it." Russell's deeper sense of connection with a roast victim and fellow survivor of changes in western life became clear in his eulogy for Pete Van. On the occasion of Van's death in 1918, Russell wrote to his "brothers" in the Great Falls Elks Club about an incident on the cattle range when Pete rescued him in a severe blizzard. Russell concluded by saying:

> It is the lonesome motherless places that tie men's hearts together in a way that time, distance or man's laws, not even death, can break. . . . [D]iscomforts pans out the good and bad in a man. Pete always showed good in the pan.[18]

Strangers, known to Russell only by similar experiences of cattle-range deprivation and hard work, typically earned Charlie's immediate friendship. He rarely condemned fellow open-range men, whether they had committed major crimes like "Kid Curry" (Harvey Logan) or, like Pete Van, attracted negative local gossip for the theft of a few unbranded calves. Special friends like Pete Van who proved themselves "good in the pan" became allies for life, worthy of roasts in stories and pictures, but never ridicule or rejection. Appreciation for lasting camaraderie pervaded Russell's depictions of the early western cattle ranges. His artistic images may have glorified a few rogues and rascals because Russell apparently overlooked minor criminal acts by people he perceived as somehow morally "good" despite their obvious flaws.

Cinch David's Voices

As an expression of this cattle-range rapport, Charlie Russell's close friends also had opportunities to deliver their own blunt roasts back in his face, whenever it seemed appropriate. But Russell held an advantage over his honored victims by his ability in later years to publish his joshing lies about them in newspapers and books. The roast of Finch David, titled "Cinch David's Voices,"[19] made fun of David's seemingly uncontrolled shifts in his vocal pitch between high falsetto and his ordinary speaking voice. Russell wrote, "'I never heered him sing,' says Rawhide Rawlins, 'but if he ever did it wouldn't be no quartet; it's a whole choir.'"[20] In this story, when Cinch David finds himself trapped under an overturned wagon, he pleads for help in so many vocal intonations that the only witness to visit the wreck refuses to help. To the potential helper, all of those victims should be able to lift up the wagon and rescue themselves.[21]

Russell's roast of Finch David teased a friend for a speech irregularity. Local accounts suggest that David frequently made a joke of his own voice, even to fooling outsiders into believing they had heard two unseen people having a conversation nearby but out of sight. In the cultures of the nineteenth-century American West, as in other rural regions, outward physical or behavioral characteristics became an immediate badge of identity, either positive or negative. Novelist Wallace Stegner understood the barbed teasing as being an unpleasant remnant of cowboy culture that he witnessed and experienced firsthand as a boy in southern Saskatchewan. As Stegner recalled:

> The folk culture sponsored every sort of crude practical joke, as it permitted the cruelist and ugliest prejudices and persecutions. Any visible difference was enough to get an individual picked on. . . . An inhumane and limited code, the value system of a life more limited and cruder than in fact ours was. We got most of it by inheritance from harsher frontiers that have preceded ours—got it, I suppose, mainly from our contacts with what was left of the cattle industry.[22]

Stegner recalled his youthful encounters with the rough challenges and teasing of his childhood in earlier western "folk culture" without much fondness or nostalgia. Later, in such writings as *Wolf Willow,* he directed attention to the emotional suffering of many people in the frontier West.

Charlie Russell seemed to thrive in the same rough atmosphere that oppressed and angered Stegner a few decades later. While he worked for eleven years as a night-wrangler or "nighthawk," Russell received the nickname "Cotton-Eye" from cattle-range cronies who noticed his penetrating gray eyes.[23] Nevertheless, there is no indication of any ridicule of his wearing the "half-breed" sash or constantly making sketches and clay figures. If there were other challenges, Russell's good humor defused the tension. Hazing or mean-spirited initiation

Cinch David's Voices

HISTORICAL RECOLLECTIONS OF RAWHIDE RAWLINS

"Speakin' of Missouri's squeaky voice, did any of you ever hear of a feller called Cinch David?" inquired Rawhide Rawlins.

"This Cinch has got all kinds of voices. He may be talkin' one minute below his belt; the next thing his voice is comin' from under his hair. I never heered him sing, but if he ever did it wouldn't be no quartet; it's a whole choir.

"One time me an' Joe Conway's night-herdin' beef. It was over in the Lone Tree country, an' we're holdin' about fifteen hundred head. There's a cold, drizzlin' rain comes up this night, hittin' the herd before they get their beds  warm. There ain't enough wind with it to keep 'em driftin' in any one direction, so these steers start to scatter, spread and walk out of the country. After Joe an' me's ridden pretty hard for a while we see there's no chance of holdin' 'em, an' knowin' there's hosses tied to the wheel in camp, Joe goes for help.

Rawhide Rawlins

" 'Tain't long till he's back, an' I can hear all kinds of men singin' and hollerin'. It's so dark you can't recognize nobody, but now and then I can see a rider agin' the sky-line. Towards mornin' we get 'em bunched an' they quiet down. It's about this time I ride on to Joe.

" 'How many men did you bring out?' says I.

" 'Only one,' he says.

" 'One,' I says, 'I'd bet I heard twenty different voices.'

"Joe laughed. 'Them was all Cinch David's,' he says.

"Another time Cinch is comin' out of the mountains with an empty wagon and a team of broncs he's been breakin'. This pair of snakes

get the bulge on him an' start hittin' the high places, finally turnin' the wagon plump over with Cinch jailed under the bed. Of course the broncs pull the pin an' start for Arizona with the double-tree.

"With the heft of the runnin' gear and bed on him, Cinch stands a good chance of starvin' to death as he can't lift this off him an' there's no chance tow 'badger' out. While he's layin' under there, studyin' ways to escape, he hears the hoofs of a hoss and the singing of a human. This is old Charlie Ferris, an Irish prospector from Yogo, who's been down the river and is returnin' happy. In his saddle pocket is a quart of joy-bringer that Ed. Morris has staked him to at Utica. About half of this is under

Charlie's hide an' he's singin' 'Bold Brennan on the Moor.'

"Charlie's worked up till he thinks he's ridin' the highways of old 're-land' with Dick Turpin. He's awakened from this day-dream by voices that he can't locate. He's a little superstitious an' sure believes in spooks, claimin' that while he's never seen any himself, his people in Ireland have all seen plenty of banshees and hobgoblins. When he first hears them voices he thinks he's kicked into a nest of 'em, but pretty soon he sees this wagon layin' wheels up, an' he finally decides that all these calls of distress is comin' from under.

"As he listens, one feller in a deep voice calls: 'Help us out of here.'

"Another voice, high an' squeaky,

yells: 'Lift the box!'

"Still another shouts: 'You ain' goin' to let us starve to death, ar you?'

"Old Charlie, sittin' on his hoss has been countin' the voices. H figures there's anyhow eight—perhaps ten men under the wagon-bed an' although he's far from stingy an would cut anything he had in two once, the idea of dividin' what's left of the quart with this band of thirst ies is too strong for his liberality.

"'What kind of min are ye, askin for help?' he inquires, addressin' th wagon box. 'If tin of ye can't rais that wagon ye're not worth savin' and he spurs on up the gulch.

"Cinch is rescued later by a coupl of men that know his outfit."

When he first hears them voices he thinks he has kicked into a nest of banshees and hobgoblins, but pretty soon he sees this wag on laying wheels up and he finally d ecides that all these calls are coming from under.

FIG. 61. "Cinch David's Voices," by Charles M. Russell, as it appeared in the *Western News* (MNA) on October 29, 1917. This friendly roast never reappeared in any books of Russell stories.

into the cowboy community may have been harsh for others, but Russell's engaging personality and entertaining artistic skills protected him from many difficulties. In his own life-summary he wrote, "Life has never been too serious with me—I lived to play and I'm playing yet. Laughs and good judgment have saved me many a black eye, but I don't laugh at other's tears."[24] No one who is ill-equipped or unwilling should have to endure such abusive rites of passage in the manner of young Wallace Stegner. Apparently, Finch David participated voluntarily in that tough frontier cowboy culture and its teasing about his variable voice without ever considering what Stegner calls "the code of the stiff upper lip."[25] If Finch David ever regarded Russell's "Cinch David" story as abusive or insulting, however, he showed no resentment and

FINCH DAVID

David has been identified with the Montana cattle industry for nearly 60 years. The photograph shows him as he was 50 years ago when he rode the range with Charles M. Russell

FIG. 62. Young Finch David, ca. 1889. Newspaper photograph printed in the 1939 article headlined "Range Partner of Russell's To Attend Cowboy Roundup Reunion, Companion of Montana's Famous Artist, Finch David Writes That He Will Be at Memorial Meeting Here," *Great Falls Tribune*, February 13, 1939.

exonerated the author in a comment to a newspaper writer, stating, "I never heard Charlie Russell insult a man nor say anything to hurt another's feelings during all the years I knew him. . . . He was one of the most considerate men I have ever known."[26]

There could be several reasons why Charlie Russell never republished "Cinch David's Voices" after 1917. He might have realized that the piece was not amusing or was simply too insulting. Russell's habit of creating roasts about his contemporaries may have crossed the line into insensitive abuse with this yarn. Of course, the friendly ridicule that Russell practiced on Finch David expressed his connection with a longtime friend rather than a sarcastic separation from a stranger or an enemy. Nevertheless, subsequent generations, from Stegner's youth gradually onward, with the exception of humorous speeches at tribute banquets, have found less humor in this mirth that focused on a person's physical, mental, or cultural quirks than did Russell's nineteenth-century cattle-range contemporaries. As one writer discussing colloquial humor expressed the change:

We can not laugh ever again with a free heart at physical deformity or at madness as people—and very good people too—did everywhere until very recently. Those

FIG. 63. Finch David, detail of photograph, 1936. Photograph courtesy of the James B. Rankin Collection, Montana Historical Society, Helena. Shown here at age sixty-five, Finch David was operating a pool hall in Utica.

sources of laughter are not sources of laughter any longer. They are gone from that list and will not be put back there, and I should be as unwilling as anybody else to see them put back. None the less, we laugh less.[27]

According to local legends, Russell told friends a humorous story about a stuttering barroom pianist, "Piano Jim and the Impotent Pumpkin Vine," but he never published it. It is impossible to know if Russell thought that the Finch David roast was inferior to his other writings or if the piece died in the hands of the Montana Newspaper Association editors.

Cultural values evolved quickly during the time of the Great War and afterward. A joke about a human disability that seemed hilarious in a nineteenth-century western saloon could have lost its charm when the Rawhide Rawlins books appeared. By the 1920s, Montana people had cultivated values that could seem alien to nineteenth-century men like Russell. This new orientation made some roasts like "Cinch David's Voices" less effective as humor or, if listeners still smirked and snickered, simply less appropriate for the printed page. As Russell commented to another old cowboy, "we usto know every body but time has made us strangers."[28] People and their cultural tastes can evolve quickly, and in the late nineteenth and early twentieth centuries the people and cultural norms in the West changed especially fast to catch up with the rest of the country.

As applied to closer friends in Charlie Russell's lifetime, the roasting story provided the mode of expression that he preferred. Many of the nature and hunting stories mentioned earlier follow the roast pattern of friendly abuse that typifies Russell's cattle-range humor. When he published "Bullard's Wolves,"[29] Russell was continuing his tradition of personal pranks and practical jokes that he had frequently inflicted on his cattle-range friend Bill Bullard. In "Lepley's Bear,"[30] Russell roasted a prominent cattleman/businessman from Fort Benton. This yarn was an exception to Russell's other published stories that focused almost exclusively on undistinguished, working-class, or merely average, local people. Nevertheless, the roast culture was not always friendly or gentle, and in tough situations, Russell showed he was no "push-over." Con Price witnessed an incident involving Charlie's circulation of a petition to release an old-time cowboy who had served about four years in the state penitentiary for rustling cattle:

> We called on people for several days and there was not a man or woman turned us down, until we met one of the wealthiest men in Great Falls. He read the petition and handed it back and said, "He can rot in the pen as far as I am concerned." Then he began to criticize Charlie for circulating the petition. There was where he made a mistake and the things he told him must have cut pretty deep into his feelings.
>
> Charlie said, "If you don't want to sign the petition, that's your business, but don't you roast me. I knew this man. He was once my friend. I don't approve of what he done, but he has a wife and two children praying for his release and he has been punished enough already." Then he looked him in the eye and said, "You know, Jim, if we all got our just dues, there would be a big bunch of us in the pen with Bill." I thought I could see the old boy's whiskers tremble because he knew what Charlie meant.[31]

Russell experienced western culture as an environment where stories like "Cinch David's Voices" and "A Pair of Outlaws" were appropriate expressions of a tough world of thick-skinned men who seldom backed away from personal challenge.

A PAIR OF OUTLAWS

Occasionally, Russell's admiration outweighed friendship in his selection of story subjects. In these circumstances, his colorful tall-tale exaggeration disappeared from the narrative. The abrasive personality of Charlie "Bowlegs" Buckley[32] made him an unlikely Russell companion and even less likely as the focus of a humorous roast. Nevertheless, since Bowlegs had ridden several times to Montana up the long cattle trail from Texas and then served as foreman on the S. T. cattle outfit around the Montana village of Big Sandy, he had earned Charlie Russell's high respect. Still, Bowlegs carried the reputation of a man who would be neither amused nor forgiving of laughter at his expense.

Two incidents attracted Charlie Russell's narrative attention—(1) Charlie Bowlegs's death-defying horseback ride to escape an onrushing Cheyenne war party and (2) his sudden

FIG. 64. Charles M. Russell, *"I'm Scarder Of Him Than I Am Of The Injuns,"* ca. 1924. Watercolor on paper, Mackay Collection, Montana Historical Society, published as an illustration for "A Pair of Outlaws" only in *Trails Plowed Under*.

demise in a card game shoot-out. Russell briefly describes Bowlegs's violent death in an illustrated letter sent to an old friend from the cattle-range days.[33] Russell published the escape yarn titled "A Pair of Outlaws" in his final collection of short stories.[34] By roping and mastering a dominant range stallion, Bowlegs barely outruns a band of hard-riding Cheyenne warriors. Ironically, years later, a barroom conflict with a mixed-blood Indian ends Bowlegs's life in a shoot-out over the Indian's demand to be included in a poker game's round of drinks. Bowlegs had saved his own life escaping from a war party's lethal game, but lost it years later when a single Indian demanded to join the white man's game:

> when [B]owlegs was playing poker he bought the drinks the breed asked if he didn't drink to[o] Bow legs told him he wasn't buying booze [for] Injuns and the ball opened Bow legs had on a over coat and [c]ouldent get his gun quick so he cashed in[35]

Russell's two "Bowlegs" pieces demonstrate the range in his narrative writings between a condensed, rough-draft summary and a longer, polished story. Considered together, the two pieces reveal a transitional shift of Indian roles from warriors who try to eliminate white

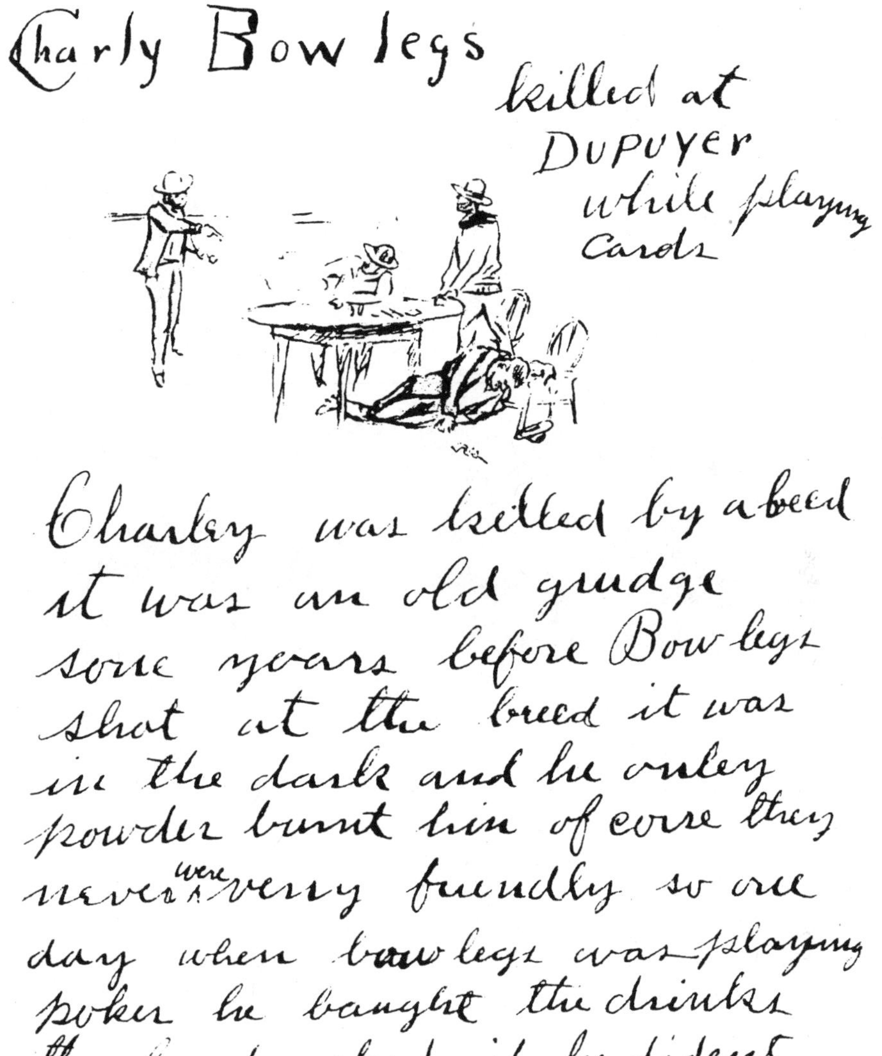

Charly Bow legs killed at
DUPUYER
while playing
Cards

Charley was killed by a breed
it was an old grudge
some years before Bow legs
shot at the breed it was
in the dark and he onley
powder burnt him of corse they
never were verry fuendly so one
day when bow legs was playing
poker he banght the drinks
the breed asked if he dident
drink to Bow legs told him
he wasent buing booze fro Inguns
and the ball opend Bow legs had
on a over coat and gouldent
get his gun quick so he cashdin

FIG. 65. Charles M. Russell, *Charly Bow legs killed in Dupuyer while playing cards,* 1901. Pen/ink, published in *Good Medicine,* 1929. Russell sent a packet of rough-sketch profiles of mutual friends to an old range pal. The group of sketches included this report on the demise of Charlie "Bowlegs" Buckley.

FIG. 66. Con Price and Charlie Russell, ca. 1905, standing in front of Russell's studio in Great Falls. Photograph courtesy of the Montana Historical Society, Helena. For several years until late 1910, Charlie and Nancy Russell were part-owners of a homestead ranch with Con Price and his wife that was located near the Canada/U.S. border.

intruders to the new circumstances several decades later when mixed-blood Indians demanded to participate in Euro-American barroom activity. Both tales about Bowlegs also demonstrate how survival in earlier frontier times might suddenly require great physical strength, quick reactions, and unyielding determination. Bowlegs's uncompromising personality that enabled him to rope and ride the wild stallion had saved him from the Indian attack out on the prairie. A few years later, however, the same asset of an unbending personality entangled him in a fatal Indian/white barroom confrontation where compromise could have meant survival.

For Charlie Russell, "A Pair of Outlaws" was nonfiction, a true story that he retold as accurately as possible, even though the "narrator" and main character (Buckley) had died years before Russell wrote down the narrative or painted the picture. In this manner, his stories celebrate friendly westerners like Con Price, as well as tougher characters like Charlie "Bowlegs" Buckley. Price worked in some of the same cattle outfits with Russell, starting in 1885, and soon became a top-hand bronc rider. Early in their marriage, Charlie and Nancy Russell bought land to become partners in Price's startup cattle-and-horse ranch located in Montana's Sweetgrass Hills along the Canada/U.S. border. After a few years of this small-scale ranching effort, however, they all gave up the ranching business and liquidated their holdings. Some losses could be absorbed by Russell's ability to make and sell art.[36] But the partners had started their unfenced ranching enterprise too late in the game, according to Price:

> The farmers filed on every water hole in the country and they all had dogs, so the cattle didn't have a chance. . . . But when I seen those farmers raise fifty bushels of wheat to the acre on that virgin soil I could see the handwriting on the wall.[37]

Even though the ranch partnership failed, the Russell/Price friendship flourished and grew through the rest of their lives.

THE GIFT HORSE

In subsequent years, Charlie Russell enjoyed roasting his friend and former business partner[38] in two published stories, "The Gift Horse"[39] and "Bronc Twisters."[40] In the first tale, a cowman named Charlie Furiman patiently struggles without success to tame an unpredictably violent horse. In despair, Furiman hands over the attractive-looking horse, without a warning disclaimer, as his wedding gift to the recently married bronc-rider Con Price. In a similar solution, Mark Twain describes his disposal of the unridable "Genuine Mexican Plug" to a passing Arkansas emigrant who "will doubtless remember the donation."[41] Russell helped his victim of the "Gift Horse" transaction to remember his questionable good fortune by publishing this story about the setup. Price found his chance to tell his version of this roasting situation when he published his own book, *Trails I Rode,* in 1947.[42]

FIG. 67. Charlie Furiman, detail of photograph of old-timers at a 1941 Miles City cowboy reunion. Photograph courtesy of the Montana Historical Society, Helena. Furiman passed off an explosively violent horse as an innocent wedding gift to former bronc-rider Con Price.

FIG. 68. Charles M. Russell, *About The Third Jump, Con Loosens.* Pen/ink on paper, Montana Historical Society, Helena. This illustration for the story "Bronc Twisters" appears in *Rawhide Rawlins Stories* and in *Trails Plowed Under,* titled "*I hit the ground a lot harder than I expected.*"

Bronc Twisters

In the first episode of the two-part piece "Bronc Twisters," Charlie Russell describes Con Price's intentional dive from a bucking horse as part of a futile attempt to gain sympathy from a settler's daughter. After staging a wreck that genuinely injured himself, Price discovered that the intended female witness was not even present in the cabin to see the fall and soothe his pain. Cattlemen, including Price and Russell, resented the intrusion of "nesters" and farmers into the unfenced cattle ranges. In telling this brief roasting yarn, Russell seems to have enjoyed the overlapping irony of a renowned bronc rider like Price who would eagerly volunteer to risk broken bones for the chance of a romantic encounter with a female nester.

In the second episode of "Bronc Twisters" Russell tells the legendary tale of Charlie Brewster's ride over a cliff. After a brief essay contrasting modern rodeo riders with earlier open-range bronc riders who tamed a cattle outfit's worst mounts, narrator "Rawhide Rawlins" singles out Charlie Brewster as one of the greatest bronc riders of bygone days, or "one of the best that ever stepped across a hoss, an' many a bad one he's tamed."[43] Charlie Brewster was the brother of Horace Brewster, who had given Charlie Russell his first job with a Judith Basin cattle company in 1882. In one observer's words, there was "[n]o outlaw horse so fierce, so untamable that Charlie Brewster would hesitate for a moment to throw his saddle on him and ride him. It was his joy, in the presence of a discriminating audience, to put a silver dollar in each stirrup, clamp his feet on them and ride the very prince of outlaws to a standstill without losing either of the silver dollars."[44]

Although Russell composed an embarrassing story to roast Con Price, this section on Charlie Brewster clearly stands as a tribute to one of the more stubbornly self-confident bronc riders in the West. In the narrative, Brewster disregards his dangerous horse ("the snakey roan") and lights a cigarette—without asking the horse's permission, according to the narrator—while riding close to the cliff rim of a thirty-foot drop-off. At the striking of the match, the horse explodes in fury, heading for the brink. Brewster has time to jump off but refuses, all the time using his full weight and strength with the reins as well as hard jabs with his sharp spurs, none of which turns the horse from its deadly trajectory. According to narrator Rawlins, "The roan's goin' high an' scary when he hits the edge of the cliff an' goes over." Here Russell, the master storyteller, delays the reader's discovery of what happened next. Brewster's companions expect the worst, that at the bottom of the cliff they would find, simply,

> a scramble of man and hoss meat. None of the bunch says nothin', but ridin' up easy, like they're goin' to a funeral, they peek over, an' what do you think they see? There, mebby ten feet below the rimrock, sits Charlie in the middle of the roan. The bronc's lookin' healthy, but uncomfortable. He's lodged in the top of a big cottonwood. Charlie's still holdin' his cigarette, an' when the boys show up he hollers: "Anybody got a match? The one I struck blowed out."[45]

This reflective pause in the narrative, as echoed in the pen/ink illustration, provides a classic western understatement for Russell's best humorous anecdote.

Both of the Brewster brothers worked for the Coburn family's Circle C cattle company northeast of Great Falls—Horace as the roundup foreman and Charlie as the bronc rider who "rode the rough string" and loved proving he was the best. One of the Coburn boys recalled that it was a pleasure to watch Charlie Brewster work a horse in the corral. He would challenge any observer sitting on the high log fence, betting a bottle of beer or a month's wages "that he could ride the bronc straight up and blow smoke from his cigarette on every jump."[46] Coburn's cigarette reference suggests that Russell presented an accurate version of Brewster in his yarn, holding the cigarette despite the chaotic wreck into the treetop.

Nevertheless, the storytelling artist may have heightened certain parts of the Charlie Brewster incident in his spoken renditions, as well as in his prose and pictures. One of several alternate story versions, attributed to a Russell contemporary known as Doc Nelson, tells of the cowboys sitting on stationary horses for a relaxing smoke. According to Nelson, the horse

FIG. 69. Charles M. Russell, *The Bronc's Lodged in the Top of An Old Cottonwood.* Pen/ink on paper, illustration for "Bronc Twisters" in *Rawhide Rawlins Stories* and *Trails Plowed Under.* Permanent Collection, C. M. Russell Museum, Great Falls, Montana. This story and picture preserved Charlie Brewster's greatest moment as a legendary western bronc rider.

merely slid off the bank into the treetop before the rider asked for a new match to relight his smoke.[47] Other than the pen/ink sketch that appeared with Russell's version of the story, no known Russell painting depicts the Brewster incident.

All of these alternative versions of Charlie Brewster's big moment suggest the variety of variations that a single legend can develop. As an eyewitness to the event, however, Charlie Brewster's brother Horace provides solid support to Russell's humorous versions. In his account, the horse was wild and unstoppable, the cliff was high, the tree was tall, and the horse escaped from the limbs only after his brother had "climbed out of the saddle and down the tree" that was then chopped down to release the horse.[48] The question about getting another match was consistent with Charlie Brewster's show-off style to smoke while riding a rough mount. These story elements may also have been part of Russell's humor that he would inject into a "true" incident simply to enliven his record of a memorable legend that actually was grounded in fact.

At the Como Art Company in Great Falls, where Nancy Russell arranged for Charlie's paintings to be framed, employee Jack Wrynn heard Russell tell Brewster's story when the artist stopped there on one of his daily downtown visits. Wrynn also remembered: "Charlie Brewster's grandsons lived just down here a block from the studio. Those kids were up here almost every day, and when I'd have customers (at the Como), they'd go get that book to show their grandfather up in the tree on his horse."[49] The incident generated enough interest to circulate as vivid local folklore. With Russell's adaptation in picture and in printed words, however, Charlie Brewster's "big jump" became a lasting legend of the American West.

RANGE HORSES

The rough "breaking" of wild or immature horses for work in the western cattle business did not strike Charlie Russell as extraordinary or cruel. He depicted men riding bucking horses in dozens of pictures and sculptures, several of which suggest the mortal danger involved in their work. Contrasting with Brewster's lighthearted attitude, Russell's watercolor, *Mankiller*, shows the perils of bronc riding (**see plate 19**). Nevertheless, the author hints at alternative ways to treat horses in "Curley's Friend." He explains, "This herder is a Bannock Injun; he can't talk much white man, but all the hosses seem to savvy Bannock. [H]e's got some language hosses seem to savvy."[50] Russell's relationships with his own horses, especially the pinto Monte, appear to have been closer to the Bannock style than to the standard brutal domination of cattle outfits. His sensitivity to horse intelligence and behavior moved him to describe the habits of wild horse herds in a brief essay, "Range Horses."[51]

Starting with a reference to the arrival of European horses in the Western Hemisphere with the Spaniards under Cortez, Russell covers topics varying from horse defenses against wolf attacks to horses' distinctive ways of drinking from a stream. At the end, narrator Rawhide Rawlins provides readers with advice about trusting a horse's instincts and intelligence, especially when traveling at night or in bad weather. "There's lots of times a hoss knows more than a man," observes Russell through his Rawhide Rawlins voice. "A man that says a hoss don't know nothin' don't know much about hosses."[52] Cowpunchers like Russell relied heavily on horses during the peak years of the open-range. Most of his peers managed horses through physical domination, while others, like Russell, used more gentle methods of persuasion. As automobiles became widely available conveniences in the early twentieth century, Russell and many rural westerners still preferred horses for their companionship and reliability.

THE OPEN RANGE

In the rangeland transitions from the final buffalo hunts in the early 1880s to the fenced control of land and water by small ranches and farms in the 1890s, the era of wide open–range cattle herding lasted approximately a decade in central Montana's Judith Basin. As Montana historian Bob Fletcher observes:

> The central part of the state was the first to succumb to the sheepmen, the small cattlemen, and the farmer. . . . From 1884–1889, the number of cattle in Fergus County declined from about 125,000 to 50,000. In 1890, alone, the Fergus County Argus estimated that nearly 28,000 head were driven north, forced out by the enclosing of land and water courses.[53]

Con Price noted that, while working as a cowboy, "Russell hated the change and followed the cattle north to Milk River country, trying to stay in the open range country."[54] One of the few published statements of Russell's opinion about the transition from open-range ranching to farming and fenced grazing appears in his brief essay "The Open Range," where he states: "There's mighty little open range left, barring the mountains—its all under wire now. . . . Most cow countries now are pastures. The Old-time roundups of the old days are almost a thing of the past."

Russell's essay avoids expressions of nostalgic regret over the loss of the open range and simply records work details of range-cattle management. In such passages as, "In old times, when they branded on the prairie . . ." and "I'm only telling about cow countries I know—different countries handled cows different ways,"[55] he reflects a matter-of-fact attitude. The focus on ethnological details demonstrates Russell's wish to preserve an awareness of their function, as reflected in his painting "The Roundup," now in the Mackay collection at the Montana Historical Society. Yet Russell never claimed he was the ultimate expert on range-cattle practices or other facets of the transitional frontier. In a detailed letter to the editors of *Adventure Magazine*, Russell concluded: "I've lived a long time in the West, but I don't know it all yet."[56]

THE STORY OF THE COWPUNCHER

Charlie Russell's published essays reflect his awareness that his reading audience exceeded his small group of cronies and other knowledgeable westerners. In a few pieces, he was also addressing those readers who needed background information about western cattle culture to appreciate his stories. Several of his brief essays stand alone as prose statements, while others accompany narrative tales. Russell's best-known dual-purpose piece, titled "The Story of the Cowpuncher," appears as the first item in *Trails Plowed Under*.[57] His handwritten first draft for the piece omits most of the essay data about cowboy clothing and personal equipment and leads directly to a yarn about the cowboy-narrator's troubled trip to Chicago. All subsequent typewritten drafts, however, contain the essay information, comprising more than half of the combined essay/story.[58] This shift may reflect the influence of editors such as Caspar Whitney who wanted nonfiction material about the West for his magazine.

Russell's narrator, "Rawhide Rawlins," begins the essay with a joke about non-westerners who misunderstand real cowpunchers.[59] The eastern girl asks her mother if cowboys actually eat grass. Her mother assures her that they do not since they are at least half-human. To counteract common misperceptions, fed by the growing popularity of "pulp" western novels and unrealistic portrayals of cowboys in silent movies, the narrator carefully describes cowboy clothes and equipment, from chaps to guns. He clarifies the contrasting variations between Texas cattle-culture traditions and the differing California styles that evolved from the same Spanish/Mexican origins. Russell's interest in these comparisons grew easily out of Montana's position as an intersection for several cattle-management traditions that coexisted in the region.

Texas outfits, dominating the southeast quarter of Montana, supplied the double cinch or "rim-fire" saddle, hemp-rope lariat, such cowboy terms as *line-riding, maverick,* and *cavvyard,* as well as the distinctive hybrid longhorn cattle. From California via Oregon, Nevada, and Utah came the buckaroo/vaquero traditions, with their hand-tooled, single-cinched Visalia or "center-fire" saddle, the longer rawhide "riatta"/lariat, and such terms as *Buckeroo, taps,* and *mayordomo.* From Midwest sources came British cattle breeds, such as the Herefords and Angus that grazed in the Sun River district between Great Falls and the Rocky Mountain Front, as well as in the Beaverhead district in southwestern Montana, with such distinctive practices as pastures divided by stacked split-rail fences, barns, haying, and hay paraphernalia such as the "beaver-slide" hay-stacking device, hay-meadow irrigation, mild-mannered domesticated cattle, and the stockmen's associations.[60] Russell's Judith Basin held elements of all three—California, British Isles, and the strongest influence of all, the Texas longhorn–versions of the Spanish/Mexican tradition.

In the 1870s and early 1880s, the quickly evolving Montana cattle cultures overlapped with earlier frontier stages. As one well-educated cowboy recalled of the Judith Basin, just before Russell's 1880 arrival:

> Our section of Montana was socially in a state of flux. The trader, hunter, and trapper were in evidence, but their day was waning; the farmer had not yet appeared. Sheepmen and cattlemen were driving their herds into the country, but neither their costumes nor their customs were then standardized.[61]

As patterns set in, so did fashion, an element that Russell found to be humorous. A few punchers soon become as self-preoccupied in their appearance as the cowboy known as "Pretty Shadow," as described by Rawhide Rawlins in "The Story of the Cowpuncher." Con Price proudly claimed to have been the narcissistic role model for "Pretty Shadow."[62] Yet whoever his role model may have been, Russell was indicating that even in the midst of their hard work and long hours far from urban civilization, the earliest American cowboys harbored a sensitive fashion consciousness.

Russell's narrator finishes the essay-piece with a story about a near-disastrous trip with a cattle shipment to Chicago. The narrative shows that a tough cowboy could be a vulnerable "fish-out-of-water" or "babe-in-the-woods" type in a tough urban setting like Chicago. Rawhide Rawlins tells how his recently purchased city "dude" disguise fools no one. Everyone in Chicago immediately understands his western mannerisms and speech to be signals of a moneymaking opportunity for themselves:

> When I put on all this rig, I sure look human; that is, I think so. But them short-horns know me, an' by the way they trim that roll, it looks like somebody's pinned a card on my back with the word "EASY" in big letters.[63]

Luckily for the narrator, the same distinctive mannerisms inspire a fellow westerner, who is lingering in Chicago, to help him escape back to his congenial prairie home. Once again, Russell uses the narrative story to demonstrate the survival benefit of the close bonds shared among men of the open range.

For his popular painting *In Without Knocking* (**see plate 20**), the artist recreates the incident when Johnny Skelton and one brother, plus Henry Keeton and Matt Price, rode their horses into a Stanford saloon in 1881 and then told Charlie Russell all about it the next day. Twenty-eight years later, Russell painted the story and impressed the participants with his rendering of specific details. Russell made such cowboys, good or bad types, the focus of narrative artworks depicting regional history.

For Charlie Russell, the open-range cowpunchers embodied the same reckless, adventure-seeking spirit as that of the fur trader, trapper, explorer, and gold seeker of earlier frontier periods. Russell understood how quickly these transitional stages had disappeared when he commented, "The cowboy was the last of this kind, and he's mighty near extinct."[64] Decades later, author Wallace Stegner understood much about the authentic cowpuncher mind, even though he had little enjoyment of the culture and social impact of the early-day cowboys, writing:

> [W]hat they themselves most respected . . . was as noble as it was limited. They honored courage, competence, self-reliance, and they honored them tacitly. They took them for granted. It was their absence, not their presence, that was cause for remark. Practicing comradeship in a rough and dangerous job, they lived a life calculated to make a man careless of everything except the few things he really valued.[65]

Despite Russell's lament that the real cowmen and cattle business had disappeared, he knew personally many ranch hands, rodeo riders, and others associated with the cattle business who continued the cowboy life and vocation into the 1920s. Nevertheless, he preferred the earlier, nomadic variety, who "left tracks in History that the farmer can't plow under. Good or bad, they were regular men and America's last frontier men."[66]

The earlier western cowboy types, like those who worked with Russell out on the fence-less prairies, seemed to the author/artist as being separate and distinctive from all who came later. One Montana participant in the early cattle-range era made this clarification:

FIG. 70. Johnny Skelton (left), Charlie Russell, and three Judith Basin pals. Photograph courtesy of Bill Skelton, Stanford, Montana. Johnny Skelton earned a wild reputation with many unsavory associates, but he also helped his relatives establish an influential family in the Stanford/Geyser area of the Judith Basin.

> Every man in the old cow days was a type by himself. He had lived alone and had had to defend himself under all kinds of circumstances without getting some one else's idea of what was the thing to do in this case or that. It made a man more individual in his ways and speech and thought. His self-reliance and independence grew because he was constantly needing them. There were plenty of strange characters among the cowmen, but there were also a lot of noble and lovable men.[67]

In his watercolor *The Trail Boss* (**see plate 21**), Russell depicts one of these independent characters smoking a hand-rolled cigarette while pondering the rivalry for range grass and water between the cattle and sheep herds. The gray mass in the upper right area of this painting may be the only known Russell depiction of a (despised) band of sheep among his thousands of verified artworks.

To people with Russell's viewpoint, the open-range cowboy appeared to be more individualistic or independent than the later participants of his trade. Clothing and other subtle outward behaviors may have signaled this difference to Russell and his peers, but the shades of difference seem minor to observers of cowboys decades later. Most ranch hands and western horsemen of later generations continue to feel and express a close affinity with Russell for the cowpunchers of the late nineteenth century. Those who have discontinued riding horses in favor of pickup trucks and the popular four-wheeled "all-terrain-vehicles" (or ATVs) typically express less interest in Russell's views and values. Even in the Judith Basin, some high school–age ranch hands in the twenty-first century report being teased by their peers for still bothering to work with saddle horses.

FIG. 71.

Charles M. Russell. Photograph courtesy of the Montana Historical Society, Helena. A decade or more after painting *Trail Boss,* Charlie stood like a regular cowpuncher while chatting with the photographer.

The open-range cowboys that Russell depicted in his narrative works had good reasons to see themselves as unique and even privileged in contrast to men in other vocations. Unlike nineteenth-century industrial workers and miners, cattle hands worked outdoors in clean air. Riding on his own horse, high above pedestrians, the cowpuncher traveled with greater freedom of direction and impulsive timing than any other worker, including railroad men. And unlike other hired laborers (except peace officers and private detectives), they frequently carried loaded guns and ammunition. When dissatisfied with a job or situation, a capable cowpuncher equipped with a gun and a horse simply rode away and sought out another cattle job elsewhere. The post–Civil War demand for beef, combined with rail lines expanding into the West, meant that most cattle outfits would quickly hire a competent-seeming stranger. Even though they were essentially laboring for wages from capitalist ranching companies in a similar manner to other wage laborers, the early-day cowboys rightly perceived themselves as relatively independent and potentially self-sufficient. Nevertheless, despite Russell's efforts to depict their distinctive clothes, hats, and working circumstances in realistic pictures, sculptures, and stories, few non-cowboys in subsequent generations perceive a meaningful difference between the open-range cowpunchers of the nineteenth century and the later types who work on fenced ranches with more docile cattle breeds than the larger, dangerous Texas Longhorns.

Hands Up!

Among the archetypal cowmen that populate western Americana and folk literature of the West, Charlie Russell chose a tough one as a lead character with seemingly ambiguous moral values in his story "Hands Up!" Narrated by "Jack Shea,"[68] this is the only published Russell tale that takes place in Colorado. In the narrative, five people are crowded into a stagecoach, including a middle-aged woman and a cowman, all unnamed. The coach has to pass through a district known for robberies, but the cowman assures the fearful woman that her last remaining money in the world, a roll of fifty dollars, will be safe under the seat cushion. He even gives her a few extra decoy dollars to "pacify these road robbers." But when the robbers do stop the stage, the cowman whispers to them the exact location of the woman's cash. After the robbers' departure, he freely admits his duplicity to his fellow passengers. "He tells it like he ain't ashamed, and finishes, sayin', 'If you don't take care of yourself, nobody else will.'"[69] The fellow passengers of this candid cowman become enraged and all of them, except the woman, agree to hang him to the nearest tree, using one of the long reins from the six-horse coach harness—for want of a rope. And in an echo of a similar joke by the Indiana humorist George Ade, one of the passengers quips grimly, "If he's as light in pounds as he is in principle, we'll slip a boulder in his pants to give him weight."[70]

The middle-aged woman pleads for the cowman's life. "She don't want to see him strung up, but thinks jail is strong enough." The cowman, although apparently facing near death, shows no fear and defiantly chides the accusers while removing his boots in anticipation of his hanging, stating:

> "'I've been a gambler all my life,' says he, draggin' off his right boot, 'but none of you shorthorns ever was; you never played nothin' but solitaire. This lady stakes me to fifty,' says he, 'and I always split my winnin's in the middle with them that stakes me.' And takin' a thousand dollars he's got tucked in his sock, he counts off five one-hundred dollar bills, and hands them to the lady. 'That's yours,' says he." [71]

The thousand dollars has escaped the robbers' notice due to the distraction of the lady's roll of fifty. The stunned passengers quickly celebrate the sudden good fortune by each taking a swig of whiskey from a shared bottle, excluding the lady. (Rather than being unfair to her, they are politely unburdening this seemingly respectable woman from the need to decline a drink, especially from a bottle used by everyone else.) Then the loudest advocate for immediate capital punishment, the owner of the nearly empty whiskey bottle, proclaims, "Here's to the gambler that pays his stakes!"[72] Finishing the whiskey, he litters the roadside with the bottle just as the stage pulls into the station and the story ends happily for all.

As in a typical George Ade fable, these characters have no names and Russell's moral for this yarn seems to be that everyone should "pay his stakes." But beyond any boisterous (and superficial) moralizing, Russell is neither roasting an old friend like Pete Van nor paying tribute to a specific survivor of a high adventure like Charlie "Bowlegs" Buckley. In "Hands Up!" Russell is relating a double-cross story with a surprise ending worthy of O. Henry. Essentially, he is celebrating an archetypal western American cattleman from the nineteenth century who stands aloof from the crowd to be true to his own moral standard and helpful to a needy female.

On the surface of this yarn, the cattleman seems brazenly self-serving in betraying the woman's cash reserve, but, ultimately, everyone learns that he privately maintains a code of honor and a survival plan. If he had wished simply to preserve his own money, the cowman could have admitted nothing to his fellow passengers and would have survived their suspicions. If he had felt guilty about the deception, he might have hurried to inform his lynchers about the money hidden in his boot. Instead, he defiantly challenges them to start the hanging, while he calmly removes his boots and hands out a share of his funds. As a result, the grateful woman receives a tenfold increase on her unwitting investment. For Russell and like-minded westerners, the cowman's intention to share his secret boot money would not be in doubt. But for readers living outside the nineteenth-century western cultural values, for whom the cowman is a stranger, his motives remain dubious—open to suspicions about self-serving convenience. Would the cowman have turned over the extra money to the female passenger if the other riders had not threatened him with an immediate roadside hanging? The story's tantalizing ambiguity balances on the question. Was it a chivalrous plan all the way or a just devious, last-minute dodge to avoid hanging?

The author's narrator and the other characters seem to accept the cattleman as an honorable western figure—the hero of this brief, humorous fable. Russell knew that such a character "type" was disappearing in the West around the turn of the century. As one commentator observed:

> There are not many of them left. Many have gone with the longhorns, which are but a memory in the northwest today. A few are living on their ranches, mostly up and down the Rocky Mountains. They were a type and that type has vanished from the west as completely as the buffalo.[73]

Near the pinnacle of his painting career and on the verge of restarting his story-publishing activity, Russell told an old friend that, among the older-style cattle-range participants, "right now I know more dead men than live ones. . . . Thirty seven years I've lived in Montana, but I am among strangers now."[74] The steady disappearance of good friends and other colorful western types saddened Russell as much as the constant changes in the cattle business and other changes in the twentieth-century West. Certainly, this sadness fed Russell's sentimental side and nostalgic impulses. Yet the same recognition that people and circumstances were changing forever also seemed to motivate him to preserve aspects of western culture in his stories and narrative art.

Charlie Russell accepted with great reluctance the changes that followed the open-range cattle era. By historian Robert Athearn's definition, Russell certainly qualified as a "romantic" witness and a participant in the transformations of western frontier regions. As Athearn defines them:

> Rather than seeing the coming of the farmer as the climax of an old tradition, romantics preferred to focus on the passing of the open range cattle business. This, they said, signified the disappearance of the Old West.[75]

Russell probably would have agreed with Athearn's definition of "The Old West," as well as his being grouped with the romantics. For Russell, the sense of western distinctiveness from other regions, including the Pacific Coast, evaporated with the transition from the cattle frontier to a region of mixed grazing and farming, mining, timber harvesting, and small-to-medium towns connected by rails, telephone lines, and gravel roads. As the work changed, so did the people, and Russell missed the distinctive characters from earlier times. In addition to the disappearance of certain types of people associated with open-range cattle practices, Russell also regretted the loss of the land itself. Open-range ranching practices dwindled gradually in Montana, according to range historian Fletcher:

> Round-up districts somewhat like those of the earlier days were still laid out by the cattlemen's convention in 1903. . . . In 1907, the round-ups had become almost entirely private affairs carried on independently by the various remaining large outfits or by two or three in cooperations. The open cattle range was gone.[76]

Russell and some of his friends might have called the open range "closed" with the cessation of the long-distance cattle drives in the 1890s, but Fletcher sees it ending a decade later. The influx of sheepmen and farming homesteaders from the East and South overwhelmed the open grazing land and overutilized the watering holes, making profitable cattle ranching even more difficult. As Con Price observed:

> I seen that country change in two years from where there was open range everywhere to where there wasn't a foot of government land left, either in Montana or across the Canadian line, and in 1910 we had a very dry year and had to gather our cattle and bring them home. So I decided to sell out.[77]

With the closing of Charlie and Con's cattle and horse operation in 1910, the artist's direct connection with ranching was severed. He lived the final sixteen years of his life as a witness and historian of the modernizing cattle culture rather than an active participant.

LONGROPE'S LAST GUARD

In Charlie Russell's published writings, the strongest sense of romantic nostalgia for the open cattle range appears in his story "Longrope's Last Guard."[78] Russell shared the cowpunchers'

FIG. 72. E. C. "Teddy Blue" Abbott and Charlie Russell, Miles City, 1919.
Photograph courtesy of the Montana Historical Society,
Helena. These longtime friends posed for several pictures
at the stockmen's convention.

high respect for the men who rode for three decades following the Civil War on the long cattle drives up the Texas Trail to Montana and he expressed that appreciation in "Longrope's Last Guard." Because Charlie Russell never participated in one of the Texas to Montana drives, he relied on the knowledge of men like Teddy Blue Abbott. Russell once stated that "Teddie [Blue] knows more about old trail men and trail days than aney man I know."[79] Russell appears to have constructed this story from several sources of inspiration, including Abbott. Teddy Blue supposedly had seen a man killed in a thunderstorm stampede on one of his rides up the trail to Montana, and J. Frank Dobie reported that one old-timer had identified Abbott as Russell's model for "Longrope's" narrator, Rawhide Rawlins. Another account informed Dobie that Russell had based "Longrope's Last Guard" on a real incident, except that Longrope somehow had survived the stampede.[80] This longer Russell yarn has received the strongest praise of any of his nonhumorous writings. Robert Gale has stated, "The whole story is masterly...a poignant lament."[81] J. Frank Dobie generously calls it "perhaps the finest story that has ever been written about cows or cowboys."[82]

More than any other Charlie Russell story or essay, "Longrope's Last Guard" completely engulfs readers with the romantic westerner's nineteenth-century perspective, idealizing this segment of the range-cattle era. "Rawhide Rawlins" narrates most of this essay/story in the present tense. Speaking in the "historical present" to replicate oral storytelling, Rawlins describes the accidental death of the man known only by the nickname "Longrope," who dies when trampled in a cattle stampede sparked by a thunderstorm's lightning blasts. Unlike most of Russell's other stories, however, "Longrope's Last Guard" lacks references to any other time or place besides the immediate moment. In the last paragraph, the narrator finally states, "It's been twenty years or more since we tucked him in with the end-gate of a bed-wagon for a headstone."[83] The story implies by omission that, in those intervening twenty years between the events and the narration, the only change along the Texas-to-Montana trail happened when the cows eventually rubbed down Longrope's grave sign. As early as the mid-1890s, however, the long cattle drives had ceased, obstructed by fences and private control of crucial water sources. The brief clarification at the close of Russell's narrative provides a sense of time passing, but no indication of an evolving American West.

An essay forms the first half of "Longrope's Last Guard," describing open-range cattle-herding practices in the present tense, as if these techniques were still in use. By the time of the first publication of "Longrope's Last Guard" in 1908, however, wire fences had segmented Montana prairies for several decades, making this essay more intellectually intriguing as cultural history than immediately relevant as practical information about "contemporary" conditions on western cattle ranges. Russell's essay and story do not portray a *passing* phase of the western cattle industry. In this story, the great trail-drive phase has never ended. When reconsidered by readers nearly a century after first publication, "Longrope's Last Guard" seems like a perfectly preserved cultural artifact, somehow frozen in time. Russell's story reveals his nostalgic cowboy vision most clearly here, not with a complaint about post-frontier conditions, but as an embrace of the nineteenth-century cattle drive as the only significant reality in the West. For this story, Russell ignored the changes and transformations that he addressed in other writings.

Other Russell stories show a broader awareness of changes in the West. In the narrative segment of "The Story of a Cowpuncher,"[84] a representative of the open range encounters the difficulties of big cities in Chicago. The barroom operators who take advantage of the guileless westerner demonstrate the threat of callous urban life. As for the impact of cities on western frontier regions, Charlie Russell never anticipated the extent or speed of urbanization in Montana. In his letter to Paris Gibson, the founder of Great Falls and, ultimately, a U.S. senator from Montana, Russell admits, "In 1883 I night herded horses where this town [Great Falls] now stands. . . . They were old men among us that spoke of it as a good beef country but there was nothing said of a town."[85] When he traveled to other states and regions to sell his artworks, Russell sent letters back to Montana friends expressing blunt opinions about large cities like Chicago and New York. He was only half-joking when predicting he would be dead as the final stages of urban degradation would engulf his Montana hometown. "I suppose," he wrote to his next-door neighbor back in Montana, "Great Falls will be lik[e] Chicago some day but I won't be there[.]"[86] Yet by the time Russell did expire in 1926 Great Falls was merely a miniature Chicago or Minneapolis, with only a fraction of those cities' populations. Nevertheless, the leading city in Montana had sprouted two railroads passing through the town, a hydro-electric dam on the Missouri River, automobiles instead of horses, electric streetcars, and a large cop-per smelter with a gigantic smokestack spewing poisonous fumes. Great Falls had achieved many economic benefits of bigger cities with only a fraction of their size.

Night Herd

Great Falls also embodied many of the scourges of urban/industrial growth. Even some of the surrounding villages experienced problems with human congestion on their own miniature scale. Charlie Russell's awareness of a particular kind of urban blight for smaller towns appears in his story "Night Herd."[87] In this roast, Russell sets up a friend as the narrator of his own embarrassing tale. Belknap "Bally" Buck[88] tells how he lost consciousness after a bout of heavy drinking in the little cow town of Big Sandy, only to wake up at dawn in what seemed to be the middle of a cattle herd. Then the narrator corrects his own tale:

> "In the middle of the herd? In the middle of hell," says he. "I'm in the center of the town dump. The steers that I have been looking at are nothing but stoves, tables, boxes; all the discard of Sandy is there. The few that's standin' are tables. That spot-ted seventy-nine steer that I know so well is a big goods box. Them spots is white paper."[89]

One observer has mentioned that Russell took liberties with the actual incident in "Night Herd" for the sake of making a good story and certainly to generate extra embarrassment.

> Ballie Buck and Russell was good friends. . . . [I]n Russell's writing about Ballie . . . up in the town dump. It didn't happen just like that, but Russ changed it to color the tale better.[90]

Even Russell's less-educated friends, including this letter writer, understood storytelling and painting as being part of the same narrative process that involves adding color when necessary. Nevertheless, this short tale reveals important information about urbanization in the West. As nineteenth-century frontier settlements grew into modest towns, urban problems of solid waste disposal also increased. Even little villages like Big Sandy had to spoil a portion of nearby land to create a community necessity—a waste dump.

Individual homesteaders also faced problems with what later generations categorize as "solid waste." Nannie Alderson settled in Montana during the same period that Charlie Russell worked in a different district as a cowpuncher. In her book of reminiscences she wrote, "Everybody in the country lived out of cans, and you would see a great heap of them outside of every little shack. But we always had a barrel for ours.[91] Describing a creative use for this kind

FIG. 73.
Belknap "Ballie" Buck.
Photography courtesy of Glenna
Buck, Helena, Montana. Ballie
was a mixed-blood Indian who
became a highly respected cattle
foreman on ranches in Montana
and southern Alberta.

of imported urban refuse, Charlie Russell told Joe DeYong about a bull-whacking freighter named "Roaring Tom Moore," who would "gather empty cans and dump them where he camped to make the other bull outfits think he was living good."[92] In the rapidly changing western frontier regions, urban trash, like the household junk surrounding the hung-over "Big Man," also could seem like a high-status achievement.

HIGHWOOD HANK QUITS

Among Charlie Russell's roasting stories of cattle-range friends, his tale "Highwood Hank Quits"[93] holds a special position. The author not only scorches his longtime friend and Great Falls neighbor Henry Keeton, he also gives himself, "Kid Russell," a thorough roasting as well. Narrator "Rawhide Rawlins" lists the damning evidence of Kid Russell's incompetence as a bronc rider and his frantic efforts to sit in the saddle while trying to stay atop the mean-tempered horses of the notorious "P" cattle outfit:

> Kid Russell tells me . . . when he quit, his fingernails was all wore off an' there wasn't a hoss in his string that had any mane from his ears to his withers. There was spur tracks all over his saddle. He couldn't eat supper thinkin' of the hoss he had to fork the next mornin', and he never made no try at breakfast. His hands are so shakey . . .

FIG. 74. Charles M. Russell, *The Bucker,* 1904. Watercolor and gouache on paper, courtesy of the Sid Richardson Collection of Western Art, Fort Worth, Texas. Russell depicts a skilled bronc rider who avoids holding the saddle ("grabbing leather") while somehow staying aboard a thrashing, bellowing, diving, bucking horse.

that he has to get a friend to roll his cigarettes. . . . [I]t takes a solid year to get the crooks out of his hands from havin' 'em clamped 'round the saddle horn.[94]

Any one of these facts would serve as embarrassing proof that Russell was a desperate rider on any jumpy horse. The accumulation of exaggerated (but plausible) details adds to the humor and Russell's widespread reputation among fellow cowpunchers as a poorer-than-average horseman.

Although he could paint someone riding the "correct" way on a pitching bronc—without grasping anything, especially parts of the saddle as in "grabbing leather"—Russell's own ability to ride was limited to mild-mannered horses. He never claimed to be a "top hand" cowboy and had no illusions about his abilities with wilder horses.[95] He became embarrassed and angry in later years when his celebrity status provoked others to misrepresent him as an excellent rider and range hand. As he told Joe DeYong, "It makes me sore when they spring a lot of my talk that I never said[.] They tell what a bronk twister and roper I am and men that know me think I been filling them up."[96] Even as an older man far removed from the open range, Russell remained immersed in cattle-culture values in which bragging, especially about nonexistent accomplishments, was considered very bad form. In a letter to an admiring fan, who must have favored Russell with a bit of flattering poetry, the artist avoids a chance to boast and, instead, gently corrects the inaccurate poem:

> Ltn R. Hoss, Dear Sir, I receved your poem It was good and well ment but would hardly do as historical as the first bronc I forked threw me so high that the boys caught him before I hit the ground an when I lit it jarred my memory so I will never forget an al tho I have ridden maney years I never reached fame as a broncho buster when riding weavers dipers sunfishers sky scrapers wornfencers I yoked my stirrups an used all advantages known to the punchers Thankin you just the same yours sincerely C M Russell[97]

In this letter, Russell reveals his sense of "history" as involving accurate depiction of known facts, despite some exaggeration, at his own expense, for comic effect. Also, by roasting himself before the reading public in "Highwood Hank," Russell fulfilled a wide appreciation among western cowpunchers for self-depreciating humor. In Russell's literary world, the roasting process included virtually anyone, including the author and chief perpetrator of many outrageous roasts.[98] As Joe DeYong recalled Russell's own words, "Nobody is important enough to feel important."[99]

The Highwood Hank roast also signals a momentary emergence of women, other than female Indians, in Russell's stories. In this narrative, Hank tries to complete the dangerous work to "break" some wild horses for use on his small ranch, despite already being an aging grandfather. He ignores his wife's timid warning and twice ends his ride earlier than intended, sitting in a heap of dust at the feet of the victorious horse. Although Hank is facing the end of his bronc-riding career, a more difficult problem surfaces. Hank not only embarrasses himself in front of his wife when he loses to the horse, he makes himself even more ridiculous by blaming her for his failure:

Where Highwood Hank Quits
HISTORICAL RECOLLECTIONS OF RAWHIDE RAWLINS

Rawhide Rawlins.

When I first knowed Highwood Hank he's a cowpuncher and is pretty handy among broncs," says Rawhide Rawlins. "In them days he's ridin' for the P, and anybody that savvies that iron knows they never owned a hoss that wasn't a snake. A man had to be a rider to work for 'em. If a hoss thief found a P hoss in his bunch at daybreak, it's a cinch he'd turn him loose. P hosses was notorious.

"Kid Russell tells me he rode one summer for Ben Phillips, who owned that brand. He claimed he didn't take on no flesh that year. When he quit his fingernails was all wore off an' there wasn't a hoss in his string that had any mane from his ears to his withers. There was spur tracks all over his saddle. He couldn't ever eat supper thinkin' of the hoss he had to fork the next mornin', and he never made no try at breakfast. His hands is so shaky all that spring that he has to get a friend to roll his cigarettes, an' if he'd worked a whole season his fingers would be wore down to the knuckles. As it is it takes a solid year to get the crooks out of his hands from havin' 'em clamped 'round the saddle horn.

"As I said before, Hank's a rider, but like all others, old Daddy Time has hung it on him. It seems these days like his backbone has growed together in places an' it don't take to the swing of a pitchin' bronc. Hank's married now, and he's a granddad. He still owns a ranch and rides, but they ain't the long circles he used to make.

"A couple of years ago Hank runs in a bunch of broncs. They're rollin' fat an' pretty snuffy. He drops his rope on to one, an' the minute his loop tightens Mr. Bronc swings 'round, comin' at Hank with his ears up, whistlin' like a bull elk. In the old days this would a-been music to Hank's ears. It takes him back to the P string.

"Mrs. Hank's lookin' through the corral fence an' begs Hubby not to crawl this one. He tells her not to worry.

"'All you got to do it sit back an' watch me scratch his shoulders,' he says. 'You won't have to pay no railroad fare to Miles City to see bronc ridin',' he tells her. 'This is goin' to be home talent.'

"'He'll throw you,' says she.

"'Yes he will,' says Hank, as he cinches his hull on.

"This bronc's got his near ear dropped down an' about half of his eye shows white. He's humped till

"Yes You Did."

you could throw a dog under the saddle skirts behind Hank's whistlin' 'Turkey in the Straw' to keep his sand up, an' his wife notices there's a tremble in his hand as he reaches for the horn.

"The minute the bronc feels weight on the near stirrup he starts for the clouds, an' the second time he comes down Hank ain't with him. He's sittin' on the ground with two hands full of corral dust.

"'I told you so,' says Wifie.

"'Yes you did,' says Hank. 'You're a fine partner, sittin' there like you're deaf an' dumb. Any time I ever rode a bronc before there's always been somebody around to yell: "Stay with him—hang an' rattle." You didn't give me no encouragement. Just lookin' at you scared me loose.'

"'All right,' says Mrs. Hank, 'I'll try and do better next time.'

"But the next one is a shorter ride than the first. His better half yells 'Stay with him,' but it's as Hank hits the ground.

"'I hollered that time,' says she.

"'Yes you did,' says Hank. 'Why didn't you wait till New Years?'

Hank hates to do it, but he has to own up that his bronc ridin' days is over."

FIG. 75. *Where Highwood Hank Quits,* by Charles M. Russell. Pen/ink, in *Harlowton Press* (MNA), December 10, 1917; also in *Rawhide Rawlins Stories* and *Trails Plowed Under.* The original caption for the illustration, "Yes you did," translates into the sarcastic slang of later generations as "Sure you did!" The caption in *Trails Plowed Under* became "Hank's sittin' on the ground with two hands full of corral dust."

FIG. 76.

Henry Keeton, detail of photograph, "Cowboys at Umbrella
Spring, Denton, 1883." Photograph
courtesy of the Montana Historical
Society, Helena. Nineteen-year-old
Charlie Russell sits in the background (right).

"You're a fine partner, sittin' there like you're deaf and dumb. Any time I ever rode
a bronc before, there's always been somebody around to tell me to stay with him—
to hang an' rattle. You didn't give me any encouragement. Just lookin' at you scared
me loose."[100]

Charlie Russell's story shows Henry Keeton's life at a low point. Hank not only must accept the
limitations of his age and give up trying to dominate wild horses all by himself, he must also
make amends for losing his temper with his wife, a supportive woman who simply cannot
appreciate his need for life-threatening, bronco-busting efforts.

Several decades after Highwood Hank learned his limits the hard way, another Montana
cattleman followed in his tracks. Rancher/writer Spike Van Cleve describes a remarkably similar incident a generation later:

when I picked myself up, I was beginning to realize that this bay bitch could buck a
little, but I caught her and got in the [saddle].

I screwed down tight, ready for her to blow the plug, and she did. I took up another homestead, and when Barbara said anxiously, "I wish you wouldn't get on her again, Spike," I told her, "Goddammit, can't you give a man a little encouragement instead of just standing there like a bump on a log?"

"OK," she said and when the filly blew again she called, "Stay with her," but the hell of it was that I heard the last two words just about the time my shoulders hit the ground.

"I'll say it quicker this time," Barbara assured me, and she did. Didn't seem to help a bit or maybe it was just plumb impossible to say it fast enough![101]

Harvard-educated, Van Cleve had evolved enough as a Montana ranchman to curse at his wife (with the kids present) and put it in his writing, thereby abandoning an earlier generation's male behavior code of "no-cursing-in-front-of-women-and-kids." And his newer version of the "can't-do-that-anymore" awakening for an aging cowboy should serve as evidence that Russell's "Highwood Hank" story actually distilled an archetypal legend out of the simple narration of a friendly roast. As Russell would articulate in his twentieth-century stories (to be examined in chapter 6), the final stages of western cattle-range evolution brought new roles for women. Hank's problems reflect an early stage of the confusing changes in work and gender roles that bewildered many nineteenth-century western men as they attempted to adjust to women in modern times.

FIG. 77. Charles M. Russell, *School Boys and Teacher* (or *We Love Our Lovin' Teacher*). Pen/ink, C. M. Russell Museum, Great Falls, Montana. Illustration for the story "When Mix Went to School," published in the *Medicine Lake Wave,* MNA, April 1, 1918, and in *Rawhide Rawlins Stories.* Charlie's boyhood schoolteachers in St. Louis enforced classroom order with brute force.

When Mix Went to School

The geographic scope of Charlie Russell's cattle-era stories spread east to west across the country, well beyond the axis extending from Con Price's home near the Canadian border down to Longrope's trail drive from Texas. Russell's story "A Ride in a Moving Cemetery" takes place in California.[102] And his humorous yarn about the lumberjack's offspring battling with schoolteachers, in "When Mix Went to School," is set in upstate New York.[103]

In the New York story, the parents hire an unemployed boxer to subdue their renegade children—a solution that reflects the author's enthusiasm for boxing. This story of violent school discipline roasted one Charlie Mix, a former operator of a Judith Basin stagecoach outpost and later a popular bartender in the mountain village of Neihart, Montana, not far from Utica.[104] Russell also wrote this story with a strong personal perspective, having clashed physically in his youth with more than one male schoolteacher. "As near as I can remember," says the narrator, "them he-schoolmarms we had was made of the same material as a bronco buster. Anyway the one I went to back in Missouri had every kid whip-broke."[105] Although "Rawhide Rawlins" supposedly provides a description of Mix's misadventures, the words also speak for Russell's own childhood. The students' fistfight brawl with the teacher stayed within the horse culture: in the end, the lumberjacks' scrappy boys were "all broke gentle."[106]

FIG. 78.
Jack Dempsey and Charlie Russell, 1923. Photograph courtesy of the Montana Historical Society. A boxing enthusiast, Charlie Russell attended the champ's Great Falls training camp and heavyweight title bout with Tommy Gibbons in Shelby, Montana. Despite Dempsey's similarities with Russell's boxer sketch, however, Charlie met the "Manassas Mauler" four years *after* publishing his illustrated story on the boxing "school marm."

A Ride in a Moving Cemetery

At the other end of the country, Charlie Russell's only California-based story signals the end of his nineteenth-century focus on the culture of the horse-and-cattle West and his shift to looking at the "modern times" of the early twentieth century. His story "A Ride in a Moving Cemetery" tells how two very drunk westerners smash their horse-drawn buggy into the side of a fast-moving freight train near the northern California town of Los Gatos. The survivor of the wreck, Russell's humorous narrator "Rawhide Rawlins," awakens several hundred miles farther north, lying on a rail flatcar full of cemetery gravestones. The disoriented narrator finally learns from a newspaper account that his buggy partner, their rig, and both horses perished in the collision.

This "Moving Cemetery" yarn resembles popular literary devices used in the nineteenth century to represent the intrusion of the industrial revolution into pastoral America. The American Studies scholar Leo Marx discusses similar themes in *The Machine in the Garden*,[107] pointing to Nathaniel Hawthorne's reverie in Sleepy Hollow (near Concord, Massachusetts) and Henry David Thoreau at Walden Pond as two writers who expressed negative reactions to a passing, loud steam locomotive. In another work, the sudden destruction of Huck and Jim's flimsy raft by a monstrous steamboat that looms suddenly out of a foggy night, in *The Adventures of Huckleberry Finn*,[108] also provided Marx with an example of destructive steam-powered machines altering nature and disturbing nature-oriented people in the nineteenth century. Art historian James Moore notes that, when compared with steamboats, "the train symbolized to some a greater degree of separation from nature, which resulted in the expression of conflicting attitudes regarding the moral worth of progress as embodied in the locomotive . . . 'that Juggernaut of Progress which everywhere violates the sacred presence of nature.'"[109] The steamboat might have seemed disruptive, but no more so than the locomotive that plows destructively through Russell's graveyard humor.

Charlie Russell's "Moving Cemetery" seems to parody Marx's examples of the literary ideal of a "pastoral heaven." In an "Eden" within fifty miles of the western coast of North America, two delirious riders find idyllic bliss driving a matched team of fine horses along the smoothest road in California. Although they artificially induce their euphoria with "corn juice" whiskey, the carefree western narrator notices that "the whole world right now looks so beautiful to me that there's no chance for an argument from religion to Teddy Roosevelt to the best brand of red-eye." The sudden impact of the collision ejects Rawhide Rawlins from the horse-and-buggy world and scrambles his transportation metaphors between airplanes and trains.

> I recollect Bill reachin' for the reins, and the next I know I've got a vague notion
> I'm in an airship and can see clear to the Mexican line. I'm wonderin' where I
> changed cars when the light goes out.[110]

Russell's representatives of the nineteenth century—two hard-drinking, horse-loving westerners—collide full-force with the primary symbol of modern industrial society for Russell's lifetime—the railroad. The self-blinded westerners have little chance to survive such an encounter and the uncaring train does not even slow down after the collision's impact. In his handling of

FIG. 79. Charles M. Russell, *He Tried to Cut a Freight in Two.* Pen/ink, illustration for the story "A Ride in A Moving Cemetery," first appeared in the *Harlowton Press* (MNA), March 19, 1917, with the story title add-on "Or How Rube the Reckless Came Close to the Cash In," which was dropped in later printings. The illustration reappeared in *Rawhide Rawlins Stories* but not in *Trails Plowed Under*.

this machine-in-the-garden theme, Russell's "Moving Cemetery" qualifies easily as an end-of-an-era allegory.

From the quickly passing cattle era, Russell crafted embarrassing legends to celebrate good people like Pete Van. He assembled Longrope's cattle drive, which is historically correct but romantically obsolete. He rose beyond the escapism of wishful nostalgia for the past, however, by providing the wake-up alarms of "Night Herd" and "Moving Cemetery." Sobering up in a small town's dump-pile or on a gravestone freight car would be painful, but Russell knew that failing to awaken quickly would mean a deadly finish like the one that Charlie Bowlegs experienced. Wide-awake adaptation became Russell's wisest theme in his cattle-era stories.

For those characters whose adaptation remains incomplete, like many of the figures in these stories, Russell makes them receive the brunt of his jokes. Without adaptive change, a nineteenth-century broncobuster wastes his efforts on an absent girlfriend. An aging rancher blames his own failures on a spouse who neither encourages victory nor sympathizes with his defeat in a struggle to dominate a horse—a fight that has lost its practical purpose. Both Con Price and Highwood Hank end up sitting bruised in the dust, disappointed for want of connection with females. They find themselves at the losing end of unstoppable changes that are making their work-identities obsolete. In the end, even the pleasures of the best whiskey and the finest horses prove to be no match for the unyielding changes brought by the industrial revolution's freight train. In Charlie Russell's cattle-range yarns, the westerners who survive must wake up from the sentimental nostalgia of Long Rope's timeless story and adapt to present-day life in the twentieth-century West.

PLATE 1. Charles M. Russell, *The Story Teller*. 1915. Watercolor on paper, from the collection of Gilcrease Museum, Tulsa, Oklahoma *(see back cover)*.

PLATE 2. Charles M. Russell, *Laugh Kills Lonesome*, 1925. Oil on canvas, Mackay Collection, Montana Historical Society, Helena *(see page 8)*.

PLATE 3.
Charles M. Russell,
The Storyteller.
Watercolor, Buffalo
Bill Historical
Center, Cody,
Wyoming;
No. L.77.86.4.;
special loan from
Mr. and Mrs.
W. D. Weiss
(see page 22).

PLATE 4.
Charles M. Russell,
Prospectors, ca. 1897.
Watercolor on paper,
courtesy of the Woody
Boudeman collection on
loan to the Kalamazoo
Institute for the Arts,
Kalamazoo, Michigan
(see page 39).

PLATE 5. Charles M. Russell, *When Blackfeet and Sioux Meet,* 1908. Oil on canvas, courtesy of the Sid Richardson Collection of Western Art, Fort Worth, Texas *(see page 60).*

PLATE 6. Charles M. Russell, *When White Men Turn Red,* 1922. Oil on canvas, courtesy of the Sid Richardson Collection of Western Art, Fort Worth, Texas *(see page 68).*

PLATE 7. Charles M. Russell, *Returning to Camp,* 1901. Oil on canvas, courtesy of the Sid Richardson Collection of Western Art, Fort Worth, Texas *(see page 70).*

PLATE 8. Charles M. Russell, *Beauty Parlor,* 1907. Watercolor, Trigg Collection, C. M. Russell Museum, Great Falls, Montana *(see page 70).*

PLATE 9. Charles M. Russell, *York,* 1909. Oil on canvas, gift of the artist, Montana Historical Society, Helena *(see page 76).*

PLATE 10. Charles M. Russell, *The Fireboat,* 1918. Oil on board, gift of Mrs. Wade George in memory of Wade Hampton George, courtesy of the C. M. Russell Museum, Great Falls, Montana *(see page 86).*

PLATE 11.
Charles M. Russell, *Bull Head Lodge*, 1906. Watercolor on birch bark, Buffalo Bill Historical Center, Cody, Wyoming; Gift of Charles Ulrick and Josephine Bay Foundation, Inc., no. 90.60 *(see page 100).*

PLATE 12. Charles M. Russell, *The Exalted Ruler*, 1912. Oil on canvas, gift of the Friends of the Exalted Ruler, C. M. Russell Museum, Great Falls, Montana *(see page 102).*

PLATE 13.

Charles M. Russell, *"Brother," said Quo-too-Quat to the Wolf, "Have You Seen the White Buffalo Lately?"* ca. 1915. Watercolor, courtesy of the Otha Wearin Family Collection, on loan to the C. M. Russell Museum, Great Falls, Montana *(see page 125).*

PLATE 14. Charles M. Russell, *Lone Wolf,* 1900. Oil on canvas, courtesy of the J. M. Hoover Collection, on loan to the C. M. Russell Museum, Great Falls, Montana *(see page 125).*

PLATE 15. Charles M. Russell, *The Wolves.* Watercolor and gouache on paper, 1914, R2028, Glenbow Museum, Calgary, Canada *(see page 125)*.

PLATE 16. Charles M. Russell, *Man's Weapons Are Useless When Nature Goes Armed* (or *Two of a Kind Win*), 1916. Oil, courtesy of the Sid Richardson Collection of Western Art, Fort Worth, Texas *(see page 128)*.

PLATE 17. Charles M. Russell, *Meat's Not Meat 'Till It's In The Pan*, 1915. Oil on canvas. From the collection of the Gilcrease Museum, Tulsa, Oklahoma *(see page 128)*.

PLATE 18.

Charles M. Russell, *When I was a Kid*, 1905. Watercolor on paper, courtesy of Ginger Renner *(see page 133)*.

PLATE 19.
Charles M. Russell, *Mankiller,* 1911. Watercolor on paper, no. 59.15.14, Glenbow Museum, Calgary, Canada. This image resembles Russell's bronze sculpture, *When the Best of Riders Quit.* *(see page 151).*

PLATE 20. Charles M. Russell, *In Without Knocking,* 1909. Oil on canvas, no. 1961.201, Amon Carter Museum, Fort Worth, Texas *(see page 154).*

PLATE 21.
Charles M. Russell,
Trail Boss, ca. 1897.
Watercolor, from
the collection of
Martha Parfet on
loan to the Kalamazoo
Institute for the Arts,
Kalamazoo, Michigan
(see page 155).

PLATE 22. Charles M. Russell, *A Quiet Day in Utica* (or *Tin Canning a Dog*), 1907. Oil on canvas, courtesy of the Sid Richardson Collection of Western Art, Fort Worth, Texas *(see page 178).*

PLATE 23. Charles M. Russell, *The Old Story* (or *The Life Lines*), 1910. Watercolor, gift of R. F. Jennings and M. A. Dutton, the C. M. Russell Museum, Great Falls, Montana *(see page 183)*.

PLATE 24. Charles M. Russell, *Hooverizing*, 1918. Watercolor on paperboard, from the collection of the Gilcrease Museum, Tulsa, Oklahoma *(see page 197)*.

PLATE 25.
Charles M. Russell, *Meat Makes Fighters*, 1918. Watercolor on paperboard, from the collection of the Gilcrease Museum, Tulsa, Oklahoma *(see page 197)*.

PLATE 26. Charles M. Russell, *Keeoma*, 1896. Oil on academy board, no. 1961.148, Amon Carter Museum, Fort Worth, Texas *(see page 199)*.

PLATE 29. Charles M. Russell, *Letter to Friend Percy* (Raban), April 20, 1914. Watercolor on paper, Buffalo Bill Historical Center, Cody, Wyoming; gift of William E. Weiss, no. 70.60 *(see page 244).*

PLATE 30. Charles M. Russell, *Fool and Knight,* 1914. Watercolor, Trigg Collection, C. M. Russell Museum, Great Falls, Montana *(see page 244).*

PLATE 31.

Cover jacket for B. M. Bower's novel *The Lure of Dim Trails*, illustrated by Charles M. Russell, frontispiece title: *Out Where the Trails of Men are Dim and Far Apart* (New York: Grosset and Dunlap, 1907) *(see page 246).*

PLATE 32.

Cover for Walt Coburn's western novel *Pardners of the Dim Trails,* cover illustrator unknown.(New York, Popular Library edition, J. B. Lippincott Company, 1940) *(see page 246).*

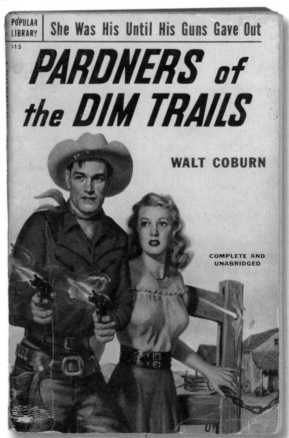

CHAPTER SIX

Modern Times in the Twentieth-Century West

A machine is made
A horse is born
No four-wheel brakes
No screaming horn
But hooves make tracks
That wheels don't know
With saddle, cinch and latigo.[1]

*I*n the early decades of the twentieth century, residents of the trans-Mississippi West moved to keep pace with other more prosperous regions by encouraging urban growth and farm mechanization. Although few of Charlie Russell's paintings reflect the transition to a new West, as noted by historian Richard Etulain,[2] the artist did not ignore the twentieth century altogether. He published stories containing many informative twentieth-century elements. Russell clearly preferred to represent colorful moments of the nineteenth-century West when he painted, sketched, and sculpted. Writing a personal letter in the early twentieth century, Russell told a fellow old-time cowpuncher, "Shaps, spurs and boots and big hat don't make riders. Neither does bib overalls and caps make pictures and stories."[3] More than his paintings and sculptures, however, Russell's stories and essays reflect influences of the bewildering twentieth-century customs and ideas that westerners began to encounter on ranches and farms and especially when they went to town. Russell recognized well enough that, in a period of accelerated

FIG. 80. Charles M. Russell, *Dude Wrangler*, 1925. Pen/ink, courtesy of the Loren Smith Collection, on loan to the C. M. Russell Museum, Great Falls, Montana. Russell provided this sketch and poem for use as letterhead stationary by the Park Saddle Horse Company, in Glacier National Park.

modernization, whether transitioning to a "New West," to an "Urban Oasis," or simply into modern times "way out west," survival was a matter of alert adaptation. In several ways, then, Russell's writing adapted to the transitional West more than his paintings and sculptures.

Despite his clear preference for the region during the nineteenth century that he called the "Old West," Charlie Russell contended with twentieth-century issues in thirteen of his forty-seven published stories and essays. The writings provide revealing scenes of nineteenth-century westerners coping with powerful railroads, horses devalued by automobiles and tractors, moralistic social reforms, independent-minded women, the Great War in Europe, and domestic tourism in the West. Reflecting Russell's bias as well as his wisdom, these published anecdotes deliver a firsthand perspective of the writer's modern-day world, often distorted in comic exaggerations, of the awkward transitions of the American West into the twentieth century.

In 1880, Charlie Russell arrived in Montana just before steam-driven riverboats on the Missouri River lost their commercial viability to overland steam railroads. These new technologies enabled large numbers of European-Americans to visit and populate Montana and other western regions. Aware of the disruptive impact of steam transportation on the wilderness and open range, Russell told a *New York Times* reporter in 1911, "If I had my way I'd put steam out of business."[4] Despite his antimechanical attitude, Russell took advantage of transportation opportunities and often enjoyed himself in the process. On some occasions, long train trips

FIG. 81. Charles M. Russell, *Take One With Me, Fred,* 1907. Watercolor and pen/ink, Permanent Collection, C. M. Russell Museum, Great Falls, Montana. A personal Christmas card for Fred Tharp, railroad engineer for the Great Northern. In the following year, Charlie Russell fully stopped drinking alcohol, but continued to socialize in saloons and to depict himself holding up a whiskey bottle to his friends.

FIG. 82.

Charles M. Russell at a train depot, 1917. Photograph courtesy of the C. M. Russell Museum, Great Falls, Montana. Charlie added a sketch with his signature on the photograph, contrasting train transport with horse-packing, telling a friend, "I'm traveling different now."

provided an opportunity for hours of storytelling with friends and strangers. Montana resident Wilford Johnson could recall the train ride to Miles City during his youth when he witnessed Russell and Teddy Blue Abbot telling astonishing stories for more than five hours, an incident that showed how Russell could make the best of a dull train ride.

BILL'S SHELBY HOTEL

Among his "modern"-era story characters, Charlie Russell also demonstrated some adaptability to rail travel. His roast of a hotel operator in "Bill's Shelby Hotel" portrays (or satirizes) Bill Ward's youthful travel techniques. "Rawhide Rawlins" explains that, when Bill attains manhood,

> he takes a dislike to work, an' after hoardin' his wages of three dollars a month for eight years, he just naturally steps underneath a freight train one mornin' with his bankroll an' takes a seat on the rods. He gives one lingerin' look at the old home-stead and tells the brakeman he can turn her loose.[5]

Russell's sense of humor plays on the nearly suicidal act of casually perching close to sudden death, when an illegal rider would stretch his body across the steel rods that hung beneath a railroad freight car passing just inches above the railroad's cross ties. Russell's listeners would have understood the humor in a hobo telling the brakeman to start the train rolling as if he were a ticket-buying passenger speaking to a train conductor. Despite packing a roll of cash, a cheapskate hobo like Bill would be hiding under the freight car, fearing discovery and arrest, and unlikely to give such an order to his adversary. The entire scene is humorously absurd in a way that would have amused Russell's knowledgeable audiences and embarrassed his roasting victim.

Western hospitality for a hobo-tourist like Bill varies from town to town as the train in Russell's story visits the urbanizing West. After several train stops, each followed by arrests, detention, and expulsion by local police, Bill disembarks in one town where he is only "as wel-come as his remainin' two dollars an' a half, which is good for just ten drinks." Eventually, Bill's train tour arrives in the new town of Shelby where he is welcomed despite his dusty face and clothes, but only welcome until he asks a skittish hotel clerk for a room with a bath. "[I]t's too much for the clerk, who has a nervous temperament and has spent the previous evenin' drinkin' Shelby Lemonade, an' he shoots Bill's hat off." Bill soon wins the hotel in a poker game, and, with it, he acquires a rough-looking "chef." Russell's description of Bill Ward's cook con-denses colorful information and innuendo that he matches with a vivid pen/ink sketch of a very unpleasant figure. As narrator "Rawhide Rawlins" puts it, Bill's chef

> hangs up a bet of a hundred dollars that with the use of a can opener, he can feed more cowpunchers an' sheep-herders than any other cook west of the Mississippi. There's never no complaint about the meat, either, for this cook's as good with a gun as he is with a can opener. In fact no one ever claims he ain't a good cook after takin' one look at him.[6]

FIG. 83. Charles M. Russell, *Bill's Chef.* Pen/ink, courtesy of the C. M. Russell Museum, Great Falls, Montana. Illustration for the (MNA) story "How Bill Broke into the Hotel Business on October 15, 1917," retitled in *Rawhide Rawlins* and *Trails Plowed Under* as "Bill's Shelby Hotel." Russell had many sour memories from unpleasant direct encounters on the cattle range with other bad-tempered camp cooks who may have resembled this one.

Bill adapts to the rough new town of Shelby and his newly acquired hotel. At the same time, his no-nonsense chef adapts to modernity by feeding customers from urban tin cans.

In this dual example, both the Russell sketch and his distilled narrative description deliver a double load of comic and cultural information about a tough western character "type." A balanced understanding of Russell's historical ideas and intent comes from the combination of his words and his picture images as a complementary unit. A basic lesson about those earlier times was that the cook is always right, no matter how he looks.

Despite the friendly sarcasm and exaggerated portrait of the "chef," Russell admitted in later years to having more vivid memories (for good or ill) of Bill's food service when compared with his more dignified professional enterprise—the Rainbow Hotel in Great Falls:

> the hotel grub is fair but dont compare with the table that Bill Ward set up in his Shelby Hotel I aint saying nothing agin the Rainbow but Ward will never run another feed joint like that one in dear old Shelby where he got his start. No one that ever fed there can forget it.[7]

Russell's nostalgia for the food at Bill Ward's Shelby hotel, however, did not prevent him from emphasizing the smoke, flies, menacing and filthy cook, and occasional violence that highlighted Shelby's transition into a twentieth-century town.

Adaptation remains the underlying message in this hotel yarn. Russell insults his friend Bill Ward with this satire of his first lodging venture, referring to the primitive hotel as a place where flies prefer to spend the cold winter months. "For a home-like, congenial place for a fly to live, you couldn't beat Bill's hotel,"[8] says Rawhide. At the same time, Bill learns from the experience of this rough first attempt, apparently, because in the beginning and ending of the piece Russell praises Bill's work in Great Falls, operating several modern hotels, and ready to open a new resort on scenic Flathead Lake.

The story of Bill Ward's hotel also shows that the town of Shelby adapts from its wild, cow-town ways, responding to James Hill's threat to relocate his east-to-west Great Northern Railroad farther to the north "an' cut out Shelby, preferrin' to climb the Sweetgrass Hills to runnin' his trains through this jolly bunch."[9] Hill's threat, apparently, was serious.[10] As one cow-puncher recalled, "Shelby at that time was one store, two saloons, and a blacksmith shop. Gold Butte [forty-five miles to the north] was the bigger town."[11] (Little remained of Gold Butte by the end of the twentieth century.) Somehow, Shelby reforms itself to reassure Hill and keep the crucial railroad service. Although reform is not always a welcome concept in Russell's stories (Russell respected only a few social reformers, such as Brother Van), in "Bill's Shelby Hotel" both the main character and the little Montana town face their shortcomings, make adaptations, and ultimately prosper. By the early 1920s, Shelby became the supply headquarters for a local oil boom at the Kevin-Sunburst oil-well field. And it gained worldwide notoriety (and a serious financial crisis) by sponsoring the 1923 heavyweight boxing championship match between Jack Dempsey and Tommy Gibbons.[12]

A less ambitious little town, like Utica, missed the blessings and problems of the railroad and tourism, and a bit of nineteenth-century prosperity from nearby cattle and mining interests proved unable to sustain much vitality in the twentieth century. Shelby continues to prosper in the twenty-first century at the intersection of a highway, an interstate freeway, and a major railroad intersection, while Utica must share a post office with nearby Hobson and can sustain only one bar-restaurant (the Oxen Yoke) plus a local museum. Attempts in the 1980s to revive a general store and gas station in Utica failed years ago. In Russell's depiction of the town, *A Quiet Day in Utica* (or *Tin Canning a Dog*) (**see plate 22**), most figures in the picture are identifiable nineteenth-century Judith Basin characters (Brian Dippie calls it "a portrait gallery"), including the artist himself, leaning on the railing, and the person second to his left—Millie Ringgold, a black woman prospector—and L. B. Divers with his hands on his knees. The sons of the general store owner, Charles Lehman (in the doorway) commissioned the painting. The picture remains a source of pride for subsequent generations of residents.

WHISKEY

Other western urban communities in Russell stories must make adaptations and adjustments for survival in the twentieth century. In "Whiskey," Russell demonstrates that even a saloon beverage can adapt to become a social force. As Dick-the-barkeep explains to Russell-the-narrator,

"No," says Dick looking wise. "This ain't no cow-town no more. It's one of the coming farmer-cities of this country, and the sellers of all this rich land don't want nothing that'll scare away farmers, and I'm here to please the folks.... The old-timer that you knew was generally on the square. When he got drunk he wanted everybody to know it and they did, if they were in the same town.... The gent that sold me this brand of booze told me there ain't a cross word in a barrel of it, and he told the truth. All these gents you see in here are pleasant without the noise. This bunch, if they stay to the finish, will whisper themselves to sleep. This booze would be safe for a burglar. I call it," says Dick, "whisperin' booze."[13]

In Russell's narration, this revolutionary "whispering booze" accommodates the new farming community by keeping the saloon patrons quiet. The timid farmers who were relocating into the arid West in the early twentieth century already were conditioned by prohibition laws in their previous home states to adopt covert drinking habits. These devious drinkers contribute to the saloon's unnatural silence with their furtive, alcoholic binges that lack the loud vocalizing that was characteristic of the supposedly honest, hard-drinking cowboys of earlier days. In Russell's view of the West, however, silent saloon patrons were as unwelcome as the real estate sellers of good grazing land to farmers.

Although Charlie Russell achieved a midlife victory over alcohol use in 1908[14] (certainly one of his most difficult adaptations to modern times), he considered mandatory social reforms like Prohibition laws to be a repressive waste of time. Russell had enjoyed Great Falls and other cattle towns when they offered amusements for the free-spending cowboy clientele, including the gambling and prostitution that later-arriving residents found unacceptable. As the cattle industry declined in western towns, reform-minded citizens gained political control.[15] Western historian William Rowley describes this "struggle for modernity," stating:

> Reformers regarded gambling houses, brothels, and the ever-present saloon as a temporary disfunction of the passing frontier stage of society that must give way to order, progress, and moral enlightenment.

Rowley finds that the western reform motive grew from a sense of economic urgency with "boosters" desiring reform of society and government in the West in order to attract more settlers, investment capital, and overall growth.[16]

Charlie Russell and his audience of like-minded older westerners resented the reforms and the population increases that these civic boosters actively encouraged. Russell expressed some amusement that he had participated in western life before the reformers brought civilized culture to the West, telling a friend from the old days:

> Im shure glad I beet those morilests to the country its hard to guess what they would have don to me. Chances are Id be making hair bridles [in jail] now for smoking sigeretts or staying up after twelve oclock. but they got here too late to hed off my fun an as I am real good now I aint worring much[17]

Regarding the "boosters" who frequently sold real estate while encouraging urban expansion and the proliferation of farming on the western cattle ranges, Russell generally scorned all of them. In a long poem, "Here's to All Old Timers," dedicated to local author, pioneer rancher, and personal art patron Robert Vaughn, Russell concluded:

> Here's to Hell with the booster
> The land is no longer free,
> The worst old timer I ever knew
> Looks dam good to me.[18]

Charlie Russell's disapproval of the changes transforming the frontier West moved him to preserve narratives of singular experiences from earlier days. He understood that population growth and urbanization would not improve the quality of life in the West that he preferred, a conclusion often shared by environmentalists and social critics of the late twentieth century. Brian Dippie has observed, "Indeed, Charlie's backward-looking conservatism made him a forward-looking environmentalist."[19] Russell blamed the disappearance of colorful frontier characters and vivid old-timers on the booster's moralistic reforms. In the process of his condemnation of the moralists, however, Russell overlooked the truly destructive impacts of unfettered alcoholism, gambling, and prostitution on the lives of the participants, their families, and peers. The only reforms he could endorse were self-imposed by individuals on themselves (like his choice and struggle to stop drinking alcohol), not those imposed by social pressure and legislation (like Prohibition laws). By expressing his skepticism about population growth in the West in personal letters and published stories, Russell was a visionary spokesman for environmental protection. In his condemnation of social reforms in the urban West, however, he proved to be shortsighted with his wisdom blurred by big-hearted enthusiasm for a spontaneous western scene populated with vivid and uncompromising characters.

How Pat Discovered the Geyser

Although Shelby quieted the cowboys' social life enough to keep their railroad, other western towns had to make a geographical adaptation. Some had to move their buildings simply to remain near the tracks. In 1907, construction of the Great Northern Railroad southeastward from Great Falls into the Judith Basin completely bypassed a few upstart cow towns like Stanford, Geyser, and Utica. These clusters of dusty shacks had to relocate or wither up. Russell demonstrates urban displacement in this roast of Pat O'Hare:

> One afternoon when Pat's asleep the railroad sneaks in an' moves the town. The minute Pat opens his eyes he's onto their hole-card, and getting' the wheelbarrow, he moves his hotel over to the new location an' has his dinin' room open for supper.[20]

In Russell's comic version of coping with modern western railroad choices, Pat must wake up (in the afternoon) to the sudden changes and act quickly. The author teases O'Hare for having a "hotel" so flimsy that a stereotypical Irish wheelbarrow could relocate it in one

FIG. 84. Charles M. Russell, *Pat Moves His Hotel*. Pen/ink, illustration for the story "How Pat Discovered the Geyser," in the October 8, 1917, MNA weekly inserts and again in *Rawhide Rawlins Stories*, but omitted from *Trails Plowed Under*. Pat's use of a wheelbarrow reflects an ethnic symbol associated with lower-class Irish laborers.

shortened afternoon. In this roast, Russell reminds his modern-day audience of how quickly young western towns might need to react. According to one local historian, Pat O'Hare founded "old Geyser" to provide a stagecoach station for the Billings and Great Falls Stage Company linking other small towns in the Judith Basin, including Lavina, Maiden, Lewistown, Cottonwood, Ubet, Stanford, Armington, and Belt. Some of these places, including Ubet and Maiden, totally disappeared decades ago, whereas others like Lewistown, Stanford, and Belt have survived into the twenty-first century as small towns of less than ten thousand residents. Pat O'Hare, fresh off the boat from Ireland in 1880, "homesteaded and ranched the site where old Geyser was laid out in 1887."[21] There he built a stage station, hotel, saloon, blacksmith shop, hall, and store buildings out of logs hauled from nearby hills. He moved his own house, the only one made of milled lumber, during the relocation in 1908 to create "new Geyser." By this time O'Hare owned approximately eight thousand acres, which he ranched in partnership with Pete Van. Despite Russell's lighthearted character assassination, O'Hare held significant property in the area.

Pat O'Hare founded and then uprooted the stagecoach stop named Geyser in response to shifting transportation systems, first the stagecoach line and then the railroad. Russell became

FIG. 85. Hotel Geyser and Geyser Saloon, ca. 1900. Photograph courtesy of the Judith Basin County Museum, Stanford, Montana. Despite Russell's roasts, Pat prospered in ranching and in hotel and saloon management.

more tolerant of rail technology just as the sudden emergence of automobiles seemed to engulf him with yet another example of excessive industrial development. In his interview with local historian A. J. Noyes, Russell announced flatly, "There is altogether too much civilization," and then went on to denounce the automobile as the primary cause for the imbalance:

> I have a saddle horse and ride each morning, but a fellow has to ride in the alleys, if he rides in the city, as the pavements are so smooth a horse can't keep his feet. There was a time when I could tie my horse in Central [A]venue in front of the Silver Dollar, but a fellow would be in a h___ of a fix now as there are too many autos; you can't get near the sidewalk. My wife has an auto and I ride with her once in a while but I just as leave go in a streetcar.[22]

In this interview, rather than making a bitter complaint, Russell may have been smiling as he delivered an ironic observation for a like-minded old friend who would appreciate the dry humor in his statement. Read decades later, Russell's words seem almost angry. Despite his

FIG. 86. Charles M. Russell, *White Man's Skunk Wagon*, 1907. Watercolor and pen/ink, printed as a commercial postcard. Charlie adopted the scornful Blackfeet term for automobiles as part of his own lingo.

role as a cultural interpreter, however, Charlie Russell's resistance to autos did not represent a universal cowpuncher attitude. Former range hands, including Pete Van and national celebrity Will Rogers, took a liking to the exciting machines that the Blackfeet and Charlie Russell referred to as "skunk-wagons."

Seeing his fellow cowpunchers getting behind the wheel inspired one of Russell's great satirical roasts. Automobiles appear in Russell's published works very few times, with the major exception being the yarn roasting Pat O'Hare. As narrator Rawhide Rawlins observes, "When automobiles get popular, Pat who's always progressive an' up-to-date, buys one." But during a casual ride to a nearby town, the car transporting O'Hare, his partner Pete Van, and an unnamed friend gradually runs out of control:

> after passin' what looks like Stanford as far as he could tell at the 80-mile gait they're goin', an' seein' they're nearin' Judith Gap, the friend asks, "What's your hurry, Pat?" "I'm in no hurry," Pat yelled, "but I'm damned if I know how to stop the thing. We'll have to let it run down."[23]

In some Russell artworks the horses and automobiles seem compatible and in others they are clearly at odds. For example, Russell painted *The Old Story* (or *The Life Lines*) (**see plate 23**) and another image of a family wagon and automobile encounter as commercial illustrations

FIG. 87. Charles M. Russell, *The Big Stack Is Our Land Mark,* 1908. Logo for the Silver Dollar Saloon, watercolor and pen/ink, courtesy of the Great Falls Elks Club Collection, Montana Historical Society, Helena. This is one of Russell's few light-hearted images either of automobiles or the imposing Anaconda smelter.

for a wagon-seat safety device. Just as the collision in his story "A Ride in A Moving Cemetery" suggests the clash between horse-centered life in the nineteenth century and the machine-driven life in subsequent decades, Pat's runaway car demonstrates Russell's sarcastic attitude about the out-of-control machines of modern times.

THE HORSE

Because of the arrival of automobiles in the West, Charlie Russell's favorite means of transportation and animal companionship—the horses—lost their economic and cultural primacy early in the twentieth century. New gasoline tractors and mechanized farm "combines" assisted the World War I bonanza wheat harvests that also put thousands of farm horses out of a job in the new century's second decade. The subsequent horse "lay-offs" added to the growing herds of abandoned and unwanted horses on western ranges.[24] In 1918, the state veterinarian of Montana estimated that two hundred thousand common range horses were crowding cattle and sheep from the state's grazing sites. In the same MNA newspaper insert sections that were publishing Russell's stories, the state vet advocated the establishment of horse slaughterhouses and meat-packing facilities to ship horse meat to Europe for human consumption.[25] Russell objected strongly to cattlemen and other friends about the abomination of killing these range horses for human food, pet feed, and fertilizer.[26] In further reaction to this trend, Charlie Russell published an especially blunt, personal statement within his story "The Horse":

> Even now [the horse] builds the roads for the automobile that has made him near-ly useless, an' I'm here to tell these machine lovers that it will take a million years for the gas wagon to catch up with the hoss in what he's done for man. To-day some of these auto drivers want to kill him off to make fertilizer out of his body. Mebby I'm sentimental, but I think its a damned hard finish for one that has been as good a friend to man as the hoss.[27]

Clearly, Charlie Russell reacted emotionally to this change in the role of horses. As Con Price explained, "Charlie loved horses almost like human beings."[28] In even more blunt terms, Russell wrote to a friend, "any man that likes a cyuse is a friend of mine. . . . I never knew a horse lover that was mean man." And in the same letter, Russell vents his scorn on any partici-pants in the horse-meat roundups: "aney old timer that ships horses to butchers is worse than a canible they only killed thair enemyes this new range hog eats his friends."[29] Many of Charlie's friends, like-minded westerners from the open-range days including Pete Van, Pat O'Hare, and even Charlie's celebrity friend Will Rogers, welcomed the chance to own and drive automobiles apparently without feeling that they had betrayed fellow range-riders or the loyal horse. Nevertheless, Charlie Russell was not alone in his strong opposition to the horse harvest. One newspaper account tells of a former Montana cowboy who attempted to dynamite an Illinois packing plant that was butchering horses for meat.[30]

Tommy Simpson's Cow

Although Charlie Russell usually ignored farming altogether or else simply scorned it as the work of unwelcome "grangers," he did produce one very short story about dairy farming, a roast built upon a colossal lie. In "Tommy Simpson's Cow" a clever Scotsman moves ahead of other scientific farmers by importing a rare breed of dairy cow from the Scottish Highlands. Late in this short anecdote, Russell's audience learns that Simpson's imported cow is "built somewhat along the lines of a lady pig," sporting three udders along the length of her belly instead of the usual single bag of four teats located near her rear legs. In such a relatively brief yarn (457 words), the narrator delivers his absurd conclusions quickly, loading the lie into the audience's mind before skeptical disbelief can catch up. Russell has delivered the lie and com-pounded the trick with an illustration by the time the reader arrives at the final sentence:

> Tommy tells me that in Scotland, where these cows eat the nutritious heather, the center bag gives pure cream, the rear one buttermilk, an' the forward one skim milk, so they don't need no separator.[31]

This droll humor seems compatible with stereotypical jokes about the extremes of Scottish ingenuity to maximize thrift. As Russell's narrator observes, "with thrift that's charac-

FIG. 88. Charles M. Russell, *Tommy Simpson's Cow.* Pen/ink, illustration for the story of the same name, appearing October 23, 1916, in the early MNA inserts, *Rawhide Rawlins Stories,* and *Trails Plowed Under.* Rural viewers familiar with bovine anatomy and breeding patterns typically appreciate this absurd cartoon sooner than "outsiders."

teristic of the family" the cow's caretaker on the voyage from Scotland to America successfully barters a free passage for both animal and himself in exchange for supplying crew and passengers with milk and cream. In the course of this brazen lie, Russell also makes passing remarks that reflect poorly on progressive attempts to improve farming as well as on the Scottish preoccupation with seemingly inconsequential place-names back in the old country. Most of the disparaging characterizations, however, fall on the main character, Tommy Simpson, in the form of an artful roast. Simpson is a natural suspect for calf stealing because many immature animals are seen following the Scottish mother cow. The narrator also reveals that Simpson left his Scottish Highland homeland "that he's run out of as a youth for poachin'." Furthering this character smear, Russell has Tommy Simpson chewing such a large wad of tobacco as to be speechless, "until he opens the stove door and nearly puts the fire out." Apparently Simpson's stream of repulsive brown saliva could extinguish all the logs burning in a wood stove.[32] As a compulsive smoker, Russell had little sympathy for tobacco chewing and the need for spittoons. Although many readers and listeners have enjoyed Russell's tough humor, this roast seems especially unflattering.

Charlie Russell usually reserved such character assassinations for close friends, but he seems to have made an exception for Tommy Simpson. Unlike the other victims of Russell's outrageous slander, Simpson does not appear in other biographical references or among the letters that Russell sent to friends and family (many of which have been published in several collections). Late twentieth-century residents of the village of Fife, a few miles east of Great Falls, have attested to Simpson's founding of the town and to his pleasure with Russell's joking yarn, but one observer suggested otherwise. Author/editor William Bleasdale Cameron reported, "I am told that Tommy was highly indignant over Russell's story of him and the Scotch cow."[33] In addition, Russell had little sympathy for dairy farming and most dairy farmers. These milkmen would have been unlikely companions for Charlie Russell and equally unlikely subjects of one of his friendly published roasts. Exaggerating the cattleman's viewpoint, Russell suggested that milk harvesting was unethical and probably worse than most crimes. "The old time cowpuncher . . . would run off a band of hosses, hold up a coach, work a brand over," Russell wrote. "Maybe he wore notches on his gun, but he wouldn't steal milk from a calf."[34] In short, "Tommy Simpson's Cow" appeared as an outrageous roast at the expense of someone not close enough to Russell to enjoy it as a measure of longstanding mutual admiration.

Mormon Zack, Fighter

Despite his limited vision on social reforms, Russell made a compelling case in his writings for appreciating rustic characters that he had encountered and admired (unlike Tommy Simpson) in the nineteenth-century West. For a colorful example of a tough old-timer who resisted modern reform, Russell presents the story of "Mormon Zack, Fighter." Zack's life spanned the western transitions from the Indian trading-post days around Reed's Fort (later to become Lewistown, Montana, in the heart of the Judith Basin) on through the range-cattle days, until the story's finish in bootlegger times of the 1920s in the border town of Havre, Montana. According to Russell's narrative, delivered by "Rawhide Rawlins," Zack survived numerous dramatic battles including gunshot wounds and being partially disemboweled when, in a fight,

> the other fellow cheats by drawin' a knife, an slippin' it into Zack's flanks he walks clean 'round him, leavin' Zack with nothin' holdin' him up but his backbone. His friends help him gather up the loose ends, and gettin' a doctor with a sackin' needle. He's soon patched up again.[35]

After Zack's wounds healed from this fight, the scar tissue around his middle made his hide as tough as thick leather. "We used to hit him in the stomach for drinks," recalled one former cowpuncher who had worked on the range with Zack Larson and withstood the "Mormon's" chuck-wagon cooking. "I was just a kid. I hit him with a neckyoke. He stuck his old stomach out and I whacked him. . . . And he was a real cook, too. A great big man."[36] Russell's story about Mormon Zack may be one of the few examples of the artist saying something favorable about roundup cooks, since several cattle-camp cooks had treated Kid Russell with neither sympathy nor generosity.

Charlie Russell finishes his tribute to Mormon Zack Larson with this sharp contrast: "Zack belonged to his time an' it was his kind and not the reformers that made Montana. These last came in with the tumble-weed."[37] One reformer whom Russell enjoyed, the Reverend William Wesley Van Orsdel, known fondly throughout Montana and Wyoming as "Brother Van," arrived in Montana several years before Russell and years before the first appearance of the Russian-thistle tumbleweed in the West. A revealing photograph of Larson standing with Russell outside his log studio also includes Brother Van. The artist enjoyed a friendship with both of these very different western men. At about the time that someone snapped the picture

FIG. 89. Charles M. Russell, "Mormon" Zack Larson, and "Brother Van"—Rev. W. W. Van Orsdell—outside Charlie's log-cabin studio. Photograph courtesy of the Homer and Helen Britzman Collection, Taylor Museum, Colorado Springs Fine Arts Center, Colorado. Russell enjoyed this specific frontier fighter and this unique frontier preacher for individual reasons, despite their opposing values and actions.

of the three men together, Russell wrote down the "Mormon Zack" piece that ends with a denunciation of reformers as being just as unwelcome as the tumbleweed.[38] In a typical split for Charlie, he could appreciate a rough old western drinking man while also holding the highest regard for the leading prohibition advocate, Brother Van. He could not disapprove of these rough types, as he explained to one friend, "maby the old timers were tuff but they were regular men and friends of mine and I havent forgotten I wasent so good myself." [39] As the population swelled in places like Great Falls, however, these rustics and curmudgeons seemed to evaporate from sight. Charlie Russell might have been more tolerant of the shift to modern times in the West had characters like Mormon Zack remained visible and still circulating through his life. The newer, civilized West cultivated different personalities and skills from those in the older days, soon leaving the coarse frontier types obsolete and unwanted.

In the same fashion that Charlie Russell condemned reformers while also praising Brother Van, the storytelling artist could generalize when condemning "boosters" while maintaining his friendship with the founder of Great Falls, U.S. Senator Paris Gibson, a primary advocate of dry-land, non-irrigated wheat farming, who also served as president of the Montana Wool Growers Association.[40] To honor this urbanizing sheepman and personal friend, Russell composed this verse as a public tribute for Gibson's eighty-sixth birthday:

MORMON ZACK, FIGHTER

HISTORICAL RECOLLECTIONS---By *Rawhide Rawlins*

"I see Mormon Zack's in the hospital with a bad front foot. This bein' crippled ain't nothin' strange for the Mormon,'" said Rawhide Rawlins, as he pulled the "makin's" out of his coat pocket and started rolling one.

Rawhide Rawlins

"If I knowed the story of every scar he's got I could hand the people a history that would make some of these scraps the kaiser's losin' look like a prayer meetin'. My knowledge of history's a little hazy, but knowin' Zack came from Norway and judgin' from his actions, he's a come-back of some of them old fightin' Norsemen. You might lick him, but you can't keep him licked and he fights as well underneath as he does on top.

"The first time I see Zack I'm a kid, helpin' throw up a log shack on the Judith river. There's a feller rides up with an Injun hoss under him. He's sittin' in an old-fashioned cow-horn saddle with 'dog-house' stirrups. In dress he's wearin' the garments of a breed—moccasins an' beaded buckskin leggin's that come to the knees. In his ca'tridge belt's a skinnin' knife an' across the front of him lays a Winchester in a 'ringed and beaded skin gun cover. One of the men that's with me tells me that's Mormon Zack.

"That'll soon be 40 years ago. At that time there's still a lot of Injun trade in the country, and that's the Mormon's business. The first time I knowed of Zack gettin' warlike is a little while after this at Reed's Fort, a tradin' post near where Lewistown stands today. It's run by Reed and Bowles.

"There's about 200 lodges of Piegans come to the post for trade. Bowles don't happen to be there, as he's gone to Benton to get whisky. While he's off gettin' this wet goods, Zack and his partner comes along and make a trade, an' when Bowles arrives there ain't as much as a skunk skin left among them Piegans. They're traded down to a breech-clout.

"This don't make Bowles pleasant to get along with an' he starts fillin' up on this trade whisky. This is the booze that made the jackrabbit spit in a wolf's eye. If they had some of this to feed our soldiers the kaiser would be up a tree right now.

"As I said before, Bowles fills up and starts tellin' Zack how much he thinks of him, and the talk Zack comes back with ain't very genteel. Zack's standin' pretty close, for all the time they're talkin' he's on to Bowles' hole-card. He knows this hog-leg that's hangin' on Bowles' hip ain't no watch-charm, so to avoid any misunderstanding, Zack hands Bowles one on the chin, knockin' him from under his hat. He's near bein' too late, for Bowles has already reached for his barker an' just when Zack's reachin' his jaw she speaks out loud, the ball nearly tearin' Zack's hind leg off at the hip.

"Bowles don't come to till next day, and then he wants to know which hoss kicked him. Zack's worse off as there ain't no doctor nearer than Benton. Of course, there's a medicine man in the Piegan camp, but Zack ain't Injun enough to believe that this red doctor can beat a tom-tom an' sing his leg together, so he forks a hoss an' pulls for the steamboat town. This little incident don't seem to take none of the fight out of Zack, and he wins and loses a few battles down there while he's healin' up.

"It's a few years later Zack comes near crossin' the range when he mixes with a fighter in Benton. The battle's Zack's from the start till the other fellow cheats by drawin' a knife, and slippin' it into Zack's flank he walks clean 'round him, leavin' Zack with nothin' holdin' him up but his backbone. His friends help him gather up the loose ends, and gettin' a doctor with a sackin' needle, he's soon patched up again.

"Another time Zack fights a feller all day. Of course they stop for drinks an' feed. There really ain't no hard feelin's; they're just tryin' to find out which is the best man. They'd a-been fightin' yet but their eyes swelled shut at last an' they couldn't find one another.

"There was one town Zack was doubtful of, an' that was Bull Hook. In them days this burg held the pennant for fighters.

"Zack had been cookin' on the Teton roundup, an' when they break up that fall he jumps a train headed east. He's got quite a bankroll and a friend stakes him to a quart that ain't grape juice. He's figurin' on winterin' in some of the towns along the road, so when the train stops at this town of Bull Hook, or Havre as they call it now, he steps off to get the air an' sizes up the citizens.

"As I was sayin', this town in the old days was the home of most of the fighters of the northwest. Zack picks out the biggest, hardest one in sight, and walkin' up friendly like hands him one in the jaw with every pound he's got. With this the ball opens, but it don't last long, an' Zack's hit him everywhere when the big feller hollers 'enough.'

"Then the stranger wants to know what it's all about and asks Zack to introduce himself an' explain just out of curiosity, what's his reason for tearin' into him. Zack tells him there's no hard feelin's and it ain't

To avoid any misunderstanding he hands Bowles one on the chin, knockin' him from under his hat. He's near bein' too late, for Bowles has already reached for his barker, and just when Zack's reachin' his jaw she speaks out loud, the ball nearly tearin' Zack's hind leg off at the hip.

no old grudge he's workin' off, but he kind of figured on winterin' in Bull Hook, an' hearin' they're all fighters there, he thinks this is the best way of introducin' himself. .

"'I picked the biggest one among you,' says the Mormon. 'If I'd a' lose, I was goin' on to Chinook, but seein' I win, I'll winter with you.' An' he did.

"Although Zack's a natural scr... per, like many of his kind he h... plenty of good traits, is good-heart... an' I never knowed him to jump o... weakling. It was always a man w... claimed to be a fighter, too. Za... belonged to his time an' it was ... kind and not the reformers that ma... Montana. These last came with t... tumble weed."

Zack picks out the biggest, hardest-lookin' citizen he can see and swings on his jaw with every pound he's

FIG. 90. Charles M. Russell, "Mormon Zack, fighter," first appearing in the *Plains Plainsman*, (MNA), October 22, 1917, featuring two pen/ink illustrations that were omitted from *Trails Plowed Under.*

There's men that claim honor or riches
Took nations with powder or lead
They never done nothin' for live ones
But built up great cities of dead.

But I drink to one with no notch in his gun
No knife or gun record to give
But on a wind-swept ground he built up a town
Where humans could come grow and live.

So here's hoping health rides herd on your camp
And sickness don't locate your smoke
For with health by your side—
Life's a mighty smooth ride
And while he's your friend—you're not broke.[41]

Russell's poster-sized tribute for Gibson showed a self-portrait of the artist on horseback holding up a whiskey bottle next to the words. Some friends understood Russell's capacity for enjoying the company of a person like Paris Gibson, whose ideas he might strongly dislike. "Charley had the kind of open-mindedness that could entertain divergent and even conflicting standards," observed Frank Linderman's daughter. "He let in, and allowed them to govern not only his thoughts but actions, often irreconcilable political and religious outlooks and personal viewpoints."[42] In matters of religion, his friend Frank Linderman tried to argue logic and sense (but to no avail) to Russell's apparent acceptance later in his life of fundamental biblical Christianity as well as the Indians' worship of the Deity embodied by the sun.

A REFORMED COWPUNCHER IN MILES CITY

Charlie Russell's public tribute to Paris Gibson included a self-portrait depicting himself as toasting the founder of Great Falls with a liquor bottle. Even though he had been abstaining from drinking for approximately ten years, Russell may have been expressing his disdain for the Prohibition law that Montana voters approved in the same year as the picture, 1916. The state law went into effect in 1919, a year ahead of the federal Eighteenth Amendment to the Constitution. By the 1920s, with wide-open defiance of the antidrinking law in towns like Havre, Butte, and Miles City,[43] prohibition reform clearly had failed in Montana. Russell incorporated the demise of prohibition and the hypocrisy of the nonenforcement into several of his stories. He mentions Bill Ward's experiences under prohibition when "no one drinks without hidin' in the cellar" and where life becomes "just one long game of hide-and-seek."[44] Russell preferred that drinking take place without guilty subterfuge—openly—the way men drank in previous times, "when the west was big and wicked folks don[e] there drinking in a saloon in frount of a bar in sted of up an alley behind a garbage can [T]he men in old times were like the pla[i]nes and mountians they lived in[:] to[o] big to hide."[45]

In "A Reformed Cowpuncher at Miles City,"[46] Russell roasted his old friend E. C. "Teddy Blue" Abbott for his wild celebrations in Miles City at the time of nineteenth-century cattle drives from Texas. Then he satirized hypocritical state lawmakers who were gambling and drinking on the train en route to the annual stockmen's meeting in Miles City, breaking their own laws in the process. In a happy coincidence, the Montana Press Association was holding a meeting in Miles City at the same time.[47] The politicians and government officials were probably headed for Miles City simply to join a good party. The overlapping events added to the sense of excitement and anticipation among the passengers. While the legislators, cattlemen, and newspapermen were drinking and playing cards, young Wilford Johnson (as reported earlier) witnessed Charlie Russell and "Teddy Blue" Abbott telling vivid yarns nonstop in another part of the train.

Charlie Russell later told Frank Linderman about the Miles City circumstances. "Ted Blue was with us on a special train that packed the bunch and we slept on the train cars[.] [T]hey tell me that this state is dry but that train and Miles town was dripping wet."[48] Russell expanded this ironical slant in the Miles City piece that he published in the MNA inserts and in subsequent books:

> There's another train from Helena, the headquarters for the lawmakers, that's filled with a bunch that acts as care-free as if they'd forgot there's such a thing as an attorney-general in their camp. They overlooked bringin' any root beer with them, so they had to fall back on stuff they was used to. Teddy looked into one of the Helena cars, he says, and what he sees through the smoke reminds him of Butte in the days of licensed gamblin'. He's told they're only playin' a few harmless games like "Old Maid," so he figures they just have the chips lyin' around to make them feel at home. . . . Ted says the friendly and trustful feelin' among this Helena crowd is fine to see. One time during daylight they pass through a tunnel, an' strikin' a match, Teddy sees every man at the table he's watchin' leanin' forward all spread out over his chips. They was undoubtedly afraid they might jolt into another train and spill the chips around, an' of course it would be a job pickin' 'em up off the floor.[49]

Obviously, Russell lampoons the nervous legislators who assume the worst from their fellow hard-drinking lawmakers and take special care to protect their illicit earnings in the momentary darkness of the tunnel. Russell also celebrates the irony of how the Prohibition law had transformed Euro-Americans into legal equals with the Indians: "It used to be agin the law to sell an Injun whiskey, but the law has made Injuns out of all of us now."[50] For this nineteenth-century former cowboy, the hypocrisy of the lawmakers and civic leaders was as bad or worse than the actual drinking.

Charlie Russell's twentieth-century stories reflect several reform ironies. Teddy Blue, who once consumed, in Russell's words, "cow-swallows of Miles City liquid fire,"[51] made a perfect lead character for "The Reformed Cowpuncher," but no more so than Russell himself. Both of these legendary carousers separately "got the jump" on the Prohibition laws and voluntarily cut drinking out of their lives several years before the antidrinking reform legislation took effect.

FIG. 91. Charles M. Russell, *Straddles It Instead of Sittin' Like a Human* (or *At The Bar*). Pen/ink, original in the Homer and Helen Britzman Collection, Taylor Museum, Colorado Springs Fine Arts Center, Colorado. Illustration for "A Reformed Cowpuncher in Miles City" in *Rawhide Rawlins Stories*, depicts Teddy Blue Abbott, Ballie Buck, and "himself" at a Miles City soda fountain. Russell must have provoked his antireform cronies to rage or laughter by including signs for buttermilk and root beer served in glasses with straws by an attractive woman bartender.

There's More Than One David

In another bit of reform satire, Russell's Bible-inspired parable "There's More Than One David" includes a wry character inversion: "There's a reformed preacher in this town runnin' a stud poker game."[52] This story also offers Russell's only partly sympathetic anecdote about sheepherders, with the meek sheepherder (the "David" in this yarn) overcoming a gun-toting bully ("Goliath") by throwing a strike with a rock to the giant's chin, followed by a pistol-whipping of his unconscious foe that would be consistent with Medicine Whip's mutilation practices. The cowboys witnessing this fight did not intervene in the giant's tormenting of the sheepherder's dog nor in the shepherd's rock-throwing response, but they do loudly encourage the shepherd to take revenge on a bully who had intimidated everyone in town. The entire story inverts the values of twentieth-century reformers who would have suppressed all of the violent conflict. Russell seems to show a redemptive quality in the process that shares a justification with the Old Testament tale about David and Goliath. The actual location, people, and events inspiring Russell's violent parable remain unknown.

Johnny Reforms Landusky

In another example of Russell's observations on the ludicrous quality in the urge for social reform, the author roasts his friend Johnny Ritch in "Johnny Reforms Landusky."[53] Although Charlie Russell did not know Ritch until later in his life, he claims that, in earlier days, this "Johnny" had earned a reputation as a rough mining-camp cook supposedly noted for a popular dish known as "vinegar pie."[54] In the first citation of Ritch's roastable character, the other miners complained about this cook's explosive cuisine and "Johnny's pet rats livin' in the flour sack." Russell grants Johnny a "pious disposition" that

> inclines him toward missionary work. . . . He picks out the Little Rockies as the most promisin' district to begin reformin'. He starts a revival there that's a cross between Mormonism an' a Sioux ghost dance.[55]

Progressive reform was automatically a joke for Russell and, consequently, missionary activity seemed especially counterproductive in the murderous Montana mining camp called "Landusky." The rough little town located in the north central Montana mountain cluster called "the Little Rockies" had earned a reputation as being "promising" for anything *except* reform. Most of Russell's Montana readers would have heard about the legendary fight between the town's founder, Pike Landusky, and "Kid Curry." Landusky died in this fight, witnessed by Ritch, that launched Kid Curry's outlaw life within the legendary "Wild Bunch" outlaw gang of Butch Cassidy and the "Sundance Kid."[56] One MNA article described Landusky as "the center of a wild, lawless border country, far removed from the more civilized sections of Montana." Among the tough men in this town was a bar owner widely known as "Jew Jake," who ran the saloon where Landusky met his end. Jake had lost part of one leg in a fight and "used a Winchester rifle for a crutch."[57] By comparison with this article, Russell's own description of Landusky uses understatement that takes advantage of the town's lurid past, a reputation already well established with readers who would appreciate the author's narrative irony:

> In them days Landusky is the principal town in the Little Rockies, an' it's a sociable camp, life there bein' far from monotonous. The leadin' industries is saloons an' gamblin' houses, with a fair sprinklin' of dance halls. For noise an' smoke there wasn't ever nothin' seen like it before the big fight in Europe starts. Little lead's wasted, as the shootin's remarkably accurate an' almost anybody serves as a target.
>
> The mayor, Jew Jake, has lost one hind leg in a argument with the sheriff, and he uses a Winchester for a crutch. Funerals in Landusky is held at night under a white flag, so that business ain't interrupted in daytime.[58]

Rather than writing gun-fighting fiction about a fantasy-based "wild west," Russell employed understated ironic satire about specific people, places, and, occasionally, violent events in a West that he and his peers knew firsthand.

In the attempt to clean up a place as rough as Landusky, according to Charlie Russell's

FIG. 92.

Charles M. Russell, *Dum Dum Bill.* Pen/ink, illustration for the story "Johnny Reforms Landusky," in *Rawhide Rawlins Stories* only. The term *dum dum* typically refers to illegally scored or hollow-tip bullets that intentionally inflict maximum damage by fragmenting upon impact. Russell's words for his boxer/school teacher also fit to this figure: "His smile, which is meant to be pleasant, is scary."

ironic roast, Ritch takes as his partner in reform the murderous bully named "Dum Dum Bill," "who's got a reputation of bein' a quiet, scholarly man with a lovable character, always shootin' to kill to save unnecessary pain an' sufferin.'" Before Dum Dum Bill's untimely end at the hands of a lynch mob, Johnny is able to effect several "progressive" reforms. Johnny's new laws include a death bounty, "a little more than they paid for a wolf," for certain citizens, but "as he's in with the reformers, Johnny's name ain't on this list," according to Russell—the unnamed narrator. "The bounty claimer must show both ears of his victims but scalpin' is frowned on as uncivilized." Landusky does have some minimal standards of civility after all, especially regarding a sense of appropriate post-battle mutilation.

    In this roast, Johnny Ritch loses his reformer job by offending the Landusky residents when he refuses the job of Mayor due to his claim to be inept with a gun. Then he alienates other citizens with his insensitivity, giving a funeral sermon over a dead gunfighter by tactlessly using for his theme "When Fools Go Forth to Fight."[59] Finally, Johnny's cooking "annoys" the rest of the town by using an old mining-camp recipe that accidentally explodes, killing several citizens. In the aftermath, Johnny is forced to leave Landusky in the same disgraceful way that

Bill Ward arrived in Shelby—by riding the rods beneath a railroad freight car. In using controlled exaggeration to tease a friend, Russell provides playful social exaggerations that satirize progressive ambitions of early twentieth-century reformers and moralists in the West.

Johnny Sees The Big Show

An international perspective occasionally arises in Russell's stories with his references to World War I or "the big fight in Europe." Of course, when Charlie Russell's satire compares tiny Landusky to the Great War, the Montana boomtown in the Little Rockies seems very tough indeed. In this wartime roast, "Johnny Sees The Big Show," the intrepid Montana newspaper correspondent notices a similarity between European battlefield clashes and "Landusky on a quiet day." On his boat trip to "over there," Johnny Ritch supposedly experiences the same motion sickness that the author had endured on his 1914 trip to and from England. According to "Rawhide Rawlins,"

> When I meet him the other day Johnny springs a lot of talk he don't hand to the public. On his trip over he tells me...he's so sick he's afraid the Dutchmen [Germans = Deutchmen = Dutchmen] won't sink the boat. One day he's hangin' with his head over the rail. Most people think it's a sailor's union suit hung out to dry, but a Red Cross nurse recognizes it as human, and puttin her arm 'round him in a motherly way, says, "Are you sick?"
>
> "Hell no," says Johnny. "I'm doin' this for fun."
>
> "Have all the fun you want," she comes back at him. "These big waves is full of jokes."
>
> Johnny tries to smile, but his countenance resembles a good job by the undertaker[60]

In a reference that Russell omitted in later printed versions, the narrator mentions in the initial MNA newspaper publication of this story that, since his return to Montana, Ritch has given a few talks in support of the Red Cross, and Russell endorsed them by stating, "it's worth your while to listen to him if he comes to your burg."[61] Ritch, the public speaker, would have been wise to incorporate Russell's seasick jokes into his speeches. Some of Russell's lines prove to be especially effective comedy writing, relying on "one-liner" phrasing still employed by America's nightclub and television comedians of the early twenty-first century. Nevertheless, this passage of anecdotal humor seems less effective than Russell's more subtle use of irony and narrative understatement that characterize his better yarns.

Russell's story "Johnny Sees the Big Show" presents a nineteenth-century westerner attempting to get close to the European war, using the old story premise of the main character in a "fish-out-of-water" situation. Russell frequently enjoyed this humorous setup in telling friends about his own travels—mishaps such as the naïve cowboy's visit to Chicago, the rural artist's experiences in New York galleries, and his social gaffe of stepping on the dowager hostess's gown train at a formal London dinner. Here, Johnny Ritch, an unsophisticated American,

FIG. 93.
John B. Ritch III.
Photograph courtesy of the
Montana Historical Society,
Helena. Sometimes called the
"Poet of the Judith," Ritch
(1868–1942), a former camp
cook and prospector, later
operated a movie theater in
Lewistown, Montana, and
ultimately served honorably
as a state legislator and as the
Montana State Historian.

suffers embarrassing setbacks but ultimately gathers his newspaper-story ideas regardless of the European wartime confusion. Despite uneven writing in this piece, Russell offers some of the best simple jokes in his published works and the story rightfully would have enhanced *Trails Plowed Under*. Unfortunately, the Doubleday editors dismissed it partly for the twentieth-century, nonwestern focus and partly because the story's jokes employ too many insider, local Montana references for unfamiliar outsiders. The local-color references to people and places are simply too numerous and obscure for most nonlocal readers.

Even with its patchwork narrative, however, "Johnny Sees the Big Show" provides insights about western American transitions to modern times. For one example, an independent, caring woman—the Red Cross nurse—clearly wins her joke-telling encounter with the seasick, western male hero. Second, both the narrator and hero express American irreverence toward the English aristocracy and their historical pretensions. Third, French linguistic sensitivities take a friendly slap when the narrator describes the French bewilderment upon hearing Johnny speak their language in a dialect supposedly learned from a Montana Sioux/French whiskey trader. The French listeners generously assume that Johnny is incoherent because he had breathed poisonous gas in the war's trenches. And, finally, Russell lampoons his own nostalgia for bygone days in the West when "Rawhide" tells how the king of Belgium gushes with sentimentality for the good old times when he supposedly lost money playing cards in Pat O'Hare's Geyser saloon or spent the evening sipping illegal booze in Shorty Young's well-known "speakeasy" club in Havre, Montana. This erratic travelogue ends abruptly with the absurd excuse that Johnny must break off his conversation with the narrator to give a Red Cross fundraising talk to some unlikely contributors—his friends, the impoverished Blackfeet Indians.

Several other stories include Charlie Russell's passing references about World War I. The unreformable Mormon Zack Larson carries scars on his body reflecting a violent history "that would make a lot of scraps the Kaiser lost look like a prayer meetin'"[62] And true to sentiments of an earlier age, Russell's story "The Horse" seriously observes that thousands of horses, gathered from the western prairies, died with American soldiers on European battlefields in helping to win "a machine-made hell."[63] These references probably seem distracting and out of place if Russell's storytelling focus supposedly should be limited to nostalgia about the Old West, but they make perfect sense as part of a humorous western view of a grim transition into the bloody and chaotic twentieth century. Westerners and their horses served and died in the war that reshaped warfare and diplomacy. Charlie Russell, like many western "diehards," felt deeply affected by World War I in far away old Europe.

Although Russell's later paintings continued to depict nineteenth-century western topics, he had other interests besides nostalgic reverie. He read newspapers every day and, even though his attention gravitated to local items about old-timers,[64] he also noticed items about social trends and the war news. In response to what he learned, Russell found a way to participate in the war effort by using his verbal talents as well as his painting skills. Charlie lent his support by responding to Herbert Hoover's call for maximum food supplies for Allied troops under the slogan "Food Will Win the War."[65] Montana food administrator Alfred Atkinson spread this message statewide through many speeches and newspaper advertisements encouraging food conservation. To help this cause, Russell contributed two paintings with accompanying verse for use as food-saving propaganda.[66] *Hooverizing* shows an older cowboy talking to his horse, while withholding the animal's oats as a substitute for wheat to cook "bannocks" (frying pan bread) over an open fire:

> *I hate to take your grub, old hoss, but then*
> *I'm leavin' meat and wheat for fightin' men;*
> *And by your handin' in your oats to me*
> *The both of us is Hooverizin', see?*
> *We're squarin' up with Uncle Sam, our friend*
> *Just kinder helpin' hold the easy end.*[67]

The title of Russell's painting *Hooverizing* refers to both Herbert Hoover's federal program for food conservation and distribution, as well as the painting's depiction of Russell's mentor, Jake Hoover (**see plate 24**). Russell's second picture for these advertisements, *Meat Makes Fighters* (**see plate 25**), shows the stubble-whiskered, aging cowboy riding beside a herd of modern,

FIG. 94.
Hooverizers, one of two advertisements that Russell provided to the food-conservation effort in Montana during World War I. Courtesy of Jim Combs. These ads, each with a picture and a poem by Russell, appeared statewide in the MNA inserts on August 29, 1918, and as handouts in retail stores and banks.

I hate to take your grub, old hoss, but then_
I'm leavin' meat and wheat for fightin' men;
And by your handin' in your oats to me
The both of us is Hooverizin'; see?
We're squarin' up with Uncle Sam, our friend;
Just kinder helpin' hold the easy end.

Painting and words by Charles M. Russell, the "cowboy artist" of Montana, for the Food Administration in Montana.

SAVE FOOD
HELP WIN THE WAR

white-faced Hereford cattle (not the Longhorns that Russell preferred). Russell seldom depicted Herefords, but in 1918, this cattle breed supplied much of the meat and leather for the U.S. effort in the Great War. The advertisement with this image, headlined "Helping to Win," included this poem as the words of the aging cowpuncher.

> *I ain't a-wearin' khaki, cause I'm too old a stag,*
> *But I'm a-handin' beef and hide to them that holds the flag.*
> *Cake and pie is good enough when folks just eat for fun,*
> *But Beef and leather plenty puts men behind the gun.*[68]

Informal gifts, especially Christmas cards, also afforded Russell the opportunity to combine writing and picture making. On the occasion of the war-support effort, the federal government published and distributed these verses and their accompanying illustrations as newspaper ads, handbills, and posters for a potentially wider audience than any of his other projects.

Charlie Russell's sincere but somewhat awkward poetic responses to the challenge of World War I harmonized with the efforts by farm and ranch communities in many western regions. Historian Robert Athearn notes that many westerners felt "increasingly ignored if not denigrated by the rising industrial society." By participating in the food-for-war effort, western-ers "found a place in world affairs, broadened their views and thought of themselves as a factor in international business."[69] Russell did his bit for the war effort by donating the two paintings and his own western verse to inspire others to support the same greater cause.

In addition to World War I, one of the largest changes of the twentieth century proved to be women's progress toward legal equality. For Russell, this threatening development culminat-ed in 1916, when Montana women gained the right to vote. It is an understatement that women were not a primary focus in most of Russell's narrative works. The few Charlie Russell artworks and published stories that depict women in the West mostly involve Native American women in their pre-reservation tribal activities. Nevertheless, these pictures and published writings do provide glimpses of his personal confusion and occasionally contradictory attitudes about the "fairer sex."

As mentioned earlier, the younger Charlie Russell indulged in a few depictions of sexual-ity. His most popular portrait formats depict an Indian woman wearing a colorful, bead-deco-rated buckskin dress with some jewelry, surrounded by typical Plains Indian housekeeping objects, while she reclines inside a tipi. Many of these so-called Keeoma portraits (**see plate 26**, for example) apparently attracted interest among Russell's peers as being sexually suggestive. With an elbow nudge, a rolling eye, and a smirking laugh, Russell's typical male viewers appar-ently reminded each other that the Indian woman represented in a Keeoma picture would typ-ically be wearing nothing else beneath her beaded buckskin dress. Some feminist critics in the late twentieth century perceived that these Russell pictures unfairly overemphasize sexuality in the lives of Indian women. As the feminist critic Corlann Gee Bush writes,

> Several other paintings seduce their viewers into believing in the truth of an obvi-ous falsity. Charles M. Russell, who should have known better, was frequently guilty of such incongruities, especially in his five Keeoma portraits. In them he presents the realistic objects of a native woman's life and then uses these to con-vince us of Keeoma's carnality and wantonness. Painted in either reclining or "hip-slung" poses, Keeoma is sexualized in a way that white women never are in western art. The message is clear: white women are too pure to be shown as specifically sex-ual creatures.[70]

Bush seems just as upset that white woman are not depicted as sexual beings as she is that Indian woman have been depicted lying down in a suggestive manner. In her own footnote to this argument, Bush acknowledges that Russell and his artworks neither routinely demean women nor fit into a simplistic anti-female category:

> Ironically we owe to Russell some of the few paintings of strong, capable, Native American women. His In The Wake of the Buffalo Runners and Indian Women Moving Camp are excellent paintings which violate all of the conventions about how Indian women were to be painted. Nonetheless, he painted few paintings of

strong, competent white women, despite the fact that his wife, Nancy Cooper Russell, was his business manager and agent.[71]

Bush's indictment incorrectly assumes that Russell's portrayals of the Keeoma figures are both inaccurate and purposefully distorted. However, the author and Russell art specialist Ginger Renner notes that Charlie's reclining Indian women reflect an established artistic style, stating, "The artist also used Indian women as objects of exotic intrigue, such as in the oil, Keeoma, done in 1896, where the cowboy artist continued the tradition of Ingres's *Odallisque*."[72] Russell's relatively sedate depictions of a Keeoma-style figure (more numerous than Bush suspects) also contrast with the more typical barroom art in western saloons noted by historian Elliot West, who has observed:

> From languid nude women to patriotic banners to (post 1896) F. Otto Becker's Custer's Last Fight . . . these illustrations and decorations made up a genre best described as Victorian macho. They spoke of women to be lusted after but still kept on a pedestal and of an admiration for muscle flexing heroics . . . in this masculine environment . . . [there existed] an exaggerated vernacular of virility and bravado.[73]

Russell's subdued depiction of fully clothed reclining Indian women that hung in Montana saloons and private homes do not fit easily the accusation of being exaggerated bravado. This differentiation between pictures of Indian women and white women bothers some feminists like Bush, but not other critics like Ginger Renner. Moreover, none of the responses by Russell's contemporaries to be found in the various archives connected with his life and works react to the Keeoma pictures negatively or suggest that Indians or non-Indians perceived these depictions as being distorted or inaccurate. Apparently, Indian women did recline within their tipi homes in the manner painted by Russell. Ethnohistorian John Ewers has noted only one inaccuracy in Russell's depictions of Indian women's garb: the female dress style shown in many of his pictures depicting Indian women in the early 1800s actually would have been appropriate only for women in the later nineteenth century. Even in nomadic Native American tribal units, women's dress fashions evolved continuously (**see pate 28**).

Bush's assertion that Russell painted few strong, competent white women feeds a popular misperception that he seldom painted *any* white women. Of the few Euro-American women who do appear in his paintings, most seem strong enough to be thriving in the difficult circumstances of the nineteenth-century West. One possible explanation for the relatively low frequency of his depictions of white women may be that so few Euro-American women actually participated in the scenes of historical periods, regions, and activities that Russell preferred to paint. Among the rare Russell depictions of white women in western scenes, one *Wagon Train* painting includes an attractive mother figure with her children (**see plate 27**).

Concerning his own realistic artistic style, Russell once expressed frustration about portraying white women as attractively as other illustrators, saying that his own pictures made these women look too "tough." As Linderman recalled the artist's statements, "'I can't paint a white woman,' Charley told me one night. . . . 'Every time I paint a white woman she looks

FIG. 95. Charles M. Russell, *Mothers Under the Skin* (or *Montana Daughters*), 1900. Pen/ink, gift of Jock Warden, C. M. Russell Museum, Great Falls, Montana.

FIG. 96. Charles M. Russell, *Thoroughman's Home on the Range,* 1897. Watercolor, Permanent Collection, C. M. Russell Museum, Great Falls, Montana. Russell painted several of these romantic ranch scenes that feature Euro-American women, including this gift for his subjects—Joe and Eula Thoroughman.

FIG. 97. Charles M. Russell, *The Last of His Race*, 1899. Pen/ink, gift of Friends of the Museum, C. M. Russell Museum, Great Falls, Montana. This sketch reflects Russell's pessimism that Indians were disappearing altogether from the urbanizing West. Over the Great Falls skyline, the toxic fumes from the Anaconda Corporation smelter's tall smokestack hold a vision of a long-discontinued Indian buffalo hunt.

tough as nails. If I paint her over again she looks tougher, like a hooker.'"[74] Perhaps another reason for the absence of white women in most of Russell's art was his perception that white women in the West were less sexually available, unless they were prostitutes. Russell did make a number of images depicting flirtatious courtship, but only between white men and white women or between Indian men and Indian women. He depicted interracial sexuality on a few occasions, but never interracial flirtation or courtship. Near the turn of the century, he made a few highly allegorical pen/ink sketches with unsympathetic images of white females, including *Mothers Under the Skin* and *The Last of His Race*, but seldom produced such politicized art during the subsequent twenty-six years of his life. Frank Linderman observed approvingly that, despite young Russell's open-minded and exuberant decade as an independent cowboy with many girlfriends and female companions, he continued to hold conservative Victorian values concerning "appropriate" gender roles typical for the nineteenth century throughout his life in the twentieth century.[75]

As Nancy Russell began to control the business of marketing his art around 1900, the artist/author apparently ceased further depictions of sexuality, even the Keeoma-style portraits.[76] By 1907, the Keeoma figure reappears in a Russell painting wearing her familiar beaded dress, but she is considerably changed. No longer reclining by the interior fire, she stands outside the tipi holding up her infant on a cradleboard in an act of solemn prayer to the rising sun. (**see plate 28**) It remains unclear how much Nancy's firm control of the marketing of her husband's art affected this change. Nevertheless, as mentioned, Nancy had attempted to eliminate any of her husband's earlier depictions of overt sexual activity. Locally, she began to emphasize more art sales in Great Falls furniture stores and art-supply shops and less in saloons. Soon she began seeking illustration assignments more aggressively while exhibiting and selling his art in larger urban art galleries throughout the country. Joe DeYong clarified that "Nancy's greatest achievement in her husband's behalf was best summed up by his longtime friend Will Rogers, who drawled: 'Nancy took an "o" out of saloon and made it read salon.'"[77]

Nancy Russell's business travels exposed Charlie not only to the works of other artists and their informative critiques of his work, but the journeys also helped him become aware of one of the largest social changes in the country. While in New York in 1911, Russell reported to a friend back in Montana about attending a voting-rights rally:

> we took in a Suffragette meeting the other night an a finer band of Hell raisers I never saw bunched according to there argument men would have littel to say in regards government I will tell you all a bout it when I see you[78]

Despite Russell's potentially humorous tone of grudging respect, several close observers have pointed to his strong dislike for these "Hell-raisers." Nevertheless, Russell also maintained that "the worst woman alive, in my opinion, is as good or better than the best man I know."[79] As Charlie Russell entrusted all his business affairs to his wife Nancy, his actions and attitudes resembled a pattern that historian Duane Smith noticed among many nineteenth-century westerners: "Men were willing to give women unheard-of privileges and a great amount of respect but hesitated to give them the vote."[80]

. . . THE BIG SHOW AT BULL HOOK AND FASHIONS

After Montana men voted-in suffrage rights for women in 1914,[81] Russell expressed a more relaxed attitude about the situation. In a piece about the new rodeo/"stampede" in Havre that Russell wrote for the MNA in 1917, he expressed some surprising acceptance of women's participation in politics. As his narrator Rawhide Rawlins states:

> When I knew cows there was plenty of cowboys, but I don't remember any she-ones. But since they got she-congressmen it seems right enough to have she-cow-punchers, and if our congresslady's as good in the capitol building as these gals are in the middle of a hoss, she'll do till something better comes along.
>
> Fanny Sperry Steele is the real thing. I've seen her ride at many contests and never yet saw her grab leather. She rides clean, with loose feet and scratches 'em[82]

In the Havre Stampede article, Russell shows that he could admire a woman bronc rider while also showing, in his story "Highwood Hank," that many nonathletic women might be utterly disinterested in dominating wild horses. In another depiction of male/female relationships, Russell's Indian story about "Lindsay" living his life married to an Indian woman includes

FIG. 98. Charles M. Russell, *Bucking Horse and Cowgirl,* ca. 1925. Ink with transparent and opaque watercolor over graphite under-drawing on paper, no. 1961.187, Amon Carter Museum, Fort Worth, Texas. When rodeos became popular in Russell's lifetime women initially were allowed to compete in bucking-horse events. Russell published expressions of admiration for the women riders.

FIG. 99. Charles M. Russell, *"Mayby you think this Lady is stripped for a bath ...,"* 1916. Watercolor, illustration from a letter to "Friend Bill," Great Falls Elks Club Collection, Montana Historical Society, Helena. Charlie Russell expressed shock at the revealing clothing and socially aggressive behavior of some stylish, twentieth-century urban women, like this cigarette-smoking, cocktail-drinking "flapper."

a statement about the dominant role of females, "It's the women that makes the men in this world."[83] Then, late in his life, about 1925, in his modern-era essay titled "Fashions," Russell expresses irritation with the evolution of modern women's clothing styles:

> It's different today. Bobbed hair, short skirts, low front and back—every rag she's wearin' wouldn't pad a crutch.... I used to think that men could stand more punishment than women, but I was wrong.... [A] woman can go further with a lipstick than a man with a winchester and a side of bacon.[84]

The clothing styles and trends among the "flappers" and other women participating in the "roaring twenties" shocked Russell, motivating him to comment about the attire of the stylish women whom he observed on the ocean liners that carried him back and forth across the Atlantic Ocean in 1914. He joked (or complained) about the women passengers who smoked in public and could outdrink their husbands, "an[d] if paint an[d] fethers is a sign of savigry Id say there [are] quite a few canibols on board."[85]

RANCHES

Eleven years later, in his 1925 essay on "Ranches," Russell expressed doubt and resentment about how a modern woman could exercise her influence over a cattle-ranching husband. He states, "But maybe the woman he's tied to is the new kind. If she is, she's got paw whip-broke. She's out for sheriff. She's that kind." This "kind" of woman, in Russell's view, abuses her power over men by dressing her obedient husband in stylish golf socks and "knickerbocker" pants that embarrass him in the presence of old friends. She drags him to Europe, "him and his checkbook," but together they never bother to see "Yallerstone or Glacier Park."[86] In Russell's understanding of personal gender politics (shaped by his experiences with Nancy), women seem to hold the upper hand over men and sometimes take unfair advantage in a modern-marriage situation.

Charlie Russell clearly meant these narrative exaggerations to amuse his friends. Nevertheless, the humorous statements also suggest some distress beneath the topical humor. Evidently, the issues of coping with capable and forceful twentieth-century women dismayed Russell, as well as many other western men. With the modernization of western ranch life (or the "urbanization" of ranches), some unresolved dilemmas about gender roles confronted western men like "Highwood Hank" when the end of the range-cattle era overlapped into modern times. Russell's essays spoke directly to the discomfort of these men and their feeling unable to resist what they saw as unwanted changes in women's traditional roles. Despite all of his misgivings about strong women, however, Russell had married one of the strongest. Overall, he seemed to be happy about his choice:

> I still love and long fer the old frontier an everything that goes with it; but I'd sacrifice it all fer Nancy. I can't stand cities or automobiles. I wouldn't drive one of them pesky cars fer love er money. My favorite's still the hoss. But jest the same, I let Nancy have her automobile, while she lets me have 2 hosses. It's a 50–50 game with us.[87]

Maintaining such a balance in their relationship required some ongoing adjustments for the "cowboy artist." A neighbor recalled Charlie Russell's skeptical first response to his wife's purchase of an automobile, soon followed by his direct involvement:

> I recall with vividness when Mrs. Russell got her first car. Charlie was passively concerned. He said, "If Mamie wants one of those stink wagons, she can have it,

FIG. 100. Nancy Russell and auto passengers, at Bull Head Lodge. Photograph courtesy of
the C. M. Russell Museum, Great Falls, Montana. The modern businesswoman
triumphant, Nancy poses proudly with her new Lincoln, driver Ted Taylor, Great
Falls Chief Librarian Louise Fernald, and Charlie—silhouetted in the back seat.

but I like the smell of horseflesh." Some way, some how, Nancy inveigled him into
trying it out, for I saw them leaving the studio one morning in the auto with
Charlie sitting in the rear seat with his feet up on the back of the front seat. He
seemed relaxed and quite confident in Nancy's handling of the "stink wagon." That
was the only time I ever saw Russell tamed to the times.[88]

Russell's attempts to cope with women in the twentieth century, as reflected in his published
writings, proved to be uneven at best. His complaints about modern females far outweigh the
praise for them in his Havre Stampede article. Nevertheless, his various attempts to express his
bewildered and often negative responses to women seem to reflect honestly the problems of
many like-minded western men of his era. Even though these pieces were perceived as humor
by his peers, they can seem to readers in the next century to be the discomforting expressions
of a man who feels overwhelmed by women.

Enthusiasm for visiting America's national parks, including "Yallerstone or Glacier Park,"
before traveling abroad, became a more popular trend following the Great War just when Russell
was publishing his stories and essays in the MNA's newspapers and books. His writings carry evidence of the new element in the economy and culture of the American West: domestic tourism.
Decades later, historian Earl Pomeroy observed in the growing appreciation for the West of this
postwar period that "[tourism] seemed to gain most strikingly in the twenties and thirties. A nos-
talgically rural and western spirit stirred as more Americans went to live in the city."[89]

 FIG. 101. Charles M. Russell, *The Boss Wears Puttees an' a Golf Cap.* Pen/ink, courtesy of the Montana Historical Society, Helena, illustration for "Ranches" in *More Rawhides,* but omitted from *Trails Plowed Under.* Russell scorned the modern rancher, whom he depicts holding an automobile starter-crank in one hand and an effeminate cigarette holder in the other, sporting an eastern snap-brim cap on his head and English riding pants over legs that are *not* bowed from riding horses, contemplating his hybrid Hereford steer that has been genetically engineered to have short legs and no horns.

On the cattle ranches of the twentieth century, Russell noticed ample evidence of the distasteful consumer materialism that reinforced his distrust of modern times. In a brief essay titled "Ranches," Rawhide Rawlins observes:

Most of the cow ranches I've seen lately was like a big farm. A bungalow with all modern improvements, a big red barn that holds white-faced bulls an' hornless milk cows. The corrals are full of fancy chickens, there's a big garage filled with all kinds of cars and at the bunkhouse that sets back where the owner and his family can't see or hear them, are the hands.

You might see a man with a big hat, boots and spurs—he's the fence rider—
but most of them wear bib overalls. The boss wears puttees and a golf cap.

The bungalow, that's got electric lights an' hot and cold water. There's a piana
that you play with your feet, and a radio, a Mah Jong set, and a phonograph.[90]

Then Russell describes the primitive ranch shacks of the early open range, but his observations of the 1920s version of the western ranch offer equally useful information, colored with the author's ironic wit. One distinguished western historian notes, "Life on the ranch was becoming not much different than life in the city had been a generation before." In citing this same passage from "Ranches," he adds, "Some westerners did not have to move to the city to enjoy its advantages; the city moved to them."[91] Apparently, many postwar cattle ranchers could embrace developments of the prosperous 1920s such as electrical appliances, automobiles, and docile cattle breeds more easily than could nineteenth-century men like Russell. Nevertheless, the artist/author observes without envy or condemnation that some former cowpunchers adapted to the changing times by finding new careers in oil drilling, employment in the national parks, as well as in distilling and transporting illegal alcohol.[92] In similar fashion, Russell made his own adjustment, leaving cow punching to embark on a twentieth-century career in fine art and, in the process, became an international success.

How Pat Discovered the Geyser

Some westerners responded to potential opportunities for tourist commerce by creating new facilities. For example, in his roast of Pat O'Hare, Russell suggests that the Irish bartender had inflated his grandiose ideas for a new resort hotel to stand beside the supposed geothermal site that gave the town its name. As "Rawhide Rawlins" describes the situation:

> Havin' heard of the Yallerstone Park, an' thinkin' he's found another one, Pat starts, a few days after, buildin' a health resort, follerin' the plans of the mammoth hotel. . . . I remember bein' there once, and after a few drinks of Pat Geyser's favorite, the measurements swells till this shack looks like the Brown Palace in Denver.[93]

Whether Pat emulates the premier hotel in Denver or the premier national park in the West, Russell's words paint the Geyser businessman as being foolishly ambitious. This story reflects a modern western trend: taking maximum financial advantage of potential tourism sites, however unattractive they might be. In Russell's narrative, the natural geyser site never shows more activity "than a keg of sour dough," except when Pat's "rest cure medicine" happens to provoke a visitor to see "northern lights at noon time, rainbows at night, an' total eclipses of the sun any time—to say nothin' of geysers of all sizes."[94]

The inevitable demise of Pat's Geyser Hotel came years later, according to local moralist and stern schoolmarm from nearby Stanford, Montana, Ms. Cassandra Phelps:

> [The hotel] has answered the call of the march of progress by being torn down and

FIG. 102. Jack Fitzgerald, Pat O'Hare, and Mike Byrne in Pat's Geyser Saloon. Photograph courtesy of the Judith Basin County Museum. Jack and Mike pose with a bottle in one hand and a pistol in the other. Was Pat hoping to promote tourism with this staged image?

made into a community dance hall where the Finnish population disport gayly when filled up with their particular brand of poison.[95]

Twentieth-century "progress" may have been marching forward with the structural dismantling of this failed tourist landmark, but Pat's tradition of volatile beverages had a life of its own with the next wave of ethnic migrants in the region.

Western tourism gained its greatest initial momentum from the expanding railroads. As Pomeroy notes, after the war, the rail companies that had been "still exhorting potential settlers to look to a smiling land of Canaan [now] switched to extolling 'the Far West, a fabled land, a story land, still a country of pioneers, still a frontier. Here are cowboys and Indians.'"[96] Although Charlie Russell's audiences as well as his story characters resented the rail-encouraged immigration, many enthusiastically adapted to taking advantage of the trains' new passengers. Russell makes light of the traveling customers, referring to Bill Ward's hobo companion whom he met beneath a Great Northern freight car as "a noted tourist, Brakebeam Ben."[97] Nevertheless, Russell understood that real tourists require gentle treatment. In his story "Bill's Shelby Hotel" the local greeting for railroad travelers proves too intense, frightening away the guests and any hope for repeat business. In "Rawhide Rawlins'" words:

> In the old times the residents there include a lot of humorists who have a habit of stoppin' trains an' entertainin' the passenger. Most of these last is from the East, an' they seemed to be serious-minded with little fun in their make-up. The Shelby folks get so jokey with one theatrical troupe that stops there that many of these actors will turn pale today at the mention of the place.[98]

These spontaneous early attempts at the business of western hospitality required some conscious readjustment. According to Russell, Shelby's resolve to reform, as mentioned earlier, drew inspiration from a threat by James Hill, owner of the Great Northern Railroad, to relocate the line far from the boisterous town. No further moral or legal admonitions proved necessary. The town abruptly faced the business realities and made the corrections necessary to exploit tourists more effectively.

In the new western world of tourism that Russell presented in several stories, Bill Ward and his first hotel were successful while Pat O'Hare's efforts were not. Ward progressed from Shelby to Great Falls and then to a venture planned for the shores of Flathead Lake, but Pat never progressed beyond a Judith Basin saloon with rooms to rent. Nevertheless, the development of a rough border town like "Bull Hook" into a nice town with rough edges, renamed "Havre" (always pronounced *"Havver"* by Montana residents), did not please old-timers like Russell. He told one friend:

> The boosters tell me that Haver has grown to be a good and moral city She may be Lady like now but when I knew her in her infantcy she was aneything but a good baby But Rube I liked her when she was young maby th old timers were tuff but they were regular men and friends of mine and I havent forgotten I wasent so good myself reforme is all right but reformers never broke trail to this or aneynother country they came with the tumble weed.[99]

In contrast with Havre, another Montana town, Miles City, made enough progress with out-of-town guests to attract Russell's praise: "Although Miles has always been a cow town, it's earned the right to be called a city, an' they handled the visitors in the old welcome way of the West."[100] By 1920, Russell was tolerant of Miles City's claim to proper urban status but earlier transformations of cow camps into cities such as Great Falls disoriented many older westerners. In the perception of Wallace Stegner, "urbanization, which is as culturally shattering an experience as the frontier itself, has often followed so hot upon settlement that the only constant in western life has been change."[101] Many of Charlie Russell's stories reflect an understanding that such constant and accelerating change necessitated more adaptation than resistance.

FIG. 103. Charlie Russell and Monte in front of the old Park Hotel (located behind the photographer) on Central Avenue in Great Falls; photograph courtesy of the Montana Historical Society, Helena. In the few years after this picture was taken, when the city paved the streets and then Monte died soon after, Russell had to ride in public streetcars or in Nancy's skunk-wagon to arrive at his afternoon storytelling sites.

Still, some Russell characters never give in. Mormon Zack Larson survives his tough western experiences without showing the need to change, but both Teddy Blue Abbott and Charlie Russell reformed voluntarily by marrying well and giving up drinking. Johnny Ritch survives both Landusky and the Great War, but Russell's favorites—the western range horses—died as beasts of burden building roads for the onrushing automobile, as canned food for pets and humans, or as cannon fodder on the battlefields of Europe helping humans wage the "machine-made hell."

The outcomes of Russell's twentieth century stories suggest mixed results consistent with life's unpredictable forces. Faced with the complexities of twentieth-century life in the West, Russell shows there is no single solution or survival lesson. Simply giving in to the new "kind" of western woman could bring harmony (and, in Russell's own case, career success and wealth), but old-fashioned western men would have to restrain their resentful outbursts better than "Highwood Hank" or be left in the dust. Expanding railroads brought permanent farmers and townsfolk, as well as closer shipping and receiving depots for livestock, but trains also carried tourists with money to spend. The new automobiles shortened distances, especially between isolated urban areas, but the loud and smelly machines also could seem uncontrollable. Just as no single dilemma lay at the heart of twentieth-century modernization, so in Russell's stories no single response works in every circumstance.

In these tales that Charlie Russell wrote more to entertain than to teach, he shared valuable information about the people and circumstances of modernization in the American West. Russell created entertainment out of real dilemmas that actual people experienced, people he knew directly. Bill Ward's hotel patrons and fellow townsfolk did frighten a theatrical troupe with gunshots in a lighthearted riot. Pat O'Hare did, indeed, relocate his flimsy hotel to be closer to the new rail line. Even though Russell exaggerated some aspects of these stories, he also preserved episodes of real people coping with the late stages of a major cultural and economic transition. With Russell's writings, later generations can sample the circumstances of both the storyteller and his audiences. By reading through these stories, students of turn-of-the-century West may understand the impact of rapid modernization as seen through the eyes of a participant.

CHAPTER SEVEN

Building the Book

"...this book is not literature—it is just Charlie Russell."
—Nancy Russell

*A*ssembling Charles M. Russell's writings and illustrations into a fine book for the national literary marketplace proved to be neither simple nor automatic for Charlie and Nancy Russell. The decision-making processes involving editing and contract negotiations for what became *Trails Plowed Under* took place almost exclusively between the determined but lightly educated Nancy Russell[1] and the seasoned professional editor for Doubleday, Page and Company, Harry Maule. Their sparring and maneuvering happened largely without direct involvement of the author. Aside from occasional conversations with Nancy about getting the book of stories published, Charlie contributed a few "new" pieces and illustrations to the project, but the majority of supposedly fresh material consisted of revived stories that he had written down or dictated decades earlier. He spent most of his remaining days during the final year of his life in light efforts at book preparation as well as sketching, painting, and sculpting.

The final book formed a composite of Russell stories, essays and illustrations arranged in a relatively arbitrary sequence, with some important illustrations omitted and others positioned far from their related text. The book almost went to print without several excellent yarns because Doubleday's New York editors misunderstood Russell's western humor. In addition, the editor's first plan for the book included neither the introduction by Will Rogers nor Russell's remarkable preface, "A Few Words About Myself." Although the finished book appeared in 1927, the interactions between Nancy Russell and Doubleday stretched from 1924 through 1935. A few brief face-to-face meetings happened in Montana and New York, but nearly all of the negotiations transpired through the sluggish U.S. mails connecting Manhattan with Great Falls or Glacier National Park. Then, in the middle of the final stages of negotiating and planning, Charlie Russell died of a sudden heart attack late in October 1926.

HARRY MAULE FIRST ENCOUNTERS CHARLIE AND NANCY RUSSELL

Two years earlier, in 1924, while he was editor of Doubleday's prestigious magazine *The Frontier*,[2] Harry Maule traveled west to gather new ideas, contacts, and material. In Montana, he hit a real jackpot. At the end of a pack-train ride through Glacier National Park, Maule happened to see the display of Charlie's art that Nancy Russell kept in a special cottage close beside John Lewis's cedar-log hotel on Lake McDonald, about ten miles by boat up the northeastern shore from the Russells' summer cabin. Maule met the artist and his wife that summer and apparently witnessed a typical Russell storytelling session before the mammoth fireplace in the Lewis Lodge's bark-timbered lounge.[3] A year later, Maule wrote to Charlie recalling their meeting and asking to "borrow" some Russell paintings for use on the frontispiece of *The Frontier*.[4] Maule would soon learn that Nancy handled all business questions. She would turn any permission request to use Russell artworks into a baited hook for other, more significant business transactions. She was trolling for a major magazine article about her husband and a nationally distributed book of Charlie's illustrated stories.

In December 1925, Nancy Russell learned that she had landed her fish. On an art-selling trip to New York, she met with Maule and either proposed or reinforced an earlier suggestion that Doubleday publish Charlie's stories. On that occasion, she handed him one of the first copies of *More Rawhides* that had just arrived from Montana with Cheely's marketing announcement letter. Only a few days after their face-to-face meeting in Manhattan, Maule wrote from Long Island to Nancy, who was still conducting business in New York, extending to her a proposal for a book that she had been struggling to secure for twenty years. "I have an idea," he wrote,

> that if Mr. Russell would write a book now and allow some of his pictures to be used as illustrations or illustrate it himself, it would be a real success. I have a book somewhat in mind somewhere between the Will James "Cowboys North and South" and Mr. Russell's own "Rawhide Rawlins." I prize mighty highly my copy of that little book of "Rawhide Rawlins" and it seems to me that if Mr. Russell would write a reminiscent book and illustrate it with black and white productions of his pictures, or even draw special pen and inks for it, it would be a greater success than any of the current cowboy books now on the market.
>
> As such, we should love to be Mr. Russell's publishers. As you know, Doubleday Page & Company publish books of all kinds—fiction, biographies, belles lettres, illustrated books, etc. . . .
>
> I hope you will talk this book idea over with Mr. Russell and let me know what you think of it before you leave. I would be glad to come in and see you again if you wanted to discuss it.[5]

When he extended this offer, Maule had *"More Rawhides"* in hand, but he also had the western-book marketplace in mind. During the early 1920s, Doubleday's publishing rival Scribner's Sons had scored a commercial success by publishing two books by a younger cowboy artist from Montana who called himself "Will James." Maule saw the chance to take advantage of a

FIG. 104.
Nancy and Charlie Russell, on
the porch of Bull Head Lodge.
Photograph courtesy of the
C. M. Russell Museum, Great
Falls, Montana. Nancy's initiative
and persistence proved crucial
to working with a large national
publisher to produce a fine book
of her husband's writings.

market trend and, additionally, to surpass Scribner's by publishing Charlie Russell's distinctive
writings and artworks.

The negotiating began with the two parties following quite different tracks. Harry Maule
soon altered his proposal to suggest that Doubleday publish two Charlie Russell books. One
volume would be like his previous suggestion for Russell's reminiscences to be styled somewhere between *Rawhide Rawlins* and the Will James books *Cowboys North and South* and *The
Drifting Cowboy*. The second project would be an art book with some pictures printed in color
as well as some in black and white, using bits of text from the first book. This book would provide a fancy, limited edition to be sold at twenty-five dollars per copy, a high price in 1926.
Maule also suggested that Nancy employ a collaborator, possibly a writer from Los Angeles,
who could transcribe and organize Russell's spoken words.

Meanwhile, Nancy Russell headed in a different direction. She tried to sell Maule outright
the two already published *Rawhide* books, plus some similar new stories that she promised

Charlie would compose right away. It did not matter to her that few of Charlie's printed stories were the kind of personal reminiscences that Maule wanted for direct competition with the Will James books. "As soon as Charlie is in the mood," Nancy firmly told Maule, "I am going to have him start on the stories whether you use them or not."[6] Harry Maule's reply moved him closer to Nancy's negative position on the possibility of a collaborator. "I agree with you," he told her, "that it would be best for Mr. Russell to write in his own way as you suggest rather than have a collaborator work with him . . . in the meantime won't you do all you can to push along the text?"[7]

SELECTING STORIES FROM THE RAWHIDE RAWLINS BOOKS

The issue of securing more text for the project came up repeatedly in the correspondence between Harry Maule and Nancy Russell. The editor was looking for material in which Charlie Russell would describe his own life, as the Will James books appeared to do. But Maule ignored Russell's clear preference for writing about people other than himself. A transcriber might have been appropriate to gather personal anecdotes since Russell's entertaining narratives about himself had to be transcribed on paper while he spoke or they would pass unrecorded. But the appropriate collaborators for Russell's completed stories up to that moment had been either his wife or his friend Percy Rabin, not someone unfamiliar with Russell's subjects and way with words. Charlie Russell thrived on a sense of intuitive compatibility with his listeners, including any potential transcriber. Maule also pushed for more text from Charlie Russell because he was not satisfied with many of the *Rawhide* stories. "[W]e see no reason why we should not use a part at least of the text of the two 'Rawhide Rawlins' books," explained the Doubleday editor.

> It is far better than a lot of stuff in other books of a similar nature. . . . We could work this out quickly according to the above outline if Mr. Russell could do just a little new text, say fifteen or twenty thousand words, like the stuff in "More Rawhides" rather than the more hilarious stories in the first book "Rawhide Rawlins."[8]

When considering the two books, Maule and his editorial staff preferred the second *Rawhide* book, with its occasionally serious tales, to the predominantly humorous pieces in the first. Complaining that he lacked ten thousand words necessary to make a well-rounded volume, Maule still proposed leaving out several of Russell's funniest yarns—"Tommy Simpson's Cow," "How Louse Creek Was Named," "Johnny Sees The Big Show," "Bill's Shelby Hotel," "Ranches," "Night Herd," "When Mix Went To School," and "Dog Eater."[9]

For her part, Nancy had unrealistically promised much more work from Charlie than he was physically able to deliver. "We are going to have a regular book of Charlie's things published," she told Joe DeYong emphatically, although Charlie had but five months to live. "He will have to write about 30,000 words more, but he has promised to do that so as to get it to New York by the first of September."[10] Neither party to this book contract faced the reality of Charlie's waning health.

The letters negotiating royalty rates reflect Nancy's preoccupation with rival author Will James. The Doubleday editor wanted to take advantage of the positive market response to cowboy-slang writings by offering Russell's presumably superior yarns and artworks. For her part, Nancy wanted to be sure her husband was paid as well, or better, than the upstart James. She agreed to accept Maule's offer of a 10-percent royalty on the first three thousand copies sold, "but I feel that after the book is well landed, Charlie's royalties should be as high as those received by Will James. Think this over and see if you don't agree with me."[11] Maule initially responded that he had no idea what Will James received for royalty rates. Later, in an effort to move Nancy to sign the final contract, he assured her that Charlie's rewards would be equal to anything that Will James earned.[12] Nancy Russell and Harry Maule finally agreed to the royalty terms. Their contract provided Charlie with 10 percent of the revenues from sales of the first three thousand copies, 12.5 percent on the next two thousand copies, and 15 percent on all copies sold after five thousand.[13] This contract arrived for the Russells' signatures accompanied by a letter from Harry Maule on October 22, 1926, just two days before C. M. Russell succumbed to a heart attack.

Months earlier, Charlie Russell's declining health had interrupted the negotiations between Great Falls and New York. On July 3, 1926, the artist underwent the routine (but long-delayed) surgical removal of a noncancerous goiter from his throat by Mayo Clinic surgeons in Rochester, Minnesota. His condition was sufficiently weakened from heart disease and smoking, among other complications, that the doctors told him he had but a year or less to live. Accordingly, the Russells rested for several weeks before returning by train to Montana.[14] Even though Nancy tried to reassure Maule at the end of July that Charlie was once again working on more stories, the editor observed Charlie's weakened condition firsthand during an August visit to Glacier Park. As a result, the editor promptly gave up hopes of publishing the book before Christmas.[15] Nancy refused to admit defeat, however, and helped Charlie assemble nine additional pieces, plus a batch of illustrations.[16]

Naming the New Book Trails Plowed Under

In addition to providing some additional text, Charlie Russell made one other significant contribution to the book project that Nancy and Harry Maule were negotiating all around him. He gave the book its distinctive name, *Trails Plowed Under*. Charlie had used the phrase in some of his letters. In a 1919 message to Teddy Blue Abbott, Charlie described reminiscing as a process when "my memory will drift back over trails long since plowed under by the nester to days when a pair of horse wranglers sat in the shadows of their horses and watched the grazing bunches of cayuses."[17] In 1924 he wrote about visiting with a neighbor who also had worked the cattle ranges. "Henery Keeton comes over once in a while and we drift back on old trails that are plowed under now."[18] The phrase had actually appeared as an earlier book title. Forty-five years previously, in 1881, a romance novel had appeared about the plight of Indians and with the title, *Ploughed Under, The Story Of An Indian Chief Told By Himself.*[19] For Russell, as well as many like-minded westerners, the phrase "Plowed Under" seemed to suggest the cessation of open-range cattle ranching, the destruction of the plains' grasslands, and the suppression of plains Indian cultures—negative connotations synonymous with destruction and the end of the "Old West." The phrase was also consistent with an Indian sign-language gesture indicating "death" or "dead" or the verb "to die" by moving one flattened, palm-down hand under the other, to symbolize going under, passing beneath the surface of life or into the earth. To plains Indians and antifarming cowboys like Russell, anything that was "plowed under" was dead, including the trails once formed by wild game and the early cattle herds crisscrossing the open prairies. Nevertheless, despite such negative connotations, editor Harry Maule was delighted by the book-title suggestion, replying weeks before Charlie's passing, "I just wanted to thank you for your telegram and to say that the title is perfectly bully."[20]

The abrupt death of her husband delivered a great blow to Nancy Russell. After less than a month of professional inactivity, however, she took up the book project again with character-istic determination. In her letter to Maule on November 19, 1926, Nancy thanked him for his sympathetic condolences. Then, she abruptly launched into the changes she wanted in the book-publishing contract. In addition to having the document redrawn in her name alone, Nancy demanded that no "publication of a cheap edition" would be allowed and that further changes in any story manuscript would have to include her written consent.[21] By forbidding all "cheap editions," Nancy Russell effectively kept *Trails Plowed Under* from being issued in any paperback format until 1996, when Doubleday allowed the University of Nebraska Press to publish a Bison Books reprint edition.[22] For seventy years, the book maintained enough sales to remain in print only in the more expensive hardcover edition.

Following Charlie Russell's death, Nancy Russell and Harry Maule looked directly at the issue of insufficient text. It was in early December of 1926 when the slim packet of nine stories and some pen/ink illustrations arrived in New York. At this moment, the two negotiators shed their earlier illusions in order to see what *Trails Plowed Under* should actually include. Maule could no longer hope for Charlie to write memoirs rather than stories. Nancy could no longer insist that Charlie would deliver 30,000 words of new stories to fill out the book. Instead, she simply invited the editor to use as much as he might care to from the *Rawhide* books. Maule was discouraged by the gap between the 50,000 new words he had anticipated receiving and the additional stories comprising just 17,400 words that Nancy had finally delivered. Two days before Christmas 1926, Maule wrote to say that he would indeed be using almost every story, including most of those he had been planning to discard. "[W]e will have to draw from "Rawhide Rawlins" and "More Rawhides" very liberally to make up the difference" for an appropriately-sized book.[23]

During the first week of January 1927, Harry Maule announced his plan to Nancy Russell for the materials he would use in the book. His final text count showed new material: 20,340 words; *Rawhide Rawlins*: 19,000; *More Rawhides*: 19,000. "Inasmuch as there are so many pic-tures," he wrote, "it will be necessary to use practically every bit of this text." He continued:

> Therefore, our plan is to use all of the stories with the single exception of "Johnny Sees the Big Show," which is topical and gives the impression of having been writ-ten during the war and seems out of date . . .

Our plan is to divide this material into four sections under these headings:

1. The Old West
2. The Many Trails
3. White Men and Injuns
4. Open Ranges[24]

Seven of the eight stories that Maule had been willing to discard back in May were now reincluded in the book, despite the editor's misgivings. From the two *Rawhide Rawlins* books, the editor rejected only "Johnny Sees the Big Show" for *Trails Plowed Under*. Actually, four additional stories that had appeared in the MNA inserts, but not the *Rawhide* books, also missed being printed by Doubleday.[25]

In this pivotal January 1927 letter to the author's widow, Maule assumed control of the sequential arrangement of the stories, creating four vague groupings. These section titles in *Trails Plowed Under* lacked specific connection with the content or themes of the stories placed within them. Section three, "White Men And Injuns," might have served as the proper gathering place for Russell's stories dealing with racial interactions, but the opportunity evaporated when Maule subsequently changed the heading to "Mavericks And Strays." The new structure offered no thematic grouping of Charlie Russell's tales that might have helped readers. Only the beginning and ending story selections reflected a bit of editorial strategy.

The book opens with "The Story of the Cowpuncher," Russell's whimsical essay about cowboys' ways in the 1880s and 1890s, thereby setting a lighthearted mood for the rest of the volume, while also delivering basic data on cowboy life. The book finishes with the especially sentimental "Longrope's Last Guard," concluding with the subject's death and burial out on the lonesome prairie. The sad ending of the anthology emphasizes a sense of mourning for all the vanishing open-range cowpunchers as well as the late author himself. This editorial decision to place a long story about death at the very end of Charlie Russell's book reinforced a sobering sense that something greater has happened than the accidental passing of a fictional character named "Longrope." *Trails Plowed Under* finishes in a way that suggests an entire era has disappeared forever.

CHOOSING WILL ROGERS FOR AN INTRODUCTION

Nancy Russell did not challenge Harry Maule's judgment on the book's structure. She actually praised him, writing, "Dividing the material into four sections, under the headings you suggested, is splendid."[26] In the same letter, however, she objected strongly to his choice of the person to write the book's introduction. As early as his Christmas letter, Maule advocated Owen Wister as his choice for this opening piece. Wister's status as a western fiction writer still remained high, despite his lack of a subsequent book as popular as his 1902 novel *The Virginian*. Before the slow mails could deliver Nancy Russell's objections to Wister, Maule contacted the author and encouraged him to begin working on the piece. In announcing his unauthorized action to Nancy, Maule tried to bolster his decision, stating, "we felt that it should have an introduction by someone with a reputation and literary distinction to treat it with the seriousness and importance Mr. Russell's work deserves. It would be very embarrassing to us now to call him off."[27]

Nancy Russell was steadfast in her choice. She knew who would be best for the introduction. "I had talked to Will Rogers," she informed Maule,

> and he was a personal friend of Charlie's and knew the West, talking the same language Charlie talked, so that is why I went to him if he would write the introduction.
>
> Mr. Wister never knew Charlie and his knowledge of the West is of an entirely different type than Will Rogers and Charlie Russell. As a literary man he undoubtedly is by far the greater, but this book is not literature,—it is just Charlie Russell. So you see how necessary it is to have Will Rogers do the work. Therefore please take up the matter with him.[28]

Nancy Russell had arranged a contract ten years earlier for her husband to illustrate a fancy edition of *The Virginian*.[29] She was well aware of Wister's high status in the world of western literature. Although she probably never met Wister personally in that transaction, and may not have read his entire book, she knew enough about the man's writing to sense its wide difference from her husband's stories. And, like Charlie's nephew Austin, she had heard her husband's comments enough to know that the bestselling book "offended" Charlie.[30] She knew without reservation that Owen Wister was wrong for this job and that Will Rogers was right for it.

Nancy's blunt assertion that *Trails Plowed Under* was not "literature" but rather an extension of her husband's personality generated a friendly retort from Maule:

> [W]hile I agree that Mr. Russell never made pretensions to literature, I still feel that his stories are, in a way, very great literature and certainly his pictures rank way up in the field of art. As such we can't have too distinguished an introducer. Of course, you understand and if Mr. Rogers does write the introduction we shall accept it gratefully.[31]

Maule seemed skeptical that Rogers could deliver anything appropriate for such an important book. When he read Rogers's introductory statement, however, the editor was very pleased. Maule wrote to Nancy to say that he saw Rogers's piece as

> one of the most remarkable introductions we ever read anywhere . . . the tremendous cleverness and deep sincerity with which he has written of his old friend. As a tribute to Mr. Russell, it is one of the most beautiful things I've ever read.[32]

Soon, Maule was proposing that the Will Rogers introduction should be reproduced as a sales poster for bookstores. The editor even suggested that Nancy Russell should persuade Rogers to praise *Trails Plowed Under* in his national newspaper column to appear on the date that Doubleday would release the finished book.[33]

Omitting Illustrations

Nancy got her way and Will Rogers wrote the introduction. But she had less success with the book's illustrations. While the focus between Nancy Russell and Harry Maule had been preoccupied with problems of text shortages, no one noticed until it was almost too late that a significant number of Charlie's pen/ink illustrations were missing. Nancy was unable to locate the original sketches used in the MNA stories that had appeared a decade earlier. Moreover, Cheely told her that the zinc plates with which he had printed the illustrations in the MNA newspapers and books were far too worn for further use. Nevertheless, Nancy believed that Maule could simply copy the pen/ink illustrations he needed from the two *Rawhide* books. The Doubleday editor, however, firmly told her that reprinting weak images of the pictures would do an injustice to Charlie's original artworks. In late May, Nancy finally located twenty-four of the missing sketches, but their early June arrival in New York proved too late for Maule. The editor was determined to have *Trails Plowed Under* printed and in the stores in time for the Christmas sales season. In addition, Maule's editorial team had already finished most of the graphic layout of the book. Maule told Nancy, "To use any large number of this twenty-four would necessitate tearing the whole thing apart and making it over again which I'm afraid would delay the publication . . . we'll work in just as many as we possibly can."[34] Nancy objected, urging Maule to reconsider and use all the illustrations that Charlie had created specifically for certain stories. In several letter exchanges about the illustrations, Maule held his ground, stating finally,

> Indeed, we held up the book for a couple of months waiting for them and finally had to go ahead without them in order to keep our publication schedule. . . . To add any more illustrations would throw the balance out from the book point of view and would, in our opinion, interfere with its excellence as a piece of book making and consequently with its success. Moreover to insert a great many more pictures now would mean doing the makeup all over again and the makeup of this book was quite a delicate and difficult job from the beginning in order to get the proper balance between type page and pictures. To do this would be expensive and would delay the publication.[35]

Months later, when proofreading the typeset galleys, Nancy wrote back to Maule, noting the specific absence of illustrations for "Bill's Shelby Hotel" (the hotel cook's deranged expression, wearing a derby hat and holding a long meat-cutting knife while a revolver handle protrudes from his greasy apron) and "A Ride In a Moving Cemetery" (one sketch showing a seated man staring at several close-by gravestones and another showing a wild collision between a freight train and a two-horse buggy ejecting two male riders). Nancy also noted an especially unfortunate omission—the absurd sketch of Tommy Simpson's Scottish cow with some of her calves and several hired men, all hard at work pulling on the numerous teats of her three udders.[36]

Although Harry Maule refused to accommodate Nancy Russell on the late-arriving illustrations, he did make one important concession. The editor included Charlie Russell's

FIG. 105. Charles M. Russell, *Milking Time*. Pen/ink, illustration for the story "Tommy
Simpson's Cow," appearing in the first MNA inserts, October 23, 1916, and *Rawhide
Rawlins Stories* but not *Trails Plowed Under*. Doubleday editor Harry Maule and his
New York staff were less enchanted by such rural humor than country people more
familiar with cows and likely to find this image hilarious.

autobiographical preface that Nancy had forwarded with the tardy sketches. "[I]t had not
occurred to me that you had wanted this used," Maule told Nancy,

> [I]t is the little introduction entitled "A Few Words About Myself" which appears
> in "More Rawhides." At the head of it we are using the sentence, "A personal intro-
> duction written by the author a few months before his death." This will explain the
> presence of the piece in the book as it is a rather unusual thing to put in a regular
> book.[37]

Maule's explanation helped to alert readers that the author had already died, providing an
opportunity for an especially sympathetic response. Once again Maule had nearly omitted one
of the outstanding facets of *Trails Plowed Under*. Charlie Russell and Will Rogers supplied two
unorthodox statements that set this book apart from other anthologies or writings about the
West. And once again, Nancy Russell's insistence on certain elements, in the face of Maule's editorial indifference, assured the book's distinctiveness. Nancy eventually wrote back to Maule, to
thank him for including Charlie's personal statement. "I am glad you followed my wishes," she
wrote, "and put in the little article that Charlie wrote about himself as everyone in the West
looks upon that as being a complete biography and think it a most remarkable piece of
work."[38] Although Harry Maule was wise enough to publish Charlie Russell's tales, he was also
detached sufficiently from rural culture in the West to have overlooked the value of many of
Russell's stories, the author's illustration choices, Russell's autobiographical statement, and the
choice of Will Rogers over Owen Wister to write the introduction.

FIG. 106. Charles M. Russell, *Trails Plowed Under*. Pen/ink, 1926, illustration for Charlie's story anthology *Trails Plowed Under*. Until Doubleday decided to print a color image on the cover of the book, this was Charlie and Nancy's selection for the cover design.

Color for Illustrations and the Book Cover

Despite his limited vision for materials included in *Trails Plowed Under*, Harry Maule did carry out several important design decisions that enhanced the book. The Russells had anticipated that a pen/ink sketch would appear on the cover of *Trails Plowed Under*, as similar ones had appeared on the two *Rawhide* books and the MNA volume *Backtrailing*. Accordingly, Charlie had prepared a sketch of a mounted cowboy and his horse being confounded by a freshly plowed field obliterating their old trails. Maule proposed to use this picture inside the book and to place a full color print of a Russell painting on the outer jacket to attract more sales.

In all of the Russells' previous experience in publishing, color printing on the outer jacket or inside illustrations had never been feasible options. Sensing a new opportunity, Nancy suggested a practical way to put some color printing inside *Trails Plowed Under*. An article about Russell in Doubleday's own *Country Life* magazine for August 1926, "The Man Behind the Brush" by Frank M. Chapman, Jr.,[39] included five prints of Russell paintings reproduced in full color. Nancy suggested that Doubleday use the same expensive color printing plates to place these images in the book.[40] Maule responded favorably, made the appropriate arrangements, and the pictures became the color illustrations and dust jacket art for *Trails Plowed Under*.[41]

First Volumes Shipped to Nancy

Nancy Russell's final contract with Doubleday for *Trails Plowed Under* arrived just before Christmas on December 23, 1926, two months after Charlie's death, accompanied by Maule's supportive letter. "I want to congratulate you," he told Nancy, "especially on the pictures for 'Trails Plowed Under.'. . . It is an achievement to have written these pieces almost as great as the pictures themselves."[42] On September 8, 1927, Harry Maule shipped two of the first completed copies of *Trails Plowed Under* to Nancy at the Russell cabin in Glacier National Park. In his accompanying note, Maule emphasized sales over any sense of status. "We all think the book looks mighty fine," Maule observed proudly. "It is a real memorial and tribute to Mr. Russell's greatness. I sincerely hope you will be able to sell a lot of them on your own hook and assure you that we are going to turn to now and do our darndest to make it a real success."[43] Maule had completed the task within his deadlines and the book was available on store shelves across the country by fall before the 1927 Christmas shopping season.

In the months that followed the release of *Trails Plowed Under,* Maule remained in contact with Nancy Russell. He told her about his sales pep-talk sessions for one hundred managers and clerks from Doubleday's twenty-one company-owned retail stores. They responded enthusiastically with suggestions that Maule get Will Rogers more involved in promoting the book. In addition, he invited her to "let me continue to serve you in every way I possibly can."[44] By November 1927, however, Maule had to disappoint Nancy with news that a manuscript for a biography of Charlie that she had commissioned a Great Falls newspaper reporter to assemble from her files and dictation was so poorly written that Doubleday had rejected it.[45] Maule later wrote to arrange the exhibition at New York's Grand Central Galleries of eighty-one pen/ink sketches and five wash drawings in connection with *Trails Plowed Under.*[46] By February 1928, Harry Maule was optimistically predicting a long commercial life for the book, stating, "It is a book which we carry in all our regular list advertising and push through the bookstores season after season, whereas most of the novels published when this was are practically dead."[47]

February also brought the business results that Nancy had been anticipating for many months. The author's widow and business collaborator received a check for $1,881.56 for the net royalties on sales of more than five thousand copies of *Trails Plowed Under,* priced at $3.50 each, calculated from September through December of 1927. Maule observed that "sales since then have been excellent and the book is going right on with remarkable life."[48] From this check onward through 1928 and after, Nancy Russell received the top royalty of 15 percent that she had negotiated in her contract. Unfortunately, the sales dropped off steadily in the months that followed. The next check for the first half of 1928 paid her just $899.73 for 1,736 copies sold, and the second half of 1928 showed sales of 769 copies and a check for only $362.00. The fifteen-month (1926–1927) total sales for the book came to more than 7,500 copies, generating total royalties of approximately $3,150.

Nancy Russell may have been delighted with these results, but she must have observed that selling art was more financially rewarding than marketing books. After Charlie's death, gallery shows were fewer and less lucrative for they lacked the presence of the charismatic artist who charmed the buyers. Nancy no longer tried to sell his larger works for the ten-thousand-

Trails Plowed Under
STORIES OF THE OLD WEST
Charles M. Russell

Forty-three robust, adventurous stories by the author
of GOOD MEDICINE illustrated with five of his
superb paintings and fifty line drawings.

WITH AN INTRODUCTION BY WILL ROGERS

FIG. 107. Early cover design for *Trails Plowed Under* by Charles M. Russell. The painting selected for the design is *Jerked Down,* now in the collection of the Gilcrease Museum in Tulsa, Oklahoma.

dollar fees that she had collected in the early 1920s. Still, the sale of a single oil painting could equal or exceed the entire royalty revenues for the first year and a half of sales of *Trails Plowed Under*. Nancy knew very well this significant difference between selling Charlie's artworks and selling his stories. About six months before the finished book arrived on store shelves, Maule had proposed a twenty-five-dollar deluxe edition, with a small original C. M. Russell line draw-ing tucked into each copy. The Doubleday editor probably imagined that he would make the proposal especially tempting to Nancy by pointing out that her 10-percent royalty, when com-bined with an extra 25-percent discount on sales she might make directly to customers, would amount to a nifty $8.75 combined royalty and profit on each book transaction.[49]

Nancy Russell was especially unimpressed with this proposal. "Regarding the deLuxe adition [*sic*]," she responded,

> it is absolutely out of the question to have original drawings or manuscript in a book and I think you will agree with me that if that is what is necessary, I would be very foolish to put them into books where I can take the one original and get five times what you sell the book for. Any special edition I have ever seen was only a lit-tle better cover and the very first off the press that made them valuable, but I know so little about publishing that I leave it to your judgment.[50]

Nancy may have known "little about publishing," but she knew more than most people about sharp intuition to control business transactions, especially when selling art. She knew better than the Doubleday editor that earning $8.75 for an original sketch by Charles M. Russell tucked into a nice book (a drawing that she could sell in a gallery for $125.00) was not a wise business strategy.

During the Great Depression years, Nancy Russell struggled financially. She still held many of Charlie's paintings and sketches for sale, and she could still order a foundry to cast a Russell bronze anytime a buyer might want one. With the ruined stock market and depressed economy, however, there were few art patrons willing and able to pay her prices. In 1929, Doubleday began distributing *Good Medicine,* Nancy's book of Charlie's illustrated letters. Eventually sales of this second book surpassed *Trails Plowed Under.* Together the two books sold well enough that Doubleday kept them both in print for decades, even when sales of one or the other might slow down. Nancy also explored other ways to generate income through Charlie's stories. She contracted with The Independent Syndicate Incorporated of Washington, D.C., to distribute his tales to newspapers around the country. In 1930 she received a check from the firm for $62.50—her half of the monthly revenues from a handful of subscribing papers. The checks that followed were progressively smaller.[51] Occasional use of one piece or another from *Trails Plowed Under* in a story anthology or collection seldom brought any significant funds. For a 1932 Harper and Brothers anthology, Nancy and Doubleday shared a dismal fifteen-dollar commission.[52] Neither syndication nor reprints in anthologies offered her any financial gain.

By 1935, Doubleday was deciding whether to reprint another run of *Trails Plowed Under.* Harry Maule contacted Nancy Russell to say that, although no longer spectacular, the sales of the book of stories remained steady enough to justify continued publishing. "We ourselves view the book as one of the most outstandingly satisfactory stock items on our list," wrote Maule. Nevertheless, sales were not high enough to justify a large printing, since even one thousand copies would last for several years. Accordingly, Maule asked for a royalty reduction down to 10 percent, or thirty-five cents per copy. In addition, he wanted to raise the price on *Good Medicine* to ten dollars per copy for the remaining stock.[53] In a single letter, Doubleday proposed to break two contracts with Nancy Russell. The price rise for one book might hurt sales or it might increase royalties. The stature of the book would surely rise, in any case, making that contract amendment easier to accept. With *Trails Plowed Under,* however, Nancy simply was in no position to resist. She had refused to allow a cut-rate version of the book to come out, presumably with the color printing removed. By relenting on the revised royalty, she kept the book available to customers in its best format and at the original price, despite the hard financial times.

A National Bestseller with a Long Life

After several years of declining health, Nancy Russell died in 1940 in Pasadena, California. The next information about the sales of *Trails Plowed Under* surfaced in the late 1950s. Harold McCracken reported in his 1957 biography, *The Charles M. Russell Book,* that the volume of Charlie Russell's stories had sold fifty-one thousand copies.[54] Back in 1926, Harry Maule had defined a "best-seller" for Nancy Russell as being "25,000 to 50,000 copies sold."[55] By the time Doubleday's subsidiary, Garden City Publishing, ceased publishing *Trails Plowed Under* in 1993, the book had entered in its twenty-eighth printing and the final count of hardback editions is not available from the publisher. Since 1996, the paperback edition published by the University of Nebraska Press, minus the color illustrations, with a brief but informative introduction by Brian Dippie, has kept Charlie Russell's stories available to contemporary readers in the twenty-first century. By early 2004, the paperback edition had sold 9,200 copies. Whatever the final numbers,[56] *Trails Plowed Under* has qualified as a bestselling classic in several fields: American folklore, colloquial literature, and American humor writing. Most significantly, it forms a critical component of the literary and cultural history of the American West.

The stories in *Trails Plowed Under* were all the literary creations of Charles M. Russell, but this book appeared in print as a consequence of an enterprising collaboration between Nancy Russell and Harry Maule. Nevertheless, the two publishing collaborators also shared responsibility for the book's shortcomings, which include a random arrangement of the stories, inappropriately placed illustrations, and the omission of several worthy pieces of writing and illustrations that would have enhanced its value even further. Despite the few shortcomings, however, Nancy Russell and Harry Maule helped ensure that *Trails Plowed Under* stayed in print and survived hard financial times, thereby assuring the continuation of Russell's literary/ storytelling legacy.

CHAPTER EIGHT

A Niche in American Literary History

"I ain't no historian, but I happen to savvy this incident."[1]
—*Rawhide Rawlins*

ost of Charles M. Russell's stories, whether spoken, written down, or published, fit naturally in a continuum of humor traditions and folkloric history in nineteenth-century America. With the appearance of his tales in the Montana Newspaper Association inserts, and then the *Rawhide Rawlins* books, and, following his death, with the 1927 publication of *Trails Plowed Under,* Russell brought many of these older American traditions into active use in twentieth-century literature. He also kept alive many regional topics, as well as the adventures and mishaps of his specific Montana friends to revive and sustain a unique component of American literature.

FRONTIER HUMORISTS OF THE OLD SOUTHWEST

Charlie Russell's brief tales and essays share many characteristics with a nineteenth-century, rural American literary tradition frequently identified as the "frontier humorists of the Old Southwest" (referring to the antebellum area that stretched approximately from Georgia to the Mississippi River).[2] Writing in *Georgia Scenes* in 1835, Augustus Baldwin Longstreet commented that the purpose of the frontier humorist "was to supply the chasm in history which has already been overlooked—the manner, customs, amusements, wit, dialect as they appear in all grades of society to an eye witness."[3] While the influx of population pressed the English-speaking "frontier" westward from the more settled southern regions, the Southwest humorists continued to write material appealing to the lighter sensibilities of rural residents in what also came to be categorized nationally as "local-color" anecdotes. Cecil Brown Williams defines local color has having settings, characters, and speech that are typical of a specific location. With special terms, syntax, and pronunciation that are unique to a specific place, characters in a local-color story "talk more like each other than like persons of another region."[4] A textbook definition of the genre distills the classification to certain distinctive "peculiarities":

> In general, local color emphasizes the setting as characteristic of a district, region, or era, and reproduces the customs, dialect, costumes, landscapes, and other peculiarities which have not been standardized. . . . As representatives of a movement the local colorists did not attract attention until after the Civil War, when they were associated with humor, with frontier tall tales, and with local traditions.[5]

Some critics cite early frontier humorists of the "old southwest," such as "William Tappan Thompson, George Washington Harris, W. T. Thorpe, Sol Smith, and Joseph G. Baldwin—who published works in the wake of A. B. Longstreet," within the definition of the local-color literary movement.[6] In contrast with the southern literature of Virginia or South Carolina that offered sentimental proslavery tributes to the plantation culture, the newspaper sketches of southwestern humor offered, instead, qualities that American Studies author Henry Nash Smith has characterized as "boisterous . . . satire."[7]

For most Southwest humorists, writing provided neither career nor prestige. Like his humor-writing predecessors, Charlie Russell also wrote for amusement rather than for gain. And like most of these earlier writers, Russell published most of his works in newspapers before they appeared in books. Russell's stories resembled the work of earlier southwestern frontier humorists who

> were quick to seize upon the comic aspects of the rough life about them and graphically sketched the humorous and colorful local happenings, the oddities in rustic pioneer character and the tall tales that were going the rounds of the locality.[8]

Creating humor out of everyday life, both Russell and the earlier Southwest writers consistently used "real incidents and real characters."[9] Seldom did they fabricate entire stories. In Russell's case, a story, sculpture, or picture celebrated or teased familiar figures and friends with a new (sometimes purposely distorted) version of the narrative account that they might have shared first with him. Nancy Russell explained to her Great Falls friends that "stories he heard were history that has never been written and would have been lost had he lacked the ability to put them on canvas."[10] Folklorist Richard Dorson praised those who collected local-color tales, describing one who

> made no distinction between the traveling fiction and the actual or embroidered incident; he listened to the townsmen with the ear of an artist, not of the

classifier . . . [working by means of] the immersion of a talented writer in the wells of folk tradition.[11]

Russell also heard local-history yarns "with the ear of an artist," as well as the heart of a humorist and the mind of a local historian. Consciously or intuitively, Charlie Russell continued many well-established Southwest humor techniques in his published pieces.

BRET HARTE AND LOCAL COLOR

Most American literary observers understand the local-color movement as emerging in the wake of the Civil War, in the years shortly after Charlie Russell was born. Walter Blair and Hamlin Hill agreed that the movement's postwar origin began in 1870, when Bret Harte seemed to launch single-handedly the local-color movement by publishing *The Luck of Roaring Camp and Other Stories* and his humorous poem "Plain Language from Truthful James."[12] Harte's poem's title referred to an American tendency to accept plain language in "local-color" writing as being especially truthful. In an 1899 essay, Harte argues that the distinctive characteristic of genuinely American literature developed in the West as humor:

> Crude at first, it [western humor] received a literary polish in the press, but its dominant quality remained. It was concise and condensed, yet suggestive. It was delightfully extravagant—or a miracle of understatement. It voiced not only the dialect, but the habits of thought of a people or locality. It gave a new interest to slang. . . . [I]t admitted no fine writing nor affectation of style. It went directly to the point. It was burdened by no conscientiousness; it was often irreverent; it was devoid of all moral responsibility—but it was original! . . . It became and still exists—as an essential feature of newspaper literature. It was the parent of the American "short story."[13]

Harte made his literary mark by merging the rural dialect and irreverent humor of the West with sentimental narrative plots. This blend of western "vulgarity" with nineteenth-century "sentimentality" formed the platform for Harte's short stories and also for the literary style of "local-color" writing. In denying that he had created this phenomenon single-handedly, Harte mentions "such writers as Harris, Cable, Page, Mark Twain in *Huckleberry Finn*," and others who had also been contributing to the literary movement. "Of such is the American short story of to-day—the germ of American literature to come."[14]

Bret Harte developed his literary reputation with sentimental short stories about the rural, uneducated people of the nineteenth century, portraying them as having hearts of gold. Harte's popularity thrived on his depiction of the everyday slang speech of rustic people of the West—speech patterns that were dismissed by some critics as being too vulgar for consideration as serious literature. Twain criticized Harte's down-home speech as inauthentic, "a dialect no man in heaven or earth had ever used until Harte invented it. With Harte it died, but it was no loss."[15] Wallace Stegner agreed, describing Harte's dialogue as "synthetic . . . with a flavor of colloquialism."[16]

Bret Harte's writing reflects little in common with Russell's vernacular stories. Harte employed an unnamed intellectual narrator who uses a condescending, non-western, or non-rural language, demonstrating that Harte wrote for an entirely different reader than the Montana artist. Charlie Russell never attempted such high-toned verbosity as seen in the following word samples from Harte's most popular work about nineteenth-century Sierra miners in California, "The Luck of Roaring Camp"[17]: "facetiousness," "ludicrous," "interdicted," "imperceptibility," "infelicitous," "lugubrious," and "tranquilizing," to cite but a few of the narrator's choices of diction. Russell may have enjoyed Harte's works, but he told and wrote stories primarily for the pleasure of his own unsophisticated Montana contemporaries.[18] These readers of Montana Newspaper Association sections and the *Rawhide Rawlins* books seemed to enjoy his portrayal of their dialect enough to give momentum to the 1927 publication of *Trails Plowed Under,* indicating a general acceptance and appreciation for Russell's versions of their own oral-tradition stories.

Some twentieth-century literary critics perceive local-color writers as mere visitors to the community they portray. For these critics, the tourist writer "insists upon the veracity of his reporting and invites his readers to marvel at the strangeness of truth."[19] In one of her popular western novels, Montana author B. M. Bower made fun of an outsider's quest for a quick dose of the magic ingredient of western culture. Her character, an unsuccessful eastern writer, provokes a friend's advice by whining:

> "My last rejection states that the local color is weak and unconvincing. Hang the local color!" . . . "The thing to do, then," [Reeve Howard] drawled, "is to go out and study up on it. Get in touch with that country, and your local color will convince."[20]

Bower hired her friend Charlie Russell to provide illustrations and a painting for the dust jacket of this novel, *The Lure of Dim Trails,* thereby giving the artist an opportunity to appreciate her satire on outsiders seeking glimmers of the very local color that he understood firsthand. For the last twenty years of his life, Russell must have been aware of the term *local color* and his involvement in its portrayal.[21] Nevertheless, he did not use the term and seemed as if he were unaware of this category that best described his paintings, sculptures, and short stories.

Henry Nash Smith and Cultural Primitivism

Without pointing at Russell's narrative works, several influential twentieth-century critics have challenged the value of local-color literature. In his landmark book *Virgin Land,* Henry Nash Smith expressed impatience with "the dying theory of cultural primitivism" that grants a sense of superiority for presumed "western freshness" versus "eastern over-sophistication." One positive side in the use of local slang, in Smith's view, has been "the creation of an American literary prose formed on the vernacular." Its greatest accomplishment was Twain's *The Adventures of Huckleberry Finn,* "the first masterpiece of vernacular prose."[22]

As a local-color writer, Charlie Russell stayed closer to the early frontier humorists than to the later local-color sentimentalists like Harte. The artist/author used some frontier-humor tricks for recreating oral-tradition storytelling on paper, techniques that his Old Southwest counterparts employed decades earlier, recreating the sense, in print, of people telling stories aloud by using the "mock oral tale" with the "framework" opening and closing that returns to the first narrator's voice.[23] Charlie Russell's stories "The Trail of the Reel Foot," "Dog Eater," and "Finger-That-Kills Wins His Squaw" employ this opening/closing framework portraying the author/storyteller as a scribe who has simply recorded on paper an overheard oral exchange.[24]

Despite his conformity with the earlier humor styles, Charlie Russell remains a difficult artist/author to contain within categories. One critic declares that local color "does not grapple seriously with the moral problem of social groups or of individuals in groups. Instead, it sermonizes and supplies innumerable demonstrations of unambiguous virtue."[25] Yet Russell's stories about Indians, especially "How Lindsay Turned Indian" and "Curley's Friend," address multiracial conflict directly and without much sentimentality. And "The War Scars of Medicine Whip" fits another critic's observation of some local-color authors with strong consciences who "were not above shocking their readers by graphic portrayals of what seemed to them social injustices unworthy of a great and proud democracy."[26] Certainly, some of Russell's brief humor sketches roast his Montana cronies with local anecdotal color that simply means to entertain. Nevertheless, the intensity and accuracy in his published narratives also informed his readers and the local culture, fulfilling Russell's basic purpose for his storytelling: entertaining his audience while passing along authentic cultural history of the West.

A drawback for most readers in subsequent generations, however, is unfamiliarity with the components of local-color narratives. As Russell's nephew observed, "There was magic in Charlie's talk: he made you see things. And yet he told none of this in detail—you just saw it. Of course, for your mind's eye to fill in the background you had to know the country."[27] Austin Russell, in his attempt to praise his uncle's storytelling, has unwittingly articulated one of the basic drawbacks of local-color literature. If the reader does not already know the country, the town, or the local characters and their life patterns, a local-color story has less impact. Charlie Russell anticipated this diminished response when he avoided telling stories to strangers and people unfamiliar with Montana. As Blair and Hill have noted,

> most readers today will find the [local color] writing sentimental in ways that we now sniff at. . . . The dialect will be too hard to read. The preachment will be too obvious. Because the writings that contain it do so many things that we find unappealing, practically all of the humor in the vast body of local-color fiction has lost its savor for modern readers.[28]

In general, Russell's published writings *are* less accessible to non-westerners or outsiders to nineteenth-century cultures of the American West. Predictably, his writings are less popular with general readers than his paintings, sketches, and sculptures. In comparison with his local-color writings, Russell's fine art expresses a more universal narrative language of color and form. Nevertheless, when delivered aloud, Russell's stories can amuse modern audiences, both urban and rural.[29] And, despite the vernacular style of *Trails Plowed Under,* the book continues to survive in print in the twenty-first century because the stories still appeal to many readers.

WALLACE STEGNER AND LOCAL COLOR

One prominent western writer who disliked local-color writing, Wallace Stegner put specific distance between his writings and the literary category defined by the works of Bret Harte. "I don't like to be called a western writer," he said, "simply because it's a limiting term, a pejorative term like 'local colorist.'" As one of the leading novelists and essayists in the twentieth-century West, Wallace Stegner's opinions about local-color literature and Charlie Russell carry unusual significance. His perfunctory opinion as expressed in a spontaneous interview may not reflect his complete thoughts, but his words are informative: "[Russell] had a cowman's prejudice. Plowing turned all the god-damned country upside down, he said. In all his attitudes and his history, though not in his gifts, he was characteristic."[30] Despite his remarkable gifts as a fine artist, Russell's values seemed too typical for a nineteenth-century cattleman to impress Stegner.

In this revealing interview, Wallace Stegner's negative comments made no mention of Russell's published stories. Stegner probably lacked detailed exposure to Russell's writings because of his distaste for local-color anecdotes. He expressed a disdain for the cowboy culture that may have been associated with the despised, western-style "rugged individualism" of his own father.[31] Adding to his intellectual distance from Russell, Stegner's family remained in Great Falls only fifteen months before settling in Utah,[32] not enough time for young Wallace to adopt the Montana town's pride and enthusiasm for their greatest local celebrity. As a young boy doing a few of Russell's lawn-mowing chores in summer, Stegner apparently never spent time with the older artist as he relaxed and told stories to his friends. Stegner recalled, "I never got into his log cabin. That was for special people from the Mint."[33] His lost opportunity compares with Russell's missed chance to hear Mark Twain speak when that author/humorist visited Great Falls on July 31, 1895, during a national lecture tour.[34] In a larger sense Stegner never really "got into" Russell's stories or personality, an ironic situation for two gifted, influential western figures of different eras whose lives crossed momentarily. One possible explanation for Stegner's disinterest in Russell's literary output could be revealed in his comment about the problem of regional isolation:

> It is the sticks I mean when I speak of the West—the last of the sticks—the subregions between the ninety-eighth meridian and the Sierra-Cascades, where patterns of local habit and belief have developed in some isolation, where they are clearer, more innocent, less diluted by outside influences, where they are bred into native sons who later, as writers, find them limited, unusable, or embarrassing.[35]

The "sub-regional" stories that Russell published to amuse his Montana friends may have been bred into some of Wallace Stegner's earliest perceptions, but they seemed inappropriate for his mature wish to create a literature of deeper self-understanding.

In the first half of the twentieth century, Hamlin Garland, Wallace Stegner, and other western writers encouraged a new literary "regionalism" to reflect more character development in narratives portraying local environmental influences. They tried to shed what Etulain calls "misleading Wild West images and the numbing sentimentalism of the local-color writers." In the 1930s, however, folklorist B. A. Botkin began "challenging regionalists to pay more attention to folk cultures" to have a better understanding of their region.[36] Decades later, in his interview with Etulain, Stegner was advocating

> using provincialism as a springboard. The most personal reaction to a landscape to people, to ways of living, is that which is rooted in the local. So long as that local is not so absolutely eccentric, so completely out of the stream that it becomes merely local color, a strange picturesque kind of oddity, then the provincial basis is as good a basis as you can get.[37]

By leading to the regional perspective, Russell's brief stories and essays have provided provincial materials for later writers who are sensitive to local western cultures.

In Charlie Russell's stories, the crucial link between local culture and the printed page required the convincing and accurate use of the local vernacular. Many successful depictions of local (uneducated) dialects in print exploit a national belief that Walter Blair has described as "a conviction that Americans long found hilarious—that there is no necessary relationship between a man's learning and his knowledge or even his wisdom."[38] This conviction runs counter to Henry Nash Smith's criticism, since it embodies the very essence of "cultural primitivism"—the rivalry between urban people and the "smarter-than-they-look-and-sound" rural characters. As one of Russell's fellow cowpunchers, John Barrows, observed, "The people of the [western] frontier were quick to resent any assumption of superiority, real or fancied"[39] by outsiders, especially from the East. Hoaxes, pranks, and lies perpetrated on the outsiders by jokers like Charlie Russell and his western contemporaries took inspiration from the East/West cultural rivalry. Folklorist B. A. Botkin notes that westerners created humor at the expense of easterners "because every tenderfoot has to be initiated or because every tourist is a natural sucker in the West, no matter how smart he may be back home."[40]

The local-color movement brought diversity to American literature preoccupied with eastern viewpoints. According to Williams, "The Local Color Movement was essentially a democratic popular literary manifestation. Hardly any wealthy persons figure as characters in Local Color stories, and intellectual aristocracy has little place."[41] Russell's story "Lepley's Bear" provided his only published work that roasts a well-to-do cattleman rather than one of the rancher's hired hands. Unlike writers such as Harte, who maintained a more elegant and grammatically correct voice for his narrator, Russell made the supposedly vulgar vernacular serve as his narrators' and his characters' language. Vernacular literature, whether *The Adventures of Huckleberry Finn* or *Trails Plowed Under,* requires "serious" readers to pay careful attention to language that often signals a lack of serious content. In this regard, critic James Austin notes that for vernacular writing to succeed, sympathetic readers "must reach out to the author and understand." Quite the opposite of sympathetic outreach was the case for the "intelligent and respectable people" on the public library committee of Concord, Massachusetts, who, in 1884, rejected *The Adventures of Huckleberry Finn* as being "rough, coarse and inelegant, dealing with a series of experiences, not elevating. . . . [It is] the veriest trash."[42] The reactions to Clemens's novel were probably more positive along the Mississippi River, where the local-color language would feel more familiar.

Forty years after the first publication of *The Adventures of Huckleberry Finn*, Russell's two vernacular *Rawhide Rawlins* books generated a broadly positive response from everyday people in Montana and from scattered western readers such as J. Frank Dobie in Texas. But critical disdain for western slang has reappeared in the late twentieth century. Historian Anne Butler has argued that such speech somehow reinforces political and social oppression. "Frontier language not only defined Americans' imagery of the West in concrete terms," concludes Butler,

> but also acted as a filter for national memory and soothed the collective conscience with the balm of honor, valor and democracy. "Screaming savages," "ambushed and massacred," "greasers," "vigilante justice," "bucks and squaws" blended into a historical collage where violence, death, oppression and racism underscored a romantic adventure fondly recalled as "the Wild West." The language imprinted a vision of the frontier that not only glorified reckless adventure and brutal conquest but also equated these with the promotion of democratic government.[43]

For one western woman who had lived closer than Butler to the nineteenth-century rural West, however, the speech patterns of the less sophisticated participants could evoke quite a different series of recollections. As she told researcher James Rankin in the 1930s, "It's always fun to meet with the old-timers—they speak a language of the old west which is fast fading. It's music in the ears of those who understood its kindness, sincerity, and honesty. It somehow soothes the heart."[44] Although Russell expected that his narrative expressions in paint or bronze would please like-minded art patrons as well as inform subsequent generations by serving as historical representations, he seems to have fashioned his published writings specifically for his immediate turn-of-the-century, rural-minded western audiences primarily with his use of familiar, colloquial language.

George Ade and Fables in Slang

Charlie Russell's historically based yarns also reflect his exposure to works of several other local-color writers. During Russell's lifetime, three men who employed rural slang in their published local-color stories were George Ade, Alfred Henry Lewis, and Andy Adams. Their books appeared in the years from 1897 to 1913, the same period when Charlie Russell experimented with writing and publishing stories. Certain Russell tales reflect similar styles and subjects with these writers' works. Russell's personal library[45] contained at least three volumes of contemporary fables by George Ade, including *More Fables in Slang*.[46] Ade's small-town Indiana world involving literary clubs, pompous colonels, and stingy farmers shared little with the characters and settings in Russell's western stories. Ade's controlled use of irony, however, seems to have left echoes in Russell's descriptive prose. In one story, Ade wrote:

> Two or three Matrons, who were too Heavy for Light Amusements, but not old

enough to remain at Home and Knit organized the Club. Nearly every Woman in town rushed to get in for fear somebody would say she hadn't been Asked.[47]

One Russell passage shows a similar dry wit that withholds crucial information until the last moment. "One heavy man," observes Russell, describing the train ride in his story "A Reformed Cowpuncher in Miles City," "the gent from Sun River Valley was lucky enough to land on his head, so he wasn't injured none."[48] Russell includes enough hints to suggest to his knowledgeable readers that the "Sun River gent" was his friend, the widely respected cattleman Belknap "Bally" Buck. Ade may have had some specific women in mind for the "Matrons," but in contrast with Russell's characters Ade's story figures seem more archetypal than specific, more cultural generality than local history.

George Ade's next book, *More Fables,* contains one story that must have caught Charlie Russell's attention if he ever opened the copy that stood on his shelf. The story carries the title "The Tale of the Inveterate Joker who Remained in Montana." In his younger days, Russell earned the right to be considered an incurable Montana joker, but his life differed from Ade's unnamed hero who finished at the end of a rope. Ade adds, "He did not hang straight enough to suit, so they brought a Keg of Nails and tied to his feet, and then stood off and Shot at the buttons on the back of his coat."[49] In addition to a similar passage about adding weight to a hanging victim in his story "Hands Up,"[50] Russell also wrote in "Johnny Reforms Landusky," about the fate of a comic villain, Dum Dum Bill, who "hasn't got enough weight below his head to break his neck, [so] his end's hastened by tuckin' an anvil into the seat of his pants."[51] Although the joke about adding weight to a hanging victim could easily be a part of widespread oral-tradition humor that reached the ears of Ade and Russell independently, the coincidence is notable, suggesting Russell's affinity for the popular Indiana humorist.

ALFRED HENRY LEWIS AND WOLFVILLE STORIES

In comparison with George Ade's urbane and grammatically formal use of colloquial language, Alfred Henry Lewis's seven volumes of *Wolfville* stories feature an especially exaggerated version of rural slang. In one story, Lewis writes:

> It's only now an' then . . . that Injuns invades Wolfville; an' when they does, we all scowls 'em outen camp—sort o' makes a sour front so as to break em early of habits of visitin' us. We shore don't hone none to have 'em hankerin' 'round.[52]

Lewis lived in the West for many years, working as a real estate agent in Dodge City and as a newspaper editor in Las Vegas, New Mexico. By the time he wrote the Wolfville stories, however, he was living in New York, writing about urban crime as a newspaper reporter. In his effort to recreate rural speech patterns from such a distance, Lewis seems to have overstated the local western slang.

While Lewis was working as a reporter in New York from 1897 to 1913, Charlie Russell made his first visit there in 1904. Upon returning to Great Falls, the artist mentioned meeting Lewis, among other celebrities.[53] Russell's nephew reported that Charlie read and enjoyed the

Wolfville stories,[54] and the artist's writings reflect some parallels with Lewis's work in his similar uses of ironic narrative. But Russell avoided Lewis's distinctive phonetic spellings to suggest rural western pronunciation in such words as "kyards" (cards), "hooman" (human), "fooneral" (funeral), "sech" (such), "thar" (there), "spechul malignant" (especially deadly), "towerists" (tourists), or numerous other examples of artificial misspelling. As Blair and Hill observe, "Even when, like Alfred Henry Lewis, local colorists somewhat sullied the pure and poetic vernacular to get laughs, they were as ostentatious as the rest in parading local habits, occupations, and backgrounds."[55] Russell also avoided Lewis's blatant racism that permeates Wolfville where, according to critic Abe Ravitz, "Chinks (Chinese), Greasers (Mexicans), Injuns and evangelists are treated with equal contempt."[56]

In one similarity noticed by Russell scholar and author Rick Stewart, Alfred Henry Lewis employs a character called "The Old Cattleman" as his primary narrator. Similarly, Charlie Russell used "Rawhide Rawlins" to narrate about half of his stories. Russell experimented with name variations before recasting several narrators into "Rawhide Rawlins." Nevertheless, many Russell narrators remained distinctive: *Jack Shea* relates "Hands Up!," *Bedrock* tells "A Savage Santa Claus," *Dad Lane* relates "The Trail of the Reel Foot," *Bowlegs* tells his own story in "A Pair of Outlaws," and so forth. Several other stories leave the narrator unnamed, suggesting that the voice is Russell's own. And "Rawhide Rawlins" does not narrate Russell's more serious Indian stories.[57] In these cross-cultural adventures, "Squaw Owens," "Dad Lane," and a few other distinct personalities describe events and their cultural context, reflecting realistic incidents and, occasionally, the fictional narrator's biased perspective. Charlie Russell may have been influenced by Alfred Henry Lewis in the use of a narrator speaking in local vernacular. In the absence of documentation that clarifies the artist's creative-writing method, the interpretation is open to speculation. Nevertheless, Russell's variety of narrators and narrative formats contrasts with Lewis's singular use of "The Old Cattleman." Whatever the impact of Lewis's narrator and exaggerated vernacular on Russell's published tale-telling, the Montana artist found numerous ways to tell a story on paper that reached well beyond the Wolfville example.

In addition to his narrator "The Old Cattleman," Alfred Henry Lewis also populated his stories with characters who lacked development, serving as bit players in comic sketches. Lewis presents such figures as "Faro Nell," "Cherokee Hall," and "Silver City Philip" to perform various tasks in "The Old Cattleman's" narratives. Their impact seems less realistic than Russell figures such as "Highwood Hank," "Mormon Zack Larson," "Bedrock Jim," or "Dad Lane." The Russell characters, in most cases, derive from actual people, whereas the lineage of Lewis's Wolfville inhabitants seems less rooted in western soil. Russell published stories that he had developed over years as oral amusements to give friendly discomfort directly to a listener who often happened to be the main character. Although his individual descriptions tend to be very brief, they typically distill one or two characteristics to achieve their comic impact. In contrast, Lewis's people seem more like cartoon caricatures than western archetypes. Obviously, Lewis enjoyed wide enough popularity to be able to publish seven Wolfville volumes, but critical readers have seldom been enthusiastic. Bernard DeVoto, for one, did not warm to Lewis's efforts, commenting that "Wolfeville [*sic*] is just a set of painted flats against a canvas backdrop."[58] Apparently, DeVoto recorded no response to Russell's stories.

ANDY ADAMS AND COWBOY CAMPFIRE STORIES

More realistic in cattle-culture details than Lewis's Wolfville tales, Andy Adams's novel *Log of a Cowboy*[59] and his other novels and stories have attracted the praise of critics such as J. Frank Dobie, who called Adams "the dean of all cowboy writers."[60]

Five years older than Russell, Adams (1859–1935) arrived in Texas in 1882 and worked for ten years in the cattle business, including participation in cattle drives in Texas, the "Indian Territories" (now Oklahoma), and Kansas, before settling in Colorado. Russell and Adams admired each other's work and exchanged correspondence in an unsuccessful effort to have Russell illustrate an Adams novel.[61] *The New York Times* quoted Adams as saying "if [Russell] painted a naked cowboy swimming across a river you'd know it was a cowpuncher."[62] And Russell told a Denver newspaper:

> Most of the writers of Western stories to-day don't seem to get just the right atmosphere of those times. There is only one exception that I know of, and that is a book by a Colorado man—"The Log of a Cowboy," by Andy Adams. I think there is nobody can say there is anything in that book that isn't the 'real thing.'[63]

Despite Adams's admiration for Russell's paintings, however, he may have had less enthusiasm for some of the artist's published stories. Charlie Russell's characterizations involve much greater use of local vernacular than Adams's. And Russell's frequent roast formats typically create humor by means of exaggeration, a technique that Adams scorned. In referring to a story told by the character "Stubbs," Adams's biographer, Wilson M. Hudson, states, "Stubbs's story is the exaggerated, wild and woolly kind that Andy heartily disliked when presented as true of the west."[64] Stubbs's fourteen-page story seems more dry and literary than "wild and wooly" when compared with the exaggerations in Russell's two pages (582 words) for "Bab's Skees" or in four pages (1,266 words) for "Dog Eater."[65]

Another, more subtle difference between Adams's and Russell's techniques is found in their selection of words. Russell chose a more subdued vernacular portrayal than Alfred Henry Lewis, and Adams took an even more formal route. Hudson explains that Andy's use of language

> is colorful and appropriate but not overdone or exaggerated. It is the language of cowboys and Rangers reworked and made smoother than it actually was. Though it has the ring of real talk, it could hardly be studied by a modern scholar as an altogether accurate and modern specimen of the language of the Southwest in the seventies and eighties. . . . he has retained the idioms and figures and improved the grammar and connection.[66]

Two examples illustrate the different styles that Adams and Russell used. Both feature a narrator's voice in the first sentences of stories about cattle stampedes. Adams wrote, "'Speaking of stampedes,' said Runt, 'reminds me of a run I was in and over which I was paid by my employer a very high complement.'"[67] In a similar comment, Russell stated, "'Whoever told you that cattle stampede without cause was talkin' like a shorthorn,' says Rawhide Rawlins. 'You can bet all you got that whenever cattle run, there's a reason for it. A whole lot of times cattle run, an' nobody knows why but the cows an' they won't tell.'"[68] Russell's style seems to be the most realistically evocative, filling the middle ground between the exaggerated overstatement of Alfred Henry Lewis and the slightly stilted formality of Andy Adams. Since Russell could make high-priced art easily yet struggled mightily to write, he lacked Adams's serious literary ambition. Consequently, Russell never wove his separate yarns into his own larger format as Adams did so successfully with *Log of Cowboy.*

Frederic Remington's Journalistic Stories

Several years before Andy Adams and Charlie Russell broke into print, Frederic Remington enhanced his stature as an expert on the American West by publishing 106 stories and articles in some of the nation's widely distributed weekly and monthly publications. Many of Remington's short pieces reappeared during his lifetime in six illustrated book collections.[69] He published most frequently in *Harper's Weekly* and several other New York–based publications, such as *Century* and *Collier's.* Remington also frequently sold illustrations to these publications, but when the illustration business was slow he encouraged other writers to publish stories that would create demand for his artworks. And when this effort came up short, the artist presented his own manuscripts for publication. According to his biographers, "The reason Remington needed to write was to get a sufficient number of his pictures printed."[70] While Russell was still working as a cowboy and honing his skill as a casual storyteller, Remington was making sure he had a steady demand for his illustrations from the nation's leading periodicals.

Frederic Remington's writings differed from Charlie Russell's sympathetic portrayals of Indian motives and ideas. Although superficially sympathetic with the Indians' difficulties in becoming farmers, as seen in "Artist Wanderings Among the Cheyennes," Remington still advocated U.S. Army control of all reservations.[71] Despite his patronizing sympathy for the defeated Indians, this artist remained loyal to his companions among the cavalry who pursued and suppressed Indian resistance. He ends his tale "Natchez's Pass" with the declaration, "What I wonder at is why highly cultivated people in America seem to side with savages as against their own soldiers."[72] Remington also proved sympathetic to the soldiers' viewpoint in his article "The Sioux Outbreak in South Dakota," which deals with the famous incident "the Wounded Knee Massacre." When his article appeared in *Harper's Weekly,* it contained no mention of the overactive killing of noncombatant Indian women and children, only the jovial, post-battle celebration by the victorious military professionals and an acknowledgment that "this professional interest in the military process of killing men sometimes rasps a citizen's nerves."[73] Conversely, Russell never wrote about the army or military conflict with Indians, and he did "side with savages," especially in his stories "The War Scars of Medicine Whip" and "Curley's Friend."

The humor that permeates most of Charlie Russell's stories and essays seems noticeably absent in Frederic Remington's writings. His few expressions of levity stand out prominently, including his droll description of an army experiment with mechanization in "The Colonel of the First Cycle Infantry" and his brief but effective try at self-depreciating humor in "How A

Trout Broke a Friendship."[74] But the humorously unpredictable encounters between man and nature found in many Russell yarns, such as "Bab's Skees" or "Dog Eater," do not appear in Remington's writings. Frederic Remington seemed to be aware of his lack of humor and admitted candidly to a friend that

> you have the faculty [*sic*] of not taking people or life seriously and that's it[:] the heart throb of modern litterary [*sic*] men. That's what makes me such a d fool— I'm too serious.[75]

Remington's best pieces about nature are serious rather than humorous and take place near his home in the canoeing waters of the Northeast, not in the West.

Frederic Remington explored several regions and events in his writings that Charlie Russell ignored, including northern Mexico, labor unrest in Chicago, the Spanish-American War in Cuba, and the U.S. cavalry in the West. Russell had little interest in writing about incidents not directly related to the northern plains and mountains. Conversely, Remington, for all his popular stature as an expert on the cowboy West, wrote very little about the cattle culture,[76] deferring to writers such as Owen Wister, Andy Adams, and Alfred Henry Lewis to publish pieces that editors would routinely match with his vivid cowboy illustrations. On a few issues, such as the preference for horses over automobiles and the disdain for mechanical advancements, Remington and Russell expressed similar attitudes. Although Russell might have read some of Remington's writings, he left no record of it and showed no indications of Remington's influence in his own writings. Unlike the situation with a few of Russell's paintings, none of the cowboy artist's writings have been singled out by modern critics as somehow following Remington's literary footsteps.

Charlie Russell showed no interest in two literary forms that Remington pursued successfully, writing novels and plays for the stage. When Russell first arrived in New York, a stage play adapted from one of Remington's two novels was experiencing moderate success: *John Ermine of the Yellowstone*.[77] The differences between these two western artist/writers in handling the subject of interracial marriage proves to be revealing. In Remington's plot about John Ermine, the white man raised by Indians gets rejected in a marriage offer to a cavalry officer's daughter. Ermine attempts to retaliate against her favored suitor but dies tragically in the effort. John Ermine pursues a self-destructive course, seeking acceptance by the white society that he cannot reenter because he has become too close culturally to the Indians.[78] In referring to a pair of Indians, Remington's novel attempts an ironic comment, stating, "Neither of the two mentioned people realized that the purpose of the present errand was to aid in bringing about the change which meant their passing."[79] Remington's story reflects little grounding in the historical West and rides on the author's stilted prose.

In contrast with Remington's fantasy of tragic interracial romance, Charlie Russell presented "How Lindsay Turned Indian," based on the historical figure Hugh Monroe, who successfully crossed the wide gap between the races. Monroe (or Lindsay) preferred to marry an Indian woman and live among her people. He survived to a ripe old age, happy with his choice, enriched by his experiences, and seemingly the envy of both the story's narrator and the author. Charlie Russell may have been nostalgic about the loss of nomadic Indian culture, but his writings demonstrate that, ultimately, he developed a mature preference for western realism over ungrounded melodrama.

Mark Twain's Appeal for Russell

Russell expressed more rapport with Samuel Clemens/Mark Twain's writings than with Frederic Remington's: he owned at least four volumes by Twain.[80] Russell seems to have had a special affinity for Twain's *A Connecticut Yankee in King Arthur's Court.* The artist added extra illustrations for one copy of Twain's novel and, upon visiting England in 1914 and wandering into an inspiring patch of forest,[81] mentioned in a personal letter his fantasy of feeling like the book's main character (**see plate 29**).

In another expression of his affinity for Twain's *Connecticut Yankee,* Russell added some extra illustrations to a friend's copy of the novel.[82] Russell shared a feeling for Twain's antiwar sentiments, expressing it through his knack for constructing rhymes in Elizabethan English. In a gift picture for his neighbor, Miss Josephine Trigg (**see plate 30**), Charlie created a confrontation between a mounted, armed knight and a court jester, who proclaims in words painted onto the surface of the picture:

> Hold and sheath thy blade I bring but merriment
> Whilst thou a slave of war, from death's own stronghold sent
> Would with thy wand of steel clame by might the way
> And turn from white to red this snow on Christmas day.
>
> I own thy greatness, noble Sir, a Fool I am thou seth
> But who is welcomed most by man, Merriment or Death?
> If merriment be ignorance and war is wisdom's school
> With gory blades as teachers, I am, thank the Saints, a Fool.[83]

The key area where Charlie Russell and Mark Twain differ in attitude concerns Indians. As mentioned earlier in chapter 3, Twain expresses a hostile attitude toward Native Americans in several essays and fiction pieces. Literary-humor critic Jesse Bier concluded that Twain's apparent scorn for Indians grew out of his disillusionment with the popular romantic stereotypes that nineteenth-century writers (especially James Fenimore Cooper) typically associated with Indians. Bier writes:

> The intransigent attitude was a counter-attack against the romanticizings. . . . The Indian, unfortunately, became one of Twain's specific symbols for all the false emotion he came to loathe after having been seduced by lies.[84]

Although they grew up generations apart, Russell shared a Missouri origin with Sam Clemens, living when local humor writers frequently produced brief pieces for newspaper publication. But despite their value in western humor and local cultural history, Russell's published works

CHAPTER XV

SANDY'S TALE

"AND so I'm proprietor of some knights," said I, as we rode off. "Who would ever have supposed that I should live to list up assets of that sort. I shan't know what to do with them; unless I raffle them off. How many of them are there, Sandy?"

"Seven, please you, sir, and their squires."

"It is a good haul. Who are they? Where do they hang out?"

"Where do they hang out?"

"Yes, where do they live?"

"Ah, I understood thee not. That will I tell eftsoons." Then she said musingly, and softly, turning the words daintily over her tongue: "Hang they out —hang they out—where hang—where do they hang out; eh, right so; where do they hang out. Of a truth the phrase hath a fair and winsome grace, and is prettily worded withal. I will repeat it anon and anon in mine idlesse, whereby I may peradventure learn it. Where do they hang out. Even so! already it falleth trippingly from my tongue, and forasmuch as—"

"Don't forget the cow-boys, Sandy."

"Cow-boys?"

"Yes; the knights, you know: You were going to

FIG. 108. Extra illustrated page from Mark Twain's *Connecticut Yankee in King Arthur's Court*. Watercolor on paper, gift of Barbara Kimball Browning, C. M. Russell Museum, Great Falls, Montana. Inspired by Twain's narrative, Russell added a few spontaneous illustrations to a friend's copy of the novel.

lack Clemens's literary complexity and proliferation. Only a few dozen oral-style, local-color stories stand as his complete literary legacy.

Owen Wister, B. M. Bower, and Romantic Western Fiction

Most of the stories published about the American West during Charlie Russell's lifetime fell into the category of "formula romances" known as "westerns." As mentioned earlier, Russell felt limited admiration for Owen Wister's *The Virginian*,[85] the novel that set the pace for popular western fiction as well as in generating stage and cinema productions. He looked at some of these westerns and apparently enjoyed a few, but he ignored the majority. Early in the twentieth century, the popular fiction writing about the West established basic formula elements that remained for decades. According to Etulain, most of these writings take place in the trans-Mississippi West during the nineteenth century and include

> a courageous hero, often a cowboy or at least a man on horseback, who combats evil by opposing villainous characters or institutions and who establishes (or reestablishes) order, frequently through violent, redeeming acts. For his deeds, he is rewarded with a virtuous young woman, who, despite her initial hesitations about the hero and his violence, is finally drawn to him.[86]

Employing most of these literary conventions, *The Virginian* addressed eastern readers' ideas about romance and violence in the West. As one cultural historian states: "Westerns did not arise in the West and go eastward to tell the world about that country and its people. They were born in the East, then marched beyond the Missouri and proceeded to change things."[87] Some longtime residents of the West also joined the trend and began writing for the popular market in western fiction. Russell knew several, including Bertha M. Bower, who produced more than one hundred short stories and several screenplays, plus sixty-eight novels, including *Chip of the Flying U,* and several others that Russell illustrated.[88] B. M. Bower paid the costs from her own pocket for Russell's illustrations when her publisher refused to meet her friend Nancy Russell's high fees (**see plate 31**).

Walt Coburn, Prolific Western Writer

Another Montana writer well known to Russell, Walt Coburn began publishing in the 1920s and proved to be almost as prolific as Bower. By the end of Charlie Russell's life, when he was encouraging young Walt Coburn to pursue the sale of stories to the pulp market, most of the commercially popular western novels no longer bothered with the specific location details that a local-color story would include. As indicated by the cover for *Pardners of the Dim Trails* (**see plate 32**), commercial designs for cheaper editions in the 1940s and '50s, including the man's blazing double guns and the woman's sexualized vulnerability, were alien to Charlie Russell's images depicting specific western people of an earlier era. By then, nearly all pulp westerns had shifted to formulas involving simple mixtures of romance, adventure, and action.[89] The overriding sentiment in the westerns expressed a nostalgic wish for an earlier, imaginary western place and people. As Etulain has noted, "Much of the formula fiction of Zane Grey and Max Brand is shot through with a crippling nostalgia for an older, more idealized West."[90]

Among the characteristics typically associated with Charlie Russell's life and art, the quality of nostalgia is frequently mentioned by critics. Several of Russell's personal letters express estrangement from the Montana residents of his later years. He often remarked that the "grangers" (farmers) and "nesters" (homesteaders) had ruined the cattle ranges. Russell made clear that he preferred the cattle-range days and his fellow "punchers" over any other time or group. One of the most extreme statements of this nostalgia may be found in a private letter sent to Harry Stanford, encouraging him to write down his memories for posterity:

> when the nester turned this country grass side down the west we loved died She was a beautiful girl that had maney lovers but today thair are onely a fiew left to morn her the farmer plowed her under but if the fiew old lovers that still camp this side of the big range would write about her she would not be forggoten the man between the plow handls was never a romance maker and when he comes history is dead fron now on Montana has no history so do your damdist.[91]

Russell mostly kept such sentiments to himself, but in occasional private letters to close friends such as Stanford, he let out his anger against the rapid changes in the western land-scape. Contributing to the nostalgic sense of loss late in Russell's lifetime, the post–World War I years brought drought and a stagnant economy to Montana, along with the collapse of farming and homesteading. According to several Montana historians:

> As prosperity vanished, so did optimism. Montana lost more in the postwar depression than its marginal farmers. To a considerable extent, it also lost its self-confidence and its faith in the future.[92]

The postwar social and economic realities contributed to Russell's nostalgic perception that Montana had, indeed, gone to hell.

Charlie Russell's preoccupation with depicting nineteenth-century incidents in his art-works, while living twenty-six years into the twentieth century, earned him a place as a lead-ing "nostalgia spokesman" for the boisterous American West. His published tales, on the other hand, articulate a less-appealing "dark side" of the American West. Russell's stories depicting Indian/white relations challenged his white peers' smug sentimentality and pride about earli-er times on the racial frontiers of the West. The genocidal conflict in "Curley's Friend," the reminder of post-buffalo starvation in "Finger-That-Kills," the moral ambiguity of self-defense in "Mormon Murphy," and the value of cultural persistence in "Dad Lane's Buffalo Yarn" undermine typical nostalgic longings for "the good old pioneer days," feelings that necessitated ignoring the suppression and removal of the Indians. Instead, Russell's Indian stories challenge his audiences to face some grim realities about the "Wild West" or the "Old West." By the twentieth-century standards of critic Larry Goodwyn, Russell's Indian stories transcended the propaganda of much writing about the West that excluded numerous groups from triumphant accounts:

> [T]he list of those who are excluded is broad: women, Mexicans, Negroes, Indians, the unmanly, urbanites, and like Dobie [removed from the University of Texas over political disputes], any number of free men. Chroniclers and folklorists would do well to remember that the demonstrably valuable aspect of frontier culture will continue to masquerade as mere propaganda unless and until they are set alongside this darker legacy.[93]

Although Russell ignored many of the groups on Goodwyn's hindsight list, the cowboy artist published unorthodox views on Indian/white relations that looked beyond superficial enthusiasms of most other western writers and artists of his time.

Charlie Russell seriously intended to preserve cultural history and wrote for a local audience, yet he was remarkably patient with Montana friends who wrote nonhistorical westerns for the commercial marketplace. He sympathized with their need to sell a product and seemed to forgive the distortions they included in their narratives to satisfy market demands for improbable violence and romance. For instance, Walt Coburn, the younger half-brother of Russell's cowpuncher friend Wallace Coburn, produced a large number of formula westerns that responded less to historical realities and more to the marketplace demands by editors and book buyers for a mythic Wild West. From 1922 to 1970, Walt Coburn published more than one thousand short stories in low-priced western magazines, plus nearly one hundred books.[94] Russell encouraged Walt early in his writing career, mentioning some of the young man's recent work:

> [I] liked both the storyes your cow punchers seemed real to me they were like those I knew in the old days. thair are maney western writers these days but fiew of them knew the range . . . all old timers who can write should tell what they know of the old west.[95]

Some of the stories that Walt Coburn could have written about historical people who lived near the Coburn ranch, including the outlaws Butch Cassidy, Kid Curry, and the Wild Bunch gang, never rolled out of his typewriter, an omission that supposedly protected Coburn's brothers from criticism.[96] Coburn also knew the difference between his commercial stories and Russell's local-color narratives. At the beginning of his publishing career in the 1920s, Coburn visited Ed Borein's art studio in Santa Barbara where, he recalled, "we would sit and listen spellbound to Charlie Russell's endless fund of original cow country and Indian anecdotes."[97]

Teddy Blue Abbott and Montana Memoir Writers

Russell's letters show that he directly encouraged many of his friends to write down their experiences and stories for publication. In the same letter with the nostalgic outburst about history dying with the arrival of farmers, Russell told Harry Stanford:

I dont see why you couldent turn out plenty of happenings in your own life of early days you have a good memory and knew the country when it was worth knowing and men good or bad who were regular men Write about them and the land they lived in.[98]

Stanford never followed this advice, but other Russell friends, such as Con Price and Tommy Tucker, wrote and found publishers for their memoirs that included occasional stories about the cowboy artist. Professor J. Frank Dobie noticed the extraordinary literary output of fiction and nonfiction from the northwest plains and mountains region when he stated, "cow people of Montana and the Northwest were more literate than those of Texas and the southwest."[99]

Among the autobiographical narratives, some works, like Russell's friend E. C. "Teddy Blue" Abbott's *We Pointed Them North*,[100] needed the assistance of a coauthor (in Abbott's case, Helena Huntington Smith) to organize the memory fragments and make a manuscript presentable for publication. Abbott told one Russell biographer that Charlie had encouraged him to publish his stories about working on the cattle drives to Montana along the Texas Trail, stating:

> "He always wanted me to write the history of the range," says Teddy Blue; "on account of me knowing so many of the men and having worked my way up through it clear to Sun River. He offered to illustrate it for free. He said he hated to think our [cowpuncher] race would die without a history. But he said I couldn't make any money out of it, so few of us are left, and the people now demand all western stories to be full of shooting and blood and thunder. I can't write fiction and it sure discouraged me."[101]

Abbott knew that writing commercial western fiction was not a viable process for his post-cattle range talents. Other memoirs such as *UBET*[102] by John Barrows or the two books by Con Price, *Montana Memories* and *Trails I Rode*,[103] also offered stories about Russell, enabling the authors to defend themselves in alternative versions to the artist/author's roasting yarns. Such anecdotes, as well as the personal letters exchanged between Russell and these authors, provide useful cross-references for understanding the cowboy artist and his writings.

One Montana memoir, titled *Riding The High Country*, by Patrick T. Tucker,[104] seemed to contain historical anecdotes but has proved to be more fiction than fact, particularly regarding Russell. Tucker's exaggerated portrayal of Charlie Russell as a young hard-drinking carouser irritated Nancy Russell when it appeared shortly following her husband's death. Although Charlie may have been friendly with Tucker during and since his cowboy days, many of the artist's contemporaries rejected episodes recounted in this book as being poorly fabricated lies.[105] In contrast with Russell's writing style, the autobiographical works by his Montana contemporaries—Price, Abbott, and Tucker—follow the tradition of writings by Charlie Siringo in his classic memoir *A Texas Cowboy*.[106] In addition, none of the autobiographers attempted to create the illusion of an oral storyteller by using a narrator's voice other than their own. And none used anything like Russell's controlled irony or included an understated lie to invert a story's impact.

Frank Bird Linderman and "Jake Hoover's Pig"

The most ambitious writer among Russell's immediate friends was Frank Bird Linderman, the only contemporary to experiment with short anecdotal stories retelling local events in oral-style yarns. Linderman also added a unique twist to a few of his stories by having a narrator speak in the French-English patois of the mixed-blood "Métis." In addition, Linderman wrote in several other formats that Russell never attempted, including short novels and longer poetry. The founder of the University of Montana's creative-writing program, Professor of English H. G. Merriam, called Linderman "the foremost writer in Montana; one of the best story tellers I know."[107]

Charlie Russell took a stronger interest in Frank Linderman's writings than in those of his other friends. Linderman also shared Russell's fascination with Indians, including their sign language. The two men exchanged bits of Indian lore and culture nearly every time they met. Charlie Russell periodically visited the Linderman family at their isolated log home on Flathead Lake and expressed concern about Linderman's ability to raise three daughters on his erratic writing income. Although Russell encouraged many of his friends to write about the West, he seemed especially intent on helping Linderman gain financial stability,[108] even to the point of suggesting that he make his writings more commercially attractive by including western romance elements. "You say you have started a new novel," observes Russell in one letter:

> that Plumer gang ought to make good stuff for a book. but dont stay to clos to the
> truth and be shure and stick in a lady and a hero. you like straight goods but the
> world dont and they are the folks that buy books.[109]

Russell knew that his friend would not willingly compromise on cultural or historical accuracy. This message most likely formed an ironic joke between the two friends. Yet Linderman's prose could be cautious and polite, leaving his books less likely to succeed in a literary marketplace full of unrealistic romance and exaggerated violence. Russell understood that Linderman needed to add some kind of special narrative spark to attract success.

When Linderman gave Russell a pre-publication look at a new book of short stories, Charlie responded with more suggestions to increase their commercial potential. "I think you might have made that Steam boat story longer an pushed in som romance," he commented:

> [C]inch your Saddle on romance hes a high headed hoss with plenty of blemishes
> but keep him moovin an theres fiew that can call the leg he limps on and most
> folks like prancers.[110]

The artist's advice to insert romantic elements, risking the loss of absolute accuracy, has attracted some critical discussion. Brian Dippie interprets this suggestion as being Russell's own "artistic creed,"[111] although it seems more like friendly advice for an author who needs more success in the commercial marketplace. Dippie also noted that Russell admired Emerson Hough's mixture of romance and history in his stories, calling this combination Russell's "artistic credo."[112] The mix may have been Russell's preferred recipe for reading matter and for

FIG. 109. Frank Bird Linderman and Charles M. Russell in Helena, 1913. Photograph courtesy of a private collection. After years spent outdoors, many old-time trappers, hunters, and cowboys, including these two longtime friends, felt more comfortable in this campfire posture than sitting on furniture.

elements in some paintings, but the artist's writings reveal very little in the way of romance. He expressed his cautious approach in another letter, when he observed:

> Romance is a beautiful lady that lives in the book case who can pull aneything from a cold deck to murder and get away with it but she's got a homely sister Reality by name that hangs around all the time.[113]

Russell might advise a friend to spice up his stories, or even use some western romance formula to increase sales, but he avoided using such elements in his own local-color yarns. By sticking to his own style, the artist/author never attempted to compete in the wider mass market for western romance tales.

Scribner's Sons published Linderman's short story collection, *On a Passing Frontier, Sketches from the Northwest,*[114] in 1920, which included Russell's story "Jake Hoover's Pig." Charlie routinely told this humorously vulgar anecdote about himself, but never published it.

Although Russell provided critical comments to Linderman on most of the other stories in this collection, he made no references to Linderman's published version of "Jake Hoover's Pig." Frank Linderman occasionally made extra income giving story-filled talks to Montana meetings and gatherings, during which he told aloud several unpublished Russell yarns, including "Jake Hoover's Pig," each time identifying Russell as their source. Linderman even dared to tell "Jake Hoover's Pig" while Charlie was present on stage at a benefit for the Santa Barbara School for the Arts in 1923.[115] Perhaps Russell simply saw the pig story as partly Linderman's to publish due to his ability to tell it aloud effectively. No records survive to show why or how Russell gave Linderman permission to publish this humorous pig tale, but the artist was known to routinely give away paintings and sculptures to almost any admirer before his bride took full control of art sales. As his would be biographer Dan Conway stated:

> His friends of that time will testify to his liberality with his pictures. If a friend admired one of his paintings, it was immediately presented to him. If someone was pleased with one of his pictures, he could see no reason why that individual should not own the painting regardless of whether it was through sale or gift. And, giving was likewise a part of his happiness.[116]

Russell may have wanted to help the sales of Linderman's book by allowing him to include this bit of barnyard banter. The local-color elements in Linderman's collection reminded some reviewers of Bret Harte, but the sales did not bring much wealth to the author. Linderman's volume anticipated Russell's *Trails Plowed Under* by seven years; though without Russell's illustrations and effective humor (despite the presence of a slightly stilted version of "Jake Hoover's Pig"), the book has remained obscure, known primarily to collectors as a worthwhile volume of northwest regional short stories. In his posthumous memoir, *Recollections of Charley Russell*, Linderman published a much better version of "Jake Hoover's Pig."[117]

RAWHIDE RAWLINS RIDES AGAIN: SECONDHAND RUSSELL ANECDOTES

Frank Linderman's accomplishment in recreating a Russell story ("Jake Hoover's Pig") in a style that effectively echoes Charlie's speaking voice becomes more impressive when contrasted with other similar attempts and failures. Many Russell friends claimed to recall dozens of his oral stories and jokes that never appeared in print. Homer Britzman's small company, Trail's End Publishing, located in Nancy Russell's former Pasadena home (which Britzman acquired after her death) gathered twenty-four of these brief secondhand anecdotes into a small, limited edition volume, titled *Rawhide Rawlins Rides Again, Or Behind The Swinging Doors, A Collection of Charlie Russell's Favorite Stories.*[118] Critic J. C. Austin correctly rejected the various tales as unrepresentative of Russell's writing:

> Much more free in references to the outhouse and the whore house, these stories represent a phase of Russell's story telling that is neglected in the more genteel publications. But, although they are retold by such professional writers as Irvin S.

Cobb and Will James, they lack the vitality of Russell's style. As readers in the 1980s, we are unimpressed by the bawdiness and let down by the anecdotal slickness. Russell was a better writer than that.[119]

J. Frank Dobie concurred. He scribbled a condemnation on the title page of his own copy, a statement that concludes, "a damned mangy dull job."[120]

If the stories in *Rawhide Rawlins Rides Again* were actually Russell's, then the artist had indulged occasionally in some lowbrow humor with his cronies. Despite their best wishes, however, such companions as Joe DeYong, Ed Borein, Will Crawford, Con Price, and eighteen others raised more questions about Russell's taste than simply the reader's laughter. Lacking Russell's way with words, or Linderman's acute memory for Charlie's speech patterns, the authors of these tales have shed a dim and less-than-flattering light on their famous friend. A similar, hypothetical circumstance might have involved a cowpuncher friend crudely shaping a lump of muddy clay, claiming "Charlie showed me something like this some years ago." Russell's actual accomplishments as a writer should not be diminished by the publishing of a few dated jokes and anecdotes of poor quality.

Just as his success with writing and publishing inspired amateur Montana writers like Con Price and Teddy Blue Abbott, Charlie Russell's success as a fine artist also encouraged many other Montana men, often cowboys or ranch hands, to take up sketching and painting. Some achieved local and regional success, including "Shorty" Shope in the Helena area, J. K. Ralston in eastern Montana, Joe DeYong and Olaf Seltzer in Great Falls, and Ace Powell in Kalispell, as well as Lone Wolf in the Browning–East Glacier district.

WILL JAMES: MONTANA'S YOUNGER STORYTELLING ARTIST

Also among this second generation following Russell's example, but in his own self-made path, Will James found greater success than the rest with painting and writing. Young Will James approached Russell for painting advice in person and by letter, and Russell responded with friendly guidance.[121] James followed Russell's painting advice by taking up oils, but he forged his own way in commercial writing without consulting Russell or imitating the older artist's local-color, anecdotal style. Scribner's published Will James's first self-illustrated book in 1924, *Cowboys North and South,* followed by *The Drifting Cowboy* (1925) and his popular first novel, *Smokey the Cowhorse* (1926).[122]

Like other rival works, these books annoyed Nancy Russell. This young upstart put his stories into national circulation before she could do the same for her more accomplished husband. But the success of these books also motivated Doubleday to publish *Trails Plowed Under* as quickly as possible. J. Frank Dobie liked James's first work best of all:

> The best one is his first, written before he became sophisticated with life—without becoming in the right way, more sophisticated in the arts of drawing and writing. Lone Cowboy . . . is without a date or a geographical location less generalized than the space between Canada and Mexico.[123]

Other contemporary western critics were less generous. Frank Linderman "smelled a rat" and suspected something false about James, stating privately in a letter to Rankin:

> James suddenly appeared in Montana. Nobody ever heard of him until his book "Smoky" (a very good thing) was published. In his "Lone Cowboy" he kills a Kodiak bear east of the Rockies in the dead of winter, deep snow, with a muzzle loading rifle loaded with birdshot.[124]

Canadian cowboy sculptor, Charlie Beil, recalled private conversations with Russell about James's writing when the younger artist told researcher James Rankin, "Mind you Russell didn't Knock him but he sayd [sic] he thought that James was writing not facts but Stuff that the Public wanted." Apparently, Russell liked James's drawings and his action in them.[125]

Will James wrote simple and direct prose that sold well to adult and juvenile markets, especially his novel about a cow pony, Smokey, and a fictional autobiography, Lone Cowboy. Before he finally succumbed to alcoholism at age fifty in 1942, Will James sold several works to the movie industry in Hollywood. One later twentieth-century critic concludes that Will James suffered from his own success in the pop-culture marketplace:

> Lone Cowboy held the public's attention because it took outrageous licence with truths that were myths—which, in James's book, were lies. The author could earn the mainstream's acceptance only by doing what the mainstream's Wild West shows, dime novels, and films had done—sensationalizing aspects of cowboy life, for the benefit of James's self-aggrandizement.[126]

Brian Dippie argues that James satisfied his readers' wishes in the 1920s for stories portraying supposedly present-day western experiences, rather than realistic events typical of the nineteenth century.[127] As a contrast, Charlie Russell did not write for the commercial marketplace, but offered westerners and rural sympathizers some old-fashioned local-color humor about his peers, several serious adventure tales and hero-stories about Indians, plus a few brief editorial essays.

At their best, Russell's stories, along with his narrative paintings and sculptures, often depict individuals in peak moments—suggesting narratives that might one day ascend into mythic status, but fit more comfortably in the status of legends. These tales passed from folklore or folk legend into literary legend when Russell wrote them down. According to Richard Dorson,

> everybody at large talks about legends. To my taste, this is the most attractive and intriguing species of United States folk tradition, for it most closely involves history, particularly local history, and most specifically reflects American experience.[128]

Dorson's comments fit Russell's stories and narrative art as being valuable mirrors of real human experience in the West.

Not all historians are convinced, however, that legends have much value in understanding past events and circumstances. Kent Ladd Steckmesser sees distortion coming from legend makers who respond too much to popular demands for beauty over truth. "There is something cold and abstract about truth," notes Steckmesser:

> Romance and legend, on the other hand, are warm and colorful, representing the ideal in aspirations. Hence it is not surprising that each legend involves a highly selective process by which the beautiful eclipses the true. The ugly or unpleasant features of life are eliminated.
>
> The historian's ruthless quest after truth frequently mars the beauty of a perfected legend. . . . Yet the people also have the right to know whether they are reading fact or fiction, and the historian has the responsibility to draw the line which separates the two.[129]

Rather than emphasizing attractive features of people in his stories, Russell's legends try to embarrass their heroes by making the all-too-human subject become the butt of the story's humor. Pete Van often fills the role of this foolish hero. Several other leading characters in non-humorous stories, such as Mormon Zack or Charlie Bowlegs, seem more like antiheroes, men whose physical accomplishments make them worthy of awe, but otherwise unwelcome in polite society. Generally, Russell's legends favor truth over beauty, but amusement including awe and humor helped to shape the storytelling.

Charlie Russell's stories about Indians, plus some of his wildlife stories, offer darker legends about what Steckmesser calls "the ugly or unpleasant features of life." Nevertheless, several Russell critics have discounted the value of his published works. Literary critic James C. Austin sees Russell's published efforts as primarily background for the illustrations in *Trails Plowed Under* and declares that "figures of speech make up almost the whole artistic value of the Rawhide Rawlins—Charles Russell stories."[130] Rather than mere escapism, however, Russell's urge to record diverse cultures, individuals, and unusual incidents of the nineteenth-century West led him to create writings, pictures, and sculptures that show generally realistic moments in specific landscapes, not idealized ones. He populated the locations depicted in his works with recognizable people, including stubborn cowboys and determined (but not always "noble") Indians, like the murderer/defender in *Mormon Murphy*. Russell's stories, more than his pictures and sculptures, mock the urbanizing, mechanizing, twentieth-century West rather than fleeing from or ignoring it. In response to urban values, Russell's published narratives deflated the pretense of modern progress with social satire and subtle irony.

Charlie Russell shared with Frank Linderman a sense of responsibility to record earlier times, or as H. G. Merriam observed of Linderman, he felt he had "a duty to, in some way, preserve the Old West, especially in Montana, in printer's ink."[131] In a region farther south, others shared a similar impulse. According to critic Larry Goodwyn, the writers J. Frank Dobie, John Lomax, Mody Boatwright, Wilson Hudson, Stith Thompson, and B. A. Botkin "expended much of their energies, as Dobie put it, 'in getting it all down before it went away on the wind,' . . . replacing the tall tales with a somewhat more authentic expression of the folk experience."[132] Rather than trying to create literary masterpieces, the storytelling artist published his tales as part of a larger western-folklore and cultural-preservation trend.

CHAPTER NINE

Critical Observers

"... find out how he stands around his home and among his kind of people."
—Will Rogers

During the late 1920s, reviewers of *Trails Plowed Under* smiled on Charlie Russell and his stories, even though some critics seemed uncertain of what to say about the odd collection of writings. Stanley Walker of *The New York Times* mentioned how different Russell's stories were from the western tales in low-priced "pulp" fiction and the popular silent movies of the time. He observed that since the stories lacked the stock-in-trade villain and helpless girl from the East, Russell's yarns "may not be always exciting, but at least they are genuine." Although this reviewer underestimated the realistic excitement inherent in many of Russell's stories, the *Times* writer sensed that the author and his works were, nevertheless, worth noting:

> When New York saw him last, a few years ago, [Russell] was attending an exhibition of his paintings—a gray, hard-bitten old eccentric with a great gift for anecdote and salty comment.
>
> "Trails Plowed Under" must represent a terrific amount of work. It contains no less than forty-three "stories," ranging all the way from inconsequential little recollections (the sort of thing that sounds gorgeous when spoken, but which is likely to be a bit thin when set down on paper) to casual essays and slightly more ambitious tales. He writes easily, however, and in the vernacular. He tells of Indians and Indian fighters, buffalo hunts, bad men, wolves, wild horses, tough hotels, drinking customs and hard-riding cowboys. . . . The writing could be the veriest [*sic*] trash, which it is not, and the illustrations would still make this a good book.[1]

The *New York Post* also endorsed the book, calling Russell "probably the greatest cowboy writer and artist that the frontier has brought to public notice" and recommended the book as a contribution to "frontier literature" that serves as "an authentic record of the of west."[2] Similarly, the New York *Literary Digest* offered a brief, positive review, and included several generous excerpts from *Trails Plowed Under*.[3] Several years after the book's publication, the *Minneapolis Tribune* observed of Russell's published tales: "These stories are the West, the Old West that exists now only in the sparkling memories of a few old-timers like the late Charles M. Russell."[4]

J. Frank Dobie and Ross Santee: Early Reviewers of Trails Plowed Under

The best critical writing about *Trails Plowed Under* appeared in a review by a young Texas writer who had worked on his family's cattle ranch as well as in the academic world as a scholar/writer/teacher. J. Frank Dobie was well aware of Russell's artworks and had read his early *Rawhide Rawlins* books. "By all odds, this is the most beautiful book of the West since Remington's 'Pony Tracks' and 'Crooked Trails' came out thirty years ago," observed Dobie.

> Russell will go down to posterity as the most important artist, excepting Remington, that ever painted the Old West, and he has an intimacy of detail, an ingeniousness, a humor and a humanity that Remington never achieved. . . . [I]t is, aside from two or three by Andy Adams, the closest [book] to the soil . . . [I]t is, in brief, a kind of Spoon River anthology of mountain and range frontiersmen, but without sophistication or patronization. Somehow, as these types are revealed and as their anecdotes are told, I have a sense of profound reality, I live a more intense life, I breathe a fresher and more wholesome air. . . . Sometimes, Russell's prose, always natural, rises to nobleness.[5]

The New York Times wisely selected a popular range-riding author/illustrator, Ross Santee, to provide a follow-up essay on Russell's book of stories a month after Stanley Walker's review. Santee roped in his older friend, Jim Thornhill, who had a firsthand familiarity with Russell for many years before relocating to Globe, Arizona.

> "Some of these I've heard him tell," says Jim, "an' the next best thing I know to hearin' him tell a thing is to get to read the story.". . . stories like Longrope's . . . that kind of pinches a man in the throat.[6]

Thornhill was admitting, as much as an old-time cowpuncher ever could, to having an emotional reaction to "Longrope's Last Guard," the final story in *Trails Plowed Under*. Most of the tales involved adventure and humor, but "Longrope" added pathos as well.

Robert Gale and Boise State's Western Writer's Series

The next moment of significant critical attention occurred fifty-two years after the first publication of *Trails Plowed Under*. In 1979, Robert Gale produced *Charles Marion Russell*, a fifty-page examination of Russell's pictures, sculptures, and writings for the Boise State *Western Writers Series*. In the brief booklet, Gale offered the first serious discussion of Charles M. Russell's published tales and essays since the reviews that appeared at the time of publication. He limited the focus of his comments and brief plot summaries to only a few stories. Generalizing about all of the pieces, Gale suggested four categories for Russell's writings—"humorous anecdotes involving white men [twenty-two items], tales of Indians [nine], informational essays [eight], and serious stories about white men [four]."[7] "Taken together—and sometimes even separately," Gale noted, "the pieces in *Trails Plowed Under* have as complicated a set of narrative stances as are to be found in Mark Twain or even Henry James."[8] Although such critical praise seems outweighed by the overall volume and variety of Mark Twain narratives, Russell did find numerous ways to portray people in the West through his roasts, hero stories, lies, tall tales, essays, and fables that involved Indians, nature, cattle, and modern times. By analyzing Russell's published writings, Robert Gale brought the work to the attention of other writers and critics, but no one else gave them closer consideration for another seventeen years. A factor in this hiatus could have been that Russell's published works, the humorous roasts, the serious adventures, and the personal-opinion essays fit no simple mold or model.

BRIAN DIPPIE AND THE FIRST PAPERBACK EDITION OF TRAILS PLOWED UNDER

After decades of unquestioning praise for the distinctiveness of Charlie Russell's life and artworks, as dominated in print by Russell scholar/author/appraiser Fred Renner, historian Brian Dippie of the University of Vancouver began publishing books and articles that pointed out a variety of influences in the cowboy artist's paintings. In 1996, Dippie turned his attention to Russell's writings when he contributed a new "Introduction" to a paperback edition of *Trails Plowed Under*. Dippie generally praises the stories and essays, but he finds that nostalgia dominates all other themes in Russell's writings. As evidence that a feeling of wishing for earlier days permeates Russell's writings, including stories about Indians, Dippie points to Russell's first published story, "Early Days on the Buffalo Range."[9] This story features a rather sentimental ending that seems especially uncharacteristic for most of Russell's subsequent writings. Nostalgia is certainly present in such Indian stories as Russell's "How Lindsay Turned Indian" and the opening paragraph of "Dunc McDonald,"[10] as well as Dippie's example in "Early Days." Many years after writing his experimental first story, however, Russell presented several rather sobering tales about Indians that provide instances of harsh tribal warfare and brutal interactions with Euro-Americans mixed with elements of critical realism that contradict sentimentality. The majority of his published writings clearly reflect a tougher self-discipline through which the author celebrates specific individuals and earlier events rather than merely wishing for an idealized past.

"Early Days on the Buffalo Range" stands as Charlie Russell's awkward first attempt at writing for publication. Moreover, in many ways, this 1897 literary experiment speaks no more effectively for Russell's mature published writings that appeared decades after "Early Days" than a watercolor sketch by teenaged Russell would define the qualities of his later oil paintings. The grim realities of Russell's racial perspective in "Curley's Friend" and "The War Scars

FIG. 110. Charles M. Russell, *Contrast in Artist's Salons—Charlie Painting in His Cabin*, ca. 1894. Ink, transparent watercolor and graphite on paper, no. 1961.305.1, Amon Carter Museum, Fort Worth, Texas. This 1891 self-portrait reveals Charlie's awareness of his local critics. The perceptions and opinions of his peers, who included Indians, concerning his depictions of their experiences and shared narratives meant far more to Russell than the reactions of academically trained writers or sophisticated art critics. Charlie discarded this picture when he departed his winter shack for the spring roundup on the cattle range.

of Medicine Whip" do not appear in "Early Days on the Buffalo Range." It was no oversight that Russell never reprinted this unpolished, beginner's work in the Montana Newspaper Association inserts, the *Rawhide Rawlins* books, or *Trails Plowed Under*. The wry social criticism embedded in Russell's mature stories about Indians transcended the "crippling nostalgia for an older, more idealized west" that Richard Etulain has noted in many widely marketed western novels.[11] Russell's personal letters clearly express nostalgia for earlier times in the West, but he moved beyond that sentiment for the most part when writing seriously for publication.

Russell's stories overlapped with his paintings and sculpture through a shared narrative purpose and a focus on the same subject matter. He mentioned this correlation on a few occasions. In 1921, a New York newspaper reviewer noticed and paraphrased Charlie Russell's personal viewpoint on art, one that had appeared in his exhibition catalog for the Babcock Galleries in New York, stating:

> In this day of broad painters, detail is laughed at. My pictures would drive an impressionist into hysterics. Mine are the foolish storytelling pictures, but I notice regular folks still like stories.[12]

Even at the height of his commercial popularity, Russell knew that his detailed, narrative artworks were out of step with sophisticated critics and twentieth-century artistic trends. But he also realized that they remained popular with the general public. Ignoring the symbolic and nonrepresentational art themes emerging in major European and American cities during the early twentieth century, Russell remained steadfastly loyal to his less-sophisticated "storytelling" priorities. Nevertheless, not all his commercially popular illustrations pleased every editor. In one of his quick notes to his apprentice Joe DeYong, Russell admitted, without further explanation, "Tower turned my picture down sa[i]d it did not tell a story[.]"[13]

WILL ROGERS AND TEDDY BLUE ABBOTT ON RUSSELL'S RURAL RAPPORT

Acceptance by editors, tributes from writers, praise from fellow artists, and grudging respect from prominent urban art critics never seemed to be Charlie Russell's primary concern. He tailored his narrative works mainly for the judgment of rural-minded audiences in Montana. His immediate, mostly male, storytelling audience consisted of cattlemen, Indians, ranch hands, fur trappers, wagon and stage drivers, bartenders, rodeo riders, prospectors, and other western types of all ages who tended to express the critical opinions he most valued. A like-minded entertainer, whom Russell encountered on his first trip to New York in 1904, observed this significant interaction in the storytelling artist's career. In his 1926 newspaper-obituary tribute for his friend, Will Rogers singled out Charlie Russell's relationship with his Montana cronies as the crucial measure of the man:

> The best way to judge just how good a man is . . . find out how he stands around his home and among his kind of people. Well he was the Cowpunchers' Painter. They swore by Russell. The Cattle Country knew if it was a Russell it was right, and they loved him personally.[14]

In a similar vein, Russell's bronc-riding pal and one-time ranching partner, Con Price, explained, "He was always more concerned about what his old-time friends cowboys an' Indians thought of his work than any body else."[15] The blunt opinions from the old-timers could be negative about almost any subject, but Russell valued their knowledge and honesty rather than seeking easy praise. The newspaper critics, magazine editors, and art gallery owners might have vanished altogether and Russell would have been satisfied with the approval or criticism of his local Montana audiences.

Charlie Russell's acceptance by his Montana constituency was especially remarkable, considering his wealthy childhood in urban St. Louis. Nevertheless, he proved himself worthy of the admiration and friendship of tough frontier types, such as the one who told the would-be biographer James Rankin:

> About all the schooling I ever had was in the school of hard knocks and they don't
> teach English or penmanship so it is hard for me to write....Charlie Russell he
> wintered one winter in the Bear Paw Mts in a log house with out a roof so you see
> he was no pink skinned hand raised cake eater like the cowpunchers you see now
> full of soda pop and conceit. And they can't cook or make a rawhide rope or never
> slept in an elkhide bed.[16]

Even though Russell had held plenty of cake in his "pink hands" during his privileged St. Louis childhood, his effective adaptation to the rough life in Montana Territory convinced most of his peers that he was "OK." In a similar tribute to Russell's solid character, one old-timer stated, "Yu can't tell a speck about a man who can roll a cigarette with one hand, mold a grizzly bear out of the inside of a biscuit with the other an' quit drinkin' without cryin' out loud."[17] All three were characteristics of Charlie Russell. In addition, Frank Linderman noticed Russell's physical courage, a highly valued characteristic in Montana. Upon returning to their hunting camp on one occasion, Linderman discovered that Charlie Russell had spent the entire afternoon pulling an infected molar out of his jaw with a pair of pliers. "The tooth had roots like those of a fur stump. Charley was full of pure grit,"[18] concluded Linderman in blunt understatement.

Russell gained general acceptance as a teenager among tough westerners, and especially standoffish cowpunchers, by doing effective cowboy work and adopting appropriate language and social behavior. His engaging verbal humor as well as his tendency to improvise anecdotes, amusing cartoons, and small figurines of everyone around also helped him overcome a relatively low level of skill as a roper and horse rider. Consequently, Russell's cattle-range comrades considered him to be a relatively typical range companion. "When I knew Charlie[,] he was no celebrity," recalled one fellow range hand, "just a common cow hand like the rest of us." In this man's words:

> There were dozens of cowboys just as clever in their lines as he was in his. Gopher
> Dick, a broncho buster who could ride anything that wore hair. Poker Pete, an old
> ranahan so slick with the cards he could cheat himself. Old Hog-tie Porter, who
> could down more cattle in an hour with a rope than most people could with a gun.
> Sugar-foot Rinnel, a stage driver who could spin a stronger "windy" than any man
> living. Big Nose George, the Bird Tail outlaw, Portage Vance, the stage stock tender
> and many others all subjects of Charlie's pictures. The stories leading up to the pic-
> ture in which each of these characters appear should be attached to each picture, if
> not they will soon be forgotten.[19]

It is tempting to imagine that C. M. Russell's numerous unpublished stories, misplaced sketches, damaged or lost paintings, and broken clay sculptures might have depicted the characters suggested above in the careful handwriting of the Montana old-timer C. J. Ellis.

One of Charlie Russell's most intelligent and perceptive companions, E. C. "Teddy Blue" Abbott, published newspaper articles and a memoir[20] that included observations of Russell. Abbott's account of his life on the cattle drives from Texas to Miles City, Montana, carries the clear sense of an insider's authority. Although his writings contain many informative anecdotes, Teddy Blue was fully aware of the drawbacks of overreliance on personal testimony, even by seemingly authoritative old-timers. Years after Russell's death, Abbott told Charlie's widow:

> the main trouble I have with old timers is they are so Poor on dates and another thing old timers have been laughed at so often for telling the truth that they retaliate by telling unheard of yarns like I did in Miles City about the 16 men hanging on one Cottonwood tree (I told it to Dan) that story told for a Dam lie in 84 is now the truth and the true story is forgotten.[21]

Abbott realized that narrative history, even from a knowledgeable, local, inside source such as himself, could still be unreliable.

FRANK LINDERMAN AND WALLY McRAE ON RUSSELL'S CELEBRITY STATUS

Occasionally, the personal testimonies from Russell's contemporaries have proved untrustworthy, especially in characteristic oral-history claims of personal friendship with the famous cowboy artist. The practice of boasting about active connections with the local hero who made a success in the world of fine art began during Charlie's lifetime. In one flagrant incident, recorded by Frank Linderman, a stranger claimed to have known the artist since childhood. This imposter happened to be seated without realizing it facing Linderman and Charlie Russell on a passenger train traveling north from Helena to Great Falls. As Linderman remembered the circumstances:

> [T]he man was talkative. "I'd like to stop off in Great Falls and have a visit with Charley Russell, the famous cowboy artist, but I can't spare the time." He looked regretfully out of the rain-streaked window.
>
> "Do you know Russell?" I asked. I felt Charley beginning to squirm in the seat beside me.
>
> "Oh my, yes. We went to school together in St. Louis when we were children. We were chums. Bright boy, Charley was."
>
> "That must have been way back in the 'nineties. [Russell had attended school in the 1870s.] Charley kicked my foot.
>
> "Are you acquainted with him?" the man asked, as though suddenly sensing possibilities.
>
> "I've seen him," I replied.
>
> I knew that the answer would clear the trail for the fellow's further lying. But Charley put an end to the entertainment.
>
> "Come on, I want a smoke," he said, leading the way to the smoker. He was thoroughly disgusted. "Hell of a lot of schoolin' he got if he went to school with me, the damned dirty liar. Went to school with me," he growled, amazed at the man's cheek. "Humph! Why he ain't dry behind the ears yet."[22]

So many old-timers have exaggerated their connections with Charlie Russell that it has become a widespread cultural joke in Montana. The situation inspired a third-generation Montana rancher and award-winning poet, Wally McRae, to observe:

> *Time was when every old-timer*
> *When storying-up a spell*
> *Would look you squarely in the eye*
> *saying, "I knowed "Kid" Russell well."*
>
> *Men that'd never misrepresent*
> *A critter they had to sell.*
> *Would often casually mention*
> *"I knowed Charlie Russell well."*
>
> *The Mint couldn't hold the 'punchers*
> *Who'd drone like a funeral knell*
> *Of drinks they'd shared with them boys*
> *Who all knowed old Charlie so well.*
>
> *They all "once had a pitcher of Charlie's"*
> *"But sold it when 'short' for a spell"*
> *"'When Horses Talked War' it was titled."*
> *"And I knowed Old Charlie damn well."*
>
> *The Devil must just love old Charlie*
> *As he pitchforks them cowboys 'round Hell*
> *That never lied 'bout nothin' else*
> *'Cept for knowin' Charlie Russell so well.*[23]

The popularity of Charles M. Russell, combined with the continuing inquiries of Montana people by curious but gullible writers and tourists, perpetuated local opportunities to claim familiarity with the "cowboy artist." Ironically, the casual day-to-day presence of the man also enabled his friends to underestimate his significance. In the range of Montana responses by Russell contemporaries, one extreme involved lying about knowing the artist, while the other included simply forgetting his oral tales. As one old-timer put it, "He was so taken for granted in Montana that people didn't retain the stories he used to tell."[24]

As for critical observers during Russell's lifetime, there were no more influential critics than his Montana contemporaries. Charlie Russell's verbal interactions with his friends provided crucial daily stimulation for both his stories and his artworks. One witness, then the president of the Great Northern Railroad, observed that Russell welcomed the local authorities' comments on his artworks even while he was creating them.

I have been in his studio several times when he was painting characteristic pictures of the early west, and it was common for him to have the studio half-filled with Indians and cowboys, who would advise him and discuss among themselves the matters of equipment, posture, etc. He was in this way able to portray with entire accuracy every detail of the western life which he was painting.[25]

Charlie Russell valued his local western critics above any professional art instructors. "These fellas can be good critics when it comes to details, let me tell you," Russell wrote to one old friend. "Why they'll see anything left out of a picture or if the colors are not right."[26] These outspoken but unsophisticated local critics frequently praised Russell's primitive early paintings and, in their enthusiasm, typically overlooked his crude composition and unrefined technique, in the same way that they enjoyed his rustic storytelling.

STITH THOMPSON ON FOLKLORE AND STORYTELLING

Beyond their role as informal critics, many of Charlie Russell's western contemporaries also inspired his narratives. Russell's artworks and written narratives frequently pass along and amplify stories that he heard from friends. Folklorists who are steeped in the storytelling process have developed insights into the typical creative adaptation that Russell seems to have used to synthesize narrative ideas into his artworks and his own stories. Indeed, a prominent folklorist in the twentieth century, Stith Thompson, has observed:

> In contrast to the modern story writer's striving for originality of plot and treatment, the teller of a folktale is proud of his ability to hand on that which he has received. He usually desires to impress his readers or his hearers with the fact that he is bringing them some thing that has the stamp of good authority, that the tale was heard from some great story-teller, or from some aged person who remembered it from old days.[27]

Russell often cited the sources for his published stories, some of which, like Dunc McDonald or Charlie Brewster, can still be verified through archival materials. And he also displayed the pride of origin that Thompson noted when the cowboy artist stated in a brief "Foreword" to his first book of oral-tradition tales, *Rawhide Rawlins Stories,* "I have tried to write down some of these yarns as nearly as possible as they were told to me."[28] This appreciation for his narrative sources seems especially obvious in the stories that Russell retold from Indian sources.

Charlie Russell displayed some caution about claiming authorship of a story. Austin Russell has noted that his uncle once expressed reluctance about claiming another author's story idea for his own. Russell told his nephew a ghost story but had refused to consider publishing it since the story was already printed in a slightly different version in Theodore Roosevelt's book *The Wilderness Hunter.*[29] Directly copying from another person's artwork seems to have been a practice that Russell consciously noticed and avoided. The comparable elements in a few Russell paintings suggesting the influence of other artists, as noted by Brian Dippie and other twentieth-century critics, could reflect unconscious influences or clear-headed choices by Russell. The artist

FIG. 111. Charles M. Russell at his easel in his log cabin studio in Great Falls, ca. 1918. Photograph courtesy of the Montana Historical Society, Helena. Charlie is working on one of his great oil paintings, *Lewis and Clark Expedition,* now at the Gilcrease Museum, Tulsa, Oklahoma.

never explained his paintings on that level and no art critic or historian in later generations knows for sure. On the other hand, broad adaptations, especially from some sense of collective consciousness or from local folklore, seem to have been a frequent part of his storytelling process in Russell's painting and writing.

Several latter-day art and history critics have appreciated the wider scope of Russell's published narratives. The Goetzmanns, father and son historians of American art and the American West, understood that "Russell was a storyteller first and a painter second," and that his greatest contribution was the world he presented of "real people seen up close."[30] Indeed, these observations apply even more to Russell's published stories. Biographer John Taliaferro defined Russell's basic attitude, stating: "In a changing world, he held steady."[31] Certainly in his storytelling, Russell held steady with nineteenth-century local-color and frontier humor, renewing it in the early twentieth century as spoken stories and published literature. Author and museum director Rick Stewart observed that, in addition to the rich legacy of Russell's stories and personal letters, "he managed to carry his narrative abilities over to his art."[32] Institution leader and accomplished author Peter Hassrick sees both Russell and Remington as "storytellers with a brush and bronze."[33] In addition to Russell's fine art, his published writings carry a special significance. "*Trails Plowed Under* is not only a western classic," observes Professor Brian Dippie, "it is one of the enduring works of American literature," adding:

> [It] helped establish the cadence and charm of cowboy vernacular. Charlie Russell caught the very rhythms of storytelling on the printed page.... [B]y making his prose simply "paper talk" he created a literature all his own."[34]

Russell archivist and author, Ginger Renner, has frequently stated that Charlie Russell wasted nothing in putting his ideas on paper. "He made every word count."[35]

Beyond the level of quaint folk literature, Charlie Russell's published writings convey aspects of local history in ways that inform wider analyses of the American West. As these published works add variety to the perspective that Russell expressed in his pictures and sculptures, they also contribute to the vivid dimension that Dobie observed when he noted, "What makes history, whether authenticated or legendary, live is that part of it that appeals to the imagination."[36] Serving as a local historian, Russell took on the job of replicating daily life as typically found in what art critics call "genre painting." His writings also performed this function, supplying useful material for observant cultural historians of the West from J. Frank Dobie to Gerald Nash, from Robert Athearn to Richard White.[37] H. G. Merriam understood this link between local-color anecdotes and history writing when he noted:

> The able historian, especially the social historian, lends a learning ear to what people of the time he is investigating have to say of that time, even when recalled in later years.[38]

Russell not only listened to the local voices and their stories, he recycled many of their narratives as artworks and published tales that achieve the level of historical legends.

Richard White on Mythmakers vs. Historians

Legends can resemble or even become cultural myths. Taking in a wide view of artworks and writings about the American West, historian Richard White makes the distinction between folklore-oriented "mythmakers" and historians. "Mythmakers usually draw from history," he observes,

> they use real people or actual incidents. They have no compunctions, however,

about changing details, adding characters, and generally rearranging events in order to make their stories clearer. . . . Historians and mythmakers thus both seek to order the past in a way that conveys meaning. Both tell stories. But historians, also by the code of their craft, cannot reorder facts or invent new ones. Historians are thus more cramped and constricted than mythmakers in their attempts to explain what the past "means."[39]

Mythmaking seems less apt for characterizing Russell's writings and artworks than legend making, but much of White's conclusion fits Russell and his works. Charlie Russell's admission, through the voice of Rawhide Rawlins, that "I ain't no historian, but I happen to savvy this incident" accurately begins a brief roast of his old friend Pete Van. Many observers have insisted that this narrative could have been about Russell himself and his own problems as a cowboy with personal infestations.[40] In this brief tale, Russell's roasting joke shifted the focus of an amusing incident onto his friend without disrupting basic cultural reality in a narrative about unpleasant body lice.

Charlie Russell clearly was willing to distort information about actual people and events for comic effect. Freed from what became the restraint and disciplined ambition of twentieth-century academic historiography, Russell's legend-making stories informally delivered aspects of cultural history that inform subsequent generations. White acknowledges this value to historians, stating that the legends or myths "themselves thus become historical sources reflecting the values and concerns of the period and people who produced them."[41]

WILLIAM CRONON AND ELLIOTT WEST ON STORIES AND NARRATIVE HISTORY

Ironically, what Charlie Russell's contemporaries once praised as "historic accuracy" in his painted depictions of people and animals some critics now call nostalgic "myth-making" partly due to his repetitive depiction of subjects in pictures, sculptures, and stories. Russell's narrative view is clearer and more enjoyable for local culture when his story has "Old Bab" tell another whopper lie. But narrative control in his stories can also be uncertain, although still intriguing, as when narrator "Dad Lane" reveals his anti-Indian bias in "Mormon Murphy's Confidence." Russell makes a game out of narrative manipulation in his published writings, but still delivers identifiable cultural history to the discerning reader. Historian William Cronon distills the advantage of a good yarn over other forms of expression, observing, "A simple story well told may reveal more about a past world than a complicated text that never finds its own center."[42]

Charlie Russell controlled the delivery of local history through his choice of details as well as his subject. The selection of narrative elements and the inclusion or exclusion of entire stories added shape and color to his presentation of local information as regional history. Just as some Russell stories are more entertaining or informative than others, some narrative histories about the West are more controversial than others, sparking debates about political interpretations. Western historian Elliott West understands how debates over stories become significant to history writing when he states:

each part of the West is also what it is because of the stories people have told about it. I am referring in particular to narratives considered as specially associated with a particular place. . . . We can think of western history as one of conflicting narratives. Just as its people have fought for control of resources and for dominance of institutions and value, so the West has been an arena where stories have contested to command that country's meaning and thus to influence how the West is treated.[43]

Understanding racial interactions in the West frequently involves the interpretation of Indian versions of an event that conflicts with white settlers' versions of the same occurrence. Where the aging Crow chief Plenty Coups saw the basic story of his people ending, a settler near the Crow reservation in southern Montana such as Nannie Alderson, the coauthor of *A Bride Goes West,* saw it as just beginning. In contrast with Alderson, Plenty Coups concludes:

> when the buffalo went away the hearts of my people fell to the ground, and they could not lift them up again. After this nothing happened.[44]

Cronon observes that the Crow chief's favorite story ended with the buffalo and that everything else is "some other plot, and there is neither joy nor sense in telling it."[45]

Charlie Russell found his favorite story ending with the shift in the West from open-range cattle ranching to the shared range of fenced ranches for cattle and sheep, plus dryland farms as well as irrigated spreads. Despite his nostalgic disappointment with the changing West, Russell persisted in telling stories about such startling twentieth-century developments as automobiles, tourist hotels, and women modernizing ranch life. He could render very few of these latter-day stories in paint or bronze, but with writing pen and paper he could tell more. Due to a few critical uncertainties and disagreements about the inspiration for Russell's folk-lyric narratives in paint, a closer look at his neglected writings seems all the more important. Charlie Russell's published works reveal the essential perspective of this witness/participant in the midst of the continuous transformation of the American West. And in their entertaining formats, Russell's writings reveal the rapidly changing West like few other documents. The process of American history-telling as expressed through the voices of people in the West is enriched because Charlie Russell's narratives live on.

According to his range companions, when words failed Russell he sketched a picture or shaped some clay. Throughout most of his life, in the right setting and mood, the words flowed easily in ways that amused those who listened. And nearing the end of his life, he helped make sure that some of those words and narratives survived him in print, telling the more complete stories that his spectacular pictures and sculptures could only suggest in a frozen moment. Charlie Russell never attempted to tell all the stories about the American West. Yet in telling about those people, animals, and places that interested him the most, he printed tales that offer rewards of information, humor, and excitement to clarify a unique time and place—in a broad collection of stories that can be found nowhere else.

When historians take a closer look at oral-tradition storytelling, they find few anecdote writers who satisfy both the readers wanting cultural amusement and those seeking concrete cultural data. A close look at the published writings of Charles M. Russell reveals a fortunate coincidence for both folktale enthusiasts and cultural historians, but this overlap does not establish a reliable theory or concept of historiography. A thorough study of any region may uncover local-color writings, but they seldom provide objective details that can be cross-referenced for time and place. Russell's unusual writings constitute the exception rather than the rule.

Charles M. Russell transformed incidents that he experienced directly or heard about from others into paintings and sculptures that have enraptured several generations of admirers. In addition, his written versions of these local events provide students and enthusiasts of the American West with an opportunity to savor nineteenth-century, rural folk culture. Historian Joan Jensen wisely concludes, "The written literature of cultures that are still close to the oral tradition is very important because it taps into these collective memories and allows us to hear what has been passed down."[46] In a similar way, Russell's published stories enable readers to experience cultural processes in speech patterns that defined the rural West.

Charlie Russell presents the vocal expressions and experiences of some but not all westerners. Some typical social groups in nineteenth-century Montana, such as Indians, cowboys, trappers, or hunters, stand out as vivid story subjects in Russell's writings. Others, such as tourists, women, and sheepherders, receive brief, incomplete mention, while some, such as Hispanics, Asians, loggers, miners, and children, simply do not appear in these tales even though they lived in and influenced the American West. Russell made no attempt to comprehensively address all facets of western life and merely published the stories he enjoyed telling that focused on topics and individuals intriguing to him, leaving his story anthology resembling a quilt of tales about western people and themes—a large and colorful patchwork with ragged borders and quite a few gaps.

Despite Russell's wide variety of inspirations beyond his own direct experiences, the influence on his works by other writers and artists of his era seems muted. The complexity of narrative elements that Russell created or adapted in his writings, pictures, and sculptures have diluted the significance of singular influences on his final synthesis for each work. Charlie Russell's stories reveal, nevertheless, the crucial influence of other people to his work. The person-to-person interaction of storytelling provided an important stimulus for Charlie Russell. Verbal exchanges with knowledgeable and supportive companions stimulated his memory for storytelling as well as narrative artworks. If Russell valued another person's narration of an adventure, incident, or situation, he might return the favor with a gift picture that recreated and celebrated the original verbal account. The artist also retold memorable stories that he heard from others, adding his own embellishments in the best tradition of lively folklore regeneration. Rather than a negatively derivative pattern, Russell's relay of another person's narrative theme celebrated the original version. On those exceptional occasions when he committed a narrative to paper, Russell typically named the source if a story came from someone else. His adaptations of another person's narrative strengthened rather than weakened his own accomplishments in sculpting, painting, or writing, as is often the case in folkloric traditions.

As social commentary, Charlie Russell's legends satirized the experience of rapid cultural transformations from the sparsely populated frontier West of the nineteenth century into zones containing farms, ranches, mining sites, Indian reservations, crossroad villages, logging camps, and tourist traps of the urbanizing West in the early twentieth century. Like many westerners of earlier times, Russell found the rapid alterations especially disorienting and dismaying. In response, his paintings mostly portray the picturesque West prior to these accelerated changes. Conversely, many of his stories and essays depict the transformative modern experiences in his present-day, early twentieth century that he declined to record in pencil, paint, or clay. Russell's light-hearted writings challenge many of the social developments, including the shift from the horse-dominated West to a region dependent on trains and automobiles, and the swift evolution from rowdy cow towns of barrooms and brothels into urbanizing centers of family homes and small shops. The social criticism in his stories did not avoid controversy. Some of Russell's writings comment negatively on the accelerated progression of western women's lives into greater personal and political power at the same time that the male-dominant culture of barrooms and saloons went into decline. In another area, he notes with little enthusiasm the replacement of large-scale cattle herding as the dominant economic activity in the rural West by small farms and fenced-pasture ranches. And he celebrates the perseverance of culturally rich Indians surviving despite the poverty of their reservation communities.

The theme of cultural transformation permeates Russell's published writings. In contrast with the predominantly romantic writings about an unchanging West that frequently appeared in print during his lifetime, most of Russell's writings depict western American life as continuously shifting and evolving. Few writers who focused on the American West have offered as much variety in narrative styles and realistic topics. Indeed, if considered as a unit, Charlie Russell's ragged but colorful tapestry of writings unfolds beyond the limits of most literary categories, including "local color." Like their author, this group of tales stands as a breed apart.

At first glance, Charlie Russell appeared to be a gifted fine artist who also happened to amuse his family, friends, and associates with an endless fount of stories and anecdotes about life in the West. On closer consideration, however, he behaved more like a storyteller first and foremost, who shared insightful moments of cultural history as well as memorable characters through several narrative disciplines. In his lifetime, Russell's fine art brought him international fame and wealth while his published tales achieved only modest status of popularity among people sharing regional legends of the West. By collecting and preserving amusing local anecdotes, Charlie Russell foreshadowed a culturally important accomplishment of the Franklin D. Roosevelt presidency: the Work's Progress Administration (WPA) and its localized Montana Writers' Project of 1935–1942. Some of the same kinds of people who supplied Russell with stories and narrative ideas seem to have spoken a few decades later with the WPA interviewers who followed in the artist/writer's footsteps to harvest a bounty of oral-tradition narratives.[47] Back in the teens and 1920s, when Russell first published his anecdotes, he set a lasting example for appreciating and preserving rural-minded stories of the West.

Through his writings, Charlie Russell matured beyond his own local-culture role as a yarn-spinner who merely entertained privileged friends and lucky contemporaries. Struggling to save his narratives as printed words on paper, Russell synthesized cultural information for wider audiences in the region and nation. In this way, Charlie Russell resembled a great Irish storyteller who (according to folklorist/historian Henry Glassie) was continuously "bundling up the past to make it a gift to the future . . . pulling the people of his place into deeper association."[48] In several artistic disciplines, Charles M. Russell eloquently and accurately portrayed the people of the American West by addressing them directly and blending their responses into his works.

Notes

INTRODUCTION

1. Napier Wilt, *Some American Humorists* (New York: Thomas Nelson and Sons, 1929), xii–xiv.
2. Dave Walter, "Introduction," in *Montana Campfire Tales, Fourteen Historical Narratives* (Helena and Billings, Mont.: Falcon Press, 1997), ix, x.
3. In the first serious discussion of Charles M. Russell's published tales and essays, Robert Gale produced a fifty-page examination of Russell's pictures, sculptures, and writings for the Boise State Western Writers Series (1979). He discusses some of Russell's stories in a few brief summaries. Gale defines his own four categories of Russell's writings as "humorous anecdotes involving white men (twenty-two items), tales of Indians (nine), informational essays (eight), and serious stories about white men (four)." Robert Gale, *Charles Marion Russell,* Western Writers Series no. 38 (Boise, Idaho: Boise State University, 1979), 25, 26.

CHAPTER ONE

1. "'He'll Give Me A Foot Up, If I Meet Him Over There,' Says Russell's Old Friend," *Great Falls Leader,* Oct. 27, 1926.
2. Horace Brewster with A. L. Jordan, "Life on the Plains," *Great Falls Tribune,* Mar. 5–Apr. 16, 1933; Dave Walter, comp. and ed., "Past Times, The Wit and Wisdom of Horace Brewster," *Montana Magazine* (May–June 2003): 78–79.
3. J. Frederick Richardson, "'Paintin' Cowpuncher's Personality Secret Of His Vivid Portrayals, He-Men, He-Horses Tell Colorful Tales of Days When Six-Gun and Sense of Justice Were Law on Montana Plains; a Genius of the Range," *Santa Barbara Morning Press,* Jan. 21, 1923.
4. Frank B. Linderman, *Recollections of Charley Russell,* ed H. G. Merriam (Norman: University of Oklahoma Press, 1963; repr., 1984), 77.
5. Richardson, "Paintin' Cowpuncher's Personality."
6. Linderman, *Recollections,* 82.
7. L. E. Falk, Aberdeen, S.Dak., letter to James B. Rankin, 1937, Montana Historical Society, Rankin Collection, no. 162, box 2, file 2.
8. Charles M. Russell, *Trails Plowed Under* (Garden City, N.Y.: Doubleday, Page and Co. 1927).
9. Sue Russell Portis, handwritten notes, p. 1, Helen E. and Homer E. Britzman Collection, Taylor Museum for Southwestern Studies of the Colorado Springs Fine Arts Center, Colo., no. E209.
10. Ibid.
11. Austin Russell, *C. M. R.: Charles M. Russell, Cowboy Artist, a Biography* (New York: Twayne Publishing, 1957), 58.

12. Ginger Renner, *A Limitless Sky: The Work of Charles M. Russell in the Collection of the Rockwell Museum, Corning, New York* (Flagstaff, Ariz.: Northland Press, 1986), 5.

13. Silas Bradford Gray, Reminiscence, 1935, unpublished typed MS, Montana Historical Society Archives, SC 766, 27.

14. A. Russell, *C. M. R.,* 84

15. H. E. Crowell, letter to James B. Rankin, May 11, 1938, Rankin Collection, box 1, file 10.

16. Mrs. Imogene [Divers] Olson, "Letters to the Editor," *Montana: The Magazine of Western History* 46:1 (spring 1996): 92. Also, see J. Frank Dobie, field notes on Florence Hotel stationary, J. Frank Dobie Collection, University of Texas at Austin, Harry Ransom Center, Russell miscellaneous file, box 1 of 2, item 14.

17. Mrs. Laura (Lolly Edgar) Whittmore, letter to James B. Rankin, 1938, Rankin Collection, box 4, file 14.

18. Lew L. Callaway, "Montana Episode, Visits with Charles M. Russell," *Montana: The Magazine of Western History* 38:3 (summer 1988): 73.

19. Al P. Andrews, to James B. Rankin, 1938, Rankin Collection, box 1, folder 1, item 1.

20. John R. Barrows, *U-BET: A Greenhorn in Old Montana* (Caldwell, Idaho: Caxton Printers, 1934; repr., Lincoln: University of Nebraska Press, 1990), 274. Also, see Stan Hoig, *The Humor of the American Cowboy* (Caldwell, Idaho: Caxton Printers, 1958; repr., Lincoln: University of Nebraska Press, 1970), 30.

21. I. D. O'Donnell, letter to James B. Rankin, 1937, Rankin Collection, box 3, folder 3.

22. In a similar circumstance, Henry B. Wonham, *Mark Twain and the Art of the Tall Tale* (New York and Oxford: Oxford University Press, 1993), 23, 95, noted that in *Roughing It,* "Twain's tenderfoot earns admission to an exclusive 'community of knowers' in the West not only by acquiring experience, but also by mastering a style of narration with which to represent and interpret his experience of the frontier."

23. Jessie Lincoln Mitchell, "C. M. Russell, The White Indian," *Montana: The Magazine of Western History* 10:1 (winter 1960): 3.

24. Joe DeYong, "Out of the Past," unpublished MS, National Cowboy Hall of Fame, Oklahoma City, Joe DeYong Collection, no. 80.18, Flood no. 849, p. 5.

25. Irvin S. Cobb, *Exit Laughing* (Indianapolis and New York: The Bobbs-Merrill Company, 1941), 403.

26. Maynard Dixon, letter to James B. Rankin, January 15, 1937, Rankin Collection, box 1, file 13.

27. J. Frank Dobie, typed notes from W. R. Pontius, August 1946, Dobie Collection, box 1 of 2, item 15.

28. Mark Twain, *Roughing It* (New York: New American Library, 1962; repr., 1980), 271, 273.

29. Joe Thoroughman, statement in Forrest Crossen, *Western Yesterdays,* vol. 9, *Charlie Russell—Friend* (Fort Collins, Colo.: Robinson Press, 1973), 24, 25.

30. William Bleasdale Cameron, "The Old West Lives Through Russell's Brush," *Canadian Cattleman* 3:1 (January 1950): 26.

31. J. Frank Dobie, field notes, Dobie Collection, box 1 of 2, item 16.

32. Joe Thoroughman, statement, 28.

33. Philip Goodwin, *Recreation Magazine* (1917), cited in Peter H. Hassrick, *Charles M. Russell* (New York: Harry N. Abrams and the National Museum of American Art, Smithsonian Institution, 1989), 116.

34. Joe DeYong, "The First of His Kind," unpublished MS, ed. Michael Kennedy, DeYong Collection, National Cowboy Hall of Fame, no. 29, Flood no. 847.

35. Ross Santee, *Lost Pony Tracks* (New York: Charles Scribner's Sons, 1953; repr., Lincoln: University of Nebraska Press, 1972), 55.

36. Frederic G. Renner, *Charles M. Russell; Paintings, Drawings, and Sculpture in the Amon Carter Museum* (New York: Harry Abrams and the Amon Carter Museum of Western Art, 1966; rev. ed., 1974), 26.

37. "Charles Russell, Cowboy Artist," *The Butte Miner,* clipping hand-dated "1908" in the Britzman Collection, no. a.185.ak.

38. Patricia M. Morris, *Charles M. Russell, Man of the West* (Casper, Wyo.: Man of the West Publishing, 1987), 21. An editorial note reads, "Pat Morris wrote this book in the early 1950s." Copy in the Mansfield Library, University of Montana, Missoula.

39. Walter Lehman, letter to James B. Rankin, Nov. 25, 1936, Montana Historical Society, box 2, file 27.

40. Walter Lehman, letter to James B. Rankin, 1939, Rankin Collection, box 2, file 2.

41. Frank M. Chapman, "The Man Behind the Brush," *Country Life* 50:4 (August 1926): 35–40.

42. "Charles Russell, Artist, Visits L.A., For Years His Brush Has Been Busy With Pictures of Cowboys, Indians," *Los Angeles Express,* Feb. 9, 1922.

43. Al Andrews, letter to James B. Rankin, Feb. 5, 1938, Rankin Collection, box 1, file 1.

44. Renner, *Charles M. Russell,* 138.

45. Sam Johns, "Linderman and Russell in Camp," *Kalispell News,* Mar. 11, 1938.

46. Lee Ford, letter to James B. Rankin, 1937, Rankin Collection, box 2, file 2.

47. Santee, *Lost Pony Tracks,* 168.

48. "Prefers Ulm To New York As Place Of Residence, Cowboy Artist Declares He Would Not Live Among Tall Teepees of Gotham," *Great Falls Tribune,* Feb. 16, 1904.

49. Joe Thoroughman, statement, 26. Thoroughman remembered the date as being 1895—the year before Charlie married Nancy. So this incident apparently took place the year before Bryan won the Democratic nomination for president with his "Cross of Gold" speech.

50. Mary Joan Boyer, "More Russell History," *The Old Gravois Coal Diggings* (Imperial, Mo., 1954), 21.

51. Jack Russell, notes to Vivian Paladin, June 15, 1970, Montana Historical Society.

52. Glenn Casey, "Letters to the Editor," *Montana: The Magazine of Western History* 34:2 (spring 1984).

53. Annie C. Bach, letter to James B. Rankin, Feb. 9, 1937, Rankin Collection, box 1, file 6.

54. Mrs. Charles Coulter, letter to Mrs. Margaret Coulter Verharen, quoted in "Mrs. Coulter Recalls Behavior of Russell," *The Kalispell Daily Inter Lake,* Mar. 21, 1954, p. 6.

55. Norma Linderman, statement, in Frank B. Linderman, *Recollections of Charley Russell,* ed H. G. Merriam (Norman: University of Oklahoma Press, 1963; repr., 1984), 135.

56. Dan Yancy [county attorney of Park County, Mont.], "The Hermit of the Yellowstone Was a Typical Montana Pioneer, 'Uncle John' Yancy Could Tell Many an Interesting Tale of the Days When the West Was Young; Was One of the Famous Pioneer Characters of Yellowstone Park District," *Fergus County Argus* (Montana Newspaper Association special inserts), Mar. 29, 1926.

57. Joe DeYong, MS notes, DeYong Collection, National Cowboy Hall of Fame, no. 34, Flood no. 853.

58. Ibid.

59. Guy Nevills, statement, in Forrest Crossen, *Western Yesterdays,* vol. 9, *Charlie Russell—Friend* (Fort Collins, Colo.: Robinson Press, 1973), 74.

60. Jack Wrynn, statement, in Patricia M. Morris, *Charles M. Russell, Man of the West* (Casper, Wyo.: Man of the West Publishing, 1987), 89.

61. Lew Callaway, "Visits With Charles M. Russell," *Montana: The Magazine of Western History* 38:3 (summer 1988): 74.

62. Nancy C. Russell, "Biographical Note," in *Good Medicine; Memories of the Real West,* by Charles M. Russell (Garden City, N.Y.: Garden City Publishing, 1929; repr., 1930), 24.

63. Lila Mackenzie, interviewed by Douglas Gaudette, Lethbridge, Jan. 16, 1977, audiotape, in the C. M. Russell Collection, Glenbow Museum, Calgary, Alberta.

64. Wilford Johnson, letter to James B. Rankin, 1937, Rankin Collection, box 2, file 13.

65. Lila Marchand Houston, letter to James B. Rankin, 1936, Rankin Collection, box 2, file 9.

66. "Prefers Ulm To New York As Place of Residence."

67. Hamlin Garland, *Companions on the Trail; A Literary Chronicle* (New York: Macmillan Company, 1931), 126.

68. Lila Marchand Houston, to James B. Rankin, 1936, Rankin Collection, box 2, file 9.

69. "Smart Set Lionizing Cowboy Artist," *The New York Press,* Jan. 31, 1904, p. 4.

70. "Cowboy Vividly Paints the Passing Life of the Plains, Worked Twenty Years as a Night Herder in Order to Utilize daylight for Sketching and Modeling—To Show His Work Here, *The New York Times,* Mar. 19, 1911, p. 5.

71. Ibid.

72. L. E. Falk, letter to James B. Rankin, 1937, Rankin Collection, box 2, file 2.

73. "Cowboy Vividly Paints."

74. "The Cowboy Painter," *The St. Louis Mirror,* Mar. 10, 1910.

75. Mitchell, "C. M. Russell, The White Indian," 6.

76. Maynard Dixon, letter to James B. Rankin, Jan. 15, 1937, Rankin Collection, box 1, file 13.

77. Joe DeYong, unpublished MS, DeYong Collection, National Cowboy Hall of Fame, Flood no. 853.

78. Joe DeYong, MS notes, DeYong Collection, National Cowboy Hall of Fame, no. 34, Flood no. 853.

79. C. M. Russell, letter to P. T. Tucker, Oct. 27, 1921, in Patrick T. Tucker, *Riding the High Country,* ed. Grace Stone Coates (Caldwell, Idaho: Caxton Printers, 1933; repr., Seattle: Fjord Press, 1987), xii.

80. J. Frank Dobie, typed MS from Mrs. Ed Neitzling, J. Frank Dobie Collection, University of Texas at Austin, Harry Ransom Center, Russell miscellaneous file, box 1, folder 14.

81. Mary Roberts Rinehart, *Through Glacier Park in 1915* (New York: P. F. Collier and Son, 1916; repr., Boulder, Colo.: Roberts Rinehart Publishing, 1983), 41.

82. Fergus Mead, letter to James B. Rankin, n.d., Rankin Collection, box 2, file 24.

83. M. O. Hammond fonds (private collection), Diaries, F 1075-5, Archives of Ontario. Also, see the photocopy in the Montana Historical Society archive. Hammond was a *Toronto Globe* reporter present at the Pablo Buffalo Roundup. This item is part of a large body of diaries documenting his personal and private life, including extensive travels through the United States.

84. Ibid.

85. Stewart Edward White, "On Cowboys," *Outlook* 78 (Sept. 3, 1904): 83–84.

86. Twain, *Roughing It,* 326.

87. Mitchell, "C. M. Russell, The White Indian," 5.

88. C. M. Russell, letter to Friend Frank, in *Charles M. Russell, Word Painter: Letters, 1887–1926,* ed. Brian Dippie (Fort Worth: Amon Carter Museum and Harry Abrams, 1993), 184.

89. Dobie Collection, box 2 of 2, item 26.

90. Lila Marchand Houston, to James B. Rankin, 1936, Rankin Collection, box 2, file 9.

91. Lee Ford, letter to James B. Rankin, 1937, Rankin Collection, no. 162, box 2, file 2.

92. Informal conversations with senior residents at Deaconess Hospital, Great Falls, 1986. Tape recordings with this writer.

93. "Famous Artist Gives First Talk Before Audience in Long Career," *The HI-LIFE, School News For Every One,* Great Falls High School, Oct. 27, 1925, vol. 5, p. 1. Original copy in bound volume at offices of Great Falls Central High School.

94. Sam Stevenson, letter to James B. Rankin, Dec. 30, 1936, Rankin Collection, box 4, file 5.

95. Aldee Bessette, letter to James B. Rankin, May 31, 1937, Rankin Collection, box 6, file 1.

96. Julius Hillgard, statement, in Forrest Crossen, *Western Yesterdays,* vol. 9, *Charlie Russell—Friend* (Fort Collins, Colo.: Robinson Press, 1973), 57–58.

97. Aldee Bessette, letter to James B. Rankin, May 31, 1937, Rankin Collection, box 6, file 1. The painting, complete with leather tepee flap, can be viewed among the stored Russell artworks at the Amon Carter Museum in Fort Worth, Texas. Commercial prints of one other example of Russell "pornographic" art are discretely displayed in a "trick" frame including one unit at the Montana Club cocktail lounge in Miles City, Montana. The visible print in the frame shows a cowboy on horseback observing an Indian woman walking nearby with her dog. When opened by its key, the frame reveals a second print showing that the cowboy's sexual activity with the woman is being interrupted because the man continues to hold the horse's reins in one hand while the horse shies away from the woman's barking dog, dragging the man with him. The whereabouts of the original watercolor paintings, titled "Anticipation and Frustration," are currently unknown.

98. Renner, *Charles M. Russell,* 270. Prints of the four *Silver Dollar* works—*Just a Little Sunshine, Just a Little Rain, Just a Little Pleasure, Just a Little Pain*—continue to be sold as a single, framed set by gift stores in museums displaying Russell artworks.

99. Ibid., 267.

100. Mitchell, "C. M. Russell, The White Indian," 6, 7.

101. A. Russell, *C. M. R.,* 173.

102. Harold Davidson, *Edward Borein, Cowboy Artist; The Life and Works of John Edward Borein, 1872–1945* (Garden City, N.Y.: Doubleday and Company, 1974), 111.

103. Ibid., 115.

104. Elizabeth Cobb, *My Wayward Parent, A Book About Irvin S. Cobb* (Indianapolis and New York: The Bobbs-Merrill Company), 201.

105. Will Rogers, "Introduction," in *Good Medicine; Memories of the Real West,* by Charles M. Russell (Garden City, N.Y.: Garden City Publishing, 1929; repr., 1930), 15–16.

CHAPTER TWO

1. C. M. Russell, "The West is Dead my Friend," *Regards to the Bunch, Letters, Poems, and Illustrations of C. M. Russell* (Great Falls: The C. M. Russell Museum, 1992), 1.

2. C. M. Russell, letter to "Friend Harry" [Stanford], Sept. 24, 1912, in *Charles M. Russell, Word Painter: Letters, 1887–1926,* ed. Brian Dippie (Fort Worth and New York: Amon Carter Museum and Harry N. Abrams, 1993), 171.

3. C. M. Russell, letter to "Friend Frank" [Linderman], Apr. 24, 1924, in *Charles M. Russell, Word Painter: Letters, 1887–1926,* ed. Brian Dippie (Fort Worth and New York: Amon Carter Museum and Harry N. Abrams, 1993), 347.

4. Joe DeYong, MS notes, Flood no. 853, document no. 34, National Cowboy Hall of Fame, Oklahoma City.

5. Charles M. Russell, *Studies of Western Life*, with Granville Stuart (New York: The Albertype Company, 1890).

6. "Russell Pictures of Western Life Drawn in Kitchen," *Helena Record-Herald*, June 30, 1929.

7. C. M. Russell, "Early Days on the Buffalo Range," *Recreation* 6 (April 1897): 227–31.

8. Untitled, handwritten, sixteen-page pencil manuscript, Helen E. and Homer E. Britzman Collection, Taylor Museum for Southwestern Studies of the Colorado Springs Fine Arts Center, Colo., no. C.8.58. A seven-page, typed MS, titled "A Buffalo Hunt," repeats the handwritten text but corrects the spelling and punctuation, while differing slightly from the *Recreation* version. Britzman collection, no. C.8.5. Harold McCracken was certain that the *Recreation* editors had rewritten Russell's story, obliterating his distinctive narrative style. McCracken, *The Charles M. Russell Book; The Life and Work of the Cowboy Artist* (Garden City, N.Y.: Doubleday and Company, 1957), 176.

9. Frederic G. Renner, *Charles M. Russell; Paintings, Drawings and Sculpture in the Amon Carter Museum* (Fort Worth: Amon Carter Museum, 1974), 25. Also, see Brian Dippie, "Introduction," in *Trails Plowed Under, Stories of the Old West,* by Charles M. Russell (Garden City, N.Y.: Doubleday, Page and Company, 1927; repr., Lincoln: University of Nebraska Press, 1996), vi. Dippie suggests a St. Louis family member or Nancy Russell moved Charlie to write for magazines. Also, see John Taliaferro, *Charles M Russell: The Life and Legend of America's Cowboy Artist* (Boston: Little, Brown and Company, 1996), 112. Taliaferro speculates that Remington's successful publishing example, as much as Nancy's influence, motivated Russell to write this story for publication.

10. Johnnie Edwards, former N/N-brand, cattle-range "Captain" and later Montana state senator, Dawson City, Montana Writers Project (Works Progress Administration), transcribed by Thomas E. Simmons, Glendive, Mont., microfilm reel 19, document no. 211.114, Mansfield Library, University of Montana.

11. Raphael Cristy, "Early Connections: The Friendship Between Charles M. Russell and James Willard Schultz," *The Piegan Storyteller* 15:2 (April 1990): 1. Schultz was publishing articles in *Forest and Stream* as early as 1880 and gave away a book of his early pieces to George Bird Grinnell in the early 1890s that Grinnell published as his own *Blackfoot Lodge Tales* in 1892. Warren Hanna, *The Life and Times of James Willard Schultz (Apikuni)* (Norman: University of Oklahoma Press, 1986), 250–52, 364.

12. Anna P. Nelson, "The Medicine Arrow," *Sports Afield* (January 1898): 20–21.

13. Elizabeth Greenfield, "The Cowboy Artist As Seen in Childhood Memory," *Montana: The Magazine of Western History* 14:1 (winter 1964): 38, 39.

14. Ibid., 38.

15. Charles M. Russell, "A Savage Santa Claus," *Great Falls Daily Tribune*, Dec. 16, 1906, p. 25.

16. P. W. Korrell, "Pioneer Tells of Historic Gulch," *Fallon County Times* (Montana Newspaper Association special inserts), Nov. 16, 1931. Russell also cast Bedrock as the leading character in his humorous yarn "Safety First, But Where Is It?" and the rescuing partner in the more serious tale "Hank Winter's Bear Story."

17. Statement by Mr. Kommers to Edith Toomer, May 3, 1941, "Anecdotes—Great Falls Yesterday," Montana Writers Project (Works Progress Administration), microfilm reel 16, p. 8, Mansfield Library, University of Montana, Missoula.

18. Charles M. Russell, *More Rawhides* (Great Falls: Montana Newspaper Association, 1925).

19. "A Savage Santa Claus," five-page, typed MS, Dec. 10, 1906, Britzman Collection, no. C.8.45.

20. "St. Louis Artist Back from the West, Charles M. Russell Declares She is Responsible for Success of work," *St. Louis Post Dispatch*, Feb. 16, 1910, clipping in Britzman Collection, no. E.185.ai.

21. Ibid.

22. C. A. Beil, letter to James B. Rankin, Dec. 5, 1936, James B. Rankin Collection, MC no. 162, box 1, file 3, Montana Historical Society archives, Helena.

23. "The Cowboy Artist Is Now Winning Fame as an Author," *Great Falls Tribune*, Dec. 16, 1906.

24. "Another Story By C. M. Russell, Demand for More Work From His Pen—Cowboy Artist and His Critics," *Great Falls Tribune*, Jan. 29, 1908, p. 4.

25. C. M. Russell stories in *Outing*: "Mormon Murphy's Misplaced Confidence," 50:5 (August 1907): 550; "How Lindsay Turned Indian," 51:3 (December 1907): 337; "Dad Lane's Buffalo Yarn," 51:5 (February 1908): 513; "Finger-That-Kills Wins His Squaw," 52:1 (April 1908): 32; "Longrope's Last Guard," 52:2 (May 1908): 176.

26. "Cowboy Artist Paints Indians, Charles Russell's Work Said to Excel Remington's. Admits That Mrs. Russell Greatly Assists Him In Creating Original Drawings and Making Wax Figures," unidentified Los Angeles newspaper clipping, dated "1906" in Britzman Collection, no. 6.185.

27. Caspar Whitney, letter to Charles M. Russell, Nov. 4, 1907, Britzman collection, no. C.5.22b.

28. Richard W. Etulain, "The Historical Development of the Western," *Journal of Popular Culture* 7:3 (winter 1973): 719.

29. Peggy Samuels and Harold Samuels, *Frederic Remington: A Biography* (Austin: University of Texas Press, 1985); Peggy Samuels and Harold Samuels, *The Collected Writings of Frederic Remington* (Garden City, N.Y.: Doubleday and Company, 1979), vii, viii.

30. Caspar Whitney, to Charles M. Russell, Jan. 4, 1908, Britzman collection, no. C.2.01.

31. Nancy C. Russell, letter to Caspar Whitney, Mar. 1, 1909, Britzman Collection, no. C.6.221.

32. C. M. Russell, handwritten note to Joe DeYong, Flood Collection, C. M. Russell Museum, Great Falls, DeYong notes no. 975-12-89 (2). Hearing-impaired Joe DeYong understood his mentor through Indian sign language, lip-reading, and scribbled notes. DeYong saved the notes; collections of them exist at the C. M. Russell Museum and at the National Cowboy Hall of Fame. Con Price claims he was the model for "Pretty Shadow" in his book *Trails I Rode* (Pasadena: Trail's End Publishing, 1947), 136–37.

33. Ibid., Mar. 1, 1909, no. C.6.221.

34. Caspar Whitney, to Nancy C. Russell, Feb. 6, 1909, Britzman Collection, no. C.6.219. The Russells seem to have corresponded with Whitney as late as 1911 but with no luck. *Collier's* was preoccupied with Remington's art and ignored Russell's stories.

35. "Montana Has 167 Publications, 16 daily and 141 Weekly Publications . . . ," *Winnett Times* (Montana Newspaper Association), July 12, 1929.

36. Sam Gilluly, *The Press Gang: A Century of Montana Newspapers, 1885–1985*, ed. Kevin S. Giles (Great Falls: Aircraft Printers, 1985), 18, 20. "Bill [Cheely], H. P. Rabin, Oliver Wadsworth and T. J. Hocking were originally all involved in the Association, but Cheely eventually became the sole owner."

37. "Specializes in Historic Anecdotes, Cheely's Publication Goes Into Thousands Of Homes In Montana / Apostle of Good Will and Cheer Renders Great Service to State," *Miles City Daily Star*, May 24, 1934, p. 19. The Montana Newspaper Association inserts cultivated a widespread and lasting appreciation in Montana for local and regional history that continued through the end of the twentieth century with the state historical society's museum, archives, and the publishing of books and a popular quarterly, *Montana: The Magazine of Western History*.

38. Pete Snelson, "Montana Loses Widely Beloved Editor in Death of William W. 'Bill' Cheely," *Judith Basin County Press* (Montana Newspaper Association), Apr. 10, 1939.

39. "Twain's Prince, Pauper Again," *Fallon County Times* (Montana Newspaper Association), Sept. 30, 1940.

40. Austin Russell, *C. M. R.: Charles M. Russell, Cowboy Artist, a Biography* (New York: Twayne Publishers, 1957), 198.

41. Ellen Shaffer, Dawson's Book Shop, Los Angeles, Aug. 29, 1939, letter to Mr. Mark Brown, copy in Rankin Collection. "It is to [Mrs. Russell] that I am indebted for the information that Raban frequently wrote out portions of the manuscript."

42. Percy Rabin, letter to James B. Rankin, n.d., Rankin Collection, box 3, file 16.

43. The first Russell/Raban collaboration appears to be "That Was Some Horse Trade When DeHart Was a Cowman," an anecdote that Russell shared with Raban, who worked it into a piece for the Montana Newspaper Association with a Russell illustration. *Dillon Examiner* (Montana Newspaper Association), Sept. 27, 1916.

44. Joe DeYong, Charles M. Russell biography (unpublished), "Introduction, section A," National Cowboy Hall of Fame no. 34, Flood no. 853.

45. No contract or documentation currently exists defining the business arrangements between the Russells and the Montana Newspaper Association for the rights to print Charlie's stories and illustrations in either the weekly insert sections or in the *Rawhide Rawlins* books.

46. "Canvas By Russell Is Sold For Five Thousand," *Great Falls Tribune,* Jan. 15, 1915, p. 6.

47. "Sale of Russell Painting for Ten Thousand Dollars Sets New Mark For Montana Artist, Does Some Fine Bronze Work," *Redstone Review* (Montana Newspaper Association), May 25, 1921.

48. Charles M. Russell, "The Story of the Cowboy As It Was Told To Me By An Old-time Rider Of The Range," *Tenth Annual Great Falls High School Roundup,* June 18, 1917, pp. 40–42. The Montana Newspaper Association reprinted the essay in 1916 and in 1921 as "The Cowboy As He Was, Reminiscences Of A Western Type That Has Passed," before it appeared in 1927 as the opening piece in *Trails Plowed Under* with the title "The Story of the Cowpuncher."

49. Charles M. Russell, "Hunting And Trapping On The Judith With Jake Hoover," *The Western News* (Montana Newspaper Association), June 18, 1917.

50. Charles M. Russell, "A Slice of Charlie's Early Life," *Eleventh Annual Great Falls High School Roundup,* June 4, 1918, p. 48.

51. Charles M. Russell, "The Olden Days," *Twelfth Annual Great Falls High School Roundup,* June 20, 1919, 147.

52. Charles M. Russell, "The Pinto," *The Moore Independent* (Montana Newspaper Association), June 30, 1919. This story appeared finally in *Trails Plowed* under the title "The Ghost Horse."

53. Nancy Russell, letter to Harry Maule, Feb. 19, 1927, Britzman Collection, no. C.6.501.

54. "Three Russell Manuscripts," Russell vertical file, Montana Historical Society Library, Helena. The documents describe the manuscript for "The Pinto" as being partly in Russell's handwriting and partly in Raban's. Apparently, Raban edited the piece only for spelling errors. The sheet listed the price of $150 for all three manuscripts.

55. Charles M. Russell, "The Ghost Horse," *Trails Plowed Under* (Garden City, N.Y.: Doubleday, Page & Co., 1927), 91.

56. Ibid.; *The Fergus County Argus* (Montana Newspaper Association), June 3, 1922.

57. Russell apparently did not seek publication opportunities in the active marketplace for juvenile literature. His long-ago friend James Willard Schultz made a large part of his income selling stories to *Youth's Companion* and other magazines continuously from 1910 through 1927. Hanna, *Life and Times of James Willard Schultz,* 361.

58. Michael Malone and Richard Roeder, *Montana: A History of Two Centuries* (Seattle: University of Washington Press, 1984), 216, 217.

59. *The Record Herald,* Helena, Mont., Nov. 21, 1921, cited in *The Charles M. Russell Book; The Life and Work of the Cowboy Artist,* by Harold McCracken (Garden City: Doubleday and Company, 1957), 221, 222.

60. McCracken, *Charles M. Russell Book,* 221, 222. In Cheely's letter to Rankin, June 17, 1937, he recalls that the first printing was ten thousand copies and the subsequent ones one thousand each. Dippie's sources offer the fifteen thousand total copies. Dippie, "Introduction," ix.

61. "Charles Russell, Artist, Visits L.A., For years His Brush Has Been Busy With Pictures of Cowboys, Indians," *Los Angeles Express,* Feb. 9, 1922.

62. Harry Maule, letter to Nancy Russell, May 20, 1926, Britzman Collection, no. C.6.566. The two republished pieces were "Some Liars of the Old West" for five dollars in the July 10, 1922, edition and "The Story of the Cowpuncher" for ten dollars in the July 25, 1922 edition.

63. Charles M. Russell, illustrator, *Back-Trailing on the Old Frontiers* (Great Falls: Cheely-Raban Syndicate, 1922).

64. Bill of sale receipt for *"Rawhide Rawlins Stories"* and *"Back-Trailing on the Old Frontiers"* inventory and copyrights, dated Oct. 15, 1923, from Percy Raban to Nancy Russell, Britzman Collection, no. C.4.245.

65. Taliaferro, *Charles M. Russell,* 242, 243.

66. "Prince of Wales Pays $10,000 For American Artist's Painting," *Los Angeles Examiner,* Feb. 27, 1923.

67. Nancy Russell, letter to Percy Raban, Oct. 8, 1923, Britzman Collection, no. C.2.19b.

68. Nancy Russell, letter to Percy Raban, Nov. 7, 1923, Britzman Collection, no. C.3.27.

69. Russell, *More Rawhides.*

70. Charles M. Russell, note to Joe DeYong, Flood Collection, C. M. Russell Museum, no. 975-12-788.

71. C. M. Russell, "A Few Words About Myself," *More Rawhides* (Great Falls: Montana Newspaper Association, 1925), 3.

72. "Charles M. Russell's New Book, 'More Rawhides,' is a Humorous Portrayal of Cowboy Life Told in Cowboy Language," *Fergus County Argus* (Montana Newspaper Association), Nov. 30, 1925.

73. "Charles M. Russell Writes New Book of Humorous Tales of the Cattle Days," *Judith Basin County Press* (Montana Newspaper Association), Nov. 23, 1925.

74. W. W. Cheely, letter to Charles and Nancy Russell, Dec. 10, 1925, Britzman Collection, no. C.2.18.

CHAPTER THREE

1. Charles M. Russell, *Good Medicine; Memories of the Real West* (Garden City, N.Y.: Garden City Publishing, 1929), 127.

2. Julie Schimmel and Robert R. White, *Bert Geer Phillips and the Taos Art Colony* (Albuquerque: University of New Mexico Press, 1994), 141.

3. David Lavender, *Bent's Fort* (Lincoln: University of Nebraska Press, 1972), 396 n. 4.

4. Austin Russell, *C. M. R.: Charles M. Russell, Cowboy Artist, a Biography* (New York: Twayne Publishers, 1957), 19, 20.

5. Mildred Taurman, statement, "The Blackfeet Indians and the Crow Indians," *Utica, Montana* (Utica, Mont.: Utica Historical Society, 1968), 20. Also, see "History of Old Utica—Most Information from Charles Waite," in *Utica, Montana* (Utica, Mont.: Utica Historical Society, 1968), 9–10; and Walter F. Waite, *Old Utica, Silver Dollar Days* (Conrad, Mont.: Marilyn and Walter Waite, 1994), 9.

6. Hugh Dempsey, interview with John Cotton—Favorite Ill Walker, "The Wise Old Ones," in *The Amazing Death of Calf Shirt and Other Blackfoot Stories: Three Hundred Years of Blackfoot History* (Norman: University of Oklahoma Press, 1994), 9–11.

7. T. J. Waddell, "Recollections. C. M. Russell," unpublished, typed MS, Greenfield Collection, Montana Historical Society Archives, no. MC166, 6–10. Also, see Finch David, letter to James B. Rankin, 1937, Rankin Collection, stating that Russell "lived for several weeks with them but came back to settlement again and announced that he liked the Indians, but it was too damn long between meals to suit him."

8. James Willard Schultz wrote the best-selling, semiautobiographical account *My Life as an Indian: The Story of a Red Woman and a White Man in the Lodges of the Blackfeet* (New York: Doubleday, Page and Company, 1907; repr., New York: Beaufort Books, 1983), as well as thirty-six other books published during his lifetime, five posthumous books, and dozens more stories and articles, all focused on the "Piegan" or "Pecunni" Blackfeet Indians.

9. Paul Dyck, "Lone Wolf Returns . . . to that long ago time," *Montana: The Magazine of Western History* 22:1 (winter 1972): 32. "Charles Russell, together with Olaf Seltzer, made summer visits to [Lone Wolf's] tipi studio seeking facts on ethnological details. He would have Lone Wolf ask old warriors like Bear Head to help solve the problems."

10. Wallace Stegner and Richard W. Etulain, *Conversations with Wallace Stegner on Western History and Literature* (Salt Lake City: University of Utah Press, 1983), 153. "I used to mow his lawn. My brother tended his furnace. . . . I never got into his log cabin. That was for special people from the Mint." Wallace Stegner, in "That Great Falls Year," in *Montana Spaces: Essays and Photographs in Celebration of Montana,* ed. William Kittredge (New York: Lyons and Burford, 1988), 123, clarifies that he mowed Russell's lawn "a couple of times."

11. Interview with Mr. and Mrs. Angus Monroe, recorded in Conrad, Mont., copy in this writer's files.

12. Dan Flores, "Bison Ecology and Bison Diplomacy: The Southern Plains from 1800 to 1850," *Journal of American History* 78:2 (September 1991): 485.

13. Robert F. Berkhofer, Jr., *The White Man's Indian: Images of the American Indian from Columbus to the Present* (New York: Random House, 1978), 196.

14. Brian Dippie, *Looking At Russell* (Fort Worth: The Amon Carter Museum, 1987), 62. Dippie did not claim to have originated the term *romantic realism.* Also, see p. 73.

15. Charles M. Russell, "The War Scars of Medicine Whip," in *Trails Plowed Under* (Garden City, N.Y.: Doubleday and Company, 1927), 177–86.

16. Brian Dippie, *Remington and Russell: The Sid Richardson Collection,* rev. ed. (Austin: University of Texas Press, 1994), 132. Rick Stewart, *Charles M. Russell, Sculptor* (Fort Worth: The Amon Carter Museum, 1994), 147–49. The authors cite the narrative letter from different sources and provide differing names for the 1902 picture, which Stewart calls *"The War Scars of Medicine Whip"* and Dippie labels *"Counting Coup* [Medicine Whip]."

17. Stewart, *Charles M. Russell, Sculptor,* 38, 147–51.

18. Nancy Russell tried to sell this story to Outing. Nancy Russell, letter to Caspar Whitney, Nov. 18, 1908, Helen E. and Homer E. Britzman Collection, Taylor Museum for Southwestern Studies of the Colorado Springs Fine Arts Center, Colo., C.5.22h. As Nancy wrote, "He has one new story finished, 'Medicine Whip's War Scars.' It's an Indian story of the old days." Whitney neither welcomed nor bought the story. First published in Charles M. Russell, *Trails Plowed Under* (Garden City, N.Y.: Doubleday and Company, 1927), 177–86.

19. Stewart, *Charles M. Russell, Sculptor*, 24.

20. Stan Steiner, "The Squaw Sachem," in *The Vanishing White Man* (Norman: University of Oklahoma Press, 1976), 186–87. During the time of the "Red Power" movement in the 1970s, Steiner and other writers and activists ridiculed the use of *squaw*, making it clear that such terms offend Indian people and others. Steiner traced the term *squaw* back to as early as the Massachusetts Bay Colony and references to John Rolfe and Pocahontas, the "squaw Sachem."

21. Russell, "War Scars of Medicine Whip," in *Trails Plowed Under*, 177, 178, 186.

22. Charles M. Russell, "Dad Lane's Buffalo Yarn," in *Trails Plowed Under* (Garden City, N.Y.: Doubleday and Company, 1927), 42.

23. Russell, "War Scars of Medicine Whip," in *Trails Plowed Under*, 180, 179.

24. William Kittredge and Steven M. Krauzer, "'Mr. Montana' Revised," *Montana: The Magazine of Western History* 36:4 (autumn 1986): 18.

25. Granville Stuart, *Pioneering in Montana: The Making of a State, 1864–1887*, ed. Paul C. Phillips (Cleveland: Arthur H. Clark Company, 1925; repr., Lincoln: University of Nebraska Press, 1977), 225, 226. Stuart's book was formerly titled *Forty Years on the Frontier as seen in the Journals and Reminiscences of Granville Stuart*.

26. Granville Stuart, Letters to the Editor, Fort Benton *River Press*, May 1881, cited by J. F. Overholser, "Livestock Growers Threatened by Indians," *The Frontier* 13:3 (March 1933): 68.

27. "The Red Devils," (unsigned), *Mineral Argus*, Maiden, Mont., Sept. 10, 1885, p. 2.

28. Russell, "War Scars of Medicine Whip," in *Trails Plowed Under*, 180.

29. Ibid., 186.

30. Mark Twain, "The Noble Red Man," *Collected Tales, Sketches, Speeches, & Essays, 1852–1890*, ed. Louis Budd (New York: Library of America, 1992), 442–46. Twain continued his expressions of contempt for Indians in 1872 with the publication of *Roughing It* and with his villain "Injun Joe," in *Tom Sawyer*, published in 1876. See "Chronology," in *Collected Tales, Sketches, Speeches, & Essays, 1852–1890*, 969, 973. Also, see Mark Twain, *Roughing It* (New York: New American Library, 1962; repr., 1980), 118, 119. For the unreliable narrator's sarcasm: "If we cannot find it in our hearts to give these poor naked creatures our Christian sympathy and compassion, in God's name let us at least not throw mud at them." Twain, *Roughing It*, 120.

31. Hugh Dempsey, "Tracking C. M. Russell in Canada, 1888–1889," *Montana: The Magazine of Western History* 39:3 (summer 1989): 4–6, 14. The American Blackfeet and Canadian Blood tribes share a language and much culture. Charlie Russell used both terms, *Blackfeet* and *Blood*, when referring to the Indians he visited near High River, Alberta, in 1888. Dempsey was unsuccessful in trying to verify the existence of anyone using the name *Medicine Whip* among the registered (American) Blackfeet or (Canadian) Blood tribal name records.

32. Helen B. West, "Starvation Winter of the Blackfeet," *Montana: The Magazine of Western History* 8:1 (winter 1958): 2.

33. Charles M. Russell, "Finger-That-Kills Wins His Squaw," in *Trails Plowed Under* (Garden City, N.Y.: Doubleday and Company, 1927), 121, 122.

34. Michael P. Malone, Richard Roeder, and William L. Lang, *Montana: A History of Two Centuries,* rev. ed. (Seattle: University of Washington Press, 1976, 1991), 17. "Misunderstanding sign language, as they often did, French traders named them the 'Gros Ventres,' meaning 'big bellies.' This was doubly unfortunate because the Atsinas had ordinary stomachs and because the Hidatsas of Dakota also became known as "Gros Ventres," leading to much confusion. . . . [The Atsinas] eventually settled directly east of the Blackfeet between the Missouri and Saskatchewan Rivers." Most live today on the Ft. Belknap Reservation in north-central Montana.

35. Russell, "Finger-That-Kills," in *Trails Plowed Under,* 122.

36. The Piegan/Blackfeet war chief Meek-I-appy (known to whites as Cut-Finger) lost fingers and nearly died in one incident closely resembling the circumstances in Russell's "Finger-That-Kills" narrative. Russell could have met the warrior or heard other storytellers' versions before he wrote "Finger-That-Kills." He probably learned the story from Robert Vaughn in his regional history/memoir *Then and Now, Thirty-six Years in the Rockies 1864–1900* (Minneapolis: Tribune Publishing Company, 1900). Vaughn was an early rancher in the Great Falls area, an older friend of Russell's, and an early art patron who hired the young artist to illustrate his book.

37. Russell, "Finger-That-Kills," in *Trails Plowed Under,* 121.

38. Ibid., 127.

39. Twain, "Noble Red Man," 444.

40. Russell, "Finger-That-Kills," in *Trails Plowed Under,* 121.

41. Ibid.

42. Ibid.

43. Jon Tuska, "Introduction," in *The Western Story: A Chronological Treasury,* ed. Jon Tuska (Lincoln: University of Nebraska Press, 1982; repr., 1995), xxxv.

44. Charles M. Russell, "How Lindsay Turned Indian," in *Trails Plowed Under* (Garden City, N.Y.: Doubleday and Company, 1927), 133.

45. Bernard DeVoto, *Across The Wide Missouri* (Boston: Houghton Mifflin Company, 1947), 376.

46. Cassandra O. Phelps, letter to James Rankin, Feb. 5, 1939, Rankin Collection, Montana Historical Society, no. 162, box 3, file 5.

47. E. C. "Teddy Blue" Abbott and Helena Huntington Smith, *We Pointed Them North: Recollections of a Cowpuncher* (New York: Farrar and Rinehart, 1939; repr., Norman and London: University of Oklahoma Press, 1986), 149.

48. J. Frank Dobie, *Life and Literature of the Southwest: Revised and Enlarged in Both Knowledge and Wisdom* (Dallas: Southern Methodist University Press, 1952), 26. Also, see "First Trial in Montana; Plaintiff Called The Presiding Judge A 'Squaw Man,' And Tragedy Was Narrowly Averted," *Fergus County Argus,* Montana Newspaper Association, June 9, 1924. "[T]he participants, court, jury, lawyers, witnesses and spectators became involved in a rough-and-tumble fist fight."

49. Russell, "How Lindsay Turned Indian," in *Trails Plowed Under,* 133.

50. John Taliaferro, *Charles M. Russell: The Life and Legend of America's Cowboy Artist* (Boston: Little, Brown and Co., 1996), 166. Taliaferro guessed that this story "is Charlie's autobiographical fantasy about taking an Indian girl as a bride."

51. James Willard Schultz, letter to James Rankin, 1937, Rankin Collection, box 4, file 1. "[I]n his pre-marriage days he drank a lot, frequented the red light houses; paid for what he got there. . . . Never had an Indian girl."

52. H. A. Bussey, letter to James Rankin, 1937, Rankin Collection, box 1, file 6.

53. Brian Dippie's commentary is in *Charles M. Russell, Word Painter: Letters, 1887–1926,* ed. Brian Dippie (Fort Worth and New York: Amon Carter Museum and Harry Abrams, 1993), 26.

54. C. M. Russell, letter to Friend Charly [Charles M. Joys], May 10, 189[2], in *Charles M. Russell, Word Painter: Letters, 1887–1926,* ed. Brian Dippie (Fort Worth and New York: Amon Carter Museum and Harry Abrams, 1993), 24, 25.

55. Waddell, "Recollections." Also, see Russell, "War Scars of Medicine Whip," in *Trails Plowed Under,* 185: "You may not know it but the Bloods are one tribe that don't eat dog, an' say it is not good to eat those who guard your camp, an' howl at your door with lonesomeness when you're gone. 'It's a poor hunter that eats his friends,' goes on Sleep-in-Blood." Also, see John Ewers, *The Horse in Blackfoot Indian Culture,* Smithsonian Institution Bureau of American Ethnology, Bulletin 159 (Washington, D.C.: United States Government Printing Office, 1955), 167: "Lazy Boy, my eldest Piegan informant could recall only one winter buffalo disappeared at a time when the weather was too bad to use horses. His band, the Skunks, remembered that year as 'when we ate dogs winter.'"

56. Taliaferro, *Charles M. Russell,* 79. Russell's watercolor *Just a Little Pleasure* depicts a white prostitute disrobing a white cowboy in her bedroom. The 1898 painting, part of a humorous series of four—*Just a Little Sunshine, Just a Little Rain, Just a Little Pleasure, Just a Little Pain*—is located in the Amon Carter Museum in Fort Worth, Texas, along with the more explicit painting cited by Taliaferro. Frederic G. Renner, *Charles M. Russell: Paintings, Drawings and Sculpture in the Amon Carter Museum* (Fort Worth: Amon Carter Museum, 1974), 268–271. Taliaferro was aware of the works and referred to the
"*Just a Little* quartet" on p. 124.

57. "Rising Wolf Mountain Is A Monument To First White Brother of Blackfeet," *The Big Timber Pioneer* (Montana Newspaper Association), Nov. 10, 1919; "Hugh Monroe, First White Man To See Splendid Scenery Of Glacier Park In 1815, Buried On Two Medicine River In 1896," *Fresno Sentinel* (Montana Newspaper Association), Apr. 19, 1920; Martha Edgerton Plassmann, "The Story Of The Adventures Of Hugh Monroe Is Perhaps The Most Thrilling Narrative Of Early Indian Life In West," *The Philipsburg Mail* (Montana Newspaper Association), Sept. 22, 1924. Hugh Monroe interview, *Ft. Benton River Press,* Feb. 19, 1890. Also, see Warren L. Hanna, *The Life and Times of James Willard Schultz (Apikuni)* (Norman: University of Oklahoma Press, 1986), 355, 358, 365.

58. Russell, "How Lindsay Turned Indian," in *Trails Plowed Under,* 138–139.

59. "How Lindsay Turns Injun," 8 pages, undated typed MS, Britzman Collection, no. C.8.54. This first-known version, a typed manuscript with several handwritten corrections, apparently based on a preliminary handwritten draft, contains Monroe's pipe trick. The revisions and textual variations such as the title suggest that this undated, typed manuscript predates the *Outing* version's dead-eye shot-and-sunlight episode. C. M. Russell, "How Lindsay Turned Indian," *Outing Magazine* 51:3 (December 1907): 340. Russell included a special black-and-white illustration of sunlight spotlighting Lindsay just after his shot.

60. Dan Conway, "A Child of the Frontier, Memoirs of Charles M. Russell (The Cowboy Artist), written under the Direction of and in Cooperation with Mrs. Nancy C. Russell," Oct. 29, 1927, p. 91, unpublished MS, Britzman Collection.

61. Audio tape interview with Mr. and Mrs. Angus Monroe, Conrad, Mont., n.d., copy with this writer.

62. "Close View of Artist Russell, His Early Inclinations and Experiences, Given at Meeting of Women's Club by Mrs. [Nancy] Russell," *Great Falls Tribune,* Mar. 1, 1914.

63. Forest Crossen, *Western Yesterdays, Charlie Russell—Friend* (Fort Collins, Colo.: Robinson Press, 1973), 16.

64. Russell, "How Lindsay Turned Indian," in *Trails Plowed Under,* 133.

65. Abbott and Smith, *We Pointed Them North,* 145. Forty dollars a month was typical cowboy wage, represented here as the wage-cost for seizing Indian lands.

66. Maynard Dixon, letter to James Rankin, Jan. 30, 1937, Rankin Collection, box 1, file 13.

67. Russell, "How Lindsay Turned Indian," in *Trails Plowed Under,* 144.

68. Russell, "Dad Lane's Buffalo Yarn," in *Trails Plowed Under,* 41–50. Also, see Robert Gale, *Charles Marion Russell,* Western Writers Series No. 38 (Boise, Idaho: Boise State University, 1979), 31, 32. Gale calls this story "complex," "captivating."

69. Flores, "Bison Ecology," 483, argues (in 1991) that mass killings by white hunters, plus Indians taking primarily female buffalo, a prolonged southern range drought, increasing Indian horse herds overgrazing prime grasses, and newer European bovine diseases, such as brucellosis, combined to increase bison mortality in the nineteenth century.

70. Gale, *Charles Marion Russell,* 32. Gale assumes that Burke's fellow Blackfeet called him "Bad Meat" because they "regarded him as a renegade." The connotations of the words to his original culture also could have been neutral or even positive.

71. Russell, "Dad Lane's Buffalo Yarns," in *Trails Plowed Under,* 47.

72. Ibid.

73. Samuel Langhorne Clemens, *Adventures of Huckleberry Finn: An Authoritative Text, Backgrounds and Sources, Criticism,* 2d ed., ed. Sculley Bradley et al. (New York: W. W. Norton and Co., 1977), 72. No proof exists of Russell reading this book.

74. Justin Kaplin, "Selling Huck Finn Down the River," *New York Times Book Review,* Mar. 17, 1996, p. 37.

75. Russell, "Longrope's Last Guard," in *Trails Plowed Under* (Garden City, N.Y.: Doubleday and Company, 1927), 204. Russell also used the same phrase describing a dark night in "Hank Winter's Bear Fight," which appeared only in the Montana Newspaper Association inserts but not in any subsequent books, as discussed in Chapter 7.

76. Tim Giago, "Magazine Should Find Time For Apologies to Indians," *Albuquerque Journal,* June 18, 1998, p. A-19.

77. C. M. Russell, note to Joe DeYong, National Cowboy Hall of Fame, Flood no. 787. "That is Clark's slave. The Indians did not believe he was black. They thought it was paint."

78. Ibid., no. 776.

79. Truman McGiffin Cheney, "Walter Jackson Montana's First Black Cowboy," in *So Long, Cowboys of the Open Range* (Helena and Billings, Mont.: Falcon Press Publishing, 1990), 102.

80. J. Frank Dobie, handwritten note, J. Frank Dobie Collection, University of Texas at Austin, Harry Ransom Center, Russell miscellaneous, box 1 of 2, item 16. "Olaf Seltzer and Russell saw Molly Reingold, one morning. Charlie recognized her and wanted to talk with her, while Seltzer wanted to escape. . . . 'You that no count Buckskin Kid. I wish you'd pay me that $20 you owe.'"

81. Cheney, *So Long,* 102. Jackson was born and raised in the Judith Basin, working throughout the region, especially at the Quarter Circle U Ranch.

82. C. M. Russell, note to Joe DeYong, Flood Collection, C. M. Russell Museum, no. 975-12-89. Regarding Mexicans, Russell says: "I believe I could get along with them treat them as an equal it will be a good country as long as it belongs to Mex if this country takes it its gon to hell they will make them ware bib over alls[.]"

83. Dippie, *Charles M. Russell, Word Painter,* 111.

84. Brian W. Dippie, *The Vanishing American: White Attitudes and U.S. Indian Policy* (Middletown, Conn.: Wesleyan University Press, 1982), 139, graph illustration.

85. Vern Dusenberry, "Montana's Displaced Persons: The Rocky Boy Indians," *Montana: The Magazine of Western History* 4:1 (winter 1954): 1.

86. "Cold Continues All Over State, Last Night The Coldest Known In Great Falls For Ten Years," *Great Falls Tribune,* Jan. 10, 1909, p. 1. Also, see "C. M. Russell Starts Fund, For the Relief of the Chippewa Indians Who Are Starving Near Helena," *Great Falls Tribune,* Jan. 10, 1909, p. 12.

87. Sam Gilluly, *The Press Gang, A Century of Montana Newspapers, 1885–1985,* ed. Kevin S. Giles (Great Falls: Aircraft Printers, 1985), 37–38. Concerning a new reservation for the landless Indians, Gilluly says: "Their work was opposed by almost everyone."

88. Charles Russell, letter to Henry L. Meyers, C. M. Russell folder, box 1, file 25, Frank B. Linderman Collection, Museum of the Plains Indian, Browning, Mont., cited by Celest River, "A Mountain in His Memory, Frank Bird Linderman: His Role in Acquiring the Rocky Boy Indian Reservation for the Montana Chippewa and Cree. . . ." (Master's thesis, University of Montana, 1990), 146, 207.

89. John Ewers, "Charlie Russell's Indians," *Montana: The Magazine of Western History* 37:3 (summer 1987): 49.

90. Gilluly, *Press Gang,* 37–38.

91. Peter H. Hassrick, *Charles M. Russell* (New York, Harry N. Abrams, and the National Museum of American Art, Smithsonian Institution, 1989), 130. Hassrick speculated that Russell acted to support the Indians only from "social guilt."

92. Charles M. Russell, "Mormon Murphy's Confidence," *Trails Plowed Under* (Garden City, N.Y.: Doubleday and Company, 1927), 69. First published in 1907 as "Mormon Murphy's Misplaced Confidence," *Outing Magazine* 50:5 (August 1907): 550. "Misplaced" disappeared from the title when the story reappeared in 1925 in Charles M. Russell, *More Rawhides* (Great Falls: Montana Newspaper Association, 1925).

93. Russell, "Mormon Murphy's Confidence," *Trails Plowed Under,* 70. His last words were "He won't hurt nobody" (71). Even in his shallow grave, Murphy "seems to be smilin' like he forgives everybody" (72).

94. Ibid., 72, 72–73.

95. Ibid., 73, 69, 72.

96. Ibid., 69–73.

97. Robert Vaughn applauded the "Baker Massacre" of two hundred sickened Blackfeet women, children and old men along the Marias River in 1869, calling it "the best thing that ever happened to northern Montana at that time." "Uncle Bob Vaughn Located First Farm In The Sun River Valley Fifty years Ago," *Joliet Independent* (Montana Newspaper Association), July 21, 1918. Also, Robert P. Thoroughman, an older recipient of Russell's gift art and letters at his homestead in Cascade, Montana, had been part of Colonel Chivington's infamous massacre of Cheyenne Indians at Sand Creek and later barely repelled a hostile Nez Perce attack on his Montana ranch—"Pioneer Who Fought Indians Fifty years Ago And Wife Celebrate Golden Wedding," *The Reed Point Review* (Montana Newspaper Association), Mar. 29, 1920.

98. Russell, *Trails Plowed Under,* 69, 173. Russell's narrator missed the correct date for the Nez Perce "break out," 1877, by one year.

99. Lew Callaway, "Nez Perce War Is Held Unjust, Blackest Chapter In American History Says Chief Justice Lew L. Callaway," *Judith Basin Press* (Montana Newspaper Association), Sept. 5, 1927.

100. Russell, "Mormon Murphy's Confidence," in *Trails Plowed Under*, 71.

101. Russell, "Curley's Friend," in *Trails Plowed Under* (Garden City, N.Y.: Doubleday and Company, 1927), 57–64.

102. "The Red Devils," *Mineral Argus*, Maiden, Mont., Sept. 10, 1885, 2.

103. "Horse Prairie Cowboys' Private Cemetery," Montana Newspaper Association, Dec. 22, 1924. A rewritten version of the same story appeared on Mar. 14, 1938, minus the mirthful attitude toward the victims.

104. C. M. Russell, "Curly's Friend," handwritten MS, Britzman Collection, no. C.8.339.

105. Russell, "Curly's Friend," in *Trails Plowed Under*, 64. Folk wisdom associates the "good Indian = dead Indian" equation with General William T. Sherman, but scholarly research has failed to confirm the origin.

106. Russell, "The Trail of the Reel Foot," in *Trails Plowed Under* (Garden City, N.Y.: Doubleday and Company, 1927), 17–21.

107. "When The Gros Ventre Indians Trailed A 'Bad Medicine' Track Through Snowbound North Country," *Chester Reporter* (Montana Newspaper Association), Dec. 22, 1924; also, see "Montana Lou" Grill, "General Nelson A. Miles Pursuit of Sitting Bull In Winter of 1876 Was Hardship on Soldiers . . . ," *Cascade Courier* (Montana Newspaper Association), May 9, 1935; apparently Miles employed Boyd as a tracker and Boyd related his story; also, see "Clubfoot Trail Puzzled Indians, Followed Tracks of Crippled Trapper To Fort Benton To Warn Whites," *Fergus County Argus* (Montana Newspaper Association), Feb. 21, 1938. Story confirmed in a 1989 conversation between this writer and (grandson) George Boyd (born 1910) of Brockton, Montana. Boyd was unaware of the similarities between his grandfather and Russell's story about "Reel Foot."

108. Russell, "Trail of the Reel Foot," in *Trails Plowed Under*, 18.

109. Coburn Maddox, letter to James B. Rankin, 1937, Rankin collection, box 2, file 27.

110. A. Russell, *C. M. R.*, 67.

111. Ibid., 211, 212.

112. Taliaferro, *Charles M. Russell*, 205. The biographer wrongly discounts Russell's talent as a sign-talker, stating that the artist used "a home-cooked sign language loosely based on the gestures he had learned from Linderman and Indians he had met over the years." Russell supposedly used sign language just for showing off—a mere parlor trick, this journalist concludes without specific evidence.

113. Russell, "Trail of the Reel Foot," in *Trails Plowed Under*, 19.

114. Ibid., 18.

115. Ibid., 21. "Dad Lane" seems serious rather than ironic: "There's one place where an Injun holds the edge on a white man—day or night you can't lose him. . . . I don't know how he does it an' I doubt if the Injun can tell himself. These people are only part human an' this is where the animal crops out." Russell, *Trails Plowed Under*, 44.

116. Russell, "The Story of the Cowpuncher," in *Trails Plowed Under* (Garden City, N.Y.: Doubleday and Company, 1927), 1.

117. Francis Parkman, *The Oregon Trail: Sketches of Prairie and Rocky Mountain Life* (New York and Avenel, N.J.: Grammercy Books and Random House Value Publishing, 1995), 68.

118. "Cold Continues All Over State, Last Night The Coldest Known In Great Falls For Ten Years"; also, see "C. M. Russell Starts Fund, For the Relief of the Chippewa Indians Who Are Starving Near Helena," pp. 1, 12.

119. A. Russell, *C. M. R.,* 165–66. Austin Russell notes the resistance of Great Falls society to spending charity funds on blankets and food for the "starving, freezing and dying" Crees. He also recorded Charlie's fury at the social resistance and criticism after Nancy had managed the fundraising event, with Charlie's participation, and distributed the surplus to the Indians.

120. Russell, letter to Josephine Trigg, Mar. 24, 1926, in Russell, *Good Medicine,* 157.

121. Malone et al., *Montana,* 46.

122. The version of "Dunc McDonald" in *Trails Plowed Under* includes the reference to "traveling with his people, The Blackfeet" (15). No earlier version, from *More Rawhides* in 1925 back to his undated, four-page handwritten manuscript "Dunc. McDonald" (Britzman Collection, no. c.8.338), contains that inaccurate reference to his Scottish/Nez Perce heritage and his Flathead (Salish) neighbors. Apparently, a Doubleday editor, Percy Raban, or Joe DeYong added the error.

123. Duncan McDonald, *New Northwest,* Deer Lodge, Mont., Jan. 10, 17, 24, 31, and Feb. 7, 21, 1879, p. 2.

124. H. T. Bailey, "Romantic Tales Still Heard About Campfire Where Indians Gather," *The Froid Tribune* (Montana Newspaper Association); also, see Walter E. Taylor, "Flatheads Add New Legends To Ancient Sagas of the Tribe," *Fallon County Times* (Montana Newspaper Association), Jan. 1, 1940. Taylor retold a very condensed version of Dunc's buffalo hunt story and claimed it had become a saga for all times among the Flathead (Salish) Indians.

125. Russell, "Dunc McDonald," in *Trails Plowed Under* (Garden City, N.Y.: Doubleday and Company, 1927), 16.

126. Dick West, "Duncan McDonald Nearly Lost an Argument When He Wounded a Buffalo; C. M. Russell Portrayed Incident," *Judith Basin County Press* (Montana Newspaper Association), July 23, 1934.

127. M. O. Hammond fonds (private collection), Diaries, F 1075-5, Archives of Ontario. Also, see the photocopy in the Montana Historical Society archives. Hammond was a *Toronto Globe* reporter present at the Pablo Buffalo Roundup.

128. Russell, "Dunc McDonald," in *Trails Plowed Under,* 15, italics added for emphasis.

129. "Duncan McDonald Was Only '49er at Meeting," *Fergus County Argus* (Montana Newspaper Association), Aug. 17, 1931.

130. Russell, *Trails Plowed Under,* 15.

131. Russell, "Injuns," in *Trails Plowed Under* (Garden City, N.Y.: Doubleday and Company, 1927), 25–29. This title did not receive an editorial upgrade from "Injun" to "Indian" in the way the manuscript "How Lindsay Turns Injun" ultimately became titled "How Lindsay Turned Indian." Britzman Collection, no. C.8.54.

132. Russell, "Injuns," in *Trails Plowed Under.* Early twentieth-century anthropologists, such as Franz Boas and Clark Wissler, shared Linderman's impression of "pre-contact native cultures as largely static." Margaret Connell Szasz, "Introduction," in *Between Indian and White Worlds: The Culture Broker,* ed. Szasz (Norman and London: University of Oklahoma Press), 7. Also, see Alice Beck Kehoe, "Introduction," in *Mythology of the Blackfoot Indians,* comp. and trans. Clark Wissler and D. C. Duvall, Anthropological Papers series 2:1 (New York: American Museum of Natural History, 1908; repr., Lincoln: University of Nebraska Press, 1995), xxiii. Also, see Frank Bird Linderman, "Out of the North," in *Blackfeet Indians* (Minneapolis: Burlington Northern, 1984), 8. "They were a changeless people, a romantically happy people, until the white man came to the plains."

133. C. M. Russell, "Injuns," handwritten MS, Britzman Collection, no. C.8.341. The typed transcription from this MS omitted Russell's words "being uncivilized" from the typed essay (Britzman Collection, no. C.8.31). The words have never reappeared in later versions.

134. Russell, "Injuns," in *Trails Plowed Under,* 28.

135. C. M. Russell, letter to "Friend [Churchill] Mehard," in *Charles M. Russell, Word Painter: Letters, 1887–1926,* ed. Brian Dippie (Fort Worth and New York: Amon Carter Museum and Harry Abrams, 1993), 229.

136. Russell, letter to "Friend Sid [Willis]," in *Charles M. Russell, Word Painter: Letters, 1887–1926,* ed. Brian Dippie (Fort Worth and New York: Amon Carter Museum and Harry Abrams, 1993), 165.

137. Russell, "Injuns," in *Trails Plowed Under,* 29.

138. C. M. Russell, letter to W. H. Smith, in *Charles M. Russell, Word Painter: Letters, 1887–1926,* ed. Brian Dippie (Fort Worth and New York: Amon Carter Museum and Harry Abrams, 1993), 154.

139. C. M. Russell, letter to Friend Ted, May 13, 1919, in *Charles M. Russell, Word Painter: Letters, 1887–1926,* ed. Brian Dippie (Fort Worth and New York: Amon Carter Museum and Harry Abrams, 1993), 280.

140. C. M. Russell, letter to "Friend Harry" (Stanford), Dec. 13, 1918, in *Charles M. Russell, Word Painter: Letters, 1887–1926,* ed. Brian Dippie (Fort Worth and New York: Amon Carter Museum and Harry Abrams, 1993), 431.

141. "Indians Give Bit To Swell Russell Fund, Blackfeet Contribute Nickels and Dimes Towards Memorial To Artist," undated and unsourced newspaper clipping in Britzman Collection.

CHAPTER FOUR

1. C. M. Russell, letter to "Friend Frank" [Linderman], undated, in Frank Bird Linderman, *Recollections of Charley Russell,* ed. H. G. Merriam (Norman: University of Oklahoma Press, 1963), illustration of letter opposite p. 66.

2. Ibid.

3. Russell, letter to Frank Linderman, in *Charles M. Russell, Word Painter: Letters, 1887–1926,* ed. Brian Dippie (Fort Worth and New York: Amon Carter Museum and Harry Abrams, 1993), 246.

4. Russell, letter to Friend Bill, in *Charles M. Russell, Word Painter: Letters, 1887–1926,* ed. Brian Dippie (Fort Worth and New York: Amon Carter Museum and Harry Abrams, 1993), 196, 197.

5. C. M. Russell, letter to Friend Mike, June 17, 1923, in *Good Medicine; Memories of the Real West,* by Charles M. Russell (Garden City, N.Y.: Garden City Publishing, 1929), 50.

6. Ramon Adams and Bob Kennon, *From the Pecos to the Powder; A Cowboy's Autobiography* (Norman: University of Oklahoma Press, 1965), 238.

7. William H. Goetzmann and William N. Goetzmann, "Russell, The Cowboy Genius," in *The West of the Imagination* (New York : W. W. Norton and Co., 1986), 261.

8. Daniel Carter Beard, letter to James Rankin, Nov. 10, 1936, Rankin Collection, box 1, file 6. D. C. Beard wrote and illustrated *The American Boy's Handy Book; What to Do and How to Do It* (New York: Charles Scribner's Sons, 1882), and *Shelters, Shacks, and Shanties* (New York: Charles Scribner's Sons, 1914). By the time he wrote these comments, Beard had become chairman of the Boy Scouts of America.

9. Granville Stuart, *Pioneering in Montana: The Making of a State, 1864–1887,* ed. Paul C. Phillips (Cleveland: Arthur H. Clark Company, 1925; repr., Lincoln: University of Nebraska Press, 1977), 188.

10. C. M. Russell, "Hunting and Trapping With Jake Hoover," *The Western News,* Montana Newspaper Association, June 18, 1917. No original manuscript exists to show whether Russell himself experimented with such grammatically correct prose, or whether an editor for the Montana Newspaper Association adjusted Russell's normally rustic word patterns into this uncharacteristic style.

11. C. M. Russell, letter to Dr. Phillip Cole, Sept. 26, 1926, in *Good Medicine; Memories of the Real West,* by Charles M. Russell (Garden City, N.Y.: Garden City Publishing, 1929), 160–61.

12. Patricia Morris, *Charles M. Russell, Man of the West* (Casper, Wyo.: Man of the West Publishing, 1987), 10. Copy in Mansfield Library, University of Montana, Missoula. Linderman, *Recollections,* 104, 96.

13. Linderman, *Recollections,* 43 n. 2.

14. C. M. Russell, "A Savage Santa Claus," *Great Falls Daily Tribune,* Dec. 16, 1906, p. 25. Story also distributed by Montana Newspaper Association for publication on Dec. 18, 1922; also, see Charles M. Russell, *More Rawhides* (Great Falls: Montana Newspaper Association, 1925), 6; also, see Russell, *Trails Plowed Under* (Garden City, N.Y.: Doubleday Page and Company, 1927), 9.

15. Ralph H. Lutts, *The Nature Fakers: Wildlife, Science and Sentiment* (Golden, Colo.: Fulcrum Publishing, 1990), 3, 4, 32, 37. Rick Stewart, *Charles M. Russell, Sculptor* (Fort Worth and New York: Amon Carter Museum and Harry Abrams, 1994), 34, 35, argues that Ernest Thompson Seton "helped shape Russell's thinking about nature and wildlife, especially with regard to his sculpture," although it remains unclear how and to what extent. Seton recalled in the 1930s, "I knew Charles Russell very slightly, mostly through meeting him in studios or at the Campfire Club. My impression of him is chiefly of a very sincere student somewhat handicapped by his modesty." Ernest Thompson Seton, to James Rankin, Feb. 8, 1937, Rankin Collection, box 4, file 3.

16. "The Strenuous Life," listed as item no. 266 in *A Bibliography of the Published Works of Charles M. Russell,* by Karl Yost and Frederic Renner (Lincoln: University of Nebraska Press, 1971), 150. Theodore Roosevelt, *Hunting the Grisly, and Other Sketches, The Wilderness Hunter Part II* (New York: G. P. Putnam's Sons, 1893; repr., The Current Literature Publishing Company, 1907), 240–47. Austin Russell, *C. M. R.: Charles M. Russell, Cowboy Artist, a Biography* (New York: Twayne Publishers, 1957), 196. *In The Mountains,* 1905, watercolor, Montana Historical Society, Helena.

17. Charles M. Russell, "Savage Santa Claus," in *Trails Plowed Under* (Garden City, N.Y.: Doubleday Page and Company, 1927), 9.

18. Ibid., 12–13. Bears seem to prefer feasting on decayed animal flesh, leaving their own meat with a rotten flavor.

19. Calvin Martin, *Keepers of the Game: Indian-Animal Relationships and the Fur Trade* (Berkeley: University of California Press, 1978), 36.

20. Russell, *Trails Plowed Under,* 14.

21. Martin, *Keepers of the Game,* 115.

22. Charles M. Russell, "Lepley's Bear," in *Trails Plowed Under* (Garden City, N.Y.: Doubleday Page and Company, 1927), 75.

23. "Charles Lepley Dead; Helped Make Montana," *Forsyth Independent* (Montana Newspaper Association), June 2, 1941. This obituary about John Lepley's nephew, Charles, stated that "Old" John Lepley already lived in Montana Territory's gold camps by 1864, the year of Charlie Russell's birth in St. Louis. Lepley family members continue to be prominent and influential in Fort Benton, Montana.

24. C. M. Russell, "Hank Winter's Bear Fight," *Plevna Herald* (Montana Newspaper Association), Jan. 5, 1920. This story appeared in neither of Russell's *Rawhide* books nor in *Trails Plowed Under.* The Montana Newspaper Association papers carried an abridged version on Aug. 24, 1936, without attribution to Russell, under the title "When Men Are Fightin' Bears With Nothin' But a Knife, Hank Winters Ain't Backin' the Human So Strong." A possible source for these stories could be a Judith Basin legend. Tom Gregory of Lewistown, Montana, recorded a similar incident about his

father's bear encounter, with many similar elements. Tom Gregory, "The Miracle That Happened For Once," transcribed by William Buchanan, Jr., for the Montana Writers Project (Works Progress Administration), June 27, 1941, document no. 214.028, microfilm reel no. 20, Mansfield Library, University of Montana, Missoula.

25. Russell, "Hank Winter's Bear Fight."

26. Charles M. Russell, *The Price of His Hide,* 1915, oil on canvas, formerly owned by Amon Carter Museum. *A Wounded Grizzly,* watercolor, in *The CMR Book,* by John Willard (Seattle: Superior Press, 1970), 59. "A Friend in Need," in *The Charles M. Russell Book,* by Harold McCracken (Garden City, N.Y.: Doubleday and Company, 1957), 185. Sketch accompanies the Montana Newspaper Association story, "Jest as Everythin's Turnin' Black I Hear Bedrock's Winchester," *Plevna Herald,* Jan. 5, 1920.

27. Stewart, *Charles M. Russell, Sculptor,* 52.

28. Martin, *Keepers of the Game,* 18.

29. Roosevelt, *Wilderness Hunter,* 2:107.

30. Charles M. Russell, "Bab's Skees," in *Trails Plowed Under* (Garden City, N.Y.: Doubleday Page and Company, 1927), 51. Stories with similar elements appeared in Montana Newspaper Association articles, indicating that such tales enjoyed local popularity and circulation where David Babcock could have heard them for elements in his story that he told Russell. "Early-Day Hunters on Skis Captured Live Elk; Practice Originated by Vic Smith," *Fergus County Argus* (Montana Newspaper Association), Jan. 17, 1938; "Hunter Makes Ride on Deer," *Winnett Times,* Nov. 28, 1927.

31. Ibid. 52.

32. Rev. George Edwards, "Some Tales of Pig-Eye Basin, Lighter Side of Pioneer Days," *Judith Basin Press* (Montana Newspaper Association), Mar. 19, 1935.

33. Charles M. Russell, "Some Liars of the Old West," in *Trails Plowed Under* (Garden City, N.Y.: Doubleday Page and Company, 1927), 192. This tall tale first appeared in "Russell The Cowboy Artist Writes of Montana Prevaricators He Has Met," *Dillon Examiner* (Montana Newspaper Association), Mar. 5, 1917. This "no-escape" story traditionally is associated with Jim Bridger, the mountain man, immigrant guide, and storyteller who lived in the Rocky Mountain West a generation before Russell. Bernard DeVoto mentioned Bridger's story about "a flight up a box canyon which ended with the pursuing Indians killing the narrator" in *Across the Wide Missouri* (Boston: Houghton Mifflin Company, 1947), p. 169. Story collections such as B. A. Botkin's *A Treasury of Western Folklore* typically include some version of Bridger's greatest lie. Another version of Bridger's lie appeared in Mrs. M. E. Plassmann, "Bridger's Tallest Yarn Ended British Captain's Curiosity on Adventures," *Fallon County Times* (Montana Newspaper Association), Feb. 24, 1930. Russell attributed the story to Babcock but could have known of Bridger's earlier versions. Pat Morris noted that Charlie "read everything he could find on Jim Bridger . . . , Russell's ideal of what a real frontiersman should be." Morris, *Charles M. Russell,* 103.

34. Russell, "Some Liars of the Old West," in *Trails Plowed Under,* 191–94, 191.

35. Henry B. Wonham, *Mark Twain and the Art of the Tall Tale* (New York and Oxford: Oxford University Press, 1993), 18, 20, 21, also identifies several other inspirations for tall tales, including a wish to exaggerate accounts of unbearable frontier hardships for outsiders and to mock overinflated Americans' grand promises and high ideals.

36. J. Lee Humfreville, "Twenty Years Among Our Hostile Indians," in *Rocky Mountain Tales,* ed. Levette J. Davidson and Forrester Blake (Norman: University of Oklahoma Press, 1947), 33.

37. "Long Bow of Pioneer, Jim Bridger, With Some of His Wild Narratives," *The Judith Basin Star* (Montana Newspaper Association), Oct. 22, 1934.

38. E. C. "Teddy Blue" Abbott, letter to Nancy Russell, July 20, 1927, Britzman Collection, no. C.4.327, Taylor Museum, Colorado Springs Fine Arts Center.

39. Mrs. M. E. Plassmann, "Mountain Guides Amuse Themselves frequently by Telling Yarns," *Winnett Times* (Montana Newspaper Association), Feb. 24, 1930.

40. Dan R. Conway, "A Child of the Frontier, Memoirs of Charles M. Russell, The Cowboy Artist," written under the direction of and in cooperation with Nancy C. Russell, unpublished typed MS, Oct. 19, 1927, p. 25, Montana Historical Society, Helena, Archives no. SC1321. This document appears to be a first draft, without editing for spelling, with direct quotes from Nancy Russell's notes of Charlie speaking. This anecdote appeared without attribution in Ramon Adams and Homer Britzman, *Charles M. Russell, The Cowboy Artist, A Biography* (Pasadena: Trail's End Publishing Company, 1948), 25.

41. Wonham, *Mark Twain and the Art of the Tall Tale,* 99, 100, points out the special narrative powers of the "perennially talkative" stagecoach drivers in Twain's *Roughing It,* men whose storytelling powers attract adulation and deference comparable to riverboat pilots.

42. Will Rogers, *New York Times,* Apr. 13, 1924.

43. A. Russell, *C. M. R.,* 118.

44. Charles M. Russell, "Safety First—But Where Is It?" in *More Rawhides* (Great Falls: Montana Newspaper Association, 1925), 32–33.

45. Ibid., 33.

46. J. Frank Dobie, handwritten comment on p. 84 of the copy of *Trails Plowed Under* in the Harry Ransom Center, University of Texas, Austin; call number: PS F 596 R 943 Dobie. Also, see O. S. Clark, *Clay Allison of the Washita, First a Cow Man and then an Extinguisher of Bad Men, RECOLLECTIONS of Colorado, New Mexico and the Texas Panhandle, Reminiscences of a '79er* (Attica, Ind.: O. S. Clark, 1922), 119, 120: "At last the fellow up the tree yelled, 'You idiot! Why don't you stay in the hole?' The chasee, with fear in his voice, and a trembling in his legs, yelled back. 'You d—— fool, there's a Bear in the hole.' There's a place here for a little moralizing. Some times we criticize when people do not respond and many times fail to help in some charitable way with donations or they fail to pay their assessments for the preacher's upkeep, resent patronizing the church suppers, etc. Did you ever stop to think that there may be a 'bear in the hole.' They may be poor in their homes and have many afflictions, sickness, helpless cripples or ill dependents. Let's be kind and charitable to them and not press them into something that is a physical impossibility for them to provide. Be more charitable ourselves, until it hurts."

47. Eugene Manlove Rhodes, "Twice Told Tales," unpublished typed MS, Britzman Collection, no. C.8.178. Rhodes's handwritten endnote to Nancy Russell indicates that he had unsuccessfully submitted this piece on folklore plagiarism to the *San Francisco Examiner.*

48. Linderman, *Recollections,* 80–82. Linderman did not own a copy of *Trails Plowed Under* because of his disdain for Nancy (as noted by James B. Rankin's letter to "Dearest," July 17, 1937, Rankin Collection, correspondence with his mother). He may have inserted his own character names to avoid copyright problems with Nancy, or Charlie may have used these alternative names when telling these yarns to him. Linderman refers to a few other Russell stories involving a man called "old Becky Sharp," but no other Russell versions refer to "old Becky Sharp" or "Dave Foot."

49. Alfred Henry Lewis, "Red Mike," in *Faro Nell and Her Friends; Wolfville Stories* (New York: G. W. Dillingham Company, 1913), 226–29. Richard Baker kindly directed this writer to the story's similarity with "Safety First."

50. Stewart, *Charles M. Russell, Sculptor,* 34.

51. Lewis, "Red Mike," 229.

52. Antti Aarne, *The Types of the Folktale, A Classification and Bibliography,* trans. Stith Thompson (Helsinki, 1961; rev. ed., 1973), 107, classification: X1133.7. Also, see in ibid., "15 ft. antlers, swears off lying—C. M. Russell, X902-A." Aarne/Thompson cite a few Russell tales on their list, such as his lie about elk antlers spanning fifteen feet, as archetypal examples of folk motifs.

53. "Charlie Russell," *Eddie's Memos* (Apgar Village, West Glacier, Mont.: Eddie's Cafe, n.d.), 4. Photocopy is in this writer's possession.

54. Richard Dorson, *Buying The Wind: Regional Folklore in the United States* (Chicago: University of Chicago Press, 1964), 3, 4.

55. Lew L. Callaway, "Visits With Charles M. Russell," *Montana: The Magazine of Western History* 38:3 (summer 1988): 74.

56. Stith Thompson, *The Folktale* (New York: Dryden Press, 1946), 214, 215, 216, 230.

57. Mody C. Boatwright, *Folk Laughter on the American Frontier* (New York: Macmillan Company, 1949), 90.

58. Ibid., 87, 87–88. Folklorists debate whether the tall tale/lie story is an American invention or an adaptation of older European customs. The unnamed Montana Newspaper Association writer concluded that once Jim Bridger found his knack for exaggerated lie-telling, "he went about [as] the Baron Manchausen [*sic*] of the new west," referring to the European tall-tale traditions often associated with the Baron (Montana Newspaper Association, Oct. 22, 1934). Also, according to R. B. Marcy, *Thirty Years of Army Life on the Border* (New York: Harper and Brothers, 1866), 403–4, cited in Davison and Blake, *Rocky Mountain Tales,* 38, 39: "Bridger seemed deeply interested in the adventures of Baron Munchausen, but admitted, after the reading was finished, that 'he be dogond ef he swallered everything that thar *Baren* Mountchawson said, and he thought he was a durn'd liar.' Yet, upon further reflection, he acknowledged that some of his own experiences among the Blackfeet would be equally marvelous 'ef writ down in a book.'"

59. J. Frank Dobie, "A Preface on Authentic Liars," in *Tall Tales From Texas Cow Camps,* by Mody C. Boatwright (Dallas: Saw Press, 1934; repr., 1982), vii, xxvi. Unfortunately, Dobie selected a truthful Russell anecdote as an example of a colorful lie—a humorous but factual reference in an illustrated letter to an aging fellow cowboy concerning the fates of several mutual friends, including one "Charly Cugar," who had progressed from cow puncher to self-employed cattle thief to horsehair craftsman in the Montana state prison. Russell, *Good Medicine,* 107.

60. Russell, "Dog Eater," in *Trails Plowed Under* (Garden City, N.Y.: Doubleday Page and Company, 1927), 129. This yarn, never published in Montana Newspaper Association inserts, first appeared in 1925 in *More Rawhides.*

61. A. Russell, *C. M. R.,* 125. "When Charlie chose he could tell [a] story in a way that would make a dog lover grind his teeth. For Charlie was sometimes perverse, and anyhow, his animal affections were for horses. Even after all these years he still had a faint prejudice against dogs because of the sheep who drove out the cattle. I don't mean that Charlie disliked dogs or any other animal; he just liked horses so much better that there was no comparison."

62. Russell, "Injuns," in *Trails Plowed Under* (Garden City, N.Y.: Doubleday Page and Company, 1927), 25. "Where meat lays too long in hot weather, it doesn't need cooking—but when you go a few days without eatin' you won't mind this."

63. Finch David, letter to James Rankin, 1937, Rankin Collection, box 1, file 11. "We worked all over the Gros Ventre and Assiniboine reservation from Milk River to the Little Rockies Mountains. Russell was popular with the Indians on account of his artist work and I was popular with them as a rider of wild horses and ability to rope cattle. So one day a chief gave us a dinner party, no one else invited. He had 2 wives. The chief dish was boiled or stewed dog. Russell tried the dog very lightly, but I did not. But they also had potatoes, biscuits, boiled beef. We were always very friendly with this old Indian as long as we worked in that country."

64. Ibid., 130–31.

65. Robert L. Gale, *Charles Marion Russell,* Western Writers Series No. 38 (Boise, Idaho: Boise State University, 1979), 29.

66. Jan Harold Brunvand, "From Western Folklore to Fiction in the Stories of Charles M. Russell," *Western Review, A Journal of the Humanities* 5:1 (summer 1968): 41, 47. Brunvand located a version of the "Dog Eater" dilemma in the Works Progress Administration Idaho Writers Project material recorded in the 1930s. This version provided a variation in which a cat's tail was cut off and the cat participated further by gnawing on the tailbones, but only after the master had eaten the stew. Appalachian folklorist/storyteller Michael "Bad-hair" Williams tells a pet-eating story involving a three-legged dog that is noticed by an urban visitor who questions the poor "hill-billy" owner. After a tortuously long retelling of many brave, life-saving deeds that the dog performed, the rural owner finally answers the city slicker's repeated question about why the dog only has three legs. "Well," goes the answer, "a dog that valuable—ya don't wanna eat it up all at once."

67. "Great Falls Area Outline, Among the 60 or 70 notorious characters in the county at this time," Montana Writers Project (Works Progress Administration), microfilm reel 17, p. 52, Mansfield Library, University of Montana. Also, see "Butte Old-Timers Claim That Younger Generation Is Ignorant of Nicknames," *Hysham Echo* (Montana Newspaper Association), Oct. 16, 1933. "Dog-Eating Jack" appears in a list including "Dandy Jim," "Three-Finger Jack," "Scar-Face Charlie," "Curley Dick," "Froggy," "Eat'em Up Jake," "Yellowstone Kelly," "Jew Jake," "Fatty The Gambler," "Nosey Ford," "Pin Pool George," "Four-Jack Bob," "Old Poison," and so on.

68. Russell, "Dog Eater," in *Trails Plowed Under,* 132.

69. Russell, "Broke Buffalo," in *Trails Plowed Under* (Garden City, N.Y.: Doubleday Page and Company, 1927), 146; it first appeared in *More Rawhides.*

70. George Ade (1890–1920), Indiana humorist, most popular with his "fables in slang" books, of which Russell owned at least three volumes. (Ellen Shaffer, *The Charles M. Russell Library* [Los Angeles: Dawson's Book Shop, 1941].) These heavily ironic tales often described the follies of unnamed characters in a style similar to "Broke Buffalo."

71. "Surplus Buffalo To Be Marketed," *Fergus County Argus* (Montana Newspaper Association), Oct. 4, 1920.

72. Harry Ward, International News Service Staff Correspondent, Washington, D.C., "Herds of Buffalo Increasing in West, American Buffalo is Far From Extinction Latest Census Shows. Are now over 3,000 in U.S.," repr. in *Great Falls Leader,* Feb. 6, 1921, p. 2.

73. Russell, "When Pete Sets a Speed Mark," first appeared in Montana Newspaper Association weekly inserts for Dec. 24, 1917; then in Russell's *Rawhide Rawlins Stories* (Great Falls: Montana Newspaper Association, 1921), 33; then, in Russell's *Trails Plowed Under* (Garden City, N.Y.: Doubleday Page and Company, 1927), 35.

74. Russell, "When Pete Sets a Speed Mark," in *Trails Plowed Under,* 41, 15.

75. Russell, "Some Liars of the Old West," in *Trails Plowed Under,* 193.

76. "William Coates, Montana Pioneer," *Judith Basin County Press* (Montana Newspaper Association), Apr. 4, 1932.

77. Ibid., 194. Also, see J. Frank Dobie, *Cow People* (Boston: Little, Brown and Company, 1964), 22. Dobie presents a similar exaggeration with a straight face, quoting an old-timer, Isaac Thomas (Ike) Pryor, San Antonio. Following a lengthy description of a vast, endless herd of uncountable buffalo, Pryor concluded, "After we were clear of them I veered northeast to intersect the Dodge City trail. I was afraid that if we kept on the way we were headed we might run into the main herd of buffaloes."

78. Stuart, *Pioneering in Montana*, 110, 125.

79. Russell, letter to Granville Stuart, spring 1915, in *Charles M. Russell, Word Painter: Letters, 1887–1926*, ed. Brian Dippie (Fort Worth and New York: Amon Carter Museum and Harry Abrams, 1993), 216.

80. Boatwright, *Folk Laughter*, 56.

81. Wonham, *Mark Twain and the Art of the Tall Tale*, 76, 66.

82. Ibid., 65.

83. Russell, letter to "Ralf Budd," Nov. 26, 1925, in *Good Medicine; Memories of the Real West*, by Charles M. Russell (Garden City, N.Y.: Garden City Publishing, 1929), 37.

84. C. M. Russell's poem, in Adams and Britzman, *Charles M. Russell*, 269.

85. Russell, "Bullard's Wolves," in *Trails Plowed Under* (Garden City, N.Y.: Doubleday Page and Company, 1927), 23; the story first appeared in Russell, *More Rawhides*, 5.

86. Russell, "Bullard's Wolves," *Trails Plowed Under*, 24, 25. Bill Bullard was a cowboy friend of Russell's with an infamous hot temper. Some of Con Price's stories tell of Charlie's narrow escapes after playing jokes on Bill.

87. 'Mon Tana Lou' Grille, "Wolves Menaced Cattle Industry," *Medicine Lake Wave* (Montana Newspaper Association), Aug. 5, 1935.

88. Truman McGiffin Cheney and Roberta Carkeek Cheney, *So Long, Cowboys of the Open Range* (Helena, Mont.: Falcon Press Publishing Company, 1990), 63, 64.

89. Margaret E. Plassmann, "Wolves," *Fergus County Argus* (Montana Newspaper Association), Mar. 21, 1927.

90. Stuart, *Pioneering in Montana*, 172.

91. Russell, letter to "Friend Beil," May 31, 1926, in Dippie, *Charles M. Russell, Word Painter*, 393, 394.

92. Canadian Senator D. E. Riley, letter to James Rankin, May 2, 1938, Rankin Collection, box 3, file 16. Also, see the statement by Charlie Beil to J. Frank Dobie, field notes, Dobie Collection, University of Texas at Austin, Harry Ransom Center, Russell miscellaneous box 1 of 2, item 16. Also see Eleanor G. Luxton (from information provided by William Henry of High River and Roy Fowler of Steveville, Dinosaur Park, Alberta), "Charles M. Russell," *Leaves From the Medicine Tree* (Lethbridge, Alberta: Lethbridge Herald, 1960), n.p.

93. Russell, "Finger-That-Kills Wins His Squaw," in *Trails Plowed Under* (Garden City, N.Y.: Doubleday Page and Company, 1927), 125–26.

94. Russell, "Range Horses," in *Trails Plowed Under* (Garden City, N.Y.: Doubleday Page and Company, 1927), 103.

95. Rick Stewart, *Charles M. Russell: Masterpieces from the Amon Carter Museum* (Fort Worth: Amon Carter Museum, 1992), 38.

96. Ginger Renner, *A Limitless Sky: The Work of Charles M. Russell in the Collection of the Rockwell Museum, Corning, New York* (Flagstaff, Ariz.: Northland Press, 1986), 120.

97. Charles Hallock, "Notes From Montana," *Nature's Realm,* New York, April, 1891, from printed brochure, Montana Historical Society Archives, MC166, box 6, file 10.

98. Stewart, *Charles M. Russell, Sculptor,* 186, 222–23, 245, 345–46.

99. William Ellsberg, "Charles, Thou Art a Rare Blade," *The American West: The Magazine of Western History* 6:2 (March 1969): 6.

100. Russell, "Finger-That-Kills," in *Trails Plowed Under,* 125–26.

101. Russell, "Injuns," in *Trails Plowed Under,* 29.

102. Martin, *Keepers of the Game,* 64.

103. C. M. Russell, "An Appreciation of Edgar Paxson," part of a post-mortem tribute, "Passing of Paxson, Montana Artist," *Jordan Gazette* (Montana Newspaper Association), Jan. 24, 1919.

104. C. M. Russell, letter to Phillip Goodwin, Apr. 10, 1920, in *Charles M. Russell, Word Painter: Letters, 1887–1926,* ed. Brian Dippie (Fort Worth and New York: Amon Carter Museum and Harry Abrams, 1993), 298.

105. Russell, letter to Dr. Phillip Cole, Sept. 26, 1926, in Russell, *Good Medicine,* 160, 161.

106. Russell, letter to My Dear Mr. Kilmer, in *Charles M. Russell, Word Painter: Letters, 1887–1926,* ed. Brian Dippie (Fort Worth and New York: Amon Carter Museum and Harry Abrams, 1993), 152.

CHAPTER FIVE

1. C. M. Russell, poem to Wallace Coburn, 1905, C. M. Russell Art Auction Catalog, 1997, poem with illustration, C. M. Russell on horseback extending a bottle.

2. Charles M. Russell, "Foreword," in *Rawhide Rawlins Stories* (Great Falls: Montana Newspaper Association, 1921), n.p.

3. Earl Talbot, letter to James Rankin, 1939, James B. Rankin Collection, no. 162, box 4, file 6, Montana Historical Society, Helena.

4. Phil Weinard, letter to James Rankin, Sept. 28, 1938, Rankin Collection, box 2, file 15.

5. Russell, letter to John B. Rich, n.d., in *Charles M. Russell, Word Painter: Letters, 1887–1926,* ed. Brian Dippie (Fort Worth and New York: Amon Carter Museum and Harry N. Abrams, 1993), 207, 208.

6. C. M. Russell, "The Ghost Horse," in *Trails Plowed Under* (Garden City, N.Y.: Doubleday and Company, 1927), 91.

7. John Taliaferro, *Charles M. Russell: The Life and Legend of America's Cowboy Artist* (Boston: Little, Brown and Company, 1996), 22, implies (without corroboration) that Russell may have fabricated or exaggerated Monte's history as an Indian-raised buffalo horse.

8. Unlike Ernest Thompson Seton and others, Russell never claimed that his animal stories or his anthropomorphic portrayals of animals were scientifically accurate.

9. Russell, "Ghost Horse," in *Trails Plowed Under,* 91, 100.

10. Walter Lehman, letter to James Rankin, Nov. 25, 1936, Rankin Collection, box 2, file 2. Also, see Lehman's undated 1939 letter.

11. C. M. Russell, "When Pete Sets A Speed Mark," in *Trails Plowed Under* (Garden City, N.Y.: Doubleday and Company, 1927), 35.

12. C. M. Russell, "How Louse Creek Was Named," in *Trails Plowed Under* (Garden City, N.Y.: Doubleday and Company, 1927), 77. This story first appeared in Montana Newspaper Association inserts for November 1916, with the narrator named "Bill Weaver." B. V. Alder told James Rankin

in a 1937 letter that it was Russell himself who was caught delousing his shirt with two rocks and who earned the stream its undignified name. May 2, 1937, Rankin Collection, box 1, file 1. Another version has Russell letting ants delouse his clothes at that site. Ramon Adams and Bob Kennon, *From the Pecos to the Powder; A Cowboy's Autobiography* (Norman: University of Oklahoma Press, 1965), 142.

13. Mrs. Mattie Phillips, statement transcribed by Don A. Myrick, Montana Writers Project (Works Progress Administration), Apr. 8, 1940, document no. 223.011, microfilm reel no. 20, "Miscellaneous Information." Not all of Russell's Judith Basin contemporaries thought Pete Van's reputation was amusing. This officially documented local gossip stated, "Peter Van—a brother-in-law of William Skelton had a small band of cattle, but most of his activities were 'of a type that cannot be written up.'" Nevertheless, Russell told a friend "when the big herds left the basin he bought a fiew mighty good cows[,] each of these cows had four or five calves a year. an Pete was mighty handy with the iron this kind [a heated cinch ring, held by two sticks, used by rustlers to alter brands on stolen cattle] he was really artistic." Russell, letter to "Friend Bill," in *Charles M. Russell, Word Painter: Letters, 1887–1926,* ed. Brian Dippie (Fort Worth and New York: Amon Carter Museum and Harry N. Abrams, 1993), 186.

14. Harold McCracken, *The Charles M. Russell Book; The Life and Work of the Cowboy Artist* (Garden City, N.Y.: Doubleday and Company, 1957), 110, 111. Russell knew firsthand about body lice. One of McCracken's best anecdotes came from a woman whose mother had refused to wash Russell's dirty laundry until he boiled it first. The daughter witnessed Russell and other cowboys boisterously betting on a mock race of their bigger body lice on a heated pie tin.

15. Russell, "How Louse Creek Was Named," in *Trails Plowed Under,* 77.

16. Mark Twain, *Mark Twain in Eruption: Hitherto Unpublished Pages About Men and Events by Mark Twain,* ed. Bernard DeVoto (New York: Harper Brothers, 1922), 361.

17. Louis J. Budd, "Chronology," in *Collected Tales, Sketches, Speeches, and Essays, 1852–1890,* by Mark Twain, ed. Louis J. Budd (New York: Library of America, 1992), 959.

18. Charles M. Russell, letter to the Great Falls Elks Club "Brothers," September 1918, authorized copy, C. M. Russell Museum inventory no. 973-11-4. "Years ago I was lost in a storm on Dry Wolf Creek with a bunch of saddle horses. I was nearly in when Pete found me so weak and cold that Pete had to saddle a fresh horse for me and helpt me mount. A few more hours would have meant the 'cash-in' for me. Several other riders were out but the storm drove them all back but Pete and if my big laughing friend had turned back I believe I would be across the big range waiting for him now."

19. Charles M. Russell, "Cinch David's Voices, Historical Recollections of Rawhide Rawlins," *Western News* (Montana Newspaper Association), Oct. 29, 1917. This story never reappeared in print until it was included in Brian Dippie, ed., *Charlie Russell Roundup: Essays on America's Favorite Cowboy Artist* (Helena: Montana Historical Society Press, 1999), 311–12.

20. Ibid.

21. Ted Owens, oral history, transcribed by Esther Johansson Murray, May 1, 1969, Montana Historical Society, no. OH 1967, 1–6, stated that the story is true but Charlie Russell himself refused to help Finch get out from under the wagon. In another version, ninety-year-old Joe Holland of Lewistown, Montana, told this writer in 1987 that the unwilling rescuer was Finch David's neighbor and feuding rival "Lying Babcock."

22. Wallace Stegner, *Wolf Willow; A History, a Story and a Memory of the Last Plains Frontier* (Lincoln: University of Nebraska Press, 1962), 128, 129, 133.

23. C. J. Ellis, letter to James Rankin, 1938, Rankin Collection, box 1, file 14. Also, see Wallace David Coburn, "Cowboy Fun," in *Rhymes from a Round-up Camp* (Great Falls, Mont.: W. T. Ridgley Press, 1899), 18. "While Cotton-Eye, the Night-Hawk, Was then a top cow-hand, As reckless as they make 'em, And, you bet, he had the sand."

24. Russell, "A Few Words About Myself," in *Trails Plowed Under* (Garden City, N.Y.: Doubleday and Company, 1927), xix.

25. Stegner, *Wolf Willow,* 130.

26. Pete Snelson, "Old-Time Cowhands Couldn't Carry A Tune In A Water Bucket, Says One Who Has Lived in 'Cow Country' for Last 40 Years," *Fallon County Times* (Montana Newspaper Association), Mar. 18, 1940.

27. John Donald Wade, "Southern Humor," in *Culture in the South,* ed. W. T. Couch (Chapel Hill: University of North Carolina Press, 1934); see M. Thomas Inge, "The Frontier Humorists," in *The Frontier Humorists: Critical Views,* ed. Inge (Hamden, Conn.: Archon Books, 1975), 44.

28. C. M. Russell, letter to Patrick T. Tucker, Oct. 27, 1921, in *Charles M. Russell, Word Painter: Letters, 1887–1926,* ed. Brian Dippie (Fort Worth and New York: Amon Carter Museum and Harry N. Abrams, 1993), 318.

29. C. M. Russell, "Bullard's Wolves," in *Trails Plowed Under* (Garden City, N.Y.: Doubleday and Company, 1927), 23.

30. C. M. Russell, "Lepley's Bear," in *Trails Plowed Under* (Garden City, N.Y.: Doubleday and Company, 1927), 75.

31. Con Price, "C. M. Russell As A Cowboy Friend, A Sidekick's Memories," *Montana: The Magazine of Western History* 8:4 (fall 1958): 33.

32. Guy Weadick, "Ballie Buck—Range Cowman," *Canadian Cattleman* 4:4 (March 1942): 165.

33. Russell, letter to H. T. Duckett, n.d., in Charles M. Russell, *Good Medicine; Memories of the Real West* (Garden City, N.Y.: Garden City Publishing, 1929), 47.

34. C. M. Russell, "A Pair of Outlaws," in *Trails Plowed Under* (Garden City, N.Y.: Doubleday and Company, 1927), 85. Nancy Russell tried to interest Caspar Whitney in this story for *Outing Magazine,* but with no luck. It did not appear in the Montana Newspaper Association inserts nor in either Rawhide Rawlins book; it first appeared in *Trails Plowed Under.*

35. Russell, letter to Harry Duckett, n.d., in *Good Medicine; Memories of the Real West,* by Charles M. Russell (Garden City, N.Y.: Garden City Publishing, 1929), 47.

36. Con Price, "C. M. Russell, As a Cowboy Friend," 50–53. As Price recalled, "'Don't worry, Con' he said, 'why I'll just get out the old paint brush and start it working and we'll soon have the price of some more dogies.'"

37. Con Price, *Memories of Old Montana* (Hollywood: Highland Press, 1946), 125.

38. Con Price, letter to James Rankin, May 16, 1938, Rankin Collection, box 3, file 6.

39. Russell, "A Gift Horse," in *Trails Plowed Under* (Garden City, N.Y.: Doubleday and Company, 1927), 7. This story first appeared in Charles M. Russell, *More Rawhides* (Great Falls: Montana Newspaper Association, 1925).

40. Russell, "Bronc Twisters," in *More Rawhides* (Great Falls: Montana Newspaper Association, 1925), 165. Under one title, Russell placed two different episodes.

41. Mark Twain, *Roughing It* (New York and Scarborough, Ontario: New American Library, 1962; repr., 1980), 145.

42. Con Price, *Trails I Rode* (Pasadena: Trail's End Publishing, 1947), 124–26. Price said he asked about the good-looking horse but received only a veiled warning from the generous donor. Russell gave Price a chance to deny or correct the story by telling it directly to Con in a 1919 letter, several years before the yarn appeared in *More Rawhides.* See Russell, *Good Medicine,* 117.

43. Russell, "Bronc Twister," in *Trails Plowed Under,* 167. An undated, handwritten manuscript on Russell's personal stationary in pencil differs slightly from the first published version in *Rawhide Rawlins Stories,* suggesting that some overall editing took place to clean up Russell's unorthodox punctuation and spelling, plus a few minor structural adjustments. The original MS resides at the C. M. Russell Museum Library, Great Falls.

44. Sidney M. Logan, "Life On Plains Described By Sidney M. Logan in Thrilling Eulogy Written by Him After Death Of Horace D. Brewster," *Ekalaka Eagle* (Montana Newspaper Association), Jan. 16, 1933.

45. Russell, "Bronc Twisters," in *Trails Plowed Under,* 168. This writer can testify, after hundreds of performances since 1985, that this story generates the most reliable laughing response of any Russell yarn when recited for twentieth- and twenty-first century audiences. It is also the Russell tale that has attracted the most spontaneous corroboration by descendants of the participants, especially near Great Falls and the Cascade County district of Montana.

46. Walt Coburn, *Pioneer Cattleman in Montana; The Story of the Circle C Ranch* (Norman: University of Oklahoma Press, 1968), 140, 141. Charlie Brewster died in Canada in 1923. Horace Brewster worked as a ranger in Glacier Park, outliving Russell by seven years before dying in 1933. Russell, letter to Con Price, Oct. 5, 1924, in *A Limitless Sky: The Work of Charles M. Russell in the Collection of the Rockwell Museum, Corning, New York,* ed. Ginger Renner (Flagstaff, Ariz.: Northland Press, 1986), 112. C. M. Russell, letter to Friend Jim, Jan. 23, 1924, in *Good Medicine; Memories of the Real West,* by Charles M. Russell (Garden City, N.Y.: Garden City Publishing, 1929), 122.

47. Truman McGiffin Cheney and Roberta Carkeek Cheney, *So Long, Cowboys of the Open Range* (Helena and Billings, Mont.: Falcon Press Publishing Co., 1990), 91:

> As they sat there rolling cigarettes, Charlie said, 'Give me a match.' Someone handed him a big wooden match. As he struck it on the brass cover of his stirrup, the match flared with a sharp crack startling his horse. As the horse jumped, the bank caved in, letting horse and rider fall into the top of a big pine tree below. Hung up—completely high-centered but with Charlie Brewster still in the saddle. Now, according to the story Russell told around the campfire that evening, Brewster looked up at his pals and said 'Throw me another match, that one went out.' Well those cowboys tossed their ropes down to Charlie and he tied them to his horse and saddle and the boys on top pulled him right out of there. Back in camp, Russell started making sketches and eventually completed a painting which depicted the humorous side of a near-tragic accident.

Other versions have drifted farther from Russell's: "Toss me a match. Mine went out on the way down": Jim Hoy, *Cowboys and Kansas: Stories From the Tallgrass Prairies* (Norman: University of Oklahoma Press, 1995), 93, 94. A similar incident recalled for the Montana Writers Project had a more serious ending. George Christenot rode his bucking horse off a twenty-foot cliff. At the bottom, the horse died of a broken neck, but the rider walked away unscratched. Mrs. Harley Newton, "Riding a Bronc," interviewed by Evelyn Rhoden, Roundup, Mont., Apr. 8, 1941, Montana Writers Project (Works Progress Administration), no. 223.069, microfilm reel no. 27, Mansfield Library, University of Montana, Missoula.

48. Horace Brewster with A. L. Jordan, "Life on the Plains," *Great Falls Tribune,* Mar. 5–Apr. 16, 1933; Dave Walter, comp. and ed., "Past Times, The Wit and Wisdom of Horace Brewster," *Montana Magazine,* Helena (May–June 2003), 81.

49. Jack Wrynn to Forrest Crossen, in *Western Yesterdays, Charlie Russell—Friend,* Vol. 9, by Crossen (Fort Collins, Colo.: Robinson Press, 1973), 38.

50. C. M. Russell, "Curley's Friend," in *Trails Plowed Under* (Garden City, N.Y.: Doubleday and Company, 1927), 57, 58.

51. C. M. Russell, "Range Horses," in *Trails Plowed Under* (Garden City, N.Y.: Doubleday and Company, 1927), 103.

52. Ibid., 105.

53. Robert S. Fletcher, "The End of the Open Range in Montana," *Mississippi Valley Historical Review* 16:2 (September 1929): 201.

54. Price, *Memories of Old Montana,* 142.

55. Russell, "The Open Range," in *Trails Plowed Under* (Garden City, N.Y.: Doubleday and Company, 1927), 163, 164.

56. Russell, letter "to Editor of Adventure," Mar. 7, 1924, in *Charles M. Russell, Word Painter: Letters, 1887–1926,* ed. Brian Dippie (Fort Worth and New York: Amon Carter Museum and Harry N. Abrams, 1993), 243.

57. Russell, "The Story of the Cowpuncher," in *Trails Plowed Under* (Garden City, N.Y.: Doubleday and Company, 1927), 2. Also published in *The Dillon Examiner* (Montana Newspaper Association), October 1916, under the title "The Story of the Cowboy As It Was Told To Me By An Old Time Rider of the Range"; in *The Redstone Review* (Montana Newspaper Association), June 1921, under the title, "The Cowboy As He Was—Reminiscences of a Western Type That Has Passed"; and in *Rawhide Rawlins Stories,* 1921, as "The Story of the Cowpuncher."

58. Untitled, handwritten, incomplete MS, 3–7, Britzman Collection, no. c.8.20; also "Cow-punchers," an incomplete MS, typed with pencil corrections, 1–2, Britzman Collection, no. c.8.23. The choice to add essay data may have come in response to Caspar Whitney's demand for nonfiction material for his magazine. Also, see "The Cowboy As He Was," a complete typed MS, 1–6, Britzman Collection, no. C.8.36. This manuscript includes a few corrections and 1.5 pages of essay material that never appeared in any published version, including expressions of disdain for sheepherders, nesters, and fighting with guns—"Where guns settle disputes, you'll find few arguments."

59. The Montana Newspaper Association version for June 1921 sets the piece within quotation marks for the first time, attributed to the voice of "an old-time cowpuncher." In the *Rawhide Rawlins Stories* format, also published in 1921, the quotation marks are attributed to "Rawhide."

60. Terry G. Jordan, *North American Cattle-Ranching Frontier: Origins, Diffusion, and Differentiation,* Histories of the American Frontier Series, ed. Ray Allen Billington (Albuquerque: University of New Mexico Press, 1993), 313.

61. John R. Barrows, *U-BET: A Greenhorn in Old Montana* (Caldwell, Idaho: Caxton Printers, 1934; repr., Lincoln: University of Nebraska Press, 1990), 49.

62. Con Price, *Trails I Rode,* 137. Price reports proudly that after he had accidentally wrecked his fancy saddle, "[t]he boss told one of the boys he was glad my rig was tore up, as he said all I did was admire my rig, fix my hat just right, and look at my shadow, so that I wasn't worth a damn."

63. Russell, "Story of the Cowpuncher," in *Trails Plowed Under,* 5.

64. Ibid., 34.

65. Stegner, *Wolf Willow*, quoted by Jackson Benson, "Where the Old West Met the New, Wallace Stegner: 1909–1993," *Montana: The Magazine of Western History* 43:4 (autumn 1993): 58.

66. Russell, letter to "Dear Mr. Geo. W. Farr," Mar. 12, 1919, in *Charles M. Russell, Word Painter: Letters, 1887–1926,* ed. Brian Dippie (Fort Worth and New York: Amon Carter Museum and Harry N. Abrams, 1993), 277.

67. Henry Keating, "Queer ways of the Cowboy," *The Medicine Lake Wave* (Montana Newspaper Association), Dec. 24, 1917.

68. Russell, "Hands Up," in *More Rawhides* (Great Falls: Montana Newspaper Association, 1925), 58–59. "Shea" is a family name originating in Ireland's County Cork and was common around the Irish enclaves of Butte and other Montana cities. Since Russell could have used "Rawhide Rawlins" to narrate any tale, Jack Shea probably existed in Montana and may have told Russell a story much like the one related here.

69. Russell, "Hands Up," in *Trails Plowed Under,* 113, 114.

70. George Ade, "The Fable of the Inveterate Joker Who Remained in Montana," *More Fables in Slang* (Chicago: Herbert Stone and Company, 1900), 126, 127. Russell owned a copy of this Ade book of humorous fables. Ellen Shaffer, ed., *The Charles M. Russell Library,* catalog no. 151 (Los Angeles: Dawson's Bookshop, 1941), copy in National Cowboy Hall of Fame, DeYong Collection, Flood no. 284. In Ade's story, "He did not Hang straight enough to suit, so they brought a Keg of Nails and tied to his feet."

71. Russell, "Hands Up," in *Trails Plowed Under,* 115.

72. Ibid.

73. "Teddy Blue" E. C. Abbott, "The Texas Trail," *Back Trailing on the Old Frontiers, Fifty-One Stories Of Noted Occurrences Along The Trails Of The Old West* (Aurora, Colo.: John Osterberg, 1990), 70.

74. C. M. Russell, letter to "Friend Kid" [Price], June 1, 1917, printed in *In The Land Of Chinook or The Story of Blaine County,* by A. J. Noyes (Helena, Mont.: State Publishing Company, 1917), 127.

75. Robert G. Athearn, *The Mythic West in Twentieth-Century America* (Lawrence: University Press of Kansas, 1986), 30.

76. Fletcher, "End of the Open Range," 209.

77. Price, *Memories of Old Montana,* 124.

78. Russell, "Longrope's Last Guard," in *Trails Plowed Under,* 199. This story first appeared in *The Outing Magazine* 52:2 (May 1908) and did not reappear in print until *Trails Plowed Under.*

79. Russell, letter to the Editor of Adventure, Mar. 7, 1924, in *Charles M. Russell, Word Painter: Letters, 1887–1926,* ed. Brian Dippie (Fort Worth and New York: Amon Carter Museum and Harry N. Abrams, 1993), 342.

80. Dobie, field notes, J. Frank Dobie Collection, University of Texas Austin, Harry Ransom Center, Russell miscellaneous box 1 of 2, item 15. Also, see Dobie's handwritten note on title page of *Rawhide Rawlins Stories,* copy in Dobie collection: "According to Jack Hawkins, Dillon, Montana, old tailer and ranger of the 70s, whom I met at San Saba ranger reunion, July 3–5, 1925, and who was for a time sheriff in Montana, Rawhide Rawlins was Teddy Blue, yet alive—1929."

81. Robert L. Gale, *Charles Marion Russell,* Western Writers Series no. 38 (Boise, Idaho: Boise State University, 1979), 42, 43.

82. J. Frank Dobie, *The Longhorns* (Boston: Little, Brown and Company, 1941), 130.

83. Russell, "Longrope's Last Guard," in *Trails Plowed Under,* 210.

84. Russell, "Story of The Cowpuncher," in *Trails Plowed Under,* 2.

85. Russell, letter to Paris Gibson, June 29, 1916, in *Good Medicine; Memories of the Real West,* by Charles M. Russell (Garden City, N.Y.: Garden City Publishing, 1929), 14.

86. Letter to "Friend Trigg," Feb. 24, 1916, in *Good Medicine; Memories of the Real West,* by Charles M. Russell (Garden City, N.Y.: Garden City Publishing, 1929), 64.

87. Russell, "Night Herd," in *Trails Plowed Under* (Garden City, N.Y.: Doubleday and Company, 1927), 55.

88. Harry Stanford, letter to James Rankin, Mar. 3, 1938, Rankin Collection, box 4, file 2. Stanford identified the primary narrator and main character as Belknap ("Baldie" or "Ballie") Buck, a longtime friend of Russell's, a mixed-blood Indian as well as a highly regarded cattleman in Montana and Alberta. Also, see "Ballie" Buck letter to James Rankin, Mar. 27, 1938, Rankin Collection, box 1, file 6. Buck confirms that he is the subject of "Night Herd," a character otherwise identified by Russell only as "Big Man."

89. Russell, "Night Herd," in *Trails Plowed Under,* 56.

90. Dan Buck, letter to J. Frank Dobie, n.d., Dobie Collection, Russell miscellaneous box 2 of 2, item 27.

91. Nannie Alderson and Helena Huntington Smith, *A Bride Goes West* (Lincoln: University of Nebraska Press, 1942; repr., 1969), 40.

92. Russell, note to Joe DeYong, undated, DeYong Collection no. 80.18, Flood no. 786, National Cowboy Hall of Fame.

93. C. M. Russell, "Highwood Hank Quits," in *Trails Plowed Under* (Garden City, N.Y.: Doubleday and Company, 1927), 195. This tale first appeared under the title "Where Highwood Hank Quits, Historical Recollections of Rawhide Rawlins," in *The Harlowton Press* (Montana Newspaper Association), Dec. 10, 1917. It reappeared in *Rawhide Rawlins Stories* in 1921. Keeton met Russell in Utica, Montana, when Charlie first came to Montana in 1880. In addition to his ranch, Keeton owned a winter house near Russell's in Great Falls during the artist's later years, enabling frequent contact.

94. Russell, "Highwood Hank Quits," in *Trails Plowed Under.* In his introduction for *More Rawhides* and *Trails,* "A Few Words About Myself," Russell wrote of being "neither a good roper nor rider." Russell also joked about being a poor rider in his letters, including one to Will James, May 12, 1920, in *Good Medicine; Memories of the Real West,* by Charles M. Russell (Garden City, N.Y.: Garden City Publishing, 1929), 68.

95. "Ballie" Buck, letter to James Rankin, Mar. 27, 1938, Rankin Collection, box 1, file 6, 4–5. Buck comments, "I think one thing that kept him from Cowboying more—he was afraid of strange horses. He couldn't ride a horse that bucked very hard."

96. Russell, pencil note to Joe DeYong, n.d., DeYong Collection, National Cowboy Hall of Fame, Flood no. 795.

97. Russell, letter to Lieutenant R. Hoss, n.d., Favell Museum, Klamath Falls, Ore.

98. Russell, "Highwood Hank Quits," in *Trails Plowed Under,* 195.

99. Joe DeYong, "Modest Son of the Old West, An intimate glimpse of the Great Master by one of his few living students," *Montana: The Magazine of Western History* 8:4 (autumn 1958): 96.

100. Russell, "Highwood Hank Quits," in *Trails Plowed Under,* 197.

101. Spike Van Cleve, *A Day Late and a Dollar Short* (Kansas City, Mo.: Lowell Press, 1982), 217.

102. C. M. Russell, "A Ride In A Moving Cemetery," *Trails Plowed Under* (Garden City, N.Y.: Doubleday and Company, 1927), 145. This story first appeared in *The Harlowton Press* (Montana Newspaper Association) on Mar. 19, 1917, under the title "A Ride In a Moving Cemetery, Or How Rube The Reckless Came Close To The Cash In." The tale reappeared in 1921 in *Rawhide Rawlins Stories* under the shorter title.

103. C. M. Russell, "When Mix Went to School," in *Trails Plowed* Under (Garden City, N.Y.: Doubleday and Company, 1927), 65. This tale first appeared in the *Medicine Lake Wave* (Montana Newspaper Association), Apr. 1, 1918, then again in *Rawhide Rawlins Stories* in 1921. David D. Anderson discussed this story at some length to show Russell's "deceptively complex artistry" in transforming folklore into literature, in "Charles M. Russell: Literary Humorist," *MIDAMERICA XII, The Yearbook of the Society for the Study of Midwestern Literature* (East Lansing: Midwestern Press, Michigan State University, 1985). Anderson correctly praises Russell's "literary artistry," but he overlooks the Montana Newspaper Association and its rural readers as Russell's primary medium and audience when he mistakenly asserts, "The readers for whom the stories were published were more genteel and literate—not to say priggish—than Russell's cronies." And contrary to Anderson's belief, the story versions actually changed little in Russell's shift from the Rawhide books to *Trails Plowed Under,* except for the unfortunate mislocation or omission of many illustrations. Anderson lacked access to Russell's original story manuscripts and mistakenly assumed that the printed versions differed from original drafts.

104. Ralph Bemis, "The Old-Time Bartender—A Lost Type," *Fairfield Times* (Montana Newspaper Association), Apr. 26, 1920.

105. Russell, "When Mix Went to School," in *Trails Plowed Under,* 65. Also, see Russell, letter to Charles Street, 1902, in *Charles M. Russell, Word Painter: Letters, 1887–1926,* ed. Brian Dippie (Fort Worth and New York: Amon Carter Museum and Harry N. Abrams, 1993), 52.

106. Ibid., 67.

107. Leo Marx, *The Machine in the Garden; Technology and the Pastoral Idea in America* (London: Oxford University Press, 1964), 15, 16.

108. Samuel Langhorne Clemens, *Adventures of Huckleberry Finn, An Authoritative Text, Backgrounds and Sources, Criticism,* ed. Sculley Bradley et al. (New York: W. W. Norton and Company, 1977), 78, 79.

109. James C. Moore, "The Storm And The Harvest, The Image of Nature in Mid-Nineteenth Century American Landscape Painting" (Ph.D. diss., Wichita State University, 1976), 216.

110. Russell, *Trails Plowed Under,* 148. Apparently, Teddy Roosevelt was controversial enough to be the subject of routine arguments.

CHAPTER SIX

1. Charles M. Russell, poem and illustration on printed stationary for Park Saddle Horse Company, Glacier National Park, A-X6, copy in Glenbow Museum Archives, Russell vertical file, Calgary, Alberta. (See fig. 80.) Also, see Britzman Collection, C. 2.11.a. Jan. 14, 1926, *Park Saddle Horse Company, Glacier National Park, Kalispell, Montana See America First:* "My dear Charley:—Well here it is and isn't it a winner. I am very pleased with it and hope you like it I am writing my first letter on the new letterhead to you, its maker. G. W. Noffsinger, President. PS—I think the piece of poetry very much a part of the picture and I wanted to give you credit but was not sure that you wrote it. It should have at least been in quotation marks."

2. Richard Etulain, *Re-Imagining the Modern American West: A Century of Fiction, History, and Art* (Tucson: University of Arizona Press, 1996), 68. "Charlie Russell refused to recognize the transition to a New West, choosing instead to champion the Old West that he knew and embraced. . . . Charlie believed in his West and persistently, lovingly, depicted that frontier in his thousands of paintings, illustrations, bronzes, and illustrated letters." Beyond most of his fine art pieces, Russell's personal letters and published stories do describe and even make fun of the twentieth-century West.

3. Russell, letter to Walt Coburn, Nov. 27, 1924, in Charles M. Russell, *Good Medicine; Memories of the Real West* (Garden City, N.Y.: Garden City Publishing, 1929), 96.

4. "Cowboy Vividly Paints the Passing Life of the Plains," *The New York Times,* Mar. 19, 1911, p. 5.

5. Charles M. Russell, "Bill's Shelby Hotel," in *Trails Plowed Under* (Garden City, N.Y.: Doubleday, Page and Company, 1927), 37. This story first appeared in print under the title "How Bill Broke Into Hotel Business When Humorists Made Shelby Hum," *The Harlowton Press,* Montana Newspaper Association, on Nov. 20, 1916. Russell assigned "the old stockman" as narrator of this version, possibly inspired by A. H. Lewis's "the Old Cattleman" who narrates the *Wolfville* books. Yet there is no solid evidence either way. Russell's first version of this yarn contains a few words and phrases that he altered in later printings, including a reference to "Shelby coco-cola" that became "Shelby lemonade." The story reappears in Russell, *Rawhide Rawlins Stories* (Great Falls: Montana Newspaper Association, 1921), 34, under the title "Bill's Shelby Hotel." In this version Russell calls the narrator simply "Rawhide," and for *Trails Plowed Under* the designated storyteller becomes "Rawhide Rawlins."

6. Ibid., 38, 39.

7. Russell, letter to Bill Rance, Apr. 2, 1913, in *Charles M. Russell, Word Painter: Letters, 1887–1926* (Fort Worth and New York: Amon Carter Museum and Harry N. Abrams, 1993), 177. Mrs. Imogene [Divers] Olson, "Letters to the Editor," *Montana: The Magazine of Western History* 46:1 (spring 1996): 92.

8. Russell, "Bill's Shelby Hotel," in *Trails Plowed Under,* 40.

9. Ibid. Some excited cowboys had scared a theater company that was visiting in Shelby. Competing for the theater women's favor and shooting their guns inside and near the troupe's rail cars, the cowboys earned the little town a bad reputation. Con Price participated in the incident and claimed the Shelby riot was merely harmless fun. Con Price, *Memories of Old Montana* (Hollywood: Highland Press, 1946), 68.

10. "Quarrel Of Jim Hill and Bob Mains Stopped A Little City in the Making," *Dillon Examiner* (Montana Newspaper Association), May 28, 1917. Shelby officials would have known of this nearby situation when Hill changed his Great Northern switching yard plans from Lohman to Bull Hook (renamed Havre) because the land price remained too high.

11. "Cowboy Was Cattle Industry's Backbone," Meager County Cowboy Annual Banquet in Great Falls, attributed to *Great Falls Tribune,* Mar. 2, 1941, listed in Montana Writers Project (Works Progress Administration) document 230.044, no. 1134, microfilm reel 24, Mansfield Library, University of Montana, Missoula.

12. James W. "Body" Johnson, *The Fight That Won't Stay Dead,* ed. John F. Kavanagh (Shelby, Mont.: Promoter Publishing Company, 1989). Because of mismanagement and confusion, the financial investors, including several Montana banks, lost their money promoting this title fight.

13. Charles M. Russell, "Whiskey," in *Trails Plowed Under* (Garden City, N.Y.: Doubleday, Page and Company, 1927), 32. This narrative essay appears to have been written only for *Trails Plowed Under* and never appeared in the Montana Newspaper Association inserts or in either Rawhide book. Russell himself seems to be the narrator.

14. Frank Bird Linderman, *Recollections of Charley Russell,* ed. H. G. Merriam (Norman: University of Oklahoma Press, 1963), 10.

15. Robert Dykstra, *The Cattle Towns* (New York: Alfred Knopf, 1968), 263.

16. William D. Rowley, "The West as Laboratory and Mirror of Reform," in *The Twentieth-Century West: Historical Interpretations,* ed. Gerald D. Nash and Richard W. Etulain (Albuquerque: University of New Mexico Press, 1989), 343, 344.

17. Russell, letter to "Friend Sweet," Mar. 24, 1909, in *Good Medicine; Memories of the Real West,* by Charles M. Russell (Garden City, N.Y.: Garden City Publishing, 1929), 108.

18. Russell, "Here's to All Old Timers," in *Good Medicine; Memories of the Real West,* by Charles M. Russell (Garden City, N.Y.: Garden City Publishing, 1929), 39.

19. Dippie, *Charles M. Russell, Word Painter,* 366.

20. Russell, "How Pat Discovered the Geyser," in *Trails Plowed Under,* 187, 188. Russell first published this story in *The Plains Plainsman* (Montana Newspaper Association), Oct. 18, 1917; then in Russell, *Rawhide Rawlins Stories,* 13.

21. Celia Lacy, "P. J. O'Hara" [*sic*], *Furrows and Trails in Judith Basin* (Stanford, Mont.: Judith Basin County Press, 1976), 31.

22. Ajax (Al) J. Noyes, *In The Land of Chinook or The Story of Blaine County* (Helena, Mont.: State Publishing Company, 1917), 122.

23. Russell, "How Pat Discovered the Geyser," in *Trails Plowed Under,* 189.

24. Robert G. Athearn, *The Mythic West in Twentieth-Century America* (Lawrence: University Press of Kansas, 1986), 40.

25. "Range Cayuse Is Offered As Food," *Medicine Lake Wave* (Montana Newspaper Association), Nov. 12, 1917. "Slaughter of Cayuses For The Eastern Market," *The Reed Point Review* (Montana Newspaper Association), Mar. 18, 1918. "200,000 Useless Range Horses in Montana Suitable for Food," *The Reed Point Review* (Montana Newspaper Association), Mar. 18, 1918. "Range Horse Go To Slaughter Pen, Butte Concern is absorbing Range Menace at rate of Hundreds Weekly," *Judith Basin County Press* (Montana Newspaper Association), Sept. 27, 1926. Also, see Robert W. Eigell, "Rounding-up 'Canners' for the 'Corned Beef and Cabbage,'" *Montana: The Magazine of Western History* 36:4 (autumn 1986): 64.

26. Con Price, letter, addressee and date unknown, in *Charles M. Russell, Man of the West,* by Patricia Morris (Casper, Wyo.: Man of the West Publishing, 1987), 87. "Charlie told them, 'I might have a horse out there on the range that nobody would know who he belonged to, and I would hate like hell to think I would never see him again only with a can opener.'"

27. Russell, "The Horse," in *Trails Plowed Under* (Garden City, N.Y.: Doubleday, Page and Company, 1927), 110; this piece first appeared in Russell, *Rawhide Rawlins,* 57. Russell's humorous speculation is in the voice of "Rawhide Rawlins."

28. Con Price, letter, addressee and date unknown, in *Charles M. Russell,* 72.

29. Russell, letter to E. McDowell, Mar. 28, 1925, Montana Historical Society archives, C. M. Russell Papers, "outgoing correspondence," box 2, file 2.

30. "Roundup Planned For Wild Horses," *Fergus County Argus* (Montana Newspaper Association), Aug. 30, 1926.

31. Russell, "Tommy Simpson's Cow," in *Trails Plowed Under* (Garden City, N.Y.: Doubleday, Page and Company, 1927), 111, 112; also, see Russell, *Rawhide Rawlins,* 11. In the opening issues of the Montana Newspaper Association's weekly inserts, this story appeared under the title "Weel I Dinna Ken Aboot That, But at Ony Rate, Tom Has a Grand Cow," *Dillon Examiner* (Montana Newspaper Association), Oct. 23, 1916. In contrast with the headline-title, this version of the story was notable by its formal and correct grammar. By the time the story reappeared in *Rawhide Rawlins* and *Trails Plowed Under,* "Tommy Simpson's Cow" had "Rawhide" narrating and the language was "Montana-rural." The first version was most likely the transcription and editing of Percy Raban, and the second, definitive version was directly by Russell.

32. Ibid., 111.

33. William Bleasdale Cameron, *Canadian Cattleman* 13:3 (March 1950): 8.

34. Russell, letter to William Armstrong, 1922, in *Good Medicine; Memories of the Real West,* by Charles M. Russell (Garden City, N.Y.: Garden City Publishing, 1929), 111.

35. Russell, "Mormon Zack, Fighter," in *Trails Plowed Under* (Garden City, N.Y.: Doubleday, Page and Company, 1927), 117, 119. First published in the *Plains Plainsman* (Montana Newspaper Association) with the additional subtitle "Historical Recollections—by Rawhide Rawlins," Oct. 22, 1917; then again in Russell, *Rawhide Rawlins,* 22. Russell's use of the term *Mormon* seems sarcastic since Zack exhibits qualities opposite to those of the pious followers of Brigham Young. Zack also seems the opposite of Russell's other character with a similar name, "Mormon Murphy."

36. Frank Kelly, interviewed by Forest Crossen, in *Western Yesterdays, Charlie Russell—Friend,* by Crossen, vol. 9 (Fort Collins, Colo.: Robinson Press, 1973), 53.

37. Russell, "Mormon Zack," in *Trails Plowed Under,* 120.

38. At the beginning of the story, Russell mentions that Zack's arm has been injured, and the photo of Zack with Russell and Brother Van shows that his right arm is wrapped up inside his shirt.

39. Russell, letter to "Friend Rube," June 20, 1917, in *Charles M. Russell, Word Painter: Letters, 1887–1926,* ed. Brian Dippie (Fort Worth and New York: Amon Carter Museum and Harry N. Abrams, 1993), 237.

40. Michael P. Malone, Richard B. Roeder, and William L. Lang, *Montana: A History of Two Centuries* (Seattle: University of Washington Press, 1976; rev. ed., 1991), 162.

41. C. M. Russell, poem to Paris Gibson, June 20, 1916, in *Charles M. Russell, Word Painter: Letters, 1887–1926,* ed. Brian Dippie (Fort Worth and New York: Amon Carter Museum and Harry N. Abrams, 1993), 228.

42. Wilda Linderman's comments, in Linderman, *Recollections,* 121. J. Frank Dobie, who never met Russell, expressed difficulty in understanding Russell's tendency to enjoy his friends despite their political or economic philosophy. Dobie wrote in the margin of Russell's tribute letter to Gibson in *Good Medicine,* "Why should Russell be complementing a politician for building a city? Looks like insincerity but I guess it's not." Russell, *Good Medicine,* 148, in Dobie Collection, Ransom Library.

43. Malone et al., *Montana,* 265.

44. Russell, "Bill's Shelby Hotel," in *Trails Plowed Under,* 38.

45. Russell, letter to Frank Linderman, "Friend Frank" Jan. 1, 1919. Photocopy in Linderman Collection, Mansfield Library, University of Montana, Missoula, MS Collection 7, box 4, file 5.

46. Russell, "A Reformed Cowpuncher in Miles City," *Trails Plowed Under* (Garden City, N.Y.: Doubleday, Page and Company, 1927), 151; first published in *Winnett Times* (Montana Newspaper Association), Apr. 28, 1919, under the title "Some Notes on the Stockmen's Meet As It Looked To A Reformed Cowman by Rawhide Rawlins," and then in Russell, *Rawhide Rawlins,* as "A Reformed Cowpuncher at Miles City," 40.

47. Sam Gilluly, *The Press Gang, A Century of Montana Newspapers, 1885–1985,* ed. Kevin S. Giles (Great Falls, Mont.: Aircraft Printers, 1985), 41. The festivities included a publication called the *Miles City Maverick* put out by *the Miles City Star*'s publisher, Joseph D. Scanlon, with the help of W. W. Cheely and Percy Raban of the Montana Newspaper Association. According to newspaper historian Sam Gilluly, "Outrageous, libelous and totally false stories about members of the press covered the Maverick's pages." The Montana Newspaper Association operators helped roast the state's newspaper leaders in similar fashion to Russell's roasts of his old friends in the Montana Newspaper Association inserts. The published roast was a popular form of humor in Montana.

48. Russell, letter to Frank Linderman, Apr. 17, 1919, photocopy in Linderman Collection, Mansfield Library, University of Montana, Missoula, MS Collection 7, box 4, file 5.

49. Russell, "Reformed Cowpuncher," in *Trails Plowed Under,* 152.

50. Russell, "Whiskey," in *Trails Plowed Under* (Garden City, N.Y.: Doubleday, Page and Company, 1927), 33.

51. Ibid., 151.

52. Russell, "There's More Than One David," in *Trails Plowed Under* (Garden City, N.Y.: Doubleday, Page and Company, 1927), 173. This piece first appeared, with the subtitle "Historical Recollections of Rawhide Rawlins," in *The Grass Range Review* (Montana Newspaper Association), Jan. 28, 1918. Also, see Russell, *Rawhide Rawlins,* 5.

53. Russell, "Johnny Reforms Landusky," in *Trails Plowed Under* (Garden City, N.Y.: Doubleday, Page and Company, 1927), 79; first published in *The Medicine Lake Wave* (Montana Newspaper Association), on May 7, 1917, under the title "Johnny Ritch, Early Day Reformer, From The Diary Of His Friend, 'Dum Dum' Bill." The version of this story that first appeared in Russell, *Rawhide Rawlins,* 54, as "Johnny Reforms Landusky," reflects editing or rewriting. The yarn remains essentially the same with the character "Dum Dum" Bill relegated to a colorful but passing figure in the narrative and no longer its source. Approximately twelve other changes of phrases, omissions, and additions of words and sentences all work for the better in the revised version. The subject, Johnny Ritch, "Poet of the Judith" (1868–1942), had come to Russell's attention as the author of a melodramatic cowboy poem that aches with nostalgia, titled "Shorty's Saloon." Russell responded with a long illustrated letter and the gift of six watercolor paintings illustrating the poem, which Russell had Miss Josephine Trigg copy in her best calligraphy. "Shorty's Saloon" with Russell's illustrations eventually appeared in Ritch's book of verse, *Horsefeathers.*

54. Ramon Adams and Bob Kennon, *From the Pecos to the Powder; A Cowboy's Autobiography* (Norman: University of Oklahoma Press, 1965), 83. "Our cook . . . Old Vinegar Jim acquired this name from making his vinegar pies, which tasted a good deal like lemon pies. I guess you'd call them 'mock lemon' today, but they sure tasted wonderful to us cowboys."

55. Russell, "Johnny Reforms Landusky," in *Trails Plowed Under,* 79, 80.

56. Johnny Ritch wrote descriptive pieces about the Curry/Landusky fight for the *Great Falls Tribune.* John B. Ritch, "True Story of Pike Landusky Better than Beadle's Best Thriller," *Great Falls Tribune,* Jan. 20, 1935; repr. in Walt Coburn, *Pioneer Cattleman in Montana: The Story of the Circle C. Ranch* (Norman: University of Oklahoma Press, 1968), 290–301. For a recent narrative version

of the Curry/Landusky feud and battle, see F. Bruce Lamb, *Kid Curry: The Life and Times of Harvey Logan and the Wild Bunch* (Boulder, Colo.: Johnson Publishing, 1991), 71.

57. "Pike Landusky, Trapper, Woodhawk, and Gold Miner; Noted As A Fighter; Bullet From 'Kid' Curry's Gun Killed Him, from facts furnished by Teddy Blue, Gilt Edge, Montana," *Joliet Independent* (Montana Newspaper Association), Sept. 20, 1920.

58. Russell, "Johnny Reforms Landusky," in *Trails Plowed Under,* 80.

59. Ibid., 80, 81.

60. Russell, "Johnny Sees The Big Show," in *Rawhide Rawlins Stories* (Great Falls: Montana Newspaper Association, 1921), 25; first published in the Roy Enterprise (Montana Newspaper Association), Feb. 25, 1918, with the subtitle "Rawhide Rawlins Gets Some Inside Facts." Doubleday's editor Harry Maule decided to omit this piece of comic writing from *Trails Plowed Under*. Years later, J. Frank Dobie agreed with the choice, noting on the contents page of his copy of *Rawhide Rawlins Stories,* "'Johnny Sees the Big Show' is not West anyhow, it's about a range lad in England." Dobie Collection. Although the piece also takes place close to the fighting lines in France, the inconsistent narrative ends abruptly and provides primarily a string of disconnected anecdotes.

61. Russell, "Johnny Sees The Big Show," *The Roy Enterprise* (Montana Newspaper Association), Feb. 25, 1918. The reference to Ritch's talks for the Red Cross did not reappear with the rest of the story in *Rawhide Rawlins Stories.*

62. Russell, "Mormon Zack," in *Trails Plowed Under,* 117.

63. Russell, "Horse," in *Trails Plowed Under,* 107.

64. Austin Russell, *C. M. R.: Charles M. Russell, Cowboy Artist, a Biography* (New York: Twayne Publishers, 1957), 150.

65. Malone et al., *Montana,* 252.

66. "Russell Aids With His Art, Great Falls Cowboy Artist Paints and Writes Poetry for Food Administrator," *Great Falls Daily Tribune,* June 15, 1918, p. 14.

67. "Russell Aids With His Art," *Great Falls Tribune,* June 21, 1918, p. 10.

68. Ibid. Beyond the copies of these designs that appeared in Montana newspapers, few (if any) of the posters still exist, suggesting that they received limited distribution.

69. Athearn, *Mythic West,* 57.

70. Corlann Gee Bush, "The Way We Weren't: Images of Women and Men in Cowboy Art," in *The Women's West,* ed. Susan Armitage and Elizabeth Jameson (Norman: University of Oklahoma Press, 1987), 26. Although Charlie seldom painted from models, a few old photos show Nancy Russell costumed and posing like some of the Keeoma-style paintings.

71. Ibid., 33 n. 5.

72. Ginger Renner, "Charlie and the Ladies in his Life," *Montana: The Magazine of Western History* 34:3 (summer 1984): 55, 56.

73. Elliot West, *The Saloon on the Rocky Mountain Mining Frontier,* Lincoln and London: Univ. of Neb. Press, 1979, p 47.

74. Linderman, *Recollections,* 48–49.

75. Ibid., 36–37.

76. Many Russell scholars, including Fred and Ginger Renner, have rejected the authenticity of William Ellsberg's description of Charlie Russell painting a nude image of a Great Falls prostitute (ca. 1915) that Ellsberg published in a magazine article, "Charles, Thou Art a Rare Blade," *The American West, The Magazine of Western History* 6:2 (March 1969). Brian Dippie has also cau-

tioned this writer about Ellsberg's work. For this citation, however, Ellsberg's comments on Russell's sign language seem consistent with other firsthand accounts.

77. Joe DeYong, "Modest Son of the Old West," *Montana: The Magazine of Western History* 8:4 (fall 1958): 96.

78. Russell, letter to A. Trigg, Apr. 10, 1911, in *Charles M. Russell, Word Painter: Letters, 1887–1926*, ed. Brian Dippie (Fort Worth and New York: Amon Carter Museum and Harry N. Abrams, 1993), 151.

79. Ramon Adams and Homer Britzman, *Charles M. Russell, The Cowboy Artist, A Biography* (Pasadena: Trails End Publishing, 1948), 291.

80. Duane Smith, *Rocky Mountain Mining Camps: The Urban Frontier* (Bloomington: Indiana University Press, 1967), 248.

81. Malone et al., *Montana*, 262.

82. C. M. Russell, "Rawhide Rawlins On Montana Stampedes; What Cowboy Of The Old Range Days Saw At The Big Show At Bull Hook," *The Medicine Lake Wave* (Montana Newspaper Association), July 23, 1917. If Fanny Sperry Steele "scratches 'em," she is using her spurs correctly on a rodeo bucking horse's shoulders. This piece never reappeared in any of Russell's books. Jeannette Rankin won election to the U.S. House of Representatives from Montana in 1918, the first woman to be elected to the U.S. Congress. She won by defeating, among others, Russell's friend Frank Bird Linderman. The piece was reprinted in Brian Dippie, ed., *Charlie Russell Roundup: Essays on America's Favorite Cowboy Artist* (Helena: Montana Historical Society Press, 1999), 308–10.

83. Russell, "How Lindsay Turned Indian," in *Trails Plowed Under* (Garden City, N.Y.: Doubleday, Page and Company, 1927), 135.

84. Russell, "Fashions," in *Trails Plowed Under* (Garden City, N.Y.: Doubleday, Page and Company, 1927), 161; also, see Russell, *More Rawhides*, 13.

85. Russell, letter to Senator Paris Gibson, May 14, 1914, in *Charles M. Russell, Word Painter: Letters, 1887–1926*, ed. Brian Dippie (Fort Worth and New York: Amon Carter Museum and Harry N. Abrams, 1993), 204.

86. Russell, "Ranches," in *Trails Plowed Under* (Garden City, N.Y.: Doubleday, Page and Company, 1927), 160; first appeared in *More Rawhides*, 23.

87. Dan Conway, "A Child of the Frontier, Memoirs of Charles M. Russell (The Cowboy Artist), written under the Direction of and in Co-operation with Mrs. Nancy C. Russell," Oct. 29, 1927, unpublished typed MS copy at Montana Historical Society, no. SC 1321, 96. With Nancy editing Conway's manuscript, the quote of Charlie's praise could seem self-serving.

88. Jessie Lincoln Mitchell, "C. M. Russell, The White Indian," *Montana: The Magazine of Western History* 10:3 (summer 1960): 12.

89. Earl Pomeroy, *In Search of the Golden West: The Tourist in Western America* (Lincoln: University of Nebraska Press, 1990), 212.

90. Russell, "Ranches," in *Trails Plowed Under*, 159.

91. Gerald D. Nash, *The American West in the Twentieth Century: A Short History of an Urban Oasis* (Englewood Cliffs, N.J.: Prentice Hall, 1973; repr., Albuquerque: University of New Mexico, 1985), 83, 84.

92. Russell, letter to Jim Thornhill, Jan. 23, 1924, in *Good Medicine; Memories of the Real West*, by Charles M. Russell (Garden City, N.Y.: Garden City Publishing, 1929), 122.

93. Russell, "How Pat Discovered the Geyser," in *Trails Plowed Under*, 187–88.

94. Ibid.

95. Cassandra Phelps, letter to James Rankin, Sept. 25, 1937, Rankin Collection, box 3, file 5.

96. Pomeroy, *In Search of the Golden West,* 213.

97. Russell, "Bill's Shelby Hotel," in *Trails Plowed Under,* 37.

98. Ibid., 39.

99. Russell, letter to "Friend Rube," June 20, 1917, in Dippie, *Charles M. Russell, Word Painter,* 237.

100. Russell, "Reformed Cowpuncher," in *Trails Plowed Under,* 154.

101. Wallace Stegner, *The Sound of Mountain Water* (Garden City, N.Y.: Doubleday and Company, 1969), 192.

CHAPTER SEVEN

1. Joan Stauffer, *Behind Every Man: The Story of Nancy Cooper Russell* (Tulsa: Daljo Publishing, 1990), 56.

2. Richard W. Etulain, "The Historical Development of the Western," *Journal of Popular Culture* 7:3 (winter 1973): 720. *The Frontier* should not be confused with either *Frontier* or *Frontier and Midland,* northwest regional literature magazines that were edited and published by H. G. Merriam at the University of Montana.

3. Harry Maule, letter to Nancy Russell, Aug. 2, 1926, Homer and Helen Britzman Collection, no. C.6.572., Taylor Museum, Colorado Springs Fine Arts Center.

4. Ibid., June 4, 1925, no. C.5.378.

5. Ibid., Dec. 7, 1925, no. C.6.559.

6. Nancy Russell, letter to Harry Maule, Apr. 8, 1926, Britzman Collection, no. C.6.561.

7. Harry Maule, letter to Nancy Russell, Apr. 17, 1926, Britzman Collection, no. C.4.481.

8. Ibid., Apr. 26, 1926, no. C.6.562.

9. Ibid., May 28, 1926, no. C.6.570.

10. Nancy Russell, letter to Harry Maule, May 20, 1926, Britzman Collection no. c.6.567.

11. Ibid., May 20, 1926, no. C.6.565.

12. Harry Maule, letter to Nancy Russell, Oct. 22, 1926, Britzman Collection, no. C.6.579.

13. Contract draft between Doubleday, Page and Co. and Charles M. Russell, Britzman Collection, no. C.6.578.

14. John Taliaferro, *Charles M. Russell: The Life and Legend of America's Cowboy Artist* (Boston: Little, Brown and Company, 1996), 255, 256.

15. Nancy Russell, letter to Harry Maule, July 27, 1926, Britzman Collection, no. C.6.573; Harry Maule, letter to Nancy Russell, Sept. 14, 1926, Britzman Collection, no. C.6.574.

16. The nine "new" stories: "The Ghost Horse," formerly printed as "The Pinto" in the Montana Newspaper Association special insert sections and as "The Olden Days" in *The Roundup* for 1919; also at least four stories prepared twenty years earlier for *Outing*—"Finger-That-Kills Wins His Squaw," "Dad Lane's Buffalo Yarn," "A Pair of Outlaws," and "The War Scars of Medicine Whip." Russell could have prepared the remaining four stories—"Injuns," "Whiskey," "Curley's Friend," and "The Open Range"—in advance of or during his final months.

17. C. M. Russell, letter to "Friend Ted" ["Teddy Blue" Abbott], May 13, 1919, in *Charles M. Russell, Word Painter: Letters, 1887–1926* (Fort Worth: Amon Carter Museum and Harry Abrams, 1993), 279.

18. C. M. Russell, letter to "Friend Con" [Price], Oct. 5, 1924, in *Charles M. Russell, Word Painter: Letters, 1887–1926* (Fort Worth: Amon Carter Museum and Harry Abrams, 1993), 357.

19. Inshta Theamba (Bright Eyes), "Introduction," *Ploughed Under, The Story of an Indian Chief, Told By Himself* (New York: Fords, Howard, and Hulbert, 1881). There is no indication that Russell ever saw this little book or knew that it advocated a policy he disliked—dissolving tribal groups in favor of mandatory allotment of Indian lands. "The key to this complicated problem is, simply, To recognize the Indian as a person and a citizen, give him a title to his lands, and place him within the jurisdiction of the courts, *as an individual.*"

20. Harry Maule, letter to Nancy Russell, Oct. 2, 1926, Britzman Collection, no. C.6.531.

21. Nancy Russell, letter to Harry Maule, Nov. 19, 1926, Britzman Collection no. C.6.580.

22. Charles M. Russell, *Trails Plowed Under, Stories of the Old West* (Garden City, N.Y.: Doubleday and Company, 1927; repr., Lincoln: University of Nebraska Press, 1996).

23. Harry Maule, letter to Nancy Russell, Dec. 23, 1926, Britzman Collection, no. C.6.369a.

24. Ibid., Jan. 7, 1927, no. C.6.376a.

25. The four Montana Newspaper Association insert pieces not selected for either the *Rawhide* books or *Trails Plowed Under* were "Rawhide Rawlins on Montana Stampedes . . . ," "Cinch David's Voices," " Hunting and Trapping on the Judith with Jake Hoover," and "Hank Winter's Bear Story."

26. Nancy Russell, letter to Harry Maule, Jan. 19, 1927, Britzman Collection, no. C.6.494.

27. Harry Maule, letter to Nancy Russell, Jan. 7, 1927, Britzman Collection, no. C.4.484.

28. Nancy Russell, letter to Harry Maule, Jan. 19, 1927, Britzman Collection, no. C.6.494.

29. Owen Wister, *The Virginian, A Horseman of the Plains,* illustrated by Charles M. Russell with drawings from western scenes by Frederic Remington (New York: The Macmillan Company, 1916).

30. Austin Russell, *C. M. R.: Charles M. Russell, Cowboy Artist, a Biography* (New York: Twayne Publishing, 1957), 142–43. "He didn't like the hanging of the hero's best friend, and such details as the hero riding the same horse all the time, riding hard day and night and never once changing horses."

31. Harry Maule, letter to Nancy Russell, Jan. 24, 1927, Britzman Collection, no. C.4.485.

32. Ibid., Mar. 24, 1927, no. C.4.486.

33. Ibid., Apr. 6, 1927, no. C.6.519; ibid., Sept. 9, 1927, no. C.6.527.

34. Ibid., June 1, 1927, no. C.6.515.

35. Ibid., July 7, 1927, no. C.6.545.

36. Nancy Russell, letter to Harry Maule, Britzman Collection, no. C.6.375a.

37. Harry Maule, letter to Nancy Russell, July 7, 1927, Britzman Collection, no. C.6.545.

38. Nancy Russell, letter to Harry Maule, Aug. 12, 1927, Britzman Collection, no. C.6.507.

39. Frank M. Chapman, Jr., "The Man Behind the Brush," *Country Life* 50:4 (August 1926): 35–40.

40. Nancy Russell, letter to Harry Maule, Apr. 8, 1926, Britzman Collection, no. C.6.561.

41. Color illustration titles: "Jerked Down," "Laugh Kills Lonesome," "Riders of the Open Range," "Taking Toll," and "Tracks Tell Tales That Rivers Make Secrets," in *Trails Plowed Under,* by Charles M. Russell (Garden City, N.Y.: Doubleday and Company, 1927), dustcover jacket, 55, 103, 157, 177. The deluxe portfolio first suggested by Maule never progressed into production partly because the book of stories satisfied the need to publish Russell's works in color and also because Nancy's next book project with Doubleday also required extensive color printing—an album of Charlie's illustrated letters titled *Good Medicine.*

42. Harry Maule, letter to Nancy Russell, Dec. 23, 1926, Britzman Collection, no. C.6.369a.

43. Ibid., Sept. 8, 1927, no. C.6.528.

44. Ibid., Sept. 22, 1927, no. C.6.530.

45. Ibid., Nov. 23, 1927, no. C.6.233.

46. Ibid., Nov. 11, 1927, no. C.6.535.

47. Ibid., Feb. 7, 1928, no. C.6.295.

48. Ibid., Feb. 9, 1928, no. C.6.294.

49. Ibid., Apr. 18, 1927, no. C.6.517.

50. Nancy Russell, letter to Harry Maule, May 20, 1927, Britzman Collection, no. C.6.498.

51. Financial statement accompanying check from The Independent Syndicate, Washington, D.C., Jan. 18, 1930, Britzman Collection, no. C.4.137; later statements: Feb. 19, 1930, Britzman Collection, no. C.4.138; Mar. 15, 1930, Britzman Collection, no. C.4.139; Nov. 20, 1930, Britzman Collection, no. C.4.140. Subscribing newspapers included: *Star Newspapers of Canada, Santa Barbara Press,* and *Salt Lake City Telegraph.*

52. Financial statement with check from Harper and Brothers to Nancy Russell, Mar. 8, 1932, Britzman Collection, no. C.6.542.

53. Harry Maule, letter to Nancy Russell, Aug. 5, 1935, Britzman Collection, no. C.6.558.

54. Harold McCracken, *The Charles M. Russell Book; The Life and Work of the Cowboy Artist* (Garden City, N.Y.: Doubleday and Company, 1957), 129.

55. Harry Maule, letter to Nancy Russell, May 28, 1926, no. C.6.570.

56. As of February 2004, the University of Nebraska Press reported selling 9,200 copies since 1996.

CHAPTER EIGHT

1. Charles M. Russell, "How Louse Creek Was Named," in *Trails Plowed Under* (Garden City, N.Y.: Garden City Publishing, 1927), 77.

2. John Donald Wade, "Southern Humor," in *Frontier Humorists: Critical Views,* ed. Thomas Inge (Hamden, Conn.: Archon Books, 1975), 35.

3. Edd Winfield Parks, "The Intent of the Ante-Bellum Southern Humorists," in *Frontier Humorists: Critical Views,* ed. Thomas Inge (Hamden, Conn.: Archon Books, 1975), 7.

4. Cecil Brown Williams, "The American Local Color Movement and Its Cultural Significance," in *Studies in American Literature Since 1850: Four Critical Essays,* Arts and Sciences Studies, Humanities Series, no. 2 (Stillwater: Oklahoma Agricultural and Mechanical College, 1951), 5–13.

5. Robert E. Spiller, Willard Thorp, Thomas H. Johnson, Henry Seidel Canby, and Richard M. Ludwig, eds., *Literary History of the United States: Bibliography,* 3d ed., rev., 2 vols. (New York, London: Macmillan Company, 1963; repr., 1971), 2:304.

6. Arthur Palmer Hudson, ed., *Humor of the Old Deep South* (New York: Macmillan Company, 1936), 530.

7. Henry Nash Smith, *Virgin Land: The American West as Symbol and Myth* (Cambridge, Mass.: Harvard University Press, 1950; repr., 1978), 152.

8. Franklin Meine, "Tall Tales of the Southwest," in *Frontier Humorists: Critical Views,* ed. Thomas Inge (Hamden, Conn.: Archon Books, 1975), 16.

9. Ibid., 28. Harte too easily ignored the short stories of Nathaniel Hawthorne, Herman Melville, and others.

10. "Close View of Artist Russell, His Early Inclinations, Given at Meeting of Woman's Club by Mrs. Russell," *Great Falls Tribune,* Mar. 1, 1914.

11. Richard Dorson, *American Folklore and the Historian* (Chicago and London: University of Chicago Press, 1971), 194.

12. Walter Blair and Hamlin Hill, *America's Humor: From Poor Richard to Doonesbury* (Oxford and New York: Oxford University Press, 1978, 1980), 264.

13. Bret Harte, "The Rise of the 'Short Story,'" *Cornhill Magazine,* new series 7 (July 1899): 1–8.

14. Ibid.

15. Bernard DeVoto, ed., *Mark Twain in Eruption: Hitherto Unpublished Pages About Men and Events by Mark Twain* (New York: Harper Brothers, 1922), 262. Some of the vehemence of Twain's denunciation might be attributed to his falling-out with Harte over their collaboration on an unsuccessful theatrical play, titled *Ah Sin,* as noted by Gary Scharnhorst, in his *Bret Harte* (New York: Twayne Publishers, 1992), 60, 61.

16. Wallace Stegner and Richard Etulain, *Conversations with Wallace Stegner on Western History and Literature* (Salt Lake City: University of Utah Press, 1983), 133.

17. Bret Harte, "The Luck of Roaring Camp," in *The Pioneer West: Narratives of the Westward March of Empire,* ed. Joseph Lewis French (Boston: Houghton Mifflin and Company, 1932; repr., 1989).

18. Charlie Russell owned a copy of one Bret Harte novel, *Trent's Trust,* no doubt because the edition included two Russell illustrations, and he may have enjoyed other works. Ellen Shaffer, *The Charles M. Russell Library,* catalog no. 152 (Los Angeles: Dawson's Book Shop, 1941), item no. 62. Bret Harte, *Trent's Trust* (Boston: Houghton Mifflin Company, 1903). Copy in National Cowboy Hall of Fame archives, Joe DeYong Collection, Flood no. 284. Russell resisted formal education and left the classroom forever at age sixteen, but continued to read actively. This catalog shows that his book collection included volumes by Mark Twain, Rudyard Kipling, Alexander Dumas, Charles Dickens, Stewart Edward White, Frank Bird Linderman, Theodore Roosevelt, and O. Henry, among many others. Some of Russell's book collection had been sold before the list was assembled.

19. Donald Dike, "Notes of Local Color and its Relation to Realism," *College English* 14:2 (November 1952): 82.

20. Bertha M. Bower, *The Lure of Dim Trails* (New York: Grosset and Dunlap Publishers, G. W. Dillingham Company, 1907), 3. "Thurston," Bower said,

> has the look, movement, dress and language of a westerner after several months of hard ranch work without being self-conscious . . . and he made practical use of the slang and colloquialisms of the plains without any mental quotation marks. . . . He was steeped to the eyes in local color—and there was the rub. The lure of it was strong upon him, and he might not loosten [*sic*] its hold. He was the son of his father; he had found himself, and he knew that, like him, he loved best to travel the dim trails. (144, 145)

21. Irvin S. Cobb's letter endorsing the *Rawhide Rawlins Stories* that the Montana Newspaper Association used in its promotional advertising praised Russell's stories as "full of good local color."

22. Smith, *Virgin Land,* 229, 230, 242, 241.

23. Walter Blair, "A Man's Voice Speaking, A Continuum in American Humor," *Harvard English Studies* 3 (1975): 187.

24. Russell, "The Trail of the Reel Foot," *Trails Plowed Under, Stories of the Old West* (Garden City, N.Y.: Doubleday and Company, 1927), 17, 21; also included are "Dog Eater," 129–32; and "Finger-That-Kills Wins His Squaw," 121–28.

25. Dike, "Notes of Local Color," 87.

26. Williams, "American Local Color," 9–10.

27. Austin Russell, *C. M. R.: Charles M. Russell, Cowboy Artist, a Biography* (New York: Twayne Publishing, 1957), 11.

28. Blair and Hill, *America's Humor,* 272.

29. This writer has performed Russell's stories to positive audience responses in thirty states, Canada, and Australia since 1985.

30. Stegner and Etulain, *Conversations,* 132, 153.

31. Jackson J. Benson, *Wallace Stegner, His Life and Work* (New York: Penguin Books, 1996), 22–23.

32. Ibid., 32.

33. Stegner and Etulain, *Conversations,* 153.

34. Alan Gribben, Nick Karannovick, et al., eds., *Overland With Mark Twain: James B. Pond's Photographs and Journal of the North American Lecture Tour of 1895* (Elmira, N.Y.: Center for Mark Twain Studies at Quarry Farm, Elmira College, 1992), 7. Also, see "When Mark Twain Made a Tour of Treasure State," *Dillon Examiner* (Montana Newspaper Association), July 19, 1920, consisting mostly of quotes from Major Pond's book *Eccentricities of a Genius.* For the first time in his tour, Twain walked around the town wanting to meet Great Falls people, but Russell was living ten miles south in Cascade, making very little money while courting his bride-to-be, Nancy. No mention of Twain's single Great Falls appearance, which apparently proved to be an off-night for the humorist, has appeared in any Russell-related document.

35. Wallace Stegner, *The Sound of Mountain Water* (Garden City, N.Y.: Doubleday and Company, 1969), 177.

36. Richard Etulain, *Re-Imagining the Modern American West: A Century of Fiction, History, and Art* (Tucson: University of Arizona Press, 1996), 90, 91.

37. Stegner and Etulain, *Conversations,* 127.

38. Blair, "A Man's Voice Speaking," 192.

39. John Barrows, letter to James B. Rankin, July 28, 1938, James Rankin Collection, Montana Historical Society Archives, no. 162, box 1, file 2.

40. B. A. Botkin, *A Treasury of Western Folklore* (New York: Bonanza Books, Random House, 1975; rev. ed., 1990), 4.

41. Williams, "American Local Color," 10.

42. Boston *Transcript,* March 1885, cited in Samuel Langhorne Clemens, *Adventures of Huckleberry Finn, An Authoritative Text, Backgrounds and Sources, Criticism,* 2d ed., ed. Sculley Bradley et al. (New York: W. W. Norton and Co., 1977), 285.

43. Anne M. Butler, "Frontier Social History," *Oxford History of the American West,* ed. Clyde Milner, Carol O'Connor, and Martha Sandweiss (New York and Oxford: Oxford University Press, 1974), 136.

44. Rachael Campbell, letter to James B. Rankin, n.d., James Rankin Collection, Montana Historical Society Archives, no. 162, box 1, file 10.

45. Shaffer, *Charles M. Russell Library,* item numbers 51, 52, 53.

46. George Ade, *More Fables in Slang* (Chicago: Herbert Stone and Company, 1900), illustrated by Clyde J. Newman. Item no. 51 in Shaffer, *Charles M. Russell Library.*

47. George Ade, "The Fable of What Happened The Night The Men Came To The Women's Club," in *More Fables in Slang* (Chicago: Herbert Stone and Company, 1900), 69. Ade emphasized words with capitalization for reasons known only to him.

48. Russell, "A Reformed Cowpuncher in Miles City," in *Trails Plowed Under* (Garden City, N.Y.: Doubleday, Page and Company, 1927), 154.

49. George Ade, "The Fable of the Inveterate Joker Who Remained in Montana," in *More Fables in Slang* (Chicago: Herbert Stone and Company, 1900), 126–27.

50. Charles M. Russell, "Hands Up," in *Trails Plowed Under* (Garden City, N.Y.: Doubleday, Page and Company, 1927), 114.

51. Charles M. Russell, "Johnny Reforms Landusky," in *Trails Plowed Under* (Garden City, N.Y.: Doubleday, Page and Company, 1927), 81.

52. Alfred Henry Lewis, "How The Raven Died," in *Old Wolfville, Chapters From The Fiction of Alfred Henry Lewis,* ed. Louis Filler (Yellow Springs, Ohio: Antioch Press, 1968), 63.

53. "Prefers Ulm to New York as Place of Residence," *Great Falls Tribune,* Feb. 16, 1904, p. 8.

54. A. Russell, *C. M. R.,* 142.

55. Blair and Hill, *America's Humor,* 267.

56. Abe C. Ravitz, *Alfred Henry Lewis,* Western Writers Series no. 32 (Boise, Idaho: Boise State University, 1978), 15.

57. Brian Dippie, "Introduction To The Bison Books Edition," in *Trails Plowed Under, Stories of the Old West,* by Charles M. Russell (Lincoln: University of Nebraska Press, 1996), ix. Dippie mistakenly states that "by the summer of 1917 all of his stories for the Montana Newspaper Association appeared under the byline 'Rawhide Rawlins.'"

58. Bernard DeVoto, cited in Louis Filler, "Wolfville, The Fiction of Alfred Henry Lewis," *New Mexico Quarterly Review,* University of New Mexico 13:1 (spring 1943): 35.

59. Andy Adams, *Log of a Cowboy, A Narrative of the Old Trail Days* (Boston: Houghton Mifflin and Company, 1903; repr., Lincoln: University of Nebraska Press, 1964).

60. J. Frank Dobie, letter to Joe DeYong, Apr. 11, 1934, National Cowboy Hall of Fame, no. 80.18, Flood no. 585.

61. Andy Adams, *The Texas Matchmaker* (Boston: Houghton Mifflin and Co., 1904).

62. "Cowboy Vividly Paints The Passing Life of the Plains," *The New York Times,* Mar. 19, 1911, p. 5.

63. Charles M. Russell quote in untitled clipping from an unnamed Denver newspaper, 1904 or 1905 [not as hand-captioned: "1911"], Helen E. and Homer E. Britzman Collection, Taylor Museum for Southwestern Studies of the Colorado Springs Fine Arts Center, Colo., e.186.aj.

64. Wilson Hudson, ed., *Andy Adams' Campfire Tales, Why The Chisholm Trail Forks and other Tales of the Cattle Country* (Lincoln: University of Nebraska Press, 1956), 184.

65. Charles M. Russell, "Bab's Skees," in *Trails Plowed Under* (Garden City, N.Y.: Doubleday, Page and Company, 1927), 51; Russell, "Dog Eater," in ibid., 129.

66. Hudson, *Andy Adams' Campfire Tales,* xxiv.

67. Andy Adams, "Button Shoes and the Big Auger," in *Andy Adams' Campfire Tales, Why The Chisholm Trail Forks and other Tales of the Cattle Country* (Lincoln: University of Nebraska Press, 1956), 116.

68. Russell, "Longrope's Last Guard," in *Trails Plowed Under* (Garden City, N.Y.: Doubleday, Page and Company, 1927), 199.

69. Harold and Peggy Samuels, eds., *The Collected Writings of Frederic Remington* (Garden City, N.Y.: Doubleday and Co., 1979).

70. Peggy Samuels and Harold Samuels, *Frederic Remington, A Biography* (Austin: University of Texas Press, 1985), 125.

71. Frederic Remington, "Artist Wanderings Among Cheyennes," *Century* 38:4 (August 1889); repr. in *Collected Writings*, 39–46.

72. Frederic Remington, "Natchez's Pass," in *The Collected Writings of Frederic Remington*, ed. Harold and Peggy Samuels (Garden City, N.Y.: Doubleday and Co., 1979), 427.

73. Frederic Remington, "The Sioux Outbreak in South Dakota," in *The Collected Writings of Frederic Remington*, ed. Harold and Peggy Samuels (Garden City, N.Y.: Doubleday and Co., 1979), 69.

74. Frederic Remington, "The Colonel of the First Cycle Infantry," 190–96; and Remington, "How a Trout Broke a Friendship," 418–20, both in *The Collected Writings of Frederic Remington*, ed. Harold and Peggy Samuels (Garden City, N.Y.: Doubleday and Co., 1979).

75. Samuels and Samuels, *Frederic Remington*, 185. Charlie Russell was not alone in his frequent misspelling in casual correspondence.

76. Remington's most notable writings about cattle culture include an essay, "Life in Cattle Country," in *The Collected Writings of Frederic Remington*, ed. Harold and Peggy Samuels (Garden City, N.Y.: Doubleday and Co., 1979), 384–88; also, see "Cracker Cowboys of Florida," in ibid., 208–12, as well as several pieces about Mexican ranch life south of the border.

77. Frederic Remington, *John Ermine of the Yellowstone*, Americans in Fiction Series (Ridgewood, N.J.: Gregg Press, 1968).

78. John Seelye, "Remington the Writer," in *Frederic Remington: The Masterworks*, ed. Peter Hassrick and Edward Shapiro (New York: Harry Abrams and the St. Louis Art Museum, 1988), 253.

79. Remington, "John Ermine of the Yellowstone," in *The Collected Writings of Frederic Remington*, ed. Harold and Peggy Samuels (Garden City, N.Y.: Doubleday and Co., 1979), 540.

80. Shaffer, *Charles M. Russell Library*, item no. 74, *The Adventures of Tom Sawyer*; no. 75, *Life on the Mississippi*; no. 76, *Personal Reflections of Joan of Arc*; no. 77, *A Tramp Abroad*.

81. Russell, letter to "Friend Percy" (Raban), Apr. 20, 1914, in *Charles M. Russell, Word Painter: Letters, 1887–1926*, ed. Brian Dippie (Fort Worth: Amon Carter Museum and Harry Abrams, 1993), 200. With Russell's affinity for Twain and local-color writing, it is ironic that no copy of *The Adventures of Huckleberry Finn* has been traced to Russell's possession. The book first appeared while Russell worked as a cowboy, many years before he began to collect books.

82. Elizabeth A. Dear, "Extra-Illustrations For 'A Connecticut Yankee At King Arthur's Court,'" *Russell's WEST, The C. M. Russell Museum Magazine* vol. 3, no. 2: 14, 15.

83. C. M. Russell, *Fool and Knight*, watercolor on paper, 1914, *Regards To The Bunch, Letters, Poems, and Illustrations of C. M. Russell* (Great Falls: C. M. Russell Museum, 1992), 51. Russell painted the words of the poem onto the painting before presenting it to the family of Josephine Trigg, the Russells' close friend and next-door neighbor whose estate helped to establish the C. M. Russell Museum with her collection of Russell gifts.

84. Jesse Bier, *The Rise and Fall of American Humor* (New York: Farrar, Straus and Giroux, 1981), 11–12.

85. Owen Wister, *The Virginian, A Horseman of the Plains* (New York: Macmillan Company, 1916), illustrated by Charles M. Russell with drawings from western scenes by Frederic Remington.

86. Etulain, *Re-Imagining the Modern American West*, 26.

87. Elliott West, "Stories, A Narrative History of the West," *Montana: The Magazine of Western History* 43:3 (summer 1995): 66.

88. Mary Clearman Blew, "Introduction," in *Chip of the Flying U* (New York: G. W. Dillingham, 1906; repr., Lincoln: University of Nebraska Press, 1995), 3. According to Blew, "Bower's commitment to Russell's brand of western realism, to his exactitude and faithfulness to detail, is plain" (6). Based on her personal experiences, Bower's stories portrayed much more romantic intrigue between female and male characters than Russell's works. Her selection of details, however, reveals similar care.

89. Richard W. Etulain, "The Historical Development of the Western," *Journal of Popular Culture* 7:3 (winter 1973): 720.

90. Richard Etulain, "Frontier and Region in Western Literature," *Southwestern American Literature* 1:3 (September 1971): 122.

91. Russell, letter to "Friend Sixapee sisstsee" (Harry Stanford), Oct. 17, 1919, in *Charles M. Russell, Word Painter: Letters, 1887–1926,* ed. Brian Dippie (Fort Worth: Amon Carter Museum and Harry Abrams, 1993), 285.

92. Michael P. Malone, Richard B. Roeder, and William L. Lang, eds., *Montana: A History of Two Centuries* (Seattle: University of Washington Press, 1976; rev. ed., 1991), 284.

93. Larry Goodwyn, "The Frontier Myth and Southwestern Literature," in *Regional Perspectives; An Examination of America's Literary Heritage,* ed. John Gordon Burke (Chicago: American Library Association, 1973), 205.

94. Walt Coburn, *Walt Coburn: Western Word Wrangler; An Autobiography* (Flagstaff, Ariz.: Northland Press, 1973), 255.

95. Russell, letter to Walt Coburn, Nov. 27, 1924, in *Good Medicine, Memories of the Real West,* by Charles M. Russell (Garden City, N.Y.: Garden City Publishing, 1929), 96.

96. Ross Santee, *Lost Pony Tracks* (New York: Charles Scribner's Sons, 1953; repr., Lincoln: University of Nebraska Press, 1972), 170. Santee expressed this opinion based on his personal familiarity with Coburn and his works, and more importantly, his contacts with Jim Thornhill, who relocated to Arizona after many years in Montana in close contact with the Coburn family, Kid Curry, and "the Wild Bunch."

97. Coburn, *Walt Coburn,* 202.

98. Russell, letter to Harry Stanford, Oct. 17, 1919, in *Charles M. Russell, Word Painter: Letters, 1887–1926,* ed. Brian Dippie (Fort Worth: Amon Carter Museum and Harry Abrams, 1993), 285.

99. J. Frank Dobie, letter to James B. Rankin, Nov. 22, 1955, Rankin Collection, no. 162, box 1, file 12.

100. E. C. "Teddy Blue" Abbott and Helena Huntington Smith, *We Pointed Them North: Recollections of a Cowpuncher* (New York: Farrar and Rinehart, 1939; repr., Norman: University of Oklahoma Press, 1954), 103. 104, 105. Abbott clarifies his version of events that Russell distorted in his roast of Teddy Blue in "A Reformed Cowpuncher in Miles City."

101. Dan Conway, "A Child of the Frontier, Memoirs of Charles M. Russell (The Cowboy Artist)," ed. Nancy Russell, unpublished MS, Oct. 29, 1927, pp. 208–9.

102. John R. Barrows, *U-BET, A Greenhorn in Old Montana* (Caldwell, Idaho: Caxton Printers, 1934; repr., Lincoln: University of Nebraska Press, 1990).

103. Con Price, *Memories of Old Montana* (Hollywood: Highland Press, 1946); also, see Price, *Trails I Rode* (Pasadena: Trail's End Publishing, 1947). In *Memories,* Price supplies details (68) about the disturbance involving the train-riding theatrical troupe that Russell mentioned in "Bill's Shelby Hotel."

104. Patrick T. Tucker, *Riding The High Country,* ed. Grace Stone Coates (Caldwell: Caxton Printers, 1933; repr., Seattle: Fjord Press, 1987).

105. Raphael Cristy, "Discredited Memoirs Resurrected," *Montana: The Magazine of Western History* 38:3 (summer 1988): 84.

106. Charles A. Siringo, *A Texas Cowboy or Fifteen Years on the Hurricane Deck of a Spanish Pony— Taken From Real Life* (Chicago: M. Umdenstock and Company, Publishers, 1885; repr., New York: William Sloane Associates, 1950), with "Bibliographic Study and Introduction" by J. Frank Dobie, illustrated by Tom Lea.

107. Harold G. Merriam, "Linderman's Tales Charm Big Audience," *Great Falls Tribune,* Feb. 27, 1937, p. 3.

108. Linderman and Russell had a brief falling out in their friendship when Russell delayed his production of some illustrations for a Linderman book in order to complete a ten-thousand-dollar painting destined for the Prince of Wales. Linderman saw this lapse as a betrayal of his family's financial needs, but the two eventually renewed their friendship. Linderman managed his hurt feelings by forgiving Charlie and blaming Nancy for the episode. Dippie, *Charles M. Russell, Word Painter,* 281, 282.

109. Charles M. Russell, letter to Frank B. Linderman, May 19, 1919, Linderman Collection, box 4, file 6, Mansfield Library, University of Montana, Missoula.

110. Russell, letter to "Friend Frank" [Linderman], Jan. 18, 1919, in *Charles M. Russell, Word Painter: Letters, 1887–1926,* ed. Brian Dippie (Fort Worth: Amon Carter Museum and Harry Abrams, 1993), 269.

111. Brian Dippie, commentary, in *Charles M. Russell, Word Painter,* by Dippie.

112. Ibid., 343.

113. Russell, letter to "Friend Bollinger," Feb. 16, 1919, in *Charles M. Russell, Word Painter: Letters, 1887–1926,* ed. Brian Dippie (Fort Worth: Amon Carter Museum and Harry Abrams, 1993), 274.

114. Frank Bird Linderman, *On a Passing Frontier; Sketches from the Northwest* (New York: Charles Scribner's Sons, 1920); repr., Linderman, *The Montana Stories of Frank B. Linderman, The Authorized Edition* (Lincoln: University of Nebraska Press, 1998). Also, see Harold G. Merriam, "Sign-Talker With Straight Tongue: Frank Bird Linderman," *Montana: The Magazine of Western History* (summer 1962), 18. Concerning "Jake Hoover's Pig," which appears on pp. 50–57, Merriam states that the volume includes "tales that circulated orally over a large territory. For instance, I have heard 'Jake Hoover's Pig' from more than one old timer." Also, see "Jake Hoover's Pig," in *Recollections of Charley Russell,* by Frank Bird Linderman, ed. H. G. Merriam (Norman: University of Oklahoma Press, 1963), 18–23.

115. Merriam, "Linderman's Tales Charm Big Audience," 3. Also, see the printed audience program for performance in Santa Barbara, photo-copy in this writer's files.

116. Conway, "Child of the Frontier," 89. This unpublished biography also contains a very similar version of "Jake Hoover's Pig" that Nancy must have transcribed while Charlie was talking. The Conway version corroborates the accuracy of Linderman's memory.

117. Linderman, *Recollections,* 18–23.

118. Homer Britzman, ed., *Rawhide Rawlins Rides Again, Or Behind The Swinging Doors, A Collection of Charlie Russell's Favorite Stories* (Pasadena: Trail's End Publishing, 1948). The editor/publisher proclaimed that the book was "Not copyrighted 1948" and invited readers to retell the stories as their own.

119. James C. Austin, "Charles M. Russell: Literary Humorist," *MIDAMERICA* XII (East Lansing, Mich.: Center For the Study of Midwestern Literature, Michigan State University, 1985), 25.

120. J. Frank Dobie, marginal comment on title page of *Rawhide Rawlins Rides Again,* copy in Harry Ransom Center, University of Texas, Austin, Library, call no. PS 3535 U673 R385 DOBIE.

121. C. M. Russell, letter to "Hello Will James," May 12, 1920, in *Good Medicine, Memories of the Real West,* by Charles M. Russell (Garden City, N.Y.: Garden City Publishing, 1929), 68.

> I know you have felt a horse under you. Nobody can tell you how to draw a horse ore cow. . . . James, you say you havent used color much dont be afraid of paint I think its easier than eather pen ore pensol. . . . James as I said before use paint but

dont get smeary let somebody elce do that keep on making real men horses and cows of corse the real artistick may never know you but nature loving regular men will and thair is more of the last kind in this old world an thair the kind you want to shake hands with[.]

122. Will James, *Cowboys North and South* (New York, Scribner's, 1924; repr., Missoula, Mont.: Mountain Press Publishing Company, 1995). Will James, *The Drifting Cowboy* (New York, Scribner's, 1925; repr., Missoula, Mont.: Mountain Press Publishing Company, 1995). Will James, *Smokey The Cowhorse* (New York, Scribner's, 1926; repr., Missoula, Mont.: Mountain Press Publishing Company, 1995).

123. J. Frank Dobie, "Range Life: Cowboys, Cattle, Sheep," *Guide to Life and Literature of the Southwest, revised and enlarged in Both Knowledge and Wisdom* (Dallas: Southern Methodist University Press, 1952), 108.

124. Frank Linderman, letter to James Rankin, Dec. 13, 1937, Rankin Collection, box 2, file 20. Will James was born in Quebec, with the name Joseph Ernest Nephtali Dufault, in 1892. Although he certainly was both an accomplished bronc rider and a gifted painter, many of his published claims to Montana experiences proved empty, according to Dippie, *Charles M. Russell, Word Painter,* 399–400, and other biographers.

125. C. A. Beil, letter to James Rankin, Dec. 15, 1936, Rankin Collection, box 1, file 3.

126. Blake Allmendinger, *The Cowboy: Representations of Labor in an American Work Culture* (New York and Oxford: Oxford University Press, 1992), 123, 125.

127. Dippie, *Charles M. Russell, Word Painter,* 400.

128. Richard Dorson, "Defining the American Folk Legend" (abstract), *Forms Upon the Frontier; Folk Life and Folk Arts in the United States,* ed. Austin and Alda Fife and Henry H. Glassie 16:2 (April 1969): 163.

129. Kent Ladd Steckmesser, *The Western Hero in History and Legend* (Norman: University of Oklahoma Press, 1965), 249, 250.

130. Austin, "Charles M. Russell," 25, 28.

131. Merriam, "Sign-Talker With Straight Tongue," 3.

132. Goodwyn, "Frontier Myth," 188.

CHAPTER NINE

1. Stanley Walker, "Tales From The West The Cowboys Knew, Charles Russell's Posthumous 'Trails Plowed Under'—Another Book by Will James," *New York Times,* Oct. 23, 1927, sec. 4, p. 4.

2. Review of *Trails Plowed Under* by C. M. Russell, newspaper clipping, handwritten: "N. Y. Post, Dec. 1927," Britzman Collection, no. e.dc.2.

3. "Cowboys, Indians, Buffaloes, and Bucking Cayuses," *Literary Digest,* Nov. 19, 1927, 44. *Vanity Fair* gave the book a positive review and recommended *Trails Plowed Under* as one of several Christmas gifts for the giver: *Archy and Mehitable,* by Don Marquis (Doubleday, Page); *Men Without Women,* by Ernest Hemingway (Scribner's); *Trails Plowed Under,* by Charles M. Russell (Doubleday, Page). "Mr. Riddell's Suggested Christmas List of Books," magazine clipping, hand-inscribed, *Vanity Fair,* December 1927, Britzman Collection.

4. *The Minneapolis Sunday Tribune,* Dec. 8, 1929, p. 3, Britzman Collection.

5. J. Frank Dobie, "Posthumous Volume is Acclaimed Most Beautiful Book of the West, 'Trails Plowed Under' is the work of Charles M. Russell," *The Dallas Morning News,* Oct. 30, 1927, book review section, p. 3. J. Frank Dobie Collection, University of Texas at Austin, Harry Ransom Center, Russell miscellaneous box 2 of 2, item 28.

6. Ross Santee, "Horses, Cattle and Men," *New York Times,* Nov. 27, 1927, p. 7.

7. Robert Gale, *Charles Marion Russell,* Western Writers Series no. 38 (Boise, Idaho: Boise State University, 1979), 25, 26.

8. Ibid., 24, 25.

9. Brian Dippie, "Introduction To The Bison Books Edition," in *Trails Plowed Under, Stories of the Old West,* by Charles M. Russell (Lincoln: University of Nebraska Press, 1996), xv.

10. Charles M. Russell, "Dunc McDonald," in *Trails Plowed Under* (Garden City, N.Y.: Garden City Publishing, 1927), 15. The humorous narrator Rawhide Rawlins states, "Like all things that happen that's worth while, it's a long time ago."

11. Richard Etulain, "Frontier and Region in Western Literature," *Southwestern American Literature* 1:3 (September 1971): 122.

12. "At the Babcock Galleries," *Brooklyn Eagle,* hand-dated 1921, clipping in the Britzman Collection, no. Ed.264.0. Also, see C. M. Russell, unsigned statement, MS typed by Nancy Russell, Joe DeYong papers, Flood no. 823, National Cowboy Hall of Fame.

13. C. M. Russell, note to Joe DeYong, Flood Collection, C. M. Russell Museum, no. 975-12-775.

14. Will Rogers, "Rogers Bows Head For Three Friends," *Los Angeles Examiner,* Nov. 28, 1926.

15. Ramon Adams and Homer Britzman, *Charles M. Russell, The Cowboy Artist, A Biography* (Pasadena: Trail's End Publishing, 1948), 181.

16. B. V. Alder, letter to James B Rankin, 1937, Rankin Collection, box 1, file 1.

17. Adams and Britzman, *Charles M. Russell,* 130.

18. Frank Bird Linderman, *Recollections of Charley Russell,* ed. H. G. Merriam (Norman: University of Oklahoma Press, 1963), 41.

19. C. J. Ellis, letter to James B. Rankin, 1938, Rankin Collection, box 1, file 14.

20. E. C. "Teddy Blue" Abbott and Helena Huntington Smith, *We Pointed Them North: Recollections of a Cowpuncher* (New York: Farrar and Rinehart, 1939; repr., Norman and London: University of Oklahoma Press, 1986).

21. Letter from E. C. "Teddy Blue" Abbott to Nancy C. Russell, July 20, 1927, Britzman Collection, no. C.4.327.

22. Linderman, *Recollections,* 14, 15.

23. Wallace McRae, "I Knowed Old Charlie Well," in *Up North is Down the Crick, Poems* (Bozeman, Mont.: Museum of the Rockies, 1985), 41. Used with author's consent.

24. Annie C. Bach, letter to James B. Rankin, Feb. 9, 1937, Rankin Collection, box 1, file 6.

25. Ralph Budd, letter to James B. Rankin, Dec. 12, 1936, Rankin Collection, box 1, file 6.

26. Adams and Britzman, *Charles M. Russell,* 199.

27. Stith Thompson, *The Folktale* (New York: Dryden Press, 1946), 4.

28. Charles M. Russell, "Foreword," in *Rawhide Rawlins Stories* (Great Falls: Montana Newspaper Association, 1921; rev. ed., 1946), n.p.

29. Austin Russell, *C. M. R.: Charles M. Russell, Cowboy Artist, a Biography* (New York: Twayne Publishing, 1957), 196.

30. William H. Goetzmann and William N. Goetzmann, "Russell: The Cowboy Genius," in *The West of the Imagination* (New York and London: W. W. Norton and Company, 1986), 258, 259.

31. John Taliaferro, "Charles M. Russell and 'Piano Jim,'" *Montana: The Magazine of Western History* 45:2 (spring 1995), 62.

32. Rick Stewart, *Charles M. Russell, Sculptor* (Fort Worth: The Amon Carter Museum, 1994), 5, 6.

33. Peter Hassrick, *Remington, Russell and the Language of Western Art* (Washington, D.C.: Trust for Museum Exhibitions, 2000), 151.

34. Dippie, "Introduction," in *Trails Plowed Under,* v.

35. Ginger Renner, personal statement made to this writer, Paradise Valley, Ariz., 1987.

36. J. Frank Dobie, statement, in B. A. Botkin, "Introduction," *A Treasury of Western Folklore,* rev. ed. (New York: Random House, 1975), xx.

37. Gerald D. Nash, *The American West in the Twentieth Century: A Short History of an Urban Oasis* (Englewood Cliffs, N.J.: Prentice Hall, 1973; repr., Albuquerque: University of New Mexico Press, 1985), 83–84. Robert G. Athearn, *The Mythic West in Twentieth-Century America* (Lawrence: University Press of Kansas, 1986), 30. Both Nash and Athearn quote the same paragraphs from Russell, "Ranches," *Trails Plowed Under,* 159–60. Richard White, "Frederick Jackson Turner and Buffalo Bill," in *The Frontier in American Culture,* ed. James R. Grossman (Berkeley: University of California Press, 1994), 46. White cites several Russell letters and a poem from the C. M. Russell Museum collection, Great Falls.

38. H. G. Merriam, "Prefatory Note," in *Way Out West; Recollections and Tales,* ed. Merriam (Norman: University of Oklahoma Press, 1969), v, vi, vii.

39. Richard White, *"It's Your Misfortune and None of My Own": A History of the American West* (Norman: University of Oklahoma Press, 1991), 615, 616.

40. Russell, "How Louse Creek Was Named," in *Trails Plowed Under* (Garden City, N.Y.: Garden City Publishing, 1927), 77.

41. White, *"It's Your Misfortune and None of My Own,"* 616.

42. William Cronon, "A Place for Stories: Nature, History, and Narrative," *Journal of American History* 78:4 (March 1992): 1371.

43. Elliott West, "Stories, A Narrative History of the West," *Montana: A Magazine of Western History* 43:3 (summer 1995): 65.

44. Frank B. Linderman, *Plenty-Coups, Chief of the Crows* (New York: John Day Company, 1930; repr., Lincoln: University of Nebraska Press, 1962), 311.

45. Cronon, "Place for Stories," 1366.

46. Joan Jensen, *One Foot in the Rockies, Women and Creativity in the Modern American West,* Calvin Horn Lectures (Albuquerque: University of New Mexico Press, 1995), 132.

47. Megan Hiller, Rick Newby, Elaine Peterson, Alexandra Swaney, eds., *An Ornery Bunch: Tales and Anecdotes Collected by the WPA Montana Writers Project, 1935–1942* (Helena, Mont.: Falcon Publishing, 1999).

48. Henry Glassie, ed., *Irish Folktales* (New York and Toronto: Pantheon Books, Random House, 1985), 10.

Selected Bibliography

Aarne, Antti. *The Types of the Folktale, A Classification and Bibliography,* trans. Stith Thompson, FFC 184, Helsinki, 1961; Bloomington: Indiana University Press, 1961, rev. ed., 1973.

Abbott, E. C. "Teddy Blue" and Helena Huntington Smith. *We Pointed Them North: Recollections of a Cowpuncher.* New York: Farrar & Rinehart, 1939; Norman: University of Oklahoma Press, 1954.

Adams, Andy. *Andy Adams' Campfire Tales,* ed. Wilson Hudson. Lincoln and London: University of Nebraska Press, 1956.

———. *Log of a Cowboy, A Narrative of the Old Trail Days.* New York: Houghton Mifflin and Company, 1903; Lincoln: University of Nebraska Press, 1964.

———. *The Texas Matchmaker.* New York: Houghton Mifflin and Company, 1904.

Adams, Ramon, and Homer Britzman. *Charles M. Russell, The Cowboy Artist, A Biography.* Pasadena: Trail's End Publishing, 1948.

———. and Bob Kennon. *From the Pecos to the Powder; A Cowboy's Autobiography.* Norman: University of Oklahoma Press, 1965.

Ade, George. *More Fables in Slang.* Chicago: Herbert Stone & Company, 1900.

———. *People You Know.* New York: Harper and Brothers, 1902.

Alderson, Nannie, and Helena Huntington Smith. *A Bride Goes West.* Lincoln: University of Nebraska Press, 1969.

Aldrich, Lanning. *The Western Art of Charles M. Russell.* New York: Ballantine–Random House, 1975.

Allen, Frederick Lewis. *Only Yesterday: An Informal History of the 1920's.* 3d ed. New York & London: Perennial Library–Harper & Row, 1931, 1959, 1964.

Allmendinger, Blake. *The Cowboy: Representations of Labor in an American Work Culture.* Oxford and New York: Oxford University Press, 1992.

Anderson, Nancy K. "'Curious Historical Artistic Data': Art History and Western American Art." In *Discovered Lands, Invented Pasts: Transforming Visions of the American West,* ed. Jules David Prown. New Haven, Conn. and London: Yale University Press, 1992.

Athearn, Robert G. *The Mythic West in Twentieth-Century America.* Lawrence: University Press of Kansas, 1986.

Axtell, James. "Through Another Glass Darkly; Early Indian Views of Europeans." In *After Columbus: Essays in the Ethnohistory of Colonial North America.* Oxford and New York: Oxford University Press, 1988.

Ballinger, James K. "Chronology." In *Frederic Remington.* New York: Harry Abrams and The National Museum of American Art, Smithsonian Institution, 1989.

Barrows, John R. *U-BET: A Greenhorn in Old Montana.* Caldwell, Idaho: Caxton Press, 1934; Lincoln: University of Nebraska Press, 1990.

Baughman, Ernest. *Type and Motif-Index of the Folktales of England and North America.* Indiana University Folklore Series no. 20. The Hague: Mouton & Company, 1966.

Beard, D. C. *The American Boy's Handy Book; What To Do and How To do It.* New York: Charles Scribner's Sons, 1882, 1889.

———. *Shelters, Shacks, and Shanties.* New York: Charles Scribner's Sons, 1914.

Benson, Jackson J. *Wallace Stegner, His Life and Work.* New York: Penguin Books, 1996.

Berkhofer, Robert F. Jr. *The White Man's Indian: Images of the American Indian from Columbus to the Present.* New York: Random House, 1978.

Bevis, William. *Ten Tough Trips: Montana Writers and the West.* Seattle: University of Washington Press, 1990.

Bier, Jesse. *The Rise and Fall of American Humor.* New York: Farrar, Straus & Groux, 1981.

Birkenhauser-Oeri, Sibylle. *The Mother: Archetypal Image in Fairy Tales.* Toronto: Inner City Books, 1988.

Blair, Walter, and Hamlin Hill. *America's Humor: From Poor Richard to Doonesbury.* Oxford and New York: Oxford University, 1978, 1980.

———. *Native American Humor.* San Francisco: Chandler Publishing, 1937, 1960.

Blew, Mary Clearman. "Introduction." In *Chip of the Flying U.* New York: G. W. Dillingham, 1906; Lincoln: University of Nebraska Press, 1995.

Boatwright, Mody. *Folk Laughter on the American Frontier.* New York: Macmillan, 1949.

Bollinger, James W. *Old Montana And Her Cowboy Artist, A Paper Read Before the Contemporary Club Davenport Iowa 1/13/50.* Shenandoah, Iowa: World Publishing Company, 1963.

Botkin, Benjamin A., ed. *A Treasury of Western Folklore.* New York: Bonanza Books, Random House, rev ed., 1975.

Bower, Bertha M. *The Lure of Dim Trails.* New York: Grosset & Dunlap Publishers, 1907.

Boyer, Mary Joan. "More Russell History." *The Old Gravois Coal Diggings.* Imperial, Missouri: 1954.

Branch, Douglas. *The Cowboy and His Interpreters.* New York: D. Appleton & Company, 1926; reprint New York: Cooper Square Publishers, 1961.

Britzman, Homer, ed. *Rawhide Rawlins Rides Again, Or Behind The Swinging Doors, A Collection of Charlie Russell's Favorite Stories.* Pasadena: Trail's End, 1948.

Broderick, Janice, ed. *Charles M. Russell: American Artist.* St. Louis: Jefferson National Expansion Historical Association, 1982.

Bronson, Edgar B. *Reminiscences of a Ranchman.* Lincoln: University of Nebraska Press, 1962.

Broun, Elizabeth. "Foreword." In *The West As America: Reinterpreting Images of the Frontier 1820–1920,* ed. William Truettner. Washington, D.C.: Smithsonian Institution, 1991.

Brown, Charles Farrar. *The Complete Works of Artemus Ward.* Rev. New York: G. Dillingham Company, 1862,1898.

Brown, Lois, ed. *Tales of the Wild West*. Introduction by B. Byron Price. New York: Rizzoli: Copublished with the National Cowboy Hall of Fame, Oklahoma City, 1993.

Brown, Milton, Sam Hunter, John Jacobus, Naomi Rosenblum, David Sokul. *American Art: Painting, Sculpture, Architecture, Decorative Arts, Photography*. New York: Harry N. Abrams, 1979.

Budd, Louis J. "Chronology." In *Mark Twain, Collected Tales, Sketches, Speeches, & Essays, 1852–1890*, ed. Louis J. Budd. New York: Library of America, 1992.

Budd, Louis J. ed. *Mark Twain, Collected Tales, Sketches, Speeches, & Essays, 1891–1910*. New York: Library of America, 1992

Bullchild, Percy. *The Sun Came Down*. San Francisco: Harper and Row, 1985.

Burke, Doreen Bolger. "In The Context of His Artistic Generation." In *Frederic Remington, The Masterworks*, eds. Michael Edward Shapiro and Peter Hassrick. New York: Harry Abrams and St. Louis Art Museum, 1988.

Bush, Corlann Gee. "The Way We Weren't: Images of Women and Men in Cowboy Art." In *The Women's West*, eds. Susan Armitage and Elizabeth Jameson. Norman: University of Oklahoma Press, 1987.

Butler, Anne M. "Frontier Social History." In *Oxford History of the American West*, eds. Clyde Milner, Carol O'Connor, Martha Sandweiss. New York and Oxford: Oxford University Press, 1995.

Campbell, Joseph. *The Complete Grimm's Fairy Tales*. Pantheon Fairy Tale and Folklore Library. New York: Random House, 1972.

Catlin, George. *Letters and Notes on the Manners, Customs, and Condition of the North American Indians*. 2 vols. London, 1841; New York: Dover, 1973.

Chapin, Louis. *Charles M. Russell, Paintings of the Old American West*. New York: Crown, 1978.

Cheney, Truman M., and Roberta C. Cheney. *So Long, Cowboys of the Open Range*. Helena, Mont.: Falcon Press, 1990.

Clark, O. S. *Clay Allison of the Washita, First a Cow Man and then an Extinguisher of Bad Men, RECOLLECTIONS of Colorado, New Mexico and the Texas Panhandle, Reminiscences of a '79er*. Attica, Ind.: O. S. Clark, 1922.

Clemens, Samuel Langhorne. *Adventures of Huckleberry Finn, An Authoritative Text, Backgrounds and Sources, Criticism*, eds. Sculley Bradley, Richmond Croom Beatty, E. Hudson Long, Tom Cooley. New York: W. W. Norton & Co., 1977.

Cobb, Elizabeth. *My Wayward Parent, A Book about Irvin S. Cobb*. Indianapolis and New York: Bobbs-Merrill, 1945.

Cobb, Irvin S. *A Laugh A Day Keeps The Doctor Away*. Garden City, N.Y.: Garden City, 1923.

———. *Exit Laughing*. Indianapolis: The Bobbs-Merrill Company, 1941.

Coburn, Wallace David. *Rhymes from a Round-up Camp*. Great Falls, Mont.: W. T. Ridgley Press, 1899.

Coburn, Walt. *Pioneer Cattleman in Montana; The Story of the Circle C Ranch*. Norman: University of Oklahoma Press, 1968.

———. *Walt Coburn: Western Word Wrangler; An Autobiography*. Flagstaff, Ariz.: Northland Press, 1973.

Cohen, Hennig, and William B. Dillingham, eds. *Humor of the Old Southwest.* Boston: Houghton Mifflin Company, 1964.

Coles, Robert. *The Call of Stories: Teaching and the Moral Imagination.* Boston: Houghton Mifflin Company, 1989.

Cox, Palmer. *Frontier Humor, Some Rather Ludicrous Experiences That Befell Myself and My Acquaintances among Frontier Characters before I Made the Acquaintance of My Esteemed Friends "The Brownies."* Chicago: Donohue, Henneberry & Co., n.d.

Crawford, Thomas Edgar. *The West of the Texas Kid, 1881–1910; Recollections of Thomas Edgar Crawford, Cowboy, Gun Fighter, Rancher, Hunter, Miner,* ed. Jeff C. Dykes. Norman: University of Oklahoma Press, 1962, 1973.

Cronon, William. "Telling Tales on Canvas: Landscape of Frontier Change." In *Discovered Lands, Invented Pasts: Transforming Visions of the American West,* ed. Jules Prown. New Haven, Conn. and London: Yale University Press, 1992.

Cross, Tom Peete. *Motif-Index of Early Irish Literature.* Folklore Series no. 7. Bloomington: Indiana University Press, 1952.

Crossen, Forrest. *Western Yesterdays, Charlie Russell—Friend.* Fort Collins, Colo.: Robinson Press, 1973.

Davidson, Harold. *Edward Borein, Cowboy Artist; The Life and Works of John Edward Borein, 1872–1945.* Garden City, N.Y.: Doubleday & Company, 1974.

Davis, Fred. *Yearning For Yesterday: A Sociology of Nostalgia.* New York: Macmillan Publishing, 1979.

Davis, Robert Murray. *Playing Cowboys: Low Culture and High Art in the Western.* Norman: University of Oklahoma Press, 1992.

Dear, Elizabeth. *The Grand Expedition of Lewis and Clark as seen by C. M. Russell.* Great Falls, Mont.: C. M. Russell Museum, 1998.

Dempsey, Hugh. Interview with John Cotton—Favorite Ill Walker, "The Wise Old Ones." In *The Amazing Death of Calf Shirt and Other Blackfoot Stories: Three Hundred Years of Blackfoot History.* Norman: University of Oklahoma Press, 1994.

DeVoto, Bernard. *Across the Wide Missouri.* Boston: Houghton Mifflin, 1947.

———. *Mark Twain's America.* Boston: Little, Brown and Company, 1932.

———. *The Portable Mark Twain.* New York: Viking Press, 1946, 1974, reprinted as "Mark Twain and the Great Valley." In *Modern Critical Views of Mark Twain,* edited by Harold Bloom. New York: Chelsea House, 1986.

———. Introduction—"Novelist of the Cattle Kingdom." In *The Hired Man on Horseback: My Story of Eugene Manlove Rhodes,* by May Davison Rhodes. Boston: Houghton Mifflin Company, 1938.

DeYong Joe. *C. M. Russell: A Legendary Man.* Great Falls, Mont.: C. M. Russell Museum, n.d.

Dippie, Brian. "Charles M. Russell: The Artist in his Prime." *Charles M. Russell, The Artist in His Heyday, 1903–1926,* ed. Kellie Keto. Santa Fe: Gerald Peters Gallery, 1995.

———. *Charlie Russell Roundup: Essays on America's Favorite Cowboy Artist.* Helena: Montana Historical Society Press, 1999.

————. "Introduction To The Bison Books Edition." In *Trails Plowed Under, Stories of the Old West,* by Charles M. Russell. Garden City, N.Y.: Doubleday & Company, 1927; Lincoln: University of Nebraska Press, 1996.

————. *Looking at Russell.* Fort Worth: Amon Carter Museum, 1987.

————. *Remington & Russell.* Austin: University of Texas Press, 1982, revised 1984.

————. *The Vanishing American: White Attitudes and U.S. Indian Policy.* Middletown: Wesleyan University Press, 1982.

————. "Two Artists From St. Louis: The Wimar-Russell Connection." In *Charles M. Russell: American Artist,* ed. Janice Broderick. St. Louis: Jefferson National Expansion Historical Association, National Park Service, 1982.

————, ed. *Charles M. Russell, Word Painter: Letters, 1887–1926.* Fort Worth and New York: Amon Carter Museum and Harry Abrams, 1992.

————, ed. *"Paper Talk": Charlie Russell's American West.* New York: Alfred Knopf and the Amon Carter Museum of Western Art, 1979.

Dobie, J. Frank. "Range Life: Cowboys, Cattle, Sheep." In *Life and Literature of the Southwest, Both Knowledge and Wisdom.* Dallas: Southern Methodist University Press, 1952.

————. Statement, Introduction to *A Treasury of Western Folklore,* by B. A. Botkin. New York: Bonanza Books, Random House, revised edition, 1975.

————. *Guide to Life and Literature of the Southwest: Revised and Enlarged in Both Knowledge and Wisdom.* Dallas: Southern Methodist University Press, 1943, revised 1952.

————. *The Longhorns.* Boston: Little, Brown & Co, 1941.

————. *Prefaces.* Boston: Little, Brown and Company, 1975.

Dorson, Richard. *American Folklore and the Historian.* Chicago: University of Chicago Press, 1971.

Driebe, Tom. *In Search of The Wild Indian, Photographs and Life Works by Karl and Grace Moon.* Moscow, Penn.: Maurose Publishing, 1997.

Dunne, Finley Peter. *Mr. Dooley on Ivrything and Ivrybody.* New York: Dover Publications, 1963.

Dykstra, Robert R. *The Cattle Towns.* New York: Alfred Knopf, 1968.

Erdoes, Richard, and Alfonzo Ortiz. *American Indian Myths and Legends.* New York: Pantheon, 1984.

Etulain, Richard. *Re-Imagining the Modern American West: A Century of Fiction, History, and Art.* Tucson: The University of Arizona Press, 1996.

————, and Jill Howard. *A Bibliographical Guide to the Study of Western American Literature,* 2d ed. Albuquerque: University of New Mexico Press, 1995.

Ewers, John. *The Blackfeet, Raiders on the Northwestern Plains.* Norman: University of Oklahoma Press, 1958.

————. *The Horse in Blackfoot Indian Culture.* Smithsonian Institution Bureau of American Ethnology, Bulletin 159. Washington, D.C.: United States Government Printing Office, 1955.

————. *Plains Indian History and Culture: Essays on Continuity and Change.* Norman: University of Oklahoma Press, 1997.

Ewing, Sherm. *The Range.* Missoula: Mountain Press Publishing, 1990.

Fraser, Frances. *The Bear Who Stole The Chinook.* "Introduction" by Hugh Dempsey. Vancouver: Douglas & McIntyre, 1959, 1968.

French, Joseph Lewis, ed. *Sixty Years of American Humor; The Best of American Humor from Mark Twain to Benchley, A Prose Anthology.* Boston: Little, Brown, and Co., 1924; reprint, Garden City, N.Y.: Garden City Publishing, 1938.

Gale, Robert. *Charles M. Russell,* Western Writers Series. Boise, Idaho: Boise State University, 1979.

Garland, Hamlin. *Companions on the Trail; A Literary Chronicle.* New York: Macmillan, 1931.

Gaston, Edwin W., Jr. *Eugene Manlove Rhodes, Cowboy Chronicler.* Southwest Writers Series no. 11. Austin: Steck-Vaughn Company, 1967.

Gilluly, Sam. *The Press Gang, A Century of Montana Newspapers, 1885–1985,* ed. Kevin S. Giles. Great Falls: Aircraft Printers, 1985.

Goetzmann, William H., and William N. Goetzmann. *West of the Imagination.* New York: W. W. Norton & Co., 1986.

Goodwyn, Larry. "The Frontier Myth and Southwestern Literature." *Regional Perspectives; An Examination of America's Literary Heritage,* ed. John Gordon Burke. Chicago: American Library Association, 1973.

Gribben, Alan, Nick Karannovick et al., eds. *Overland With Mark Twain: James B. Pond's Photographs and Journal of the North American Lecture Tour of 1895.* Elmira, New York: Center for Mark Twain Studies at Quarry Farm, Elmira College, 1992.

Griffith, Nancy Snell. *Humor of the Old Southwest: An Annotated Bibliography of Primary and Secondary Sources.* New York: Greenwood Press, 1989.

Grinnell, George Bird. *Blackfoot Lodge Tales; The Story of a Prairie People.* Lincoln: University of Nebraska Press, 1962.

———. *By Cheyenne Campfires.* Lincoln: University of Nebraska Press, 1926, 1971.

Hanna, Warren L. *The Life and Times of James Willard Schultz (Apikuni).* Norman: University of Oklahoma Press, 1986.

Harris, Joel Chandler. *Uncle Remus Returns.* New York: McKinlay, Stone & Mackenzie, 1918.

———. *Nights With Uncle Remus.* New York: McKinlay, Stone & Mackenzie, 1918.

Hart, William S. *My Life East and West.* Boston: Houghton Mifflin Company, 1929.

Harte, Bret. *The Luck of Roaring Camp.* Boston: Houghton Mifflin Company, 1899; reprinted as *The Pioneer West,* ed. Joseph French. Boston: Little, Brown and Company.

———. *Trent's Trust.* Boston, Houghton Mifflin Company, 1903.

Hassrick, Peter H. *Charles M. Russell.* Washington, D.C.: Harry Abrams, in association with The National Museum of American Art, Smithsonian Institution, 1989.

———. "The Painter." In *Frederic Remington, The Masterworks,* edited by Michael Edward Shapiro and Peter Hassrick. New York: Harry Abrams and The St. Louis Art Museum, 1988.

———. *Frederic Remington: Paintings, Drawings, and Sculpture in the Amon Carter Museum and The Sid Richardson Foundation Collections.* New York: Harry Abrams and The Amon Carter Museum of Western Art, 1986.

———. *Remington, Russell and the Language of Western Art.* Washington, D.C.: Trust for Museum Exhibitions, 2000.

Hilger, Bryan. *Building the Herd.* Helena, Mont.: Tailight Studio, 1989.

Hillerman, Tony. *The Best of the West: An Anthology of Classic Writing from the American West.* New York: Harper Collins, 1991.

Hoffmann, Werner. *Turning Points in Twentieth-Century Art: 1890–1917,* trans. Charles Kessler. New York: George Braziller, n.d.

Hoig, Stan. *The Humor of the American Cowboy.* Lincoln: University of Nebraska Press, 1958.

Home, Henry (Lord Kaims). *Six Sketches on the History of Man.* Philadelphia: R. Bell and R. Aitken, 1776.

Hough, Emerson. *The Covered Wagon.* New York: Grosset & Dunlap, 1922.

Hoy, Jim. *Cowboys and Kansas: Stories From the Tallgrass Prairies.* Norman: University of Oklahoma Press, 1995.

Hudson, Arthur Palmer. *Humor of the Old Deep South.* New York: Macmillan, 1936.

Hudson, Wilson, ed. *Andy Adams' Campfire Tales, Why The Chisholm Trail Forks and other Tales of the Cattle Country.* Lincoln : University of Nebraska Press, 1956.

Hughes, Robert. *American Visions: The Epic History of Art in America.* New York: Alfred A. Knopf, 1997.

Humfreville, J. Lee. "Twenty Years Among Our Hostile Indians." In *Rocky Mountain Tales,* eds. Levette J. Davidson and Forrester Blake. Norman: University of Oklahoma Press, 1947.

Huntington, Bill. *Bill Huntington's Good Men and Salty Cusses.* Billings, Mont.: Western Livestock Reporter, 1952.

Hyde, George E. *Life of George Bent.* Norman: University of Oklahoma Press, 1968.

Hyer, Sally. "Pablita Velarde: The Pueblo Artist as Cultural Broker." In *Between Indian and White Worlds: The Cultural Broker,* ed. Margaret Connell Szasz. Norman: University of Oklahoma Press, 1994.

Inge, Thomas, ed. *Frontier Humorists, Critical Views.* Hamden, Conn.: Archon Books, 1975.

James, Will. *Cowboys North and South.* New York: Scribner's, 1924; Missoula, Mont.: Mountain Press Publishing Co., 1995.

———. *The Drifting Cowboy.* New York: Scribner's, 1925; Missoula, Mont.: Mountain Press Publishing Co., 1995.

———. *Smokey the Cowhorse.* New York, Scribner's, 1926; Missoula, Mont.: Mountain Press Publishing Co., 1995.

Jensen, Joan. *One Foot in the Rockies: Women and Creativity in the Modern American West.* Calvin Horn Lectures. Albuquerque: University of New Mexico Press, 1995.

Jewell, Edward Allen. *Have We An American Art?* New York: Longmans, Green & Company, 1939.

Johnson, James W. *The Fight That Won't Stay Dead,* ed. John F. Kavanagh. Shelby, Mont.: Promoter Publishing Co., 1989.

Jordan, Terry G. *North American Cattle-Ranching Frontiers: Origins, Diffusion, and Differentiation.* Histories of the American Frontier Series, ed. Ray Allen Billington. Albuquerque: University of New Mexico Press, 1993.

"The Justin Boys." "To Charles M. Russell, The Cowboy Artist." In *Justin Boots.* Fort Worth: Justin Boot Co., 1923.

Jussim, Estelle. *Frederick Remington, The Camera, and the Old West.* Fort Worth: Amon Carter Museum, 1983.

Kaplan, Justin. *Mr. Clemens and Mark Twain: A Biography.* New York: Simon & Shuster, 1966, 1983.

Kehoe, Alice Beck. "Introduction." In *Mythology of the Blackfoot Indians.* Compiled and translated by Clark Wissler and D. C. Duvall, Anthropological Papers series 2:1. New York: American Museum of Natural History, 1908; Lincoln and London: University of Nebraska Press, 1995.

Keller, Robert. *American Protestantism and U.S. Indian Policy, 1869–1882.* Lincoln: University of Nebraska Press, 1985.

Kennedy, Michael Stephen. *O. C. Seltzer: Meticulous Master of Western Art.* Helena, Mont.: Historical Society Press, n.d.

Kesterson, David B. *Josh Billings (Henry Wheeler Shaw).* New York: Twayne, 1973.

King, Joan. *Charles Russell: Cowboy and Artist.* Lincoln: Media Publishers, 1991.

Kittredge, William, and Annick Smith, eds. *The Last Best Place: A Montana Anthology.* Helena: Montana Historical Society Press, 1988.

Knowles, Thomas W., and Joe R. Lansdale. *Wild West Show!* New York and London: Wings/Random House, 1994.

Lacy, Celia. "P. J. O'Hara" [sic]. *Furrows and Trails in Judith Basin.* Stanford, Mont.: Judith Basin Co. Press, 1976.

Lamb, F. Bruce. *Kid Curry: The Life and Times of Harvey Logan and the Wild Bunch: An Old West Narrative.* Boulder: Johnson Books, 1991.

Lavender, David. *Bent's Fort.* Lincoln: University of Nebraska Press, 1954, 1972.

Lawson, Anita. *Irvin S. Cobb.* Bowling Green, Ohio: Bowling Green State University Press, 1984.

Lewis, Alfred Henry. "How The Raven Died." In *Old Wolfville. Chapters From the Fiction of Alfred Henry Lewis,* ed. Louis Filler. Yellow Springs: Antioch Press, 1968.

———. *Wolfville Days.* New York: Grosset & Dunlap, 1902.

Limerick, Patricia Nelson. *The Legacy of Conquest: The Unbroken Past of the American West.* New York and London: W. W. Norton & Company, 1987.

Linderman, Frank B. *On a Passing Frontier; Sketches from the Northwest.* New York: Charles Scribner's Sons, 1920; reprinted as *The Montana Stories of Frank B. Linderman, The Authorized Edition.* Lincoln: University of Nebraska Press, 1998.

———. "Out of the North." In *Blackfeet Indians.* Minneapolis: Burlington Northern, 1984.

———. *Recollections of Charley Russell,* edited by H. G. Merriam. Norman: University of Oklahoma Press, 1963.

Linderman, Norma. "Afterword." In *Recollections of Charley Russell,* by Frank B. Linderman. Edited by H. G. Merriam. Norman: University of Oklahoma Press, 1963.

Lutts, Ralph H. *The Nature Fakers: Wildlife, Science & Sentiment.* Golden, Colo.: Fulcrum Publishing, 1990.

Lynn, Kenneth. *Mark Twain and Southwest Humor.* Boston: Little, Brown and Co., 1959.

Malone, Michael P., and Richard Roeder. *Montana: A History of Two Centuries.* Seattle: University of Washington Press, 1984.

————, Richard Roeder, and William L. Lang. *Montana: A History of Two Centuries.* Rev. ed. Seattle: University of Washington Press, 1991.

Martin, Calvin. *Keepers of the Game: Indian-Animal Relationships and the Fur Trade.* Berkeley: University of California Press, 1978.

Marx, Leo. *The Machine in the Garden: Technology and the Pastoral Ideal in America.* Oxford and New York: Oxford University Press, 1964.

McClure, Colonel Alexander K. *Lincoln's Yarns and Stories; A Complete Collection of the Funny and Witty Anecdotes that made Abraham Lincoln Famous as America's Greatest Story Teller.* Chicago: The John C. Winston Company, n.d.

McCracken, Harold. *The Charles M. Russell Book; The Life and Work of the Cowboy Artist.* Garden City, N.Y.: Doubleday, 1957.

McFee, Malcolm. *Modern Blackfeet; Montanans on a Reservation.* Prospect Heights, Ill.: Waveland Press, 1972.

McRae, Wallace. "I Knowed Old Charlie Well." In *Up North is Down the Crick, Poems.* Bozeman, Mont.: Museum of the Rockies, 1985.

Meine, Franklin J., ed. *Tall Tales of the Southwest: An Anthology of Southern and Southwestern Humor 1830–1860.* New York: Alfred A Knopf, 1930.

Merriam, H. G., ed. *Way Out West; Recollections and Tales.* Norman: University of Oklahoma Press, 1969.

Morris, Patricia. *Charles M. Russell, Man of the West.* Casper, Wyo.: Man of the West Publishers, 1987.

Nash, Gerald D. *The American West in the Twentieth Century: A Short History of an Urban Oasis.* Englewood Cliffs, N.J.: Prentice-Hall, 1973; reprint, Albuquerque: University of New Mexico Press, 1985.

Nash, Roderick. *Wilderness and the American Mind.* 3d ed. New Haven, Conn.: Yale University Press, 1967, 1973, 1982.

Neilson, Helen Parson. *What the Cow Said to the Calf: Stories and Sketches by Ballie Buck, a Legendary Indian Cowboy.* Gig Harbor, Wash.: Red Apple Publishing, 1993.

Nemerov, Alexander. "'Doing the "Old America,"' The Image of the American West, 1880–1920." In *The West As America: Reinterpreting Images of the Frontier, 1820–1920,* ed. William Truetner. Washington, D.C.: Smithsonian Institution Press, 1991.

————. *Frederic Remington and Turn of the Century America.* New Haven, Conn.: Yale University Press, 1995.

Noyes, Ajax J. *In The Land of Chinook or the Story of Blaine County.* Helena, Mont.: State Publishing Co., 1917.

Nye, Bill. "The Annual Wail." In *Bill Nye's Western Humor,* ed. T. A. Larson. Lincoln: University of Nebraska Press, 1968.

Oppel, Frank, ed. *Tales of the West.* Secaucus, N.J.: Castle Book Sales, 1984.

Parkman, Francis. The *Oregon Trail: Sketches of Prairie and Rocky Mountain Life.* New York and Avenel, N.J.: Grammercy Books and Random House Value Publishing, 1995.

Parks, Edd Winfield. "The Intent of the Ante-Bellum Southern Humorists." In *Frontier Humorists, Critical Views,* ed. Thomas Inge. Hamden, Conn.: Archon Books, 1975.

Peters, Gerald, ed. *Charles M. Russell, The Artist in His Heyday.* Santa Fe: The Peters Corporation, 1995.

Peterson, Larry Len. *Charles M. Russell, Legacy: Published and Printed Works of Montana's Cowboy Artist.* Helena and Great Falls: Falcon Publishing and the C. M. Russell Museum, 1999.

———. *Philip R. Goodwyn: America's Sporting & Wildlife Artist.* Hayden, Idaho & Tucson, Ariz.: The Coeur D'Alene Art Auction and Settlers West Galleries, 2001.

Pomeroy, Earl. *In Search of the Golden West: The Tourist in Western America.* New York: Knopf, 1957; Lincoln: University of Nebraska Press, 1990.

Price, Con. *Memories of Old Montana.* Hollywood: Highland Press, 1946.

———. *Trails I Rode.* Pasadena: Trail's End Publishing, 1947.

Prucha, Francis Paul. *The Great Father: The United States and the American Indians,* 2 vols. Lincoln: University of Nebraska Press, 1984.

Ravitz, Abe C. *Alfred Henry Lewis.* Western Writers Series, no. 32. Boise, Idaho: Boise State University Press, 1978.

Reed, Walt, and Roger Reed, eds. *The Illustrator in America, 1880–1980: A Century of Illustration.* New York: Madison Square Press, 1984.

Remington, Frederic. *The Collected Writings of Frederic Remington,* eds. Harold Samuels and Peggy Samuels. Garden City, N.Y.: Doubleday and Company, 1979.

———. *Crooked Trails.* New York: Harper's, 1898.

———. *John Ermine of the Yellowstone.* New York: Harper's, 1902; Ridgewood, N.J.: Gregg Press, 1968.

———. *Men With the Bark On.* New York: Harper's, 1900.

———. *Pony Tracks.* New York: Harper's, 1895; Norman: University of Oklahoma Press, 1961.

———. *A Rogers Ranger in the French and Indian War, 1757–59.* New York: Harper's, 1897.

———. *Stories of Peace and War.* New York: Harper's, 1899.

———. *Sun-Down Leflare.* New York: Harper's, 1899.

———. *The Way of an Indian.* New York: Harper's, 1906.

Renner, Frederic. *Charles M. Russell: Paintings, Drawings and Sculpture in the Amon Carter Museum.* New York: H. N. Abrams, 1974.

———. *Charles M. Russell: The Frederic G. Renner Collection.* Phoenix: The Phoenix Art Museum, 1981.

———, "Introduction." In *The C. M. Russell Boyhood Sketchbook,* by R. D. Warden. Bozeman, Mont.: Treasure Products, 1972.

———, ed. *Paper Talk; Illustrated Letters of Charles M. Russell.* Fort Worth: Amon Carter Museum of Western Art, 1962.

Renner, Ginger. *A Limitless Sky: The Work of Charles M. Russell in the Collection of the Rockwell Museum, Corning, New York.* Flagstaff, Ariz.: Northland Press, 1986.

———. "Foreword." In *Charles M. Russell: The Frederic G. Renner Collection.* Phoenix: Phoenix Art Museum, 1981.

Rhodes, May Davison. *The Hired Man on Horseback: My Story of Eugene Manlove Rhodes.* Boston: Houghton Mifflin Company, 1938.

Richardson, E. P. *A Short History of Painting in America; The Story of 450 Years.* New York: Harper & Row, 1963.

Rinehart, Mary Roberts. *Through Glacier Park in 1915.* New York: P. F. Collier & Son, 1916; Boston: Houghton Mifflin & Company, 1930; Boulder: Roberts Rinehart, 1983.

Rogers, Will. *The Best of Will Rogers: A Collection of Rogers' Wit and Wisdom Astonishingly Relevant for Today's World,* edited by Bryan Sterling. New York: M. Evans & Co. Inc., 1979.

———. *Will Rogers' Illiterate Digest.* New York: Albert and Charles Boni, 1936.

Roosevelt, Theodore. *Hunting the Grisly and Other Sketches, The Wilderness Hunter Part II.* New York: G. P. Putnam's Sons, 1893; Current Literature Publishing Company, 1907.

Rourke, Constance. *American Humor; A Study of the National Character.* New York: Harcourt Brace Jovanovich, 1931; Tallahassee: Florida State University Press, 1959.

Rowley, William. "The West as a Laboratory and Mirror of Reform." In *The Twentieth Century West,* eds. Gerald Nash and Richard Etulain. Albuquerque: University of New Mexico Press, 1989.

Rush, Oscar. *The Open Range and Bunk House Philosophy.* Denver: Colorado Herald Publishing Company, 1930.

Russell, Austin. *C. M. R.: Charles M. Russell, Cowboy Artist, a Biography.* New York: Twayne, 1957.

Russell, Charles M. *Good Medicine, Memories of the Real West.* Garden City, N.Y.: Garden City Publishers, 1929.

———. *More Rawhides.* Great Falls: Montana Newspaper Association, 1925.

———. "The Olden Days." In *Twelfth Annual Great Falls High School Roundup.* Great Falls, Mont.: Great Falls High, 1919.

———. *Paper Talk; Illustrated Letters of Charles M. Russell,* ed. Frederic G. Renner. Fort Worth: Amon Carter Museum of Western Art, 1962.

———. *"Paper Talk": Charlie Russell's American West,* ed. Brian Dippie. New York: Alfred Knopf, 1979.

———. *Rawhide Rawlins Stories.* Great Falls: Montana Newspaper Association, 1921.

———. *Regards to the Bunch, Letters, Poems, and Illustrations of C. M. Russell.* Great Falls: C. M. Russell Museum, 1992.

———. "A Slice of Charlie's Early Life." In *Eleventh Annual Great Falls High School Roundup.* Great Falls, Mont.: Great Falls High School, 1918.

———. "The Story of the Cowboy As It Was Told To Me By An Old-time Rider Of The Range." In *Tenth Annual Great Falls High School Roundup.* Great Falls, Mont.: Great Falls High School, 1917.

———. *Studies in Western Life.* New York: Albertype, 1890.

———. *Trails Plowed Under, Stories of the Old West.* Garden City: Doubleday, 1927.

Russell, Nancy C. "Biographical Note." In *Good Medicine, Memories of the Real West,* by Charles M. Russell. Garden City, N.Y.: Garden City Publishing, 1929, 1930.

Samek, Hana. *The Blackfoot Confederacy, 1880–1920: A Comparative Study of Canadian and U.S. Indian Policy.* Albuquerque: University of New Mexico Press, 1987.

Samuels, Harold and Peggy Samuels, eds. *The Collected Writings of Frederic Remington.* Garden City, N.Y.: Doubleday & Company, 1979.

———. *Frederic Remington: A Biography.* Garden City, N.Y.: Doubleday & Company, 1982; Austin: University of Texas Press, 1985.

Santee, Ross. *Lost Pony Tracks.* New York: Charles Scribner's Sons, 1953; Lincoln: University of Nebraska Press, 1972.

Scharnhorst, Gary. *Bret Harte.* New York: Twayne Publishers, 1992.

Schimmel, Julie, and Robert R. White. *Bert Geer Phillips and the Taos Art Colony.* Albuquerque: University of New Mexico Press, 1994.

Schultz, James Willard. *My Life as an Indian.* New York: Forest and Stream Publishing Co., 1907; New York and Bozeman, Mont.: Beaufort Books and Museum of the Rockies, 1983.

Seelye, John. "Remington the Writer." In *Frederic Remington: The Masterworks,* eds. Peter Hassrick and Edward Shapiro. New York: Harry Abrams and the St. Louis Art Museum, 1988.

Seton, Ernest Thompson. *Wild Animals I Have Known.* New York: Charles Scribner's Sons, 1898; New York and London: Viking Penguin, 1987.

Shaffer, Ellen, ed. *The Charles M. Russell Library.* Los Angeles: Dawson's Book Shop, 1941.

Shelton, Lola. *Charles Marion Russell: Cowboy, Artist, Friend.* New York: Dodd, Mead, 1962.

Shillaber, B. P. *Mrs. Partington's Knitting-Work; and What Was Done By Her Plaguy Boy Ike. A Web of Many Textures, As Wrought by The Old Lady Herself.* Philadelphia: John E. Potter and Company, 1868.

Siringo, Charles. *A Texas Cowboy or Fifteen Years on the Hurricane Deck of a Spanish Pony—Taken From Real Life.* Chicago: M. Umbdenstock & Company Publishers, 1885; New York: William Sloane Associates, 1950.

Slotkin, Richard. *The Fatal Environment: The Myth of the Frontier in the Age of Industrialization, 1800–1890.* New York: Athenaeum, 1985; New York: Harper Collins, 1994.

Smith, Duane. *Rocky Mountain Mining Camps: The Urban Frontier.* Bloomington: Indiana University Press, 1967.

Smith, Henry Nash. *Virgin Land: The American West as Symbol and Myth.* Cambridge, Mass.: Harvard University Press, 1950, 1978.

Spiller, Robert E., Willard Thorp, Thomas H. Johnson, Henry Seidel Canby, Richard M. Ludwig, eds. *Literary History of the United States: Bibliography.* New York: Macmillan Company, 3d ed., rev., vol. 2, 1971.

Stauffer, Joan. *Behind Every Man: The Story of Nancy Cooper Russell.* Tulsa, Okla.: Daljo Publishing Co., 1990.

Steckmesser, Kent Ladd. *The Western Hero in History and Legend.* Norman: University of Oklahoma Press, 1965.

Stegner, Wallace. *The Sound of Mountain Water.* Garden City, N.Y.: Doubleday & Company, 1969.

———. *Wolf Willow.* Lincoln: University of Nebraska Press, 1980.

———, and Richard Etulain. *Conversations with Wallace Stegner on Western History and Literature.* Salt Lake City: University of Utah Press, 1983.

Steiner, Stan. "The Squaw Sachem." In *The Vanishing White Man.* Norman: University of Oklahoma Press, 1976.

Stewart, Rick. *Charles M. Russell: Masterpieces from the Amon Carter Museum.* Fort Worth: Amon Carter Museum, 1990.

———. *Charles M. Russell, Sculptor.* Fort Worth and New York: Amon Carter Museum and Harry Abrams, 1994.

Stowe, Harriet Beecher. *Uncle Tom's Cabin.* New York and London: Bantam Books, 1981.

Stuart, Granville. *Pioneering in Montana: The Making of a State, 1864–1887,* ed. Paul C. Phillips. (Originally titled *Forty Years on the Frontier as seen in the Journals and Reminiscences of Granville Stuart, Gold Miner, Trade, Merchant, Rancher and Politician,* Volume II.) Cleveland: Arthur H. Clark Company, 1925; Lincoln: Bison Book Edition, University of Nebraska Press, 1977.

Szasz, Margaret Connell, ed. *Between Indian and White Worlds: The Cultural Broker.* Norman and London: University of Oklahoma Press, 1994.

Taggett, Sherry Clayton, and Ted Schwarz. *Paintbrushes and Pistols: How the Taos Artists Sold the West.* Santa Fe: John Muir Publications, 1990.

Taliaferro, John. *Charles M. Russell: The Life and Legend of America's Cowboy Artist.* Boston: Little, Brown and Company, 1996.

Tatum, Stephen. *Inventing Billy the Kid: Visions of the Outlaw in America, 1881–1981.* Albuquerque: University of New Mexico Press, 1982.

Theamba, Inshta (Bright Eyes). "Introduction." In *Ploughed Under, The Story of an Indian Chief, Told By Himself.* New York: Fords, Howard, & Hulbert, 1881.

Thompson, Stith. *European Tales among the North American Indians.* Boulder: Colorado College Publications Language Series vol. II, no. 34., April–May 1919.

———. *The Folktale.* New York: Dryden Press, 1946.

———, ed. *Tales of the North American Indians.* 4th ed. Bloomington: Indiana University Press, 1929; Midland Books, 1966, 1971.

Tompkins, Jane. *West of Everything: The Inner Life of Westerns.* Oxford and New York: Oxford University Press, 1992.

Truettner, William, ed. *The West As America: Reinterpreting Images of the Frontier, 1820–1920.* Washington, D.C.: Smithsonian Institution Press, 1991.

Tucker, Patrick T. *Riding The High Country.* Caldwell, Idaho: Caxton Press, 1933; Seattle: Fjord Press, 1987.

Turner, Frederick Jackson. "The Significance of the Frontier in American History." In *The Frontier in American History.* New York: H. Holt and Co., 1920.

Tuska, Jon, ed. *The Western Story: A Chronological Treasury.* Lincoln and London: University of Nebraska Press, 1995.

Twain, Mark. *Collected Tales, Sketches, Speeches, & Essays, 1852–1890,* ed. Louis J. Budd. New York: Library Classics of the United States, 1992.

———. *Collected Tales, Sketches, Speeches, & Essays, 1891–1910,* ed. Louis J. Budd. New York: Library Classics of the United States, 1992.

———. *A Connecticut Yankee in King Arthur's Court.* New York: Signet Classic–New American Library, n.d.

———. *Mark Twain in Eruption: Hitherto Unpublished Pages About Men and Events,* by Mark Twain, ed. Bernard DeVoto. New York: Harper Bros., 1922.

———. "The Noble Red Man." In *Collected Tales, Sketches, Speeches, & Essays, 1852–1890,* ed. Louis Budd. New York: The Library of America, 1992.

———. *Roughing It.* New York: The New American Library, 1980.

Van Cleve, Spike. *A Day Late and A Dollar Short.* Kansas City: The Lowell Press, 1982.

Vaughn, Robert. *Then and Now, Thirty-Six Years in the Rockies 1864–1900.* Minneapolis, Minn.: Tribune Publishing Company, 1900.

Vichorek, Dan. *Montana's High Line.* Helena: American and World Geographic Press, 1992.

Vorpahl, Ben Merchant. *My Dear Wister: The Frederic Remington–Owen Wister Letters.* Palo Alto, Calif.: American West, 1972.

Wade, John Donald. "Southern Humor." In *Frontier Humorists, Critical Views,* ed. Thomas Inge. Hamden, Conn.: Archon Books, 1975.

Waite, Walter F. *Old Utica, Silver Dollar Tales.* Conrad, Mont.: Marilyn and Walter Waite, 1994.

Walter, Dave. *Montana Campfire Tales: Fourteen Historical Narratives.* Helena and Billings, Mont.: Falcon Press, 1997.

Warden, R. D. *The C. M. Russell Boyhood Sketchbook.* Bozeman, Mont.: Treasure Products, 1972.

Webb, Walter Prescott. *The Great Plains: A Study in Institutions and Environment.* Boston and New York: Houghton Mifflin Company, 1931, 1936.

West, Elliott. *The Saloon on the Rocky Mountain Mining Frontier.* Lincoln: University of Nebraska Press, 1979.

West, John O. *Cowboy Folk Humor: Life and Laughter in the American West.* Little Rock, Ark.: August House, 1990.

Westermeier, Clifford P., ed. *Trailing the Cowboy, His Life and Lore as Told by Frontier Journalists.* Caldwell, Idaho: Caxton Printers, 1955.

White, E. B., and Katharine S. White, eds. *A Subtreasury of American Humor.* New York: Coward-McCann Inc., 1941.

White, G. Edward. *The Eastern Establishment and the Western Experience: The West of Frederic Remington, Theodore Roosevelt, and Owen Wister.* New Haven, Conn.: Yale University Press, 1968; reprint, Austin: University of Texas Press, 1989.

White, Richard. *"It's Your Misfortune and None of My Own": A History of the American West.* Norman: University of Oklahoma Press, 1991.

———, and Patricia Nelson Limerick. *The Frontier in American Culture: An Exhibition at the Newberry Library, August 26, 1994–January 7, 1995.* Berkeley: University of California Press, 1994.

Willard, John. *The CMR Book.* Seattle: Superior Press, 1970.

Williams, Cecil Brown. "The American Local Color Movement and Its Cultural Significance." In *Studies in American Literature Since 1850, Four Critical Essays.* Arts and Sciences Studies, Humanities Series, no. 2. Stillwater: Oklahoma Agricultural and Mechanical College, 1951.

Wister, Owen. *The Virginian, A Horseman of the Plains.* Illustrated by Charles M. Russell with drawings from western scenes by Frederic Remington. New York: Macmillan Company, 1916.

Wonham, Henry B. *Mark Twain and the Art of the Tall Tale.* Oxford and New York: Oxford University Press, 1993.

Yost, Karl, and Frederic Renner. *A Bibliography of the Published Works of Charles M. Russell.* Lincoln: University of Nebraska Press, 1971.

Primary Sources—Unpublished Manuscripts

Cristy, Raphael J. "Legend Maker: Charles M. Russell's Historical Perspective In His Published Stories and Essays." Unpublished Master's thesis, University of Montana, Department of History, 1992.

Grant, Frank. "Embattled Voice for the Montana Farmers, Robert Sutherlin's Rocky Mountain Husbandman." Unpublished Ph.D. dissertation, University of Montana, Department of History, 1984.

Moore, James C. "The Storm And The Harvest, The Image of Nature in Mid-Nineteenth Century American Landscape Painting." Unpublished Ph.D. dissertation, Wichita State University, 1976.

River, Celeste. "A Mountain In His Memory, Frank Bird Linderman, His Role In Acquiring the Rocky Boy Indian Reservation for the Montana Chippewa and Cree. . . ." Unpublished Master's Thesis, University of Montana, 1990.

Archive Collections

C. M. Russell Museum, Library & Archives, Flood Collection.

Colorado Springs Fine Arts Center, Taylor Museum for Southwestern Studies, The Helen E. And Homer E. Britzman Collection, Nancy Russell's Story-Publishing Correspondence, Manuscripts and Periodical Clippings.

Harry Ransom Center, University of Texas, Austin, J. Frank Dobie Collection, C. M. Russell, Documents.

Mansfield Library Archives, University of Montana, Missoula, Frank B. Linderman Collection.

Montana Historical Society, Helena, Montana, the James B. Rankin Collection.

National Cowboy Hall of Fame Library/Archives, Joe DeYong Collection.

Other Sources

Hill, Hamlin. Public lecture, "Voices of Mark Twain," July 2, 1997, Popejoy Hall Performing Arts Center, University of New Mexico, Albuquerque.

Monroe, Mr. and Mrs. Angus. Audiotape interview, n.d., recorded in Conrad, Montana. Copy with this writer.

Montana Writers Project (W.P.A.), microfilm, Montana Historical Society, Helena.

Renner, Frederic G. *Charles M. Russell, An American Artist.* Film/video produced by Schwartz & Associates. St. Louis: Jefferson National Expansion Historical Association, 1982.

Periodicals

American Art 8:1 (winter 1994).

American Heritage: The Magazine of History 24:3 (April 1973).

The American West: The Magazine of Western History 6:2 (March 1969), 14:6 (November/December 1977).

Art News 80:10 (December 1981).

The Art Bulletin 70:2 (June 1988).

The Bellman 26:669 (May 10, 1919).

C. M. Russell Art Auction Catalog, 1997.

Canadian Cattleman 4:4 (March 1943), 13:3 (March 1950), 13:4 (April 1950).

The Cattleman 33:9 (February 1947).

College English 4:2 (November 1952).

Collier's 62:13 (December 12, 1908).

Cornhill Magazine, new series 7 (July 1899).

Country Life 50:4 (August 1926).

Forms Upon the Frontier: Folk Life and Folk Arts in the United States 16:2 (April 1961).

Fort Benton River Press, May 1881.

The Frontier 13:3 (March 1933).

Harvard English Studies 3 (1975).

The HI-LIFE, Great Falls High School, vol. 5, p. 1, October 27, 1925.

Journal of American Culture 3:1 (spring 1980).

Journal of American History 78:4 (March 1992), 78:2 (September 1991).

Journal of Popular Culture 7 (winter 1973), 5 (spring 1972).

MIDAMERICA: The Yearbook of the Society for the Study of Midwestern Literature 12 (1985).

Mississippi Valley Historical Review 16:2 (September 1929).

Montana: The Magazine of Western History.

National Geographic Magazine 169:1 (January 1987).

The New Yorker 71:38 (November 27, 1995).

Outing Magazine 50:5 (August 1907), 51:3 (December 1907), 51:5 (February 1908), 52:1 (April 1908), 52:2 (May 1908).

Pacific Monthly 12 (December 1904).

Persimmon Hill 11:3/4 (summer/fall 1982).

The Piegan Storyteller 15:2 (April 1990).

Recreation Magazine 6:4 (1897).

Russell's West: The C. M. Russell Museum Magazine 1:1, 3:1, 4:2, 6:2.

Scribner's Magazine 2 (March 1892).

Southwestern American Literature 1:3 (September 1971).

Sports Afield 20:1 (January 1898).

Western Historical Quarterly 20 (February 1989).

Western Review: A Journal of the Humanities 5:1 (summer 1968).

NEWSPAPERS

Albuquerque Journal

Anaconda Standard

Brooklyn Eagle

Butte Miner

Chicago Evening Post

Dallas Morning News

Deer Lodge New Northwest

Fort Benton River Press

Great Falls Leader

Great Falls Tribune

Hamilton Ravalli Republic

Helena Record-Herald

Kalispell Inter-Lake

Los Angeles Examiner

Los Angeles Times

Miles City Daily Star

Minneapolis Journal .

Minneapolis Tribune

Montana Newspaper Association

New York Globe

New York Herald

New York Press

New York Times

Pasadena Star News

Rocky Mountain News

Santa Barbara Morning Press

St. Louis Mirror

St. Louis Post Dispatch

St. Paul Daily News

Winnipeg Tribune

Index

Note: Page numbers in italics refer to illustrations.